Capitalism
as if the World Matters

Capitalism
as if the World Matters

Jonathon Porritt

London • Sterling, VA

First published by Earthscan in the UK and USA in 2005
Reprinted 2006 (twice)

ISBN-10: 1-84407-192-8
ISBN-13: 978-1-84407-192-0

Typesetting by JS Typesetting Ltd, Porthcawl, Mid Glamorgan
Printed and bound in the UK by Bath Press
Cover design by Susanne Harris

For a full list of publications please contact:

Earthscan
8–12 Camden High Street
London, NW1 0JH, UK
Tel: +44 (0)20 7387 8558
Fax: +44 (0)20 7387 8998
Email: earthinfo@earthscan.co.uk
Web: **www.earthscan.co.uk**

22883 Quicksilver Drive, Sterling, VA 20166-2012, USA

Earthscan is an imprint of James and James (Science Publishers) Ltd and publishes in
association with the International Institute for Environment and Development

A catalogue record for this book is available from the British Library

Library of Congress Cataloging-in-Publication Data

Porritt, Jonathon.
    Capitalism : as if the world matters / Jonathon Porritt.
       p. cm.
    Includes bibliographical references and index.
    ISBN 1-84407-192-8
    1. Sustainable development. 2. Capitalism. I. Title.
    HC79.E5P667 2005
    330.12'2—dc22
                        2005021488

The paper used for the text pages of this book is FSC
certified. FSC (the Forest Stewardship Council)
is an international network to promote responsible
management of the world's forests.

Mixed Sources

Product group from well-managed
forests and other controlled sources
www.fsc.org Cert no. SGS-COC-2121
© 1996 Forest Stewardship Council

for ELEANOR and REBECCA

and for a generation
that depends so much
on our generation
coming to its senses

Contents

PART II A FRAMEWORK FOR SUSTAINABLE CAPITALISM

Acknowledgements

This book started out as a collaborative enterprise involving a large number of colleagues at Forum for the Future. Having worked hard since our inception in 1996 to operationalize the concept of an economic framework based on five different kinds of capital (natural, human, social, manufactured and financial) through our various partnership schemes, we subsequently felt the need to develop some of the intellectual foundations behind that Framework – a rare example, perhaps, of theory following practice!

That work was done during 2002 and 2003, and particular thanks are due to James Wilsdon for his work on social capital, to Rupert Howes and Brian Pearce for their work on financial capital, to David Bent and David Aeron-Thomas for their work on environmental cost accounting, to Mark Everard and David Cook for their work on manufactured capital, to Martin Wright for his work on security issues and sustainability, and to Peter Price-Thomas and Simon Slater for their work on spiritual capital.

But the real origins of the work go back to discussions between myself and Paul Ekins in the mid 1990s when we were drawing up plans for the organization that would eventually become Forum for the Future. Paul had already done substantial work on the whole question of economic growth and sustainability, and the degree to which the two could be reconciled within a capitalist economy. The idea of using the five different kinds of capital to demonstrate what a genuinely sustainable economy would look like in practice emerged from those discussions, and an internal Forum paper written by Paul in 1997 became the source document for a lot of the work that the Forum has done in this area since then.

I should add that Paul's own book, *Economic Growth and Environmental Sustainability*, has done more to help me get my head around these issues than any other single work.

And there have been many other works over the last couple of years as what started out as a quite self-contained presentation of the Forum's Five Capitals Framework broadened out into an exploration of many other aspects of the economics and politics of sustainability. This book could not have been written without that intellectual feast having been available to me, and I have drawn on it unhesitatingly to lend substance and coherence to my own exploratory journey.

Where I hope I've been able to add something a little different is in the synthesizing of all those different inputs. It is only fair to say, in that context, that for all the guidance I've drawn on from colleagues both within and beyond the

Forum, *Capitalism as if the World Matters* is an expression of my own personal views rather than those of Forum for the Future as an organization. It's there that responsibility must lie for any misinterpretations or analytical inadequacies.

FORUM FOR THE FUTURE

Forum for the Future is the UK's leading sustainable development charity. Its mission is to accelerate the change to a sustainable way of life, taking a positive, solutions-oriented approach in everything it does. That mission is shared with partners drawn from business, finance, local authorities, regional bodies and higher education. We communicate what we learn with our partners to a wide network of decision-makers and opinion-formers.

www.forumforthefuture.org.uk

info@forumforthefuture.org.uk

All royalties from the sales of *Capitalism as if the World Matters* are being paid to Forum for the Future to support its ongoing work.

Introduction

In December 2004, the world looked on aghast as the horrifying impacts of the Indian Ocean earthquake and resulting tsunami filled our television screens night after night. More than 300,000 dead, 5 million people homeless. Economic damage ran into untold billions of US dollars. It was, without a doubt, the worst natural disaster in living memory.

The response of people across the developed world was extraordinary. In the UK, hundreds of millions of pounds were raised in just a few weeks in response to a constant stream of images of suffering and loss. Disaster-hardened professionals were almost as astonished at the scale and intensity of this response as they were at the scale of the disaster itself.

By one of those bizarre coincidences, a global campaign 'to make poverty history' was launched at almost exactly the same time, poignantly reminding people of the ongoing reality of a planet still so starkly divided between rich and poor – over and above the cataclysmic horror of any one natural disaster. And despite a year in which the challenge of global poverty has assumed a far more prominent part in international gatherings such as the G8 Summit, the Commission for Africa, various United Nations (UN) conferences and the deliberations of the European Union (EU), poverty campaigners have inevitably found themselves reflecting somewhat wearily upon the intensity of the response to the tsunami compared to the 'slow burn' of shifting public opinion on the critical urgency of dealing with chronic poverty across the world.

It is, of course, unreasonable to expect people to relate as emotionally to long-term problems with which they feel they have little connection. In this respect, both global poverty and environmental degradation tend to feature episodically in people's lives, rather than as a constant – especially when the episode in hand is a particularly awful natural or man-made disaster. But part of the hope upon which this book is premised is that fewer people in the rich world are any longer prepared to turn a blind eye to what they see going on around them. Whether or not the Indian Ocean tsunami will be seen in retrospect to have ushered in a more compassionate and responsible era must inevitably remain somewhat speculative at this stage. But optimism on that score did not seem as irrational during the first half of 2005 as it did even a year ago.

It's that optimism that I very much want to give breathing space to in these pages. For the best part of ten years, I have been fortunate enough to end up working with a large number of people at senior level in both government and business – through Forum for the Future, the UK Sustainable Development Commission and the Prince of Wales's Business and the Environment Programme. Although it is, of course, possible that the wool is being pulled over my eyes by all of these people all of the time, my overwhelming impression is that more and more of them are now intent upon seriously pushing forward on more sustainable ways of doing their jobs. These are not radical people. They are not activists. They would not dream of looking for change outside the system: if it can't be made to happen inside the system, then for them it just won't work. Given the urgency now required, the length of time it takes to get the basics sorted and the extraordinary reluctance to take any real risks remain hugely frustrating – but it is still the case that almost all key policy processes continue to move slowly in the right direction. Incremental change is the name of the game, not transformation.

And that, of course, means that the emerging solutions have to be made to work within the embrace of capitalism. Like it or not (and the vast majority of people *do*), capitalism is now the only economic game in town. The drive to extend the reach of markets into every aspect of every economy is an irresistible force, and the benefits of today's globalization process still outweigh the costs – however substantive those costs may be, as we shall see. The adaptability and inherent strengths of market-based, for-profit economic systems have proved themselves time after time, and there will be few reading this book who are not the direct beneficiaries of those systems.

It's as well to acknowledge both the power and the enduring appeal of capitalism up front. Much of what follows will seek to harness the strengths of that system to the pursuit of sustainable development, while simultaneously challenging our dependence upon today's particular model of capitalism. For fear, perhaps, of arriving at a different conclusion, there is an unspoken (and largely untested) assumption that there need be no fundamental contradiction between sustainable development and capitalism. That assumption stands in stark contrast to the prevailing view of many radical academics and non-governmental organizations (NGOs) that there are profound (and possibly unmanageable) contradictions which demand a completely different world order.

Those critics point to two interlocking data sets. The first is social, and addresses enduring poverty and inequity across so much of the world. In the next hour, more than 1000 children under the age of five will die from illnesses linked to poverty – half of them in Africa. That is a death toll equivalent to at least two tsunamis a month – and in this case, the vast majority of those deaths are easily preventable. The UN's Millennium Development Goals (MDGs) remind us just how many challenges of this order we still have to confront.

The second data set is ecological and is summarized in Chapter 1. The price that we are now paying for the ongoing destruction of the 'natural capital' upon which we depend is becoming more and more visible. Even the natural disaster of the Indian Ocean tsunami was severely exacerbated by several man-made factors. As people began to reflect upon the impacts of the tsunami, it became apparent that some of the areas worst affected were those that had seen their mangrove swamps, coral reefs and coastal forests most seriously depleted over the last few years – often to make way for intensive shrimp farms or new tourist developments. A very similar set of contributory, man-made factors are now becoming apparent as the US reflects on the horrendous consequences of Hurricane Katrina in Louisiana and Mississippi, where coastal defences have been systematically degraded by intensive development over the last few decades.

These interlocking concerns now press in harder than ever on the somewhat complacent assumption that contemporary capitalism will, in time, deliver a more sustainable, equitable world. That assumption will be rigorously tested in Part I, as will the relationship between most governments' good intentions on sustainable development and the prevailing political and economic framework through which they seek to deliver on those good intentions. Sustainable development is still a relatively young and unfinished concept, and has had to establish itself over the last 20 years or so at precisely the time when those political philosophies which would have given it more space (social democracy and democratic socialism) were giving ground to today's dominant, neo-liberal free market ideology.

This may help to explain why organizations and individuals championing sustainable development as a radically different model of progress for humankind have had their work cut out simply trying to mitigate the worst externalities of today's global economy. There has been little time or opportunity to map out more positive visions of what a sustainable world would look like, to stop hammering on and on about the necessity of change and start focusing instead upon the desirability of change in terms of improved quality of life, greater security, and more fulfilled ways of working and living. We are so preoccupied with avoiding nightmares in the future that we have pretty much given up on offering our dreams of a better world today.

Capitalism as if the World Matters sets out to address that imbalance. It does so on the basis of a new political convergence that I believe is beginning to emerge around the twin concepts of *sustainability* and *wellbeing*. With the exception of the current US Administration, most governments around the world are now struggling to reconcile legitimate material aspirations with the need to protect the natural environment far more effectively than we have been able to do until now. They would, of course, prefer it if there were no such environmental constraints; but the costs of mismanaging our natural capital are now so great as to demand a new and lasting resolution to this long-running dilemma.

At the same time, though even less purposefully, governments are beginning to wake up to the problems of trying to achieve *everything* via the medium of constant economic growth. As we'll see in Chapter 3, growth clearly provides the wherewithal for delivering many of the improvements that people ask of their governments (better public services, security, renewed infrastructure and so on), as well as many of the material benefits that people seek through increased personal wealth and consumption. But it also gives rise to substantial social and environmental costs, and does not appear to be making people any happier or any more contented with their lot in life. So should governments be shifting the focus more towards the promotion of wellbeing and contentment, rather than towards economic growth per se?

This conclusion has been available to Organisation for Economic Co-operation and Development (OECD) governments for a very long time. But our economies are now so geared towards year-on-year increases in personal consumption (in order to keep business growth buoyant and tax revenues flowing) that politicians are extremely reluctant even to question this particular paradigm of progress. Companies have been equally hostile to the notion that people might actually be better off by consuming *less*, and see any such discourse as a direct attack on the self-evident benefits of free market economics. For most business people, this has positioned sustainable development in the wrong psychological box – the one labelled 'regulation and red tape', 'constraint on business', 'increased costs' or 'high risks'. Only during the last few years have we seen the other box – labelled 'opportunity', 'innovation', 'increased market share' and 'stronger brands' – opening up in such a way as to provide wealth creators with an entirely different and far more positive proposition. Given the dominant role of business in the world today, this particular mindset transition is critically important: however necessary or desirable something may be, it is unlikely to obtain the necessary traction in today's world unless the business community can be inspired and motivated to get behind it.

Opportunity is, thus, the third key element in the case made for a rapid transition to a very different variant of capitalism: capitalism as if the world matters. The politics of sustainability makes change *necessary*: we literally don't have any choice unless we want to see the natural world collapse around us, and with it our dreams of a better world for humankind. The politics of wellbeing makes change *desirable*: we really do have a choice in finding better ways of improving people's lives than those we are currently relying upon. Responding to both those challenges will generate extraordinary opportunities for the wealth creators of the future. When something is both necessary and desirable, and can be pitched to demanding electorates in terms of both *opportunity* and *progress*, then it becomes politically viable – and that's the threshold that I believe we have now, at long last, reached.

PART I

OUR UNSUSTAINABLE WORLD

1

Conflicting Imperatives

INTRODUCTION

Wouldn't it be great if any book dealing with sustainability could open with a resolutely upbeat account of the state of the planet? But that's just not possible – not in this decade, at least. As this chapter confirms, things *are* going from bad to worse, and they'll get worse yet. Despite a growing number of countervailing success stories, almost all of the trends are still heading in the wrong direction. There is no mystery here: burgeoning human numbers, a spectacularly vibrant, consumption-driven economy and a continuing inability to accept that there really are natural limits, makes for a lethal combination. But no politician can currently gainsay that drive for increased prosperity – offering people more (at almost any cost) has become the number one political imperative. The resulting impasse poses the greatest challenge we face today: we know that change is necessary, but that doesn't necessarily make it desirable. Nevertheless, this chapter ends with a brief and optimistic account of what it would be like to live in a more sustainable world, just to show how close that already is to most people's idea of a better life.

BIOLOGICAL AND POLITICAL IMPERATIVES

At the start of the 21st century, our lives are bounded by two very different and potentially irreconcilable imperatives. The first is a biological imperative: to learn to live sustainably on this planet. This is an *absolute* imperative in that it is determined by the laws of nature and, hence, is non-negotiable – this side of extinction, it permits no choice. The second is a political imperative: to aspire to improve our material standard of living year on year. This is a *relative* imperative in that it is politically determined, with a number of alternative economic paradigms available to us. These imperatives are therefore very different in both kind and degree.

The need to find some reconciliation between these imperatives has never been more urgent. The world has been completely transformed over the last 60 years, with a combination of rapid population growth and massively increased economic activity (driven by access to relatively cheap sources of coal, oil and gas) exacting a harsh and continuing toll on the physical environment.

It has become fashionable in some quarters to disparage this kind of sweeping assertion. Predominantly right-wing media in the US and the UK have taken to their hearts a succession of dissenting scientists and commentators anxious to reassure people that the environmental and social problems we face today are not nearly as serious as environmental activists and poverty campaigners make out. Accusations of exaggeration and scaremongering abound. Given that environmentalists started talking in these apocalyptic terms back in the 1970s, how is it that there has been no hint of a serious breakdown during the last 30 years? The understandable consequence of this barrage of complacency is that many people really don't know who to trust in terms of gauging just how serious things are, especially on issues such as climate change (to which I will return at the end of this chapter) where the ongoing controversies about both the science and the politics are at their fiercest.

Yet, these days, most of the information about the state of the physical environment (and, indeed, about the state of people living in the world's poorest countries) comes from government departments, the United Nations (UN) or other international agencies, and independent academics. Non-governmental organizations (NGOs) are rarely involved in commissioning original research, and concentrate primarily upon disseminating and interpreting the data that comes into the public domain from official sources. With the best will in the world, I find it very difficult to explain how these official sources might have been subverted to falsify information, peddle untruths or generally seek to play games with the general public by exaggerating the seriousness of today's environmental dilemmas. For most environmentalists, this continuing denial on the part of 'contrarians' such as Bjorn Lomborg (2001) is but the last gasp of a 40-year endeavour to make out that all is well with the world, even as our impact upon it grows exponentially year on year.

THE ASSAULT ON NATURE

It may be helpful to briefly review the official position on some of these key environmental problems. In country after country, the data reveals a similar state of affairs: we are continuing to destroy natural habitats of every kind through conversion for human purposes. More than half of the world's original forest area has been lost and one third of what is left will be gone in the next 20 years at current rates of deforestation. An even larger proportion of original wetlands has been destroyed, and more than one third of the world's coral reefs are either dead or severely damaged. Not surprisingly, this habitat destruction has had a huge impact upon wild species, with various estimates of loss of biodiversity from the World Conservation Union (IUCN) and other international bodies a source of intense concern. This situation has often been exacerbated by the impact of alien species on many indigenous ecosystems, with billions of dollars now being spent across the world on control and eradication programmes.

In terms of managed (rather than wild) areas, we have seen little improvement in management techniques over the last two decades. Soil erosion is a chronic problem in many parts of the world, as is salinization, often caused by hugely wasteful and poorly designed irrigation schemes. There are different estimates as to the collective impact of all this upon farmland; but the UN Food and Agriculture Organization (FAO) believes that a minimum of 20 per cent of total cultivated acreage is now seriously damaged. Overgrazing of grasslands has resulted in a similar loss of productivity in literally dozens of countries.

More recently, there has been growing concern about freshwater impacts, both in terms of quantity (with severe water shortages now affecting a large number of countries) and quality, as both rivers and groundwater aquifers are increasingly affected by diffuse pollution of many different kinds. It is true that river quality has often improved substantially in many Organisation for Economic Co-operation and Development (OECD) countries during the last decade through much tighter regulation and a growing reluctance to allow companies to use rivers and streams as their private sewers. But the situation continues to worsen in most developing countries. The same is true with local air quality.

When the will is there, it has occasionally proved possible to get on top of major environmental problems. Quite rightly, the phasing out of gases such as chlorofluorocarbons (CFCs) that were having such a damaging impact upon the protective ozone layer in the upper atmosphere is seen as one of the most effective examples of international diplomacy working to protect the environment and people's health. But even here, we're not exactly out of the woods. There is a thriving black market in banned CFCs, and growing resistance in the US and elsewhere to further measures to phase out other ozone-depleting substances such as methyl bromide. The United Nations Environment Programme (UNEP) still reminds politicians that it is likely to be another 40 years before levels of ozone in the atmosphere are restored to where they were during the 1980s, and in 2004 scientists recorded some of the worst-ever levels of ozone depletion over the Arctic Circle.

Many of these issues can only be resolved at the global level. Although it is true, for instance, that responsibility for commercial fisheries lies partly with nation states and partly with trading blocs such as the European Union (EU), many fisheries issues require binding international agreements – and these are proving extremely hard to broker in the face of competing national interests. Unfortunately, mismanagement is standard at every level, as depicted with depressing clarity in Charles Clover's definitive work on over-fishing, *The End of the Line*. As he says:

> Fish were once seen as renewable resources, creatures that would replenish their stocks forever for our benefit. But around the world there is evidence that numerous types of fish are not recovering. Reassurance from official sources on both sides of the Atlantic that the seas are being 'managed' scientifically is increasingly hard to believe. Enforcement of the rules that are meant to prevail in the oceans has proved wanting almost everywhere.

> *Even in some of the best-governed democracies, experts admit that over-fishing is out of control.* (Clover, 2004)

One of the biggest problems in all of these areas is that the deterioration is usually incremental, acre by acre, town by town, pollution incident by pollution incident, species by species – and hence all but invisible to people living in the midst of this progressive decline. The position in any one year may not be much worse than in the preceding year, but go back 30 or 40 years and the changes are stark. It is death by a thousand cuts rather than by some traumatic shock to the system, which would be far harder for citizens and politicians to ignore.

Hopefully, that danger will now be averted through the publication of the Millennium Ecosystem Assessment report (MA, 2005) in April. This extraordinary study took four years to compile, involving dozens of scientists all over the world, assessing literally thousands of peer-reviewed papers covering all of the principal aspects of the relationship between ourselves and the natural world, and bringing those findings together in a single, extremely powerful analysis.

Its principal focus is upon what are known as 'ecosystem services' – in other words, the benefits that people obtain from different ecosystems (see Figure 1.1). The MA describes 'services' in four categories: 'provisioning services', such as food, water, timber and fibre; 'regulating services', which affect climate, flood control, disease, waste and water quality; 'cultural services' that provide recreational, aesthetic and spiritual benefits; and 'supporting services', such as soil formation, photosynthesis and nutrient cycling. This serves to remind us, however buffered against the impact of environmental damage we may think we are through new technology, that we are still fundamentally dependent upon the constant and reliable flow of ecosystem services to secure our own wellbeing. The MA identifies the essential constituents of human wellbeing as having access to the basic materials for a good life (such as food, shelter and clothing), sound health, good social relations, security and freedom of choice and action (see Figure 1.2). Apart from the first of those, most commentators would see little direct linkage between the healthy functioning of the planet and the healthy functioning of the planet's most powerful species. So it's worth tracking out those connections that the MA makes (see Figure 1.3).

The overall conclusions of the Millennium Ecosystem Assessment are predictably disconcerting:

- Over the past 50 years, humans have changed ecosystems more rapidly and extensively than in any comparable period of time in human history, primarily in order to meet rapidly growing demands for food, freshwater, timber, fibre and fuel. This has resulted in a substantial and largely irreversible loss in the diversity of life on Earth.
- The changes that have been made to ecosystems have contributed to substantial net gains in human wellbeing and economic development; but these gains have been achieved at growing costs in the form of the degradation of many ecosystem services.

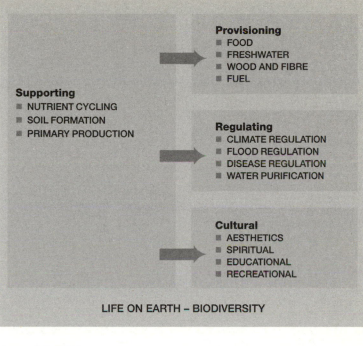

Source: MA (2005)

Figure 1.1 *Ecosystem services*

- Approximately 60 per cent (15 out of 24) of the ecosystem services examined are being degraded or used unsustainably, including freshwater; fisheries; air and water purification; and the regulation of regional and local climate, natural hazards and pests.
- The full costs of the loss and degradation of these ecosystem services are difficult to measure, but the available evidence demonstrates that they are substantial and growing.
- The harmful effects of this degradation are being borne disproportionately by the poor, are contributing to growing inequities and disparities across groups of people, and are sometimes the principal factor causing poverty and social conflict.
- The degradation of ecosystem services is already a significant barrier to achieving the Millennium Development Goals (MDGs), and the harmful consequences of this could grow significantly worse during the next 50 years.
- There is established but incomplete evidence that changes being made in ecosystems are increasing the likelihood of non-linear changes in ecosystems (including accelerating, abrupt and potentially irreversible changes) that have important consequences for human wellbeing.

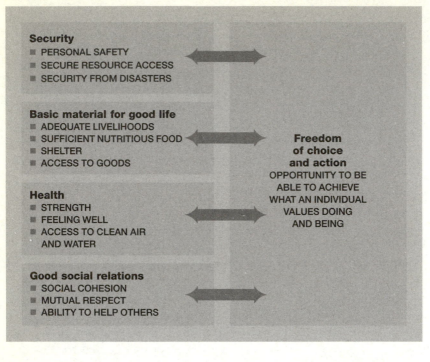

Source: MA (2005)

Figure 1.2 *Constituents of wellbeing*

Blind optimism in the face of such a litany of continuing destruction and mis-management is a strange phenomenon. It is premised on the hope that the planet's self-healing capacity remains resilient enough to weather these constant assaults despite growing evidence of irreversibility in terms of lost productivity and diversity. There is something deeply unhistorical about this cornucopian optimism, as if there wasn't a robust body of evidence available to us – captured authoritatively in Clive Ponting's *A Green History of the World* (1991) and, more recently, in Jared Diamond's *Collapse* (2005) – demonstrating that there really are 'points of no return' when ecosystems are systematically overexploited and abused. A rather more historical perspective would be helpful in all sorts of ways.

BIOPHYSICAL SUSTAINABILITY

Over the last 550 million years, there have been five mass extinctions on planet Earth, the last one just 65 million years ago when the dinosaurs disappeared. For one reason or another (meteor or asteroid impact, dramatic climate change, volcanic or other planetary traumas, or the normal process of speciation and extinction as evolution unfolded), most life forms that have appeared on planet Earth have turned out to be unsustainable. We are the first species (as far as we

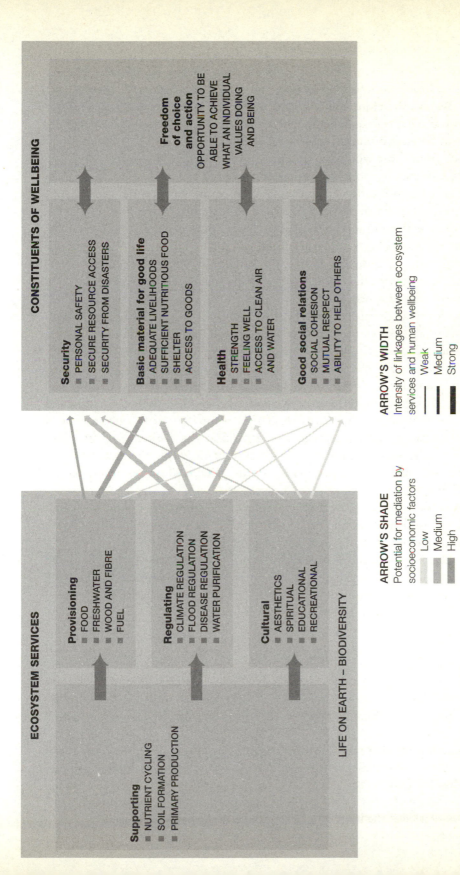

ECOSYSTEM SERVICES

Supporting
- NUTRIENT CYCLING
- SOIL FORMATION
- PRIMARY PRODUCTION

Provisioning
- FOOD
- FRESHWATER
- WOOD AND FIBRE
- FUEL

Regulating
- CLIMATE REGULATION
- FLOOD REGULATION
- DISEASE REGULATION
- WATER PURIFICATION

Cultural
- AESTHETICS
- SPIRITUAL
- EDUCATIONAL
- RECREATIONAL

LIFE ON EARTH – BIODIVERSITY

CONSTITUENTS OF WELLBEING

Security
- PERSONAL SAFETY
- SECURE RESOURCE ACCESS
- SECURITY FROM DISASTERS

Basic material for good life
- ADEQUATE LIVELIHOODS
- SUFFICIENT NUTRITIOUS FOOD
- SHELTER
- ACCESS TO GOODS

Health
- STRENGTH
- FEELING WELL
- ACCESS TO CLEAN AIR AND WATER

Good social relations
- SOCIAL COHESION
- MUTUAL RESPECT
- ABILITY TO HELP OTHERS

Freedom of choice and action
OPPORTUNITY TO BE ABLE TO ACHIEVE WHAT AN INDIVIDUAL VALUES DOING AND BEING

ARROW'S SHADE
Potential for mediation by socioeconomic factors
- Low
- Medium
- High

ARROW'S WIDTH
Intensity of linkages between ecosystem services and human wellbeing
- Weak
- Medium
- Strong

Figure 1.3 *Ecosystem services and wellbeing*

Source: MA (2005)

know) that is able to reflect upon where we have come from and where we are headed. We are, therefore, able to conceptualize the necessary conditions for our own survival as a species and, in the light of that understanding, so shape our living patterns in order to optimize our survival chances.

Apart from those who have subscribed over the centuries to an apocalyptic vision of Christianity (in which the second coming of Christ ushers in a 'mass extinction' of a very different kind), our continuing, apparently 'permanent', presence on planet Earth has been taken as a philosophical given. It is only in the last few decades that our survival as a species has become an issue. Slowly, painfully, we are coming to realize that there is nothing automatic or guaranteed about our continued existence. If we don't learn to live sustainably within the natural systems and limits that provide the foundation for *all* life forms, then we will go the same way as every other life form that failed to adapt to those changing systems and limits. Deep down in our collective psyche, after hundreds of years of industrialization that systematically suppressed a proper understanding of our continuing and total dependency upon the natural world, that atavistic reality is beginning to resurface.

All else depends upon this. If we can't secure our own biophysical survival, then it is game over for every other noble aspiration or venal self-interest that we may entertain. With great respect to those who assert the so-called 'primacy' of key social and economic goals (such as the elimination of poverty or the attainment of universal human rights), it must be said loud and clear that these are *secondary* goals: all else is conditional upon learning to live sustainably within the Earth's systems and limits. Not only is the pursuit of biophysical sustainability non-negotiable; it's preconditional.

Having said that, these are really two sides of the same coin. On the one hand, social sustainability is entirely dependent upon ecological sustainability. As we continue to undermine nature's capacity to provide humans with essential services (such as clean water, a stable climate and so on) and resources (such as food and raw materials), both individuals and nation states will be subjected to growing amounts of pressure. Conflict will grow, and threats to public health and personal safety will increase in the face of ecological degradation.

On the other hand, ecological sustainability has become dependent upon social sustainability. With a growing number of people living within a social system that systematically constrains their ability to meet their needs, it becomes increasingly difficult to protect the natural environment. Forests are cleared to make way for land-hungry farmers; grazing lands are overstocked, aquifers depleted, rivers over-fished; and the rest of nature is driven back into ever smaller reserves or natural parks.

Regardless of where an individual organization places the primary focus of interest in the sustainability debate – on the social or the ecological side – it should be emphasized that the social questions are the key leverage points for stopping these undesirable feedback loops. It is human behaviour and the resulting social dynamics that lie at the heart of today's social and ecological problems.

Fortunately, all species have a deep survival instinct. Ultimately, they do everything they can to secure their own survival chances. And that is as true of humans as it is of the Siberian tiger or the lowliest of bacteria. We humans have now coined a name for our survival instinct: it's called 'sustainable development', which means, quite simply, living on this planet as if we intended to go on living here forever.

With the publication of Rachel Carson's *Silent Spring* in 1962, it started to dawn on people that our survival instincts had somehow become buried in the pursuit of ever greater material prosperity. To generate that prosperity, we have been literally laying waste the planet, tearing down forests, damming rivers, polluting the air, eroding topsoil, warming the atmosphere, depleting fish stocks, and covering everything with concrete and tarmac. And as our numbers grow, by an additional 85 million or so a year, the pressures on the planet and its life-support systems (upon which *all* species depend, including ourselves) continue to mount year by year. We can no longer go on ignoring the challenge of biophysical sustainability.

ECONOMIC PROSPERITY

Even as we witness this unfolding in front of our eyes, it seems that we have no choice in the rich world but to go on getting richer, even though it will undoubtedly jar with some people to describe the continuing pursuit of greater prosperity as an 'imperative'. Historians will reflect upon the fact that the current model of progress, premised on year-on-year increases in material prosperity, can only be traced back a few centuries; life without any expectation of increased prosperity has, in fact, been the historical norm. And anthropologists might point to the Kalahari Bushmen or other indigenous people as living proof that constant improvements in our material standard of living are not a *necessary* condition of human existence.

Environmentalists argue that the pursuit of increased prosperity is a second-order political aspiration rather than a first-order imperative, and should in no way be set alongside the pursuit of sustainability – a point to which we return later. Exponents of the art of 'voluntary simplicity' (maximizing one's quality of life while minimizing one's dependence upon a wasteful, energy-intensive standard of living) point to the falsehood that increased prosperity automatically leads to a higher quality of life. And adherents of the world's leading religions are able to call upon concepts such as 'right livelihood' or warnings about camels passing through eyes of needles to demonstrate that God and Mammon still inhabit different spheres.

That's all well and good; but the vast majority of people alive today both want to be better off themselves and want their children (if they have them) to be better off than them. This would appear to be as true of citizens in the world's richest nations as of those in the poorest.

There are clearly enormous differences in different people's material aspirations. Although there is still serious poverty in almost all OECD countries, what are defined as 'basic human needs' are now largely met in those countries. But as far back as 1930, John Maynard Keynes pointed out that our *absolute* wants (those which we feel regardless of our relative position in society) are limited and finite; it is our *relative* wants (those which we feel in comparison to what others have in society) that are apparently insatiable – and it is these relative wants that keep the wheels of our growth machine spinning merrily away.

This is eloquently summarized in the United Nations Development Programme's *Human Development Report*, published in September 2005, immediately prior to the UN Summit assessing progress on the Millennium Development Goals. It describes progress as 'depressingly slow', despite some encouraging signs – an extra 30 million children in school, child death cut by 3 million a year, overall life expectancy up by two years, and so on. But more than 460 million people now live in countries with a *lower score* on the Human Development Index than in 1990 – an 'unprecedented reversal', as the report puts it.

> *In the midst of an increasingly prosperous global economy, 10.7 million children every year do not live to see their fifth birthday, and more than 1 billion people survive in abject poverty on less than $1 a day. One fifth of humanity live in countries where many people think nothing of spending $2 a day on a cappuccino. Another fifth of humanity survive on less than a dollar a day, and live in countries where children die for want of a simple anti-mosquito bed net.* (UNDP, 2005)

Reaffirming that 'deep-rooted human development inequality is at the heart of the problem', it pointedly comments that for every $1 spent on aid in rich countries $10 is spent on arms and military expenditure. Just the *increase* in defence spending since 2000, if devoted to aid instead, would have been sufficient to reach the UN's target of 0.7 per cent of GDP being devoted to international aid. It concludes: 'this development disaster is as unavoidable as it is predictable'.

In rich countries or poor, with different justifications, it is the pursuit of greater prosperity that drives the political process. Those who claim that many people, deep down, know that increased prosperity won't necessarily make them happier, may well be right. But that is not the way they vote. Those who inveigh against today's 'ideological vacuum' (where the pursuit of economic growth has become an all too inadequate surrogate for real politics) may do so with overwhelming justification; but such protestations would appear to count for little across the political scene as a whole.

Francis Fukuyama was clearly a little premature when he asserted that the demise of communism heralded 'the end of history'. Nothing lasts forever, and there's little doubt that viable alternatives to capitalism (or, at least, a very different model of capitalism) will emerge over time. The question is 'when' not 'whether', and in which direction. In mapping out the kind of transformation that I believe is now both necessary and desirable, I will be emphasizing the potential of a 'soft landing' for contemporary capitalism, seizing hold of the wealth of opportunity entailed in fashioning genuinely sustainable livelihoods for the 9 billion people with whom we will be sharing this planet by the middle of the century. Capitalism is a complex, adaptive system, and is clearly capable of profound and rapid shifts.

Even those who do not share the kind of analysis presented here, based upon an understanding of environmental limits, have good reason to be concerned about the durability of this particular model of capitalism. A combination of different factors – the deregulation of cross-border capital flows; the emergence of currency trading on an unprecedented scale in today's 'casino economy'; increased liberalization exerting downward pressure on wages and prices; growing disparities in wealth both within and between countries; extraordinarily high levels of debt in so many counties and particularly in the US; oil trading at around $60 dollars a barrel – makes the maintenance of our current global economy look like an extremely dangerous high-wire act, with the prospects of a vertiginous collapse seeming ever more likely.

Indeed, many of today's most trenchant critics of global capitalism believe that the collapse of capitalism could be upon us far sooner than anyone anticipates, often summoning up the analogy of the dramatic collapse of communism in a manner and at a time that defied all of the prognostications of the world's smartest think tanks and academics. The collapse of global capitalism, it is often argued, would usher in more self-reliant, compassionate and sustainable economies, with none of today's frenetic consumerism or aggressive self-interest.

Looking at the state of the world today, this seems an improbable scenario, both in its assumption of a rapid rather than a long-term transition, and in its assumption that such a transition would be benign. Whatever personal or ideological sympathy one may feel for these alternatives, prevailing geopolitical reality would seem to indicate a very different prospect – in which the process of globalization accelerates still further, the phenomenon of mass denial continues as the majority of people continue to press for improvements in their material standard of living, and 'reform from within' remains the most realistic option of all of the political options available.

For anyone concerned about sustainability, such *realpolitik* is extraordinarily challenging on two counts. First, the reconciliation (in part or in whole) of these two imperatives (sustainability and increased prosperity) must therefore be achieved through market-based systems in predominantly capitalist economies. By implication, the more 'market friendly' any proposed reform may be, the greater the likelihood of its adoption. Yet, as we will see, many of the changes that are now required can only be twisted to fit these market disciplines with great difficulty.

Second, it means that measures to achieve reconciliation must win widespread political acceptance within the democratic systems that set the boundaries for those economic markets. They cannot be imposed against the wishes of an electorate;

they must be agreed to be either necessary or desirable (and preferably both) given the nature of the challenge we now face. What is more, the public policy measures required to achieve that level of democratic ownership are unlikely to come about through a simple return to the tried and tested precepts of 'top-down' social democracy. As Tom Bentley of the UK think tank Demos says:

> *The values of individualism, diversity and open exchange, which have been fought for over centuries, have won out in the modern world. They are embodied in the structure of capitalism, which now constitutes the only viable possibility for organizing economies. This combination of forces will not go away: the impulse to personal choice and freedom of expression is more deep-rooted than any specific political project and has a long way to run. It is aided and fuelled by the progress of consumer capitalism, which systematically promotes the idea that the use of individual purchasing power to make lifestyle choices creates fulfilment since such choices are the key engine of capitalism's growth and renewal.*
> (Bentley, 2002)

That puts the highest possible premium on political leadership in an age when such leadership seems more and more elusive. As we will see in Chapter 3, ecological reality is usually ignored if it is identified as any kind of serious barrier to increased material prosperity. Nowhere has this been more evident than in the response of the US to the phenomenon of climate change. Its basic rule of thumb was definitively mapped out by George Bush senior when he arrived at the 1992 Earth Summit in Rio de Janeiro warning all and sundry that 'the American way of life' was not up for grabs in the negotiations around the United Nations Framework Convention on Climate Change. The US did, eventually, sign up to the Convention; but that was the last positive thing it has done on the international climate change agenda since that time.

OUR CHANGING CLIMATE

The hard evidence that our climate is already changing as a consequence of the emission of carbon dioxide (CO_2) and other greenhouse gases has been getting firmer and firmer. Computer models of what *might* happen have come increasingly in line with what *is* happening; even the US Administration now accepts that the 0.6°C warming that has occurred since the middle of the last century is, 'in all probability', the direct consequence of man-made emissions – a huge step forward in terms of the US beginning to acknowledge the scale of the problem.

All around the world, people are witnessing climate change for themselves in terms of extreme weather events, natural phenomena 'out of sync' (for instance, early flowering of trees and plants, or egg-laying in birds); and scientists are tracking in enormous detail the shrinkage of glaciers, the thawing out of the permafrost, and the late freezing and earlier break-up of ice on rivers and lakes. *High Tide* by Mark Lynas (2004) records the very personal accounts of the impact of changing weather and seasons upon the lives of people in China, the Pacific, Peru, Alaska and so on. Behind the dry scientific data are the real-life stories of people already devastated by a phenomenon too many of us still think of as one of those problems for tomorrow, not today:

> *If there's one message above all that I want people to take from these pages, it's this: that all the impacts described here are just the first whispers of the hurricane of future climate change which is now bearing down on us. Like the canary in the coal mine, those who live closest to the land – the Eskimos in Alaska and the Pacific islanders – have been the first to notice. But they won't be alone for long. As I suspected when I first began to undertake this mission, the first signs are evident to anyone who chooses to look.* (Lynas, 2004)

Estimates vary as to the scale of this 'hurricane'. The official forecasts of the Inter-governmental Panel on Climate Change (IPCC) talk of a range of temperature increases of between 1.4°C and 5.8°C this century. At a major conference in the UK in February 2005 (convened by the UK Government as part of its presidency of the G8 Group of Nations), a wide range of much grimmer scenarios was explored. The uncertainties here depend upon how quickly the West Antarctic and Greenland ice sheets continue to melt, upon how much more carbon trees and soils can absorb, upon levels of methane leakage from permafrost and ocean sediments, and so on.

As a member of the International Climate Change Taskforce (involving politicians, business people and leading academics from the US, Australia and the UK), I was able to observe at first hand how hard it is to establish any kind of durable consensus on likely temperature increases, let alone appropriate responses. But we did, indeed, arrive at such a consensus. Having reviewed all the latest evidence, our principal recommendation to governments was that they should set a long-term objective of preventing average global temperatures from rising by more than 2°C above pre-industrial levels before the end of the century. Anything beyond that, and the likelihood of 'dangerous climate change' is dramatically increased.

Our choice of wording here was very deliberate. The original United Nations Framework Convention on Climate Change (UNFCCC), which came into force in 1995, secured the agreement of 189 nations (including the US) to the goal of 'stabilization of greenhouse gas concentrations in the atmosphere, at levels that would prevent dangerous anthropogenic interference with the climate system'. Since then, no specific limit has been set, and the Americans spent the next ten years trying to prevent the Kyoto Protocol (the first legally binding agreement emerging from the UNFCCC) getting off the ground. Fortunately, they failed in this endeavour, and the Protocol came into force on 16 February 2005.

This is not the place to go into any great detail regarding the political and economic responses to climate change forthcoming from governments around the world, though I will obviously revert to the 'politics of climate change' at a number of points in later chapters. Suffice it to say that progress remains incredibly slow and massively out of line with the scale and urgency of the challenge – notwithstanding the fact that the costs of climate change are already substantial. The 2003 heatwave in Europe was responsible for more than 30,000 premature deaths and caused 13.5 billion Euros in direct costs; the 2002 European floods caused 16 billion Euros in direct costs. Reinsurance companies such as SwissRe and MunichRe are increasingly outspoken in flagging up both today's rising costs associated with extreme weather events and even more steeply rising costs in the future.

All of this is just water off a duck's back as far as today's 'climate contrarians' are concerned. A small number of dissenting scientists (almost all funded directly or indirectly by US corporates, and by the oil industry in particular) continue to give the impression that the science of climate change is still hotly contested and that no real consensus exists. When the science historian Naomi Oreskes analysed the 928 peer-reviewed papers on climate change published between 1993 and 2003, she came to the very different conclusion that today's consensus is almost universal. 'Politicians, economists, journalists and others may have the impression of confusion, disagreement and discord among climate scientists, but that impression is incorrect' (Oreskes, 2004). Bob May, president of the Royal Society in the UK and a former chief scientific adviser to the UK Government, puts it rather more robustly:

> So there we have it. On the one hand, we have the Intergovernmental Panel on Climate Change, the rest of the world's major scientific organizations and the Government's Chief Scientific Adviser all pointing to the need to cut emissions. On the other hand, we have a small band of sceptics, including lobbyists funded by the US oil industry, a sci-fi writer (in the shape of Michael Crichton) and the Daily Mail who deny the scientists are right. It is reminiscent of the tobacco lobby's attempts to persuade us that smoking does not cause lung cancer. There is no danger this lobby will influence the scientists. But they don't need to. It is the influence on the media that is so poisonous. (May, 2005)

Having been routed scientifically, most contrarians have now shifted their argument to the *economics* of climate change: even if it is happening, and even if it is going to have extremely severe impacts upon humankind in terms of rising sea levels, extreme weather events, disrupted agriculture and so on, the costs of doing anything to mitigate these impacts are deemed by contrarians to be far too onerous. Marshalled by Bjorn Lomborg in Europe, and by a host of right-wing think tanks (such as the Cato Institute and the Competitive Enterprise Institute), they are succeeding yet again in giving politicians a pretext for endless delay and half-hearted half measures. Yet here's what it really means, as explained by Clive Hamilton in *Growth Fetish*:

> *They typically conclude that cutting emissions as mandated in the Kyoto Protocol would see the GNP [gross national product] of the United States reduced by 1 per cent by 2012. What does this figure mean? It means that with the required emission reductions, GNP in 2012 is expected to be 1 per cent lower than it would otherwise have been. 1 per cent is a tiny amount. If nothing is done, and the economy grows at 3 per cent a year over the period, GNP will be 40 per cent higher by 2012. According to the models, if policies to reduce emissions as specified in the Kyoto Protocol were implemented, GNP would be 39 per cent higher by 2012. Put another way, instead of GNP reaching a level 40 per cent higher by, say, 1 June 2012, it will not reach that level until 1 October 2012. This is the growth fetish taken to an absurd degree.* (Hamilton, 2003)

The root causes of this kind of persistent denial are investigated in Chapter 12. Suffice it to say, for the time being, that it has kept most people in the world's richest countries almost entirely detached from the physical reality of our continuing dependence upon the natural world, deprived of the information and knowledge that they need to make sense of these conflicting imperatives, and wholly unprepared for the kind of transformation that is now required to secure a sustainable future for humankind.

A GLIMPSE INTO A SUSTAINABLE FUTURE

Nevertheless, as I will keep pointing out, the fact that something is necessary doesn't necessarily make it desirable. And desirability is something that advocates of sustainable development are not very good at. They are often hampered by the fact that the origins of much of what they stand for today were cast in the crucible of radical opposition to the established political and economic order back in the 1970s and 1980s. Like all opposition movements, environmental campaigners became better known for what they stood against rather than what they stood for, and to a certain extent that is still true today. As we will see in the next chapter, sustainable development embraces a far wider range of concerns than environmentalism per se, but it still suffers from the same problem as far as the general public is concerned: we know what you don't want to see happen, and we know that you're broadly in favour of environmental protection and helping the developing world, but what would our lives actually be like if everything suddenly went sustainable?

At one level, it is tempting to say that things probably wouldn't look very different – on the surface, at least. A sustainable society will still need a highly sophisticated infrastructure, and a mix of housing, industry, offices, recreational facilities, open spaces and so on. But construction techniques will be radically different, with energy efficiency and renewables pushed to the absolute maximum. There will still be roads – but fewer of them, and carrying cars that are four or five times as efficient as today's models. People will, indeed, be walking and cycling a lot more than they do today! And there will still be airports – though the numbers of people flying will not increase much as the costs of flying gradually rise to reflect the impacts of aviation upon the environment, and upon climate change in particular.

In terms of the kind of aspirations that most people have today, I very much doubt that these will be very different either. We all want the best possible schools and hospitals, the safest streets, the highest physical quality of life, and the fairest and most effective democratic processes. And we will go on seeking them just as keenly in a sustainable society as we do today. The likelihood that things will, in all probability, be more decentralized, with a lot more going on at the human scale and the community level, won't actually change any of that.

But it is probably on economic issues that people feel least confident about the ability of 'more sustainable ways of creating wealth' to provide them with the kind of material comfort and security that they are looking for. Some of the theoretical thinking behind the idea of a sustainable economy provides the core of Chapters 10 and 11; but some of the basics are not that much different here either: fair prices in properly regulated markets; efficient and reliable public services; a commitment to ensure access to job opportunities and fulfilling work; and so on. No hair-shirt asceticism, but far less frenetic consumerism, less shopping for the sake of shopping, less conspicuous consumption, less waste, less keeping up with the Joneses – with more time, therefore, to do more of the things that people today always claim to regret not having the time to do.

There will also be a lot less international trade. A watchword of sustainable economics is self-reliance – not self-sufficiency, which I believe holds very few attractions. Self-reliance entails combining judicious and necessary trade with other countries with an unapologetic emphasis on each country maintaining security of supply in terms of energy, food and even manufacturing. The idea that today's neo-liberal, no-holds-barred model of globalization will last much longer seems fantastical anyway, as nation after nation feels the pain of China and other lowest-cost economies making it all but impossible to compete in any serious sense.

With oil trading at well over $100 dollars a barrel, some of the most absurd anomalies of international trade and travel (apples from New Zealand, £10 flights to dozens of destinations, and so on) will have long since disappeared. As part of our efforts to mitigate the worst threats of climate change, each individual will have his/her own carbon quota, allocated on an annual basis, and finding ways of living elegant, low-carbon lives will be both fashionable and profitable. This should usher in the first moment in modern history where cyclists have the edge on the owners of the next generation of gas-guzzling SUVs!

And there is no point beating around the bush on one other thing: people who are better off will almost certainly be paying higher taxes than they do today. Two of the cornerstones of a sustainable economy are increased efficiency (in terms of resources, energy, raw materials, value for money, capital allocation and so on) and social justice. No serious definition of the word 'sustainable' could possibly allow for a continuation of the grotesque disparities in wealth that we see today, both within countries and between countries. This is not egalitarianism (at least, not in the market-based model of sustainable capitalism that I will be exploring in this book), but an uncompromising commitment to greater equity and to the elimination of the kind of poverty that still blights the lives of so many hundreds of millions of people.

No amount of enthusiastic visioning processes will make it any easier to reconcile the two conflicting imperatives outlined in this chapter. This will require years of hard practical and ideological graft, and the harsh truth of it is that the majority of protagonists for a 'more sustainable future' are ill-prepared for a journey of that kind. So here, in summary, is the alternative case that I will be laying out over the next 16 chapters:

- It is all but impossible any longer to deny the need for profound change in the face of today's gathering ecological crises. The science upon which that analysis is based is rock solid and more than sufficient to justify far more radical political interventions than are currently occurring.
- The fact that profound change is necessary is obviously not sufficient in itself – the pace of change remains hopelessly inadequate. Conventional environmentalism has so far failed to win over hearts and minds either within the electorate at large or within today's political elites.
- Change will not come by threatening people with yet more ecological doom and gloom. The necessary changes have also to be seen as desirable changes: good for people, their health and their quality of life – and not just good for the prospects of future generations. This is a 'here and now' agenda, as well as an agenda for tomorrow.
- This means working with the grain of markets and free choice, not against it. It means embracing capitalism as the only overarching system capable of achieving any kind of reconciliation between ecological sustainability, on the one hand, and the pursuit of prosperity and personal wellbeing, on the other.
- That said, today's particular model of capitalism is clearly incapable of delivering this kind of reconciliation, dependent as it is upon the accelerating liquidation of the natural capital upon which we depend and upon worsening divides between the rich and the poor worldwide.
- At its heart, therefore, sustainable development comes right down to one all-important challenge: is it possible to conceptualize and then operationalize an alternative model of capitalism – one that allows for the sustainable management of the different capital assets upon which we rely so that the yield from those different assets sustains us now, as well as in the future?

- The case for sustainable development must be reframed if that is to happen. It must be as much about new opportunities for responsible wealth creation as about outlawing irresponsible wealth creation; it must draw upon a core of ideas and values that speaks directly to people's desire for a higher quality of life, emphasizing enlightened self-interest and personal wellbeing of a different kind.
- It is only this combination (sustainable development perceived as answering the unavoidable challenge of living within natural limits, providing unprecedented opportunities for responsible and innovative wealth creators, and offering people a more balanced and more rewarding way of life) that is likely to provide any serious political alternative to today's economic and political orthodoxy.
- Unless it throws in its lot with this kind of progressive political agenda, conventional environmentalism will continue to decline.
- All things considered, what is the alternative anyway? If not genuinely sustainable development, then what? And if not now, when?

All of these points assume at least a working knowledge of what we mean by sustainable development, which leads us to the next chapter.

REFERENCES

Bentley, T. (2002) 'Letting go: Complexity, individualism and the left', *Renewal*, vol 10

Carson, R. (1962) *Silent Spring*, Houghton Mifflin, Boston, MA

Clover, C. (2004) *The End of the Line*, Ebury Press, London

Diamond, J. (2005) *Collapse: How Societies Choose to Fail or Succeed*, Allen Lane, London

Hamilton, C. (2003) *Growth Fetish*, Allen and Unwin, Sydney

Lomborg, B. (2001) *The Skeptical Environmentalist: Measuring the Real State of the World*, Cambridge University Press, Cambridge, UK

Lynas, M. (2004) *High Tide*, Flamingo, London

MA (2005) *Ecosystems and Human Well-being: Opportunities and Challenges for Business and Industry*, the fourth Millennium Ecosystem Assessment report, available at www.millenniumassessment.org

May, R. (2005) 'Under-informed, over here', *Guardian*, 27 January

Oreskes, N. (2004) 'Beyond the ivory tower: The scientific consensus on climate change', *Science*, vol 306, issue 5702, 3 December

Ponting, C. (1991) *A Green History of the World: The Environment and the Collapse of Great Civilizations*, Penguin Books, New York

UNDP (2005) *Human Development Report 2005: International Cooperation at a Crossroads – Aid, Trade and Security in an Unequal World*, United Nations Development Programme, available at http://hdr.undp.org/reports/global/2005/

2

Sustainable Development for Real

INTRODUCTION

It's important to get the definitions out of the way early on – and most people are still very confused as to what sustainable development does or doesn't mean. And is sustainable development the same thing as sustainability? For me, it's the *science of sustainability* that provides the rock-solid foundations upon which the structures of sustainable development are now being raised – still somewhat tentatively and haphazardly, it has to be said. That science takes us back to the core principles of ecological limits, with a brief historical excursion to consider why so many earlier civilizations brought upon themselves their own collapse by ignoring those limits. For most businesses today, however, this remains far too unworldly: here, the language of the triple bottom line (economic, environmental *and* social bottom lines) still prevails, or 'stakeholder strategies', or corporate social responsibility, all jumbled together in a goulash of jargon and lofty aspiration that somehow still serves to keep physical reality at bay.

DISENTANGLING THE DEFINITIONS

Given that these two concepts of sustainability and sustainable development are very different (although used interchangeably and very confusingly by almost everyone), some brief definitions are necessary.

Sustainability may best be defined as the *capacity for continuance into the long-term future*. Anything that can go on being done on an indefinite basis is sustainable. Anything that cannot go on being done indefinitely is unsustainable. In that respect, sustainability is the end goal, or desired destination, for the human species as much as for any other species.

By contrast, sustainable development is the process by which we move towards sustainability. There have been many attempts to define sustainable development; the most widely used is the definition that first appeared in the Brundtland Report in 1987: 'Development that meets the needs of the present without compromising the ability of future generations to meet their own needs' (WCED, 1987). But the limitations of this definition are becoming more and more obvious. Above all, it fails to convey the idea that there are biophysical limits within which society must operate if the natural capital upon which we depend is not to be eroded. The alternative adopted by Forum for the Future – 'Sustainable development is a dynamic process which enables all people to realize their potential and to improve their quality of life in ways which simultaneously protect and enhance the Earth's life-support systems' – both affirms sustainable development as a dynamic process and emphasizes the importance of social justice and equity in that it has to be made to work for *all* people. It also makes it clear that achieving sustainable development is not simply about managing the environment more effectively, while people pursue their business as usual. It is a social and economic project as much as an environmental project, with the very positive objective of optimizing human wellbeing.

Since 1987, sustainable development has become the principal conceptual framework within which government, business and non-governmental organizations (NGOs) have sought to reconcile the potentially conflicting imperatives referred to in Chapter 1. It remains a highly contestable (and contested) concept, with many diverging definitions and operational manifestations. Until now, that flexibility and inclusivity has been seen as a strength, allowing representatives of all sectors to 'buy in' to sustainable development from a host of different economic and ideological positions. More recently, this 'plasticity' has come under growing attack on a number of different counts: that sustainable development is so vague and indeterminate a concept as to allow almost infinite abuse by politicians and business people who have no real intention of changing their ways any more than they are absolutely required to; that it is a contradiction in terms since it provides no guidance as to how sustainability and development can be made mutually consistent; that it oversimplifies a hugely complex set of interlocking issues; that it inadvertently obscures the truth about impending ecological collapse; and that in its widest definition (embracing social sustainability, equity and justice as much as ecological sustainability) it may even be obstructing the development of sufficiently clear-cut and radical measures to protect the physical environment. Furthermore, there is real concern that sustainable development is an exceptionally difficult bit of jargon, with almost zero sex appeal or political 'street cred'.

Putting to one side that final point (for one really has to ask just how hard politicians beyond today's green parties have made any serious efforts to get to grips with sustainable development), such misgivings need to be urgently addressed. If sustainable development continues to mean all (often mutually exclusive) things to all people, then it cannot possibly carry the intellectual weight required of it at this crucial turning point in human history.

Part of the problem lies in the fact that people have very different views of what is meant by development itself. From the 1960s onwards, the seductive notion of 'development as growth' has been dominant, both in terms of the academic literature and the actual policies of Western governments. This carried over into the 1987 Brundtland Report (WCED, 1987), which ended up invalidating much of its own analysis of unsustainable development by calling for substantially higher levels of economic growth throughout the developing world – without, for a second, questioning what kind of growth would deliver *real* development and what kind of growth actually undermines development by continuing to damage the environment, erode the value of social capital and put all of a country's eggs in the one basket of export-led commodity production. As the Johannesburg Memo *Fairness in a Fragile World* puts it:

> *It was politically expedient for everybody, the North, the South and the ex-communist countries, not to question the development-as-growth philosophy. Both the South and the economies in transition could continue to phrase their demands for justice and recognition as demands for unlimited economic growth without making crucial distinctions as to 'what kind of growth', 'for whose benefit', 'growth in which direction'. In this way, the elites in the South and the North could reconcile themselves with the outcome of the 1992 Earth Summit. Indeed, it was an unholy alliance between Southern and Northern governments in favour of development as growth that largely emasculated the spirit of Rio.* (Johannesburg Memo, 2002)

It is therefore important to be crystal clear about what development means from a more rigorous sustainable development perspective. Ever since the concept of sustainable development was first used by Dame Barbara Ward (one of the founders of the International Institute for Environment and Development, IIED) and picked up in the 1980 World Conservation Strategy (seven years before the Brundtland Report), development has been seen as being as much about health, education, democracy and freedom as it is about increased material prosperity and economic growth. Without ignoring the importance of growth in gross domestic product (GDP) or personal income, any radical conception of development must go way beyond it.

The most eloquent and powerful articulation of 'development as freedom' rather than development as growth is Amartya Sen's book of the same title, published in 1999. 'Development as freedom' puts the removal of lack of freedom as the most important priority facing multilateral bodies and individual nation states across the world:

> *Development requires the removal of major sources of unfreedom: poverty as well as tyranny, poor economic opportunities as well as systematic social deprivation, neglect of public facilities as well as intolerance or over-activity of repressive states. Despite unprecedented increases in overall opulence, the contemporary world denies elementary freedoms to vast numbers – perhaps even the majority – of people.* (Sen, 1999)

In that spirit, Sen is contemptuous of those who have argued (as some, astonishingly, still do today) that the systematic denial of political freedoms and civil rights is good for rapid economic development. He compares one view of development as 'a fierce process' in which toughness and market disciplines postpone social interventions to establish welfare safety nets or improve access to health and education, with his own view of development as 'a friendly process', with a strong, early emphasis on institutions other than the market, and on civil liberties and social development.

Sen distinguishes between freedom as the 'primary end of development' – expanding human freedoms including 'elementary capabilities like being able to avoid such deprivations as starvation, under-nourishment, escapable morbidity and premature mortality', as well as the freedoms that are associated with being literate and numerate, enjoying political participation and uncensored speech and so on – and freedom as the 'principal means of development', under which he includes political freedoms, economic facilities, social opportunities, transparency guarantees and protective security.

It is hard to exaggerate the dramatic difference between this kind of approach to development and the so-called Washington Consensus, promoted with such extraordinary ideological fervour over the last few decades by the International Monetary Fund (IMF), the World Bank, the World Trade Organization (WTO) and so on. We are not just talking about different models of development here, but very different models of capitalism.

So, definitions do matter. It may well be true that sustainable development still sounds very 'geeky' as far as most people are concerned, and that it has more than its fair share of potentially alienating jargon, especially from a business perspective. But opting out of any rigorous application of what sustainable development really means will be much more damaging in the long run. Comfortable euphemisms such as 'improving our quality of life', 'adding sustainable economic value', or 'protecting and enhancing the environment' are all well and good, but do little to advance any real understanding of the intellectual and ideological power that is subsumed within the all too self-effacing concept of sustainable development.

THE SCIENCE OF SUSTAINABILITY

Many of the notional weaknesses attributed to sustainable development link back to the chronic failure (mostly on the part of its critics) to understand both the differences and the linkages between sustainable development and sustainability. The usefulness of sustainable development depends upon being absolutely clear about what sustainability itself means, principally by reference to the biophysical parameters within which all human activity must be constrained.

So, how do we determine those parameters and then ensure that we stay within them? Contrary to popular opinion (which sees sustainability as something rather fuzzy and hard to pin down), biophysical sustainability is capable of scientific explanation, definition and measurement. It is now well understood that there are basically three sets of *services* provided by the natural world upon which we still totally depend:

1 the provision of *resources* for human activities;
2 the absorption and recycling of wastes caused by those human activities (through a variety of different *sinks*);
3 the provision of additional ecological *services* (such as climate regulation, pollination and enhancing soil fertility).

Based upon that kind of high-level analysis, many different efforts have been made over the years to identify the underlying principles behind the concept of sustainability. From this kind of scientific perspective, sustainability can only be understood according to the basic principles of thermodynamics and cell biology. It is this desire to ground sustainability in basic science which has led to the development of The Natural Step (TNS) and other science-based initiatives. At the heart of The Natural Step lie four key concepts, or 'System Conditions', which collectively define the conditions that must be met for society to be able to live sustainably within the Earth's supporting biosphere (see Table 2.1) It is only by understanding how the world around us works that we can properly understand how we need to manage our human systems so that they do not breach the limits set by the biophysical world.

Table 2.1 *The four system conditions for a sustainable society*

1 In a sustainable society, nature is not subject to having systematically increasing concentrations of substances extracted from the Earth's crust.	This means substituting certain minerals that are scarce in nature with others that are more abundant, using all mined materials efficiently, and systematically reducing dependence upon fossil fuels.
2 In a sustainable society, nature is not subject to systematically increasing concentrations of substances produced by society.	This means systematically substituting certain persistent and unnatural compounds with ones that are normally abundant or break down more easily in nature, and using all substances produced by society as efficiently as possible.
3 In a sustainable society, nature is not subject to systematically increasing degradation by physical means.	This means drawing resources only from well-managed ecosystems, systematically pursuing the most productive and efficient use of those resources and of land, and exercising caution in modifying nature.
4 And in that society, human needs are met worldwide.	This means using all of our resources efficiently, fairly and responsibly so that the needs of all people, and the future needs of people who are not yet born, stand the best chance of being met.

Source: The Natural Step

Jared Diamond's new book *Collapse: How Societies Choose to Fail or Succeed* (2005) provides a wealth of historical examples of societies that have breached those limits and, subsequently, have collapsed – from the Vikings in Greenland to the Mayans in Central America, from Easter Island to Angkor Wat. His analysis confirms that many of those 'mysterious abandonments' were *partly* triggered by people inadvertently undermining the natural systems and resources upon which they depended. But this process of 'ecocide' (as he describes it) has to be contextualized within a broader framework of contributory factors, including hostile neighbours, trading relations and climate change:

> *Those past collapses tended to follow somewhat similar courses constituting variations on a theme. Population growth forced people to adopt intensified means of agricultural production (such as irrigation, double-cropping or terracing) and to expand farming from the prime lands first chosen on to more marginal land in order to feed the growing number of hungry mouths. Unsustainable practices led to environmental damage, resulting in agriculturally marginal lands having to be abandoned again. Consequences for society included food shortages, starvation, wars among too many people fighting for too few resources, and overthrows of governing elites by disillusioned masses.* (Diamond, 2005)

I will return later to some of the lessons that Jared Diamond draws from this survey of ecocidal societies. There is a huge amount to learn that is of direct relevance to world leaders today. But it is also important not to claim too much on behalf of the science of sustainability. Of itself, it delivers few answers – merely the secure foundations upon which those answers can be constructed. And sustainability should certainly not be confused with some 'ideal state' where absolutely no damage is done to humans or nature. Sustainability simply means that human society can continue to exist because ecosystems are able to go on providing life-sustaining services (such as clean water, soil fertility, climate regulation and so on) and that society is capable of organizing itself so that people have the opportunity to fulfil their needs.

And there is no 'survival guarantee' here either. Imagine, optimistically, that a universal consensus emerges over the next decade regarding what we have to do (economically, politically and technologically) for the whole of humankind to be able to live within those natural limits. Then imagine, even more optimistically, that over the next few decades we actually succeed in reaching that goal. Humankind could, at that very moment, be obliterated from the face of the Earth by some cataclysmic event such as a meteorite impact or see its numbers dramatically cut back in a few thousand years by the inexorable onset of the next Ice Age. Viewed from a more cosmological perspective, literally *nothing* is truly sustainable inasmuch as the sun itself will, in a few billion years, cease to provide the energy upon which all life depends. We can't buck nature just by learning to live sustainably in this particular fragment of time.

In the short term, however, if sustainability is the *destination* (the point at which we can genuinely claim to be living within those biophysical parameters), then sustainable development is the *process* or *journey* which we must undertake in order to get to that destination. For this reason, sustainable development as a concept remains less scientific, more imprecise and more politically determined. But that does not mean to say that sustainable development, in contrast to sustainability, is somehow a 'science-free' zone. In 1990, Herman Daly put forward four core principles to underpin the sustainable development journey:

1   *Limit the human scale (or economic throughput) to that which is within the Earth's current capacity.*
2   *Ensure that technological progress is efficiency increasing rather than throughput increasing.*
3   *For renewable resources, harvesting rates should not exceed regeneration rates (sustained yield); waste emissions should not exceed the assimilative capacities of the receiving environment.*
4   *Non-renewable resources should be exploited no faster than the rate of creation of renewable substitutes.* (Daly, 1990)

FRAMING SUSTAINABLE DEVELOPMENT IN GOVERNMENT

Daly's four core principles have been elaborated upon many times since then. Unfortunately, they have proved to be of only limited use to politicians, given that such principles in themselves still shed little light on the social and economic aspects of sustainable development – and politicians still don't quite accept that the environmental leg of sustainable development's 'three-legged stool' is as important as the social and economic legs. That has led to all sorts of less scientifically rigorous formulations of sustainable development, as exemplified in the UK Government's 1999 sustainable development strategy based on the following objectives:

• social progress that recognizes the needs of everyone;
• effective protection of the environment;
• prudent use of natural resources; and
• maintenance of high and stable levels of economic growth and employment.

Despite a tokenistic reference to the importance of considering all four objectives 'simultaneously', this particular articulation of sustainable development resulted inevitably in the automatic preferencing of the 'economic growth' objective over the other three objectives. Over the last five years, however, the UK Government's understanding of sustainable development has moved forward significantly, and in 2005 a much improved 'framework goal' was adopted in the new UK strategy: *Securing the Future* (see Box 2.1).

BOX 2.1 UK GOVERNMENT'S SUSTAINABLE DEVELOPMENT GOAL

The goal of sustainable development is to enable all people throughout the world to satisfy their basic needs and to enjoy a better quality of life without compromising the quality of life of future generations.

For the UK Government and the devolved administrations, that goal will be pursued in an integrated way through a sustainable, innovative and productive economy that delivers high levels of employment, and a just society that promotes social inclusion, sustainable communities and personal wellbeing. This will be done in ways that protect and enhance the physical and natural environment, and use resources and energy as efficiently as possible.

Government must promote a clear understanding of, and commitment to, sustainable development so that all people can contribute to the overall goal through their individual decisions.

Similar objectives will inform all our international endeavours, with the UK actively promoting multilateral and sustainable solutions to today's most pressing environmental, economic and social problems. There is a clear obligation on more prosperous nations both to put their own house in order and to support other countries in the transitions towards a more equitable and sustainable world.

Source: HM Government (2005)

This represents a real step forward, with much more emphasis on 'basic needs' – as in the original Brundtland Report (WCED, 1987) definition – on a genuinely integrated approach, and on the international dimension of what we need to make happen here in the UK. This more balanced approach is made even clearer in the way in which the five basic principles underpinning sustainable development (see Figure 2.1) are articulated in the new strategy, reminding people that what we are really striving for through sustainable development is a way of 'living within environmental limits' and 'a strong, healthy and just society'. The economy, our systems of governance and the way in which we use science are all means to those two overarching *goals* – and it is important to bear in mind, when thinking of the economy in this way, that *Securing the Future* is as much the strategy of the UK Treasury as it is of the UK Department for Environment, Food and Rural Affairs (DEFRA).

It is the equivalent pairing of those two goals (living within environmental limits, and a strong, healthy and just society) that explains why sustainable development has such leverage in political terms. Prior to its arrival on the scene, many conservationists and environmentalists showed little interest or concern in the problems facing humankind, especially in the world's poorer countries. Although it is often strenuously denied by the current leadership of organizations such as the World Wide Fund for Nature (WWF) and Conservation International

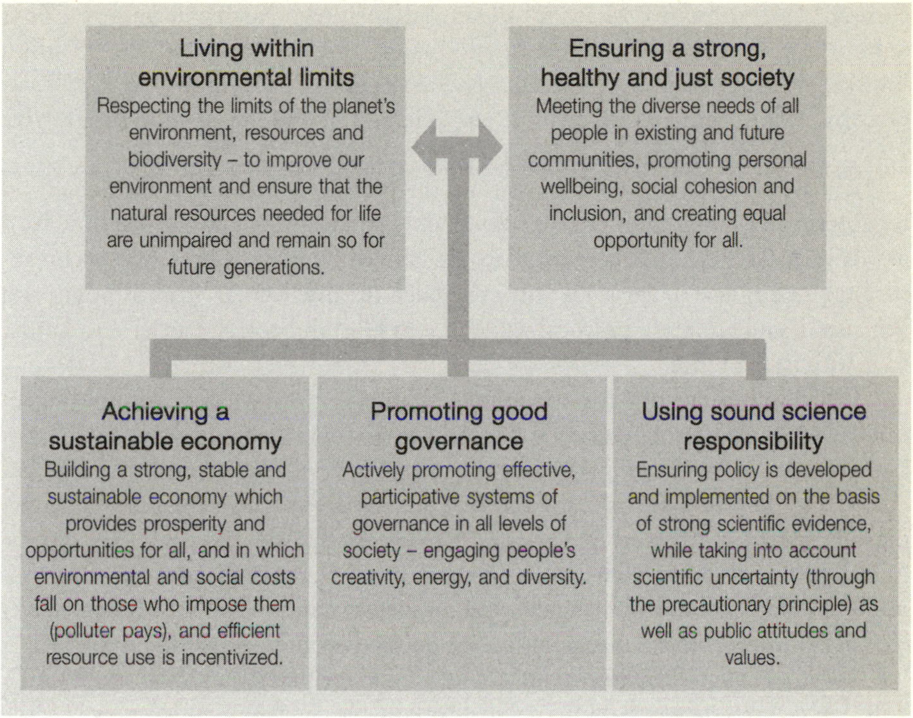

Living within environmental limits
Respecting the limits of the planet's environment, resources and biodiversity – to improve our environment and ensure that the natural resources needed for life are unimpaired and remain so for future generations.

Ensuring a strong, healthy and just society
Meeting the diverse needs of all people in existing and future communities, promoting personal wellbeing, social cohesion and inclusion, and creating equal opportunity for all.

Achieving a sustainable economy
Building a strong, stable and sustainable economy which provides prosperity and opportunities for all, and in which environmental and social costs fall on those who impose them (polluter pays), and efficient resource use is incentivized.

Promoting good governance
Actively promoting effective, participative systems of governance in all levels of society – engaging people's creativity, energy, and diversity.

Using sound science responsibility
Ensuring policy is developed and implemented on the basis of strong scientific evidence, while taking into account scientific uncertainty (through the precautionary principle) as well as public attitudes and values.

Source: HM Government (2005)

Figure 2.1 *Five principles of sustainable development*

(CI), there was an unapologetic elitism about those organizations in the past and a much narrower focus on the natural world, with the human element somehow abstracted from it. Indeed, the tendency of some environmental organizations even today – particularly in the US – to try and keep the environment in some depoliticized zone, stripped of human complexity and controversy, may be one of the reasons why the environment movement in its own right has had less political impact than notional levels of public support might indicate.

By the same token, the vast majority of organizations addressing the social agenda (poverty, justice, human rights, health and so on) had little if any time for thinking about the environment, consigning it to the category of nice-to-do things for the affluent middle classes, while real progressives got on with the serious business of making a better world for humankind. Over the years, strenuous efforts have been made to bring 'the environmental' and 'the social' aspects of sustainable development into more effective organizational forms, but often with little real impact.

One of the most ambitious of these initiatives was Real World, a coalition of around 35 NGOs across a whole range of social and environmental concerns, which came together during the mid 1990s to give voice to what they held in common over and above what they pursued as their own particular interests. That common ground was sustainable development, and the book that the coalition brought out just before the 1997 UK general election, *The Politics of the Real World* (Jacobs, 1996), remains a powerful and effective statement of how progressive NGOs can work together to achieve a common cause.

But Real World did not flourish. As the person who brought that coalition together, and chaired it for the first few years, I still bear the scars of just how hard it was to make Real World more than the sum of its parts! There was no break-through in political or electoral terms to match the intellectual breakthrough, and because it could not add political value of that kind, it became harder and harder to justify its existence.

But things move on: cross-sectoral 'coalitions of the willing' are now much more evident, addressing specific issues rather than some ideological but still distant high ground. In 2005, for instance, most of the big development and environment charities in the UK (under the aegis of the Climate Group) came together to ratchet up their pressure on government regarding climate change. Ten years on from the founding of Real World, with a lot of new data available, the motivation for the development organizations in getting involved in such a coalition was now much clearer in that the impact of climate change on the poor is becoming more and more severe.

Twenty years on from its first full articulation in the Brundtland Report (WCED, 1987), it is therefore justifiable to say that sustainable development has now become the conceptual umbrella under which many diverse organizations find increasingly robust common ground. It is also right to acknowledge that this common ground is unambiguously progressive in ideological terms, with its emphasis on justice and redistributive equity, as well as on biophysical sustainability. That makes for an interesting and sometimes problematic combination, with the neutral and hope-fully 'objective' science of sustainability underpinning the first goal in the UK Government's 2005 strategy ('living within environmental limits'), and the values-driven politics of global justice and progressive governance underpinning the second goal ('a strong, healthy and just society'). As we will see, this combination has led many people of a more conservative ideological persuasion to dismiss sustainable development out of hand, and it may, in part, also explain the nervousness that many large companies still feel about embracing the language of sustainable development rather than the much cosier language of corporate social responsibility.

THE TRIPLE BOTTOM LINE

Sustainable development still remains a frustratingly elusive and abstract concept as far as most businesses are concerned, a 'wrap around' for more operational business drivers, such as eco-efficiency and corporate social responsibility. The familiar notion of the 'triple bottom line' (with companies demonstrating a growing readiness to attend not just to the economic bottom line but to the environmental and social bottom lines as well) has been seized upon both by business practitioners and commentators as the easiest way of 'grounding' the often stratospheric debate surrounding sustainable development.

Inasmuch as it has been successful in this important but limited purpose, and has enabled some companies to think in a much more integrated way in addressing their environmental and social responsibilities, the triple bottom line has played an important part in the evolution of sustainable development consciousness. But it has clear limitations, particularly with regard to the way in which each of the respective 'bottom lines' is interpreted.

The *environmental bottom line* has come to be associated with the practice of environmental management – as in the International Organization for Standardization's ISO 14001 or the Eco-management and Audit Scheme (EMAS) – and the pursuit of eco-efficiency, defined by the World Business Council for Sustainable Development (WBCSD) as 'the delivery of competitively priced goods and services that satisfy human needs and bring quality of life while progressively reducing ecological impacts and resource intensity throughout the life cycle to a level at least in line with the Earth's estimated carrying capacity' (WBCSD, 2002).

No problem so far. But if interpreted in a minimalist way (as it almost always is), such an approach fails to shed much light on whether or not a company is moving towards genuine sustainability (as defined by The Natural Step, for instance), and can even discourage scrutiny of much harder questions than 'how' something is produced, such as 'why' it is being produced at all. In that context, it is still surprising to hear people talking about 'environment-friendly landmines' or 'sustainable nuclear power'.

Attention to the *social bottom line* has accelerated a lot of new thinking about corporate social responsibility, in general, helping to reinforce what is referred to by some as the 'stakeholder' model of capitalism in which the interest of stakeholders beyond the shareholder are given growing prominence. However, in comparison to the environmental bottom line, this is still a relatively new area, and there is considerable, if creative, confusion regarding different ways of measuring corporate social responsibility, let alone 'mainstreaming' it into corporate strategies.

Perhaps paradoxically, it is around the interpretation of the *'economic bottom line'* that the most serious problems have emerged. Economic sustainability has been helpfully defined by academics as 'non-declining economic welfare projected indefinitely into the future'. Yet, there is almost no correlation between that particular definition and the day-to-day use of the economic bottom line by businesses themselves. Given the continuing supremacy of the so-called 'shareholder model' of capitalism (in which a company is seen to have legal or fiduciary obligations only to its shareholders or owners, and to the governments that set the legal boundaries within which it operates), the economic bottom line has come to mean little more than 'business as usual': profits, dividends, return on investments, productivity, growth – in other words, financial performance in the time-honoured sense. Even information about environmental and social expenditures or savings are only rarely included in company accounts or stand-alone environment or corporate responsibility reports.

While it is clearly true that companies need to stay in business to be sustainable, this overall approach (profitable business as usual, plus as much of the green and social 'stuff' that does not conflict with that priority) leaves us – and often the companies themselves – in the dark with regard to their overall economic sustainability. Companies can add substantial economic and social value in all sorts of different ways – through their supply chain and procurement policies; through investment in staff training and development; through their employment practices, seeking out best practice beyond that which is mandated through employment law; through their investment and innovation strategies; through the taxes they pay; through their investment in the local economy or community enterprises; and so on. Indirectly, companies also have a substantial impact upon society through their products and the way in which these products are used. Only very rarely will a company even allude to these important economic multipliers, focusing much more narrowly upon what should more accurately be described as its *financial* bottom line.

Although less pervasive than the concept of the triple bottom line, the idea of the stakeholder company has also been taken up with some enthusiasm, both by individual companies and NGOs. In his book *A Stake in the Future: The Stakeholding Solution*, John Plender outlined the basics of stakeholder theory:

> *Stakeholder theory proposed a view of the managerial role which came closer to trusteeship, where the trustees' role was to balance the interests of the various constituencies in the business and to recognize a wider responsibility to society. In the modern world, large, professionally run companies more closely resembled social entities in which investors enjoyed few rights of possession and control, and failed to exercise many of the rights that they did have. This, indeed, was how many business men had long seen things. The chairman of Standard Oil Company of New Jersey, Frank Abrams, gave an address in 1951 in which he said: 'The job of management is to maintain an equitable and working balance among the claims of the various directly interested groups – stock holders, employers, customers and the public at large.'* (Plender, 1997)

In reality, the notion of the stakeholder company has added little to evolving ideas about corporate social responsibility (CSR) or sustainable development, and has settled more pragmatically around the narrow concept of 'stakeholder dialogue', with companies as diverse as Nike, Shell and Novo carefully defining their respective stakeholders, developing a strategy for engagement (either with each stakeholder separately or together) and then allowing these inputs to shape policy in a number of key areas. While such dialogue processes are greatly to be welcomed, they do not in themselves accelerate the transition to a more sustainable society.

In January 2005, the *Economist* made its contribution to that dialogue by devoting an entire supplement to CSR. Drawing copiously on the work of David Henderson (2001), whose *Misguided Virtue* provides perhaps the most elegant attack on CSR today, Wilfred Beckerman and Elaine Sternberg, it set out to fashion an army of straw men and then gleefully pulled them to pieces.

As it happens, many people (without sympathy for the ideological positioning of the *Economist*) do indeed have deep reservations about both the intellectual rigour and the practical usefulness of CSR, and I will return to these in Chapter 14. But the *Economist* was not interested in that kind of enquiry. By mischievously confusing CSR with corporate philanthropy, accusing all CSR practitioners as having 'a paranoid fear of capitalism', and falling back on a sequence of heinous misinterpretations of the work of Adam Smith, it failed completely to get to grips with the genuine dilemma of our time: what further interventions by government are necessary to secure a more effective working relationship between the dynamism of a capitalist economy and the discipline of living within the Earth's limits? Geoffrey Chandler, founder and former chair of Amnesty International's UK Business Group, was quick to reply:

> *The premise for any sensible definition of CSR is not that 'unadorned capitalism fails to serve the public interest', but that unprincipled capitalism inflicts collateral damage on all its stakeholders, including ultimately its shareholders. The responsibility of the company to society is not about benevolence, philanthropy or solving the problems of the world, but about conducting its business profitably in a way which matches the values of contemporary society in its treatment of its employees and the physical and social environment wherever it operates. Certainly, a company whose practices are based on 'ordinary decency' will thrive; but this attractively naive concept is unlikely to be helpful to those who actually have to manage in the many countries today characterized by unrepresentative government, corruption, discrimination, violence and human rights violations. Capitalism, the most effective mechanism the world has so far known for providing goods and services and creating financial wealth, is under threat from itself and its lack of underlying principle, not from without.* (Chandler, 2005)

The *Economist* adamantly adheres to the belief, as an article of revealed truth, that the primary, if not exclusive, objective of business is to maximize profit, and that success in this goal will of itself provide the greatest public good. Hence, its reference to Adam Smith's oft-quoted 'nostrum' that 'it is not from the benevolence of the butcher, the brewer or the baker that we expect our dinner, but from their regard to their own interest'. The *Economist* goes on to say: 'This is not the fatal defect of capitalism as CSR advocates appear to believe; it is the very reason capitalism works' (*Economist*, 2005). Markets should therefore be permitted to operate in a strictly amoral way, with individuals empowered to pursue their own self-interest as circumscribed only by the law.

This is disingenuous, if not dishonest. Adam Smith was the author not only of the *Wealth of Nations*, but of the *Theory of the Moral Sentiments*, where he asserts time after time that self-interest has to be pursued by people of conscience, informed by their capacity for moral awareness. Without that, the 'invisible hand' of self-interest will not work for the public good. The dominant form of enterprise in Adam Smith's time was the partnership, in which ownership and management were one and the same thing. As we will see in Chapter 5, it was the emergence of the limited liability corporation that began to erode the freedom of managers to act with conscience on behalf of the public good – a process which Adam Smith himself predicted would lead to dangerous consequences. For those keen to advance the benefits of 'moral capitalism' over today's 'brute, amoral capitalism', Adam Smith is undoubtedly their founding father.

CONFRONTING THE FUNDAMENTALISTS

Reclaiming the inheritance of Adam Smith may be something of a distraction, but there are good reasons not to be seduced by those who would have us believe that the way capitalism is today is the way it has always been and always should be. In this regard, the *Economist* represents the moderate wing of today's neo-conservative establishment. Advocates of sustainable development (especially in the US) are increasingly under attack from a more extremist school of neo-conservative thought, neatly captured in this quote from the American Policy Center: 'If you want to keep your guns, your property, your children and your God, then sustainable development is your enemy!'

Sustainable development activists are themselves often unaware of the high ideological stakes for which they are playing. With debates modulated through the reassuring pursuit of centrist, consensus politics across most of Europe, the real battleground in the US remains obscure and somehow too 'exotic' to worry about. But worry we should. The combination of aggressive unilateralism in pursuit of a new American imperium, an unprecedentedly radical application of liberal, neo-conservative economic policies, and the mind-boggling (to the average European mind, at least) adherence of large numbers of Americans to various forms of religious fundamentalism poses perhaps the greatest single threat to the prospect of sustainable development gradually becoming the dominant political framework within which today's complex dilemmas should be worked through.

In *An Angel Directs the Storm: Apocalyptic Religion and American Empire*, Michael Northcott (2004) provides an insightful critique of the 'deformation of Christianity' being practised by so many adherents of today's fundamentalist churches in the US, and of the naivety of Europeans in not understanding what we are really dealing with in contemporary America. Opinion polls there regularly indicate that at least one quarter of all Americans think they are living 'in the end times', subscribing to a set of pre-millennialist beliefs that cast a dark cloud of fatalism and fanaticism over the US's role in the world today:

> *Pre-millennialists believe they are living in the end time, and it is an era of growing lawlessness and dreadful wars which threaten to extinguish human life on Earth. Only after these events will Christ return to inaugurate a literal 'thousand-year reign of peace', which millennialists believe is predicted by the* Book of Revelation. *Pre-millennialists also believe that true believers will be 'raptured' or plucked off the planet by God before the Great Tribulation, so that only those 'left behind' will have to face the terrors of the end time – the last great conflagration of Armageddon, or World War III, which will happen as a result of the escalation of crisis in the Middle East.* (Northcott, 2004)

According to a Gallup poll carried out just before the 2004 presidential election, around one third of the US electorate believe that the Bible is *literally* true in every particular. Just under 50 per cent of congressmen are backed – politically and financially – by the religious right. A 2002 CNN poll found that 59 per cent of Americans believe that the prophecies found in the *Book of Revelation* are going to come true and, indeed, are almost upon us. As Bill Moyers, one of the best-known public service broadcasters in the US puts it: 'The delusional is no longer marginal.'

Indeed, it is not marginal at all. More than 1600 radio stations and 250 television stations churn this stuff out hour after hour, day after day. And the knock-on impacts for the environment in the US are proving dramatic. The US Administration wants to rewrite and radically dilute the Clean Air Act, the Clean Water Act, the Endangered Species Act and the National Environmental Policy Act – the four pillars of US environment policy. It wants to open up the Arctic National Wildlife Refuge, and extend both grazing and logging rights on public land. And why not? Despite a growing awareness on the part of moderate evangelicals across the US that they have given away far too much of the moral high ground to their more extreme co-religionists, particularly in terms of standing up for God's creation, this rearguard action is long overdue. In October 2004, the National Association of Evangelicals adopted an 'evangelical call to civic responsibility', affirming that 'God-given dominion is a sacred responsibility to steward the Earth, and not a licence to abuse the creation of which we are a part.' However, there are still millions of Christian fundamentalists in the US who believe that environmental destruction is not just unimportant, but something to be positively welcomed – even hastened – as a sign of the coming apocalypse. Environmental activists are regularly castigated as both crypto-communists and godless heretics:

> *Why care about the Earth when the droughts, floods, famine and pestilence brought by ecological collapse are signs of the apocalypse*

*foretold in the Bible? Why care about global climate change when you
and yours will be rescued in the rapture? And why care about converting
from oil to solar when the same God who performed the miracle of the
loaves and fishes can whip up a few billion barrels of light crude with a
word?* (Moyers, 2005)

Most Europeans are prone to dismiss all of this as yet another bizarre manifestation
of a nation dominated by 'stupid white men', to use Michael Moore's phrase. But
that seems complacent. The successful advocacy of sustainable development, as
articulated in this chapter, depends utterly upon some sense of shared purpose
across the world as a whole, including, and especially, the US, as well as upon a
wholly rational, evidence-based analysis of the urgent need to change our ways.
Bringing the Americans on board over climate change has proved to be a nightmare,
in part because the same body of evidence is being processed in completely different
ways on either side of the Atlantic. But the Bush Administration's approach to
climate change is just the visible tip of an iceberg of environment-wrecking policies.
In *Crimes Against Nature* (2004), Robert Kennedy Jr has provided the most chilling
account of the way in which the Bush Administration has set out covertly but
systematically to dismantle every single principal building block of his country's
environmental legislation. He cites more than 300 major roll-backs in President
Bush's first four years in office. Most of these are directly or indirectly connected
to financial contributions to the Republican party, with tens of millions of dollars
changing hands in a way that makes this particular Administration one of the most
shamelessly corrupt governments anywhere in the world.

This assault on the environment has only been possible by subverting the work
of the Environmental Protection Agency and every other regulatory body. In case
after case, Robert Kennedy Jr itemizes how data have been suppressed, key reports
amended to downplay the evidence, and individual scientists harassed and victim-
ized. In February 2004, the Union of Concerned Scientists issued an unprecedented report signed by 60 world-renowned scientists, including 20 Nobel
laureates, asserting that the scope and scale of 'the manipulation, suppression and
misrepresentation of science by the Bush Administration is unprecedented'. (Union
of Concerned Scientists, 2004). As Robert Kennedy Jr says:

*Science, like theology, reveals transcendent truths about a changing
world. The best scientists are moral individuals whose business is to seek
the truth. Corruption of this process undermines not just democracy but
civilization itself.* (Kennedy, 2004)

Against that backdrop, there is now an extremely lively debate in the US (under
the provocative heading 'the death of environmentalism') about the environment
movement's complicity in the triumph of anti-environmental, neo-conservative
politics in America. Many now believe that an excessively technocratic, regulation-

driven approach to protecting the environment has allowed the neo-conservatives to win the battle for people's hearts and minds, appealing unapologetically to their sense of themselves as fair, hard-working, entrepreneurial citizens – oppressed rather than liberated by their environmental protectors. Between the apocalyptic warnings of imminent eco-doom, on the one hand, and high-tech eco-utopias on the other, it is true that there has not been as much positive engagement with consumers and citizens as will be required to win people over to the practicalities of living more sustainably on planet Earth.

THE CHALLENGE TO ENVIRONMENTALISTS

Environmental concerns are usually framed very technically as something to be sorted out by legislators and experts. They are neatly boxed up in discrete self-contained packages: air quality, biological diversity, national parks, toxic waste, climate change and so on. The focus is fixed firmly on the environment as such, without widening the frame to embrace people, their communities or the economy. Coalitions with other progressive causes are usually seen as too difficult to handle, diluting the environmental message, potentially alienating funders and inviting unnecessary controversy. For instance, why speak out against the war in Iraq or HIV/AIDS or systematized cruelty to animals if these are clearly not 'environmental' issues as such?

All this has led Adam Werbach, a former executive director of the Sierra Club, to the following rather sober conclusion:

> The signs of environmentalism's death are all around us: we speak in terms of technical policies, not vision and values; we propose 20th-century solutions to 21st-century problems; we are failing to attract young people, the physical embodiment of the future, to our cause; we're failing to attract the disenfranchised, the disempowered, the dispossessed and the disengaged; we treat our mental categories, ourselves and other elements of nature as things; most of all, environmentalism is no longer capable of generating the power it needs to deal with the world's most serious ecological problems. (Werbach, 2004)

I suspect that most European environmentalists would want to see themselves exempted from such charges. And it is certainly true that they have, to a considerable extent, managed to avoid such constricting demarcation lines. Friends of the Earth continues to campaign with passion on human rights, international trade, governance issues and so on; Greenpeace has steadfastly maintained its work on security issues and nuclear weapons; WWF has found itself increasingly involved in community-based social and economic initiatives, if only to ensure that its biodiversity work can be more effectively prosecuted. Sustainable development is more of a lived reality this side of the Atlantic than on the other – even if those organizations still find it difficult to embrace its language and more radical intellectual analysis.

But questions will need to be asked in Europe too. The EU's renewed emphasis on economic growth and competitiveness at almost all costs is having a massively damaging impact upon a number of key environmental issues. People are accustomed to seeing Europe's green parties still winning relatively low percentages in elections (even though those green parties remain by far the most articulate and realistic exponents of what the politics of sustainable development must eventually come to look like), and few in the UK will have been surprised at the UK Green Party's very low vote in the 2005 general election. But they must have been somewhat taken aback to see how little attention environmental issues warranted throughout the election campaign. Even climate change barely crossed the visibility threshold despite politicians in *every* major party acknowledging (outside the general election campaign, it has to be said) that this is one of the biggest – if not *the* biggest – challenge that we face in the longer term.

It is easy to blame the politicians for the usual combination of short-sightedness and poor leadership; but some have already started to question just how effective the UK environment movement has been over the last eight years since the Labour government was first elected. There have been very few out-and-out successes, a huge amount of effort devoted to holding the ground won under preceding Tory governments, and a great string of disappointments and setbacks that certainly were not part of the forward thinking when environmentalists so warmly welcomed the Labour victory in 1997. So have we lost the plot? Have we sold out to a government that talks as green as they come, but defaults on almost every occasion to classic 'growth' responses? Even if we aren't necessarily contemplating 'the death of environmentalism' as such, in the UK or in Europe more generally, I would argue that we can now talk with some justification of the *demise* of conventional environmentalism in the face of 20 years of unreconstructed, neo-conservative economic liberalization.

In that regard, the challenge is the same both here and in the US: how to reframe the social and environmental problems we now face in such a way as to win back the progressive ground lost to the conservatives during that time. Conventional environmentalism is demonstrably incapable of rising to that challenge: its appeal is too narrow, too technical, too anti-business, too depressing, often too dowdy, and too 'heard it all before'. Unless environmentalism can reposition itself within the more progressive and radical frame that sustainable development provides – a frame that allows the inevitable (as in the need for change) to be made desirable – then a continuing decline in influence seems the most likely outcome.

This debate has yet to ignite here in the UK. In the US, it's been fizzing away since 2004, with environmentalists arguing passionately about the language they use, the core precepts that lie behind their movement, the balance between top down and bottom up, the appropriateness of the networks and institutions upon which they rely, and the potential for bringing together a much broader coalition of progressive causes to take on the neo-conservatives in that battle for hearts and minds – not so much through the issues themselves, but through clear moral repositioning and a clear appeal to people's core values. That will inevitably entail a profound shift of mood:

> *Martin Luther King's 'I Have a Dream' speech is famous because it put forward an inspiring, positive vision that carried a critique of the current moment within it. Imagine how history would have turned out had King given an 'I Have a Nightmare' speech instead. In the absence of a bold vision and a reconsideration of the problem, environmental leaders are effectively giving the 'I Have a Nightmare' speech, not just in our press interviews but also in the way we make our proposals. The world's most effective leaders are not issue identified, but rather vision and value identified. These leaders distinguish themselves by inspiring hope against fear, love against injustice and power against powerlessness. A positive, transformative vision doesn't just inspire, it also creates the cognitive space for assumptions to be challenged and new ideas to surface.* (Schellenberger and Norhaus, 2005)

These comments by Michael Schellenberger and Ted Norhaus were made in the context of climate change, and it is interesting to see how things are now beginning to shift in the US. With oil prices soaring, the focus has shifted dramatically from climate change itself to the question of energy security: two-thirds of oil consumption in the US is used for transportation, and there is growing concern about the source of that oil. 'Much of the world's oil is controlled by countries that are sponsors of or allied with radical Islamists who foment hatred against the United States.' That quote features on the website of the Set America Free Coalition (www.setamericafree.org), which includes not just a powerful line-up of right-wing Republicans, but the Natural Resources Defense Council and other environmental groups. By the same token, the Energy Future Coalition is another bipartisan think tank taking an equally strong line, as explained by Reid Detchon, its executive director: 'We are arguing forcefully that if you look at oil independence as a national security concern – which it is – then the US should be investing in it as we are in other national security areas, instead of nickel and diming the development of energy alternatives' (Detchon, 2005).

But it is not just on climate change that we need to discover that kind of innovative and stereotype-busting 'cognitive space'. The neo-conservative elite in Washington is equally reluctant to engage in any serious exploration about the need to transform today's prevailing economic paradigm – the so-called Washington Consensus. While it's true that some sort of understanding has now emerged about the critical importance of reducing, if not eliminating, the burden of international debt for the world's poorest countries, the determination of the Bush Administration to hold the ideological ground it has won was aggressively demonstrated in March 2005 by the appointment of Paul Wolfowitz as the new president of the World Bank. Wolfowitz was not just one of the prime movers of the Iraq war, but is a leading light in the ongoing efforts of the neo-conservatives systematically to take control of all the key levers of power in Washington. In his previous roles (as US ambassador in Indonesia, an investment banker and, latterly, at the Pentagon), his unapologetic focus has been on enhancing US-led globalization and the specific interests of US corporate power.

These problems are further compounded by the appointment of John Bolton as US ambassador to the United Nations and Ann Veneman as head of the United Nations International Children's Fund (UNICEF). Veneman is another staunch neo-conservative, actively involved in dismantling the legislation that protects US forests. Bolton has been the Bush Administration's leading unilateralist, under-mining not just the international negotiations around climate change, but a host of other key global treaties and agreements painstakingly built up over the last 20 years or so. It is difficult to imagine that such appointments to the UN are being made without some deep game plan in mind, a suspicion amply confirmed by Bolton's astonishing intervention in August 2005 when he set out to destroy the UN's new draft global strategy by putting forward 750 wrecking amendments right at the last moment – including the deletion of any reference to the Millennium Development Goals, to the Kyoto Protocol, or to the commitment by G8 nations to raising levels of aid to developing nations to 0.7 per cent of their GDP.

At a more abstract level, many other aspects of today's economic orthodoxy remain as firmly off-limits as ever, in terms of any public debate, particularly the notion that progress is best served by the uncomplicated pursuit of ever higher levels of economic growth and personal consumption. This has a huge impact upon the quality of debate about sustainable development, and what it really means in terms of transforming conventional economic policies and practice. There are many in government and business, across the world, who are only too happy to see the concept of sustainable development remain totally detached from the debate about economic growth. But that cannot be.

To engage purposefully in debates about the nature of economic growth and its compatibility/incompatibility with the pursuit of sustainability is surely within the 'manageable universe' of what politicians can and cannot cope with. So why exactly has this become yet another taboo territory, shunned even by those politicians who have fallen off the greasy pole of personal ambition and have nothing to lose in challenging the shibboleths of today's political economy? Is it complacency? A lingering belief that this is an impossibly 'black-and-white area' of debate (it's either gung-ho growth at all costs, as we have it today, or zero growth as espoused by fundamentalist greens back in the early 1970s) – even though this is patently not the case? An unthinking sense of 'if it ain't broke, don't fix it' – even though the most cursory examination would reveal just how 'broke' our depend-ency upon conventional GDP-driven economic growth really is? Or a feeling (rarely acknowledged in public) that the rich world can probably get away it with it anyway, just a little bit longer, so long as the poor world isn't allowed to gatecrash the party?

REFERENCES

Chandler, G. (2005) Unpublished letter to the *Economist*, 27 January

Daly, H. (1990) 'Toward some operational principles of sustainable development', *Ecological Economics*, vol 2

Detchon, R. (2005) 'Patriot games', *Guardian*, 18 May

Diamond, J. (2005) *Collapse: How Societies Choose to Fail or Succeed*, Allen Lane, London

Economist (2005) 'The good company: Survey of CSR', *Economist*, 22 January

Henderson, D. (2001) *Misguided Virtue: False Notions of Corporate Social Responsibility*, Institute of Economic Affairs, London

HM Government (2005) *Securing the Future: Delivering UK Sustainable Development Strategy*, TSO, London

Jacobs, M. (ed) (1996) *The Politics of the Real World*, Earthscan, London

Johannesburg Memo (2002) *Fairness in a Fragile World*, Heinrich Böll Foundation, Berlin

Kennedy, R. (2004) *Crimes Against Nature*, Penguin, London

Moyers, B. (2005) 'Welcome to Doomsday', *New York Review of Books*, vol 52, no 5

Northcott, M. (2004) *An Angel Directs the Storm: Apocalyptic Religion and American Empire*, I. B. Tauris, London

Plender, J. (1997) *A Stake in the Future: The Stakeholding Solution*, Nicholas Brealey, London

Schellenburger, M. and Norhaus, T. (2005) 'The death of environmentalism: Global warming politics in a post-environmental world', *Grist Magazine*, www.grist.org

Sen, A. (1999) *Development as Freedom*, Oxford University Press, Oxford

Union of Concerned Scientists (2004) 'Scientific integrity in policy making', report available at www.ucsusa.org/global_environment/rsi/page.cfm?pageID=1642

WBCSD (World Business Council for Sustainable Development) (2002) *Walking the Talk: The Business Case for Sustainable Development*, WBCSD, Geneva

WCED (World Commission on Environment and Development) (1987) *Our Common Future*, the Brundtland Report, Oxford University Press, Oxford

Werbach, A. (2004) *Is Environmentalism Dead?*, speech at The Commonwealth Club, San Francisco, 8 December. Text available at www.grist.org/news/maindish/2005/01/13/werbach-reprint/

3

Re-engaging with Economic Growth

INTRODUCTION

At the heart of contemporary capitalism lies the concept of economic growth. So one can't assess the compatibility of sustainable development and capitalism without first getting to grips with growth. This remains a critical debate, though much less current than it was during the 1970s – perhaps because the laws of thermodynamics have proved such indigestible fare for modern politicians! But today's critique of growth is no anti-growth or zero-growth diatribe: economic growth can still be great, and billions of people all around the world still need a lot more of it. But what *kind* of growth? For *whom*? Within what *limits*? And measured against what kind of *benchmarks*? To shed light on these questions, this chapter considers the so-called 'peak oil debate': how soon will the extraction of oil and gas peak in terms of their contribution to global energy supplies? A lot rests on the answer to this question, given the critical role that access to reliable and relatively cheap oil and gas has played in driving our growth economies over the last 50 years.

THE LIMITS TO GROWTH

Astonishingly, the whole question of sustainability and economic growth has been more or less sidelined over the last couple of decades. The 'limits to growth' debate during the 1970s may well have been somewhat cruder and more polarized than environmentalists would have wanted, but at least it opened up some of the 'killer questions' about economic growth that far too few people are prepared to engage in today.

In 2005, Jorgen Randers and Dennis Meadows brought out their *Limits to Growth: The 30-Year Update* of the original *Limits to Growth* (the third author of the original work, Donella Meadows, died in 2001). It provides a compelling account of the 'growth and sustainability' conundrum, is as relevant now as it was back in 1972, and is required reading for anyone trying to think these issues through from an integrated, systems perspective. As such, it remains one of the most important contributions to the sustainable development debate that has ever been written.

If that sounds a bit assertive, it may well be because some people still retain a vague folk-memory that the original *Limits to Growth* 'got it all wrong' in predicting the end of life as we know it, was based on faulty computer modelling and was 'seen off' (especially in the US) by a group of growth-fixated economists – the proto-contrarians, as we might see them today. None of these perceptions is accurate. As the *30-Year Update* demonstrates, the many different models that the original work explored have proved to be remarkably robust, and the core analysis about natural limits and the dangers of overshooting these limits is, if anything, more critical now than it was then. It did *not* claim that economic growth leads inevitably to collapse, and it did *not* advocate a zero-growth alternative:

> *Our analysis did not foresee abrupt limits – absent one day, totally binding the next. In our scenarios, the expansion of population and physical capital gradually forces humanity to divert more and more capital to cope with the problems arising from a combination of constraints. Eventually, so much capital is diverted to solving these problems that it becomes impossible to sustain further growth in industrial output. When industry declines, society can no longer sustain greater and greater output in the other economic sectors: food, services and other consumption. When those sectors quit growing, population growth also ceases.* (Randers and Meadows, 2005)

It is the notion of 'overshoot' that makes the analysis so powerful – meaning, quite simply, to go too far, to cross the line, to go beyond limits without necessarily knowing that this is what one has done. On a finite Earth, physical growth must eventually end. The idea that we can sustain the kind of growth we have seen since 1950 in key areas of economic activity, knowing what we already know about the state of the planet, is simply fantastical. In fact, as can be seen from Table 3.1, adapted from *Limits to Growth: The 30-Year Update*, rates of growth between 1975 and 2000 were already a great deal slower than rates of growth between 1950 and 1975.

The principal conclusion of the research conducted by Randers and Meadows over a 30-year period is simple:

> *... we worry that current policies will produce global overshoot and collapse through ineffective efforts to anticipate and cope with ecological limits. We believe that the human economy is exceeding important limits now, and that this overshoot will intensify greatly over the coming decades.* (Randers and Meadows, 2005)

And overshoot can lead to only two outcomes: a crash of some description, or a deliberate, planned turnaround through a series of corrections that will be more or less painful depending upon the timeframe within which they are made.

Table 3.1 *30-year update to Limits to Growth*

	1950	25-year change (percentage)	1975	25-year change (percentage)	2000
Human population (millions)	2520	160	4077	150	6067
Registered vehicles (millions)	70	470	328	220	723
Oil consumption (million barrels per year)	3800	540	20,512	130	27,635
Natural gas consumption (trillion cubic feet per year)	6.5	680	44.4	210	94.5
Coal consumption (million metric tonnes per year)	1400	230	3300	150	5100
Electrical generation capacity (million kilowatts)	154	1040	1606	200	3240
Corn (maize) production (million metric tonnes per year)	131	260	342	170	594
Wheat production (million metric tonnes per year)	143	250	356	160	584
Rice production (million metric tonnes per year)	150	240	357	170	598
Cotton production (million metric tonnes per year)	5.4	230	12	150	18
Wood pulp production (million metric tonnes per year)	12	830	102	170	171
Iron production (million metric tonnes per year)	134	350	468	120	580
Steel production (million metric tonnes per year)	185	350	651	120	788
Aluminium production (million metric tonnes per year)	1.5	800	12	190	23

Source: adapted from Randers and Meadows (2005)

It is for this reason that any serious analysis of the potential compatibility of sustainability, on the one hand, and capitalism, on the other, must surely address the question of economic growth more systematically than any other. Of all the defining characteristics of post-World War II capitalism, the centrality of economic growth as the overarching policy objective is perhaps the most important. It has driven turnover in the global economy to a staggering $45 trillion per annum, doubling in just 25 years, with the volume of world trade now 12 times what it was in 1945. Hundreds of millions of people's lives have been enriched, often dramatically, in the process.

Yet, as we also know, those dramatic increases in economic activity and material wellbeing have failed to solve many of the world's worst problems (particularly chronic poverty in developing countries) and have created a host of additional problems as a consequence of the environmental and social externalities. That has left some environmentalists arguing that sustainability and the pursuit of economic growth – of any kind – are totally incompatible. But is that really the case?

Going right back to the work of Reverend Thomas Malthus – who examined the impact of population growth in 1798 and reached the conclusion that population growth would naturally check itself in the form of famine, wars and disease – people have always tended to underestimate both the resilience of biophysical systems in accommodating the expansion of the human species, and the sheer genius of the human species in finding new resources, bringing on substitutes for diminishing resources and increasing the efficiency of resource use through market forces. Conventional economics holds that so long as the price of something provides a sufficiently realistic measure of its value, then rising prices for diminishing resources will encourage both greater efficiencies in its use and the development of substitutes. As we will see later in the chapter, this is precisely how most economists address the problem that levels of oil production are likely to peak within the next decade. So what is the problem?

Unfortunately, past performance provides no guarantee as to future performance. What if – as the empirical data would now seem to suggest in the Millennium Ecosystem Assessment report (MA, 2005) – the biophysical indicators of scarcity and environmental degradation are telling a very different story from the economic indicators upon which we almost exclusively rely? What if the hidden, cumulative costs of our current model of progress threaten to offset all of the benefits that it is still generating?

SUSTAINABLE SYSTEMS

At the heart of the growth conundrum is a misconception so gross that it makes a complete nonsense of the way in which the vast majority of economists and politicians think about economic growth. For them, the global economy is *the* system, within which all else (human society, the planet and all other species) can be subsumed as subsystems. And once the global economy is seen as the overarching, self-contained system, it can then define its own operational boundaries and, theoretically, expand both permanently and exponentially, with constant increases in the throughput of both matter and energy.

Unfortunately, this is as close to biological and thermodynamic illiteracy as it is possible to get. The economy is, in the first instance, a subsystem of human society (the economy may well have appropriated more and more of that broader societal territory, but there is still a lot more to human life than the economic activity we engage in), which is itself, in the second instance, a subsystem of the totality of life on Earth (the biosphere). *And no subsystem can expand beyond the capacity of the total system of which it is a part* (see Figure 3.1).

That may sound so obvious as to insult the reader's intelligence. Yet, despite the re-uttering of it over the years by scores of 'maverick' economists and environmentalists, it remains steadfastly outside the canon of what passes for conventional neo-classical economics, with increasingly disturbing consequences.

It means that the majority of economists (and the politicians whom they advise) still do not appreciate that as an open subsystem of the much larger but essentially closed ecosystem, it is the physical limits of that ecosystem which will constrain the speed and scale at which the economic subsystem can expand. In the long run, it *cannot* grow beyond the capacity of the surrounding ecosystem to sustain that growth – and the planet (or overarching ecosystem) *cannot* grow. What

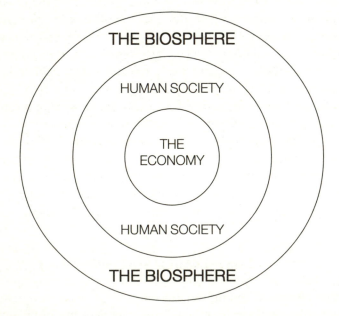

Source: Forum for the Future

Figure 3.1 *Sustainable systems*

we have is what we've got. Come what may, therefore, the scale of the economic subsystem will eventually be determined by the overall scale of the ecosystem, by its ability to provide high-grade resources and to absorb low-grade waste, and by the interdependency of all interlocking elements within that ecosystem. As eco-entrepreneur Paul Hawken puts it:

> *Contrary to what many people might believe, the rate and capacity of the Earth to create material quality depends not upon human-driven activities, but upon the sun. Virtually all our human activities remove or consume quality. As ingenious and important as industrial practices are, they also use up quality and order. Nature has the capacity to recycle wastes and reconstitute them into new resources of concentrated material quality. However, its capacity is regulated by sunlight and photosynthesis, not by economic theory or politics. Today's extraction and processing of resources is overwhelming that capacity, while the waste from these processes systematically builds up in our water, air, soil, wildlife – and in ourselves.* (Hawken, 1993)

Trying to buck the laws of thermodynamics is not sensible. The first law of thermodynamics (or conservation law) states quite simply that energy is neither created nor destroyed as it is changed from one form to another (heat, light, motion, etc.). The second law of thermodynamics states that the availability of that energy to perform useful work is reduced as it passes through successive transformations. This is sometimes described as the law of entropy – entropy being a measure of the amount of energy no longer capable of further conversions to perform useful work. Entropy within any closed system inevitably increases over time; it is only the fact that our system is open to incoming solar radiation that prevents an inexorable decline into chaos.

These laws lead to two simple but all-important conclusions. First, nothing ever disappears. Every atom in the universe today has been part of the universe since the Big Bang, and will continue to be part of the universe until the end of time. Everything has to go somewhere, and 'stuff' has a way of spreading. And, second, every time energy and matter are converted into another form, their quality is degraded and they become less useful to us. We know all of this from our own daily experience. Natural resources that are extracted or harvested to power our economy must eventually return to nature. Steel eventually rusts, fossil fuels are burned, wood rots, carpets turn to dust – not the other way round. And the value of these resources (and the products in which we incorporate them) is directly related to their *order*, by which we mean the quality or concentration of energy and matter. As that concentration is dispersed, its value drops.

As a result, it is not things or molecules that we are consuming, but the order inherent in them. When we burn a gallon of petrol in an internal combustion engine, we do not really consume those hydrocarbons, but benefit from the work they perform as they are being transformed. When we drink water, we are not only consuming it physically, but also consuming its quality in terms of the concentration of clean molecules. It's that which has value. It is the availability and maintenance of this quality that determines the prosperity of humankind, and if society consumes quality more quickly than it can be reconstituted through biophysical systems, then we are, in effect, becoming poorer not richer.

THE EXPONENTIAL DILEMMA

The laws of thermodynamics are therefore fundamental to an understanding of our growth dilemma. From Nicolas Georgescu-Roegen during the mid-20th century onwards, alternative economists have sought to persuade mainstream economists that they must link increases in economic growth with increases in entropy. As Paul Ekins puts it:

> Economic activity increases entropy by depleting resources and producing wastes. Entropy on Earth can only be decreased by importing low entropy resources (solar energy) from outside it. This energy can renew resources and neutralize and recycle waste. To the extent that the human economy is powered by solar energy, it is limited only by the flow of that energy. Growth in physical production and throughput that is not based on solar energy must increase entropy and make environmental problems worse, implying an eventual limit to such growth. Gross national product (GNP) can free itself from these limits only to the extent that it 'decouples' itself from growth in physical production. Such decoupling has occurred to some extent; but the entropy law decrees that it can never be complete. Optimists believe that the decoupling can be substantial and continuous; pessimists are more sceptical. (Ekins, 2000)

Optimists do, indeed, point to the so-called 'invisible environmental hand', where economic growth can actually help to reduce pollution if it accelerates resource productivity at a faster rate than both resource consumption and population growth. Wilfred Beckerman, for instance, asserts that 'in the longer run, the surest way to improve your environment is to become rich' (Beckerman, 1974). The pessimists promptly point to the 'rebound effect' (whereby any additional 'environmental space' created by increased resource efficiency is immediately offset by additional consumption), and simply invite people to re-examine the irrefutable empirical evidence of continuing and worsening ecological damage.

That situation is further worsened by the fact that we don't just continue to grow, but to grow exponentially. There is a crucial distinction between *linear* growth (when a quantity of something grows by the same amount over each time period, regardless of what is already there), and *exponential* growth (when the increase is not constant, but is proportional to what is already there). It is the difference between 10 per cent on £100 producing £10 per annum year after year, and 10 per cent on £100 producing £10 in year one, £11 in year two (10 per cent of £110), £12.10 in year three (10 per cent of £121), £13.31 in year four and so on. It may not sound much, but as Box 3.1 shows, it leads to dramatic consequences. And a growth rate of 3 per cent per annum means a doubling of the quantity involved in just 23 years.

BOX 3.1 BEYOND THE LIMITS

The surprising consequences of exponential growth have fascinated people for centuries.

There is an old Persian legend about a clever courtier who presented a beautiful chessboard to his king and requested that the king give him in exchange 1 grain of rice for the first square on the board, 2 grains for the second square, 4 grains for the third, and so forth. The king readily agreed and ordered rice to be brought from his stores. The fourth square on the chessboard required 8 grains, the tenth square took 512 grains, the 15th required 16,384, and 21st square gave the courtier more than 1 million grains of rice. By the 40th square, 1 million million rice grains had to be piled up. The payment could never have continued to the 64th square; it would have taken more rice than there was in the whole world.

A French riddle for children illustrates another aspect of exponential growth – the apparent suddenness with which an exponentially growing quantity approaches a fixed limit:

> *Suppose you own a pond on which a water lily is growing. The lily plant doubles in size each day. If the plant were allowed to grow unchecked, it would completely cover the pond in 30 days, choking off the other forms of life in the water. For a long time the lily plant seems small, so you decide not to worry about it until it covers half the pond. On what day will that be? On the 29th day. You have just one day to act to save your pond.*

Source: Meadows et al (1992)

As Paul Ekins (2000) points out, this makes it all the more important to distinguish between different kinds of growth:

- *growth in the economy's biophysical throughput (in a world bound by the laws of thermodynamics, indefinite growth of this kind is physically impossible);*
- *growth in the economic value of that throughput (decoupled from the level of biophysical throughput itself);*
- *growth in economic welfare (which is much harder to calculate and very different from the growth in the economic value of biophysical throughput, although invariably treated as one and the same).*

Growth in economic welfare is what matters most; growth in the economic value of biophysical throughput can, of course, generate precisely that (although it often does not), and can certainly do so without any corresponding growth in biophysical throughput – as we will see in Chapter 10. This leads Paul Ekins to the following conclusion:

> *It is clear from past experience that the relationship between the economy's value and its physical scale is variable, and that it is possible to reduce the material intensity of GNP. This establishes the theoretical possibility of GNP growing indefinitely in a finite material world. However, neither such a possibility nor previous experience says much about the kind of change in the physical impacts of current economic activity which are required for that activity to become environmentally sustainable in the real world, or whether the technological and economic opportunities exist for these changes to be brought about such that the value of economic activity (GNP) is increased rather than reduced.* (Ekins, 2000)

RAISING THE HAPPINESS STAKES

The truth of it is that economic growth, like the process of globalization, has become fixed in people's minds as a given – indeed, 'a force beyond human control'. As Clive Hamilton's (2003) wonderfully provocative *Growth Fetish* makes clear, governments of all persuasions are now mesmerized by economic growth. Not only has it become synonymous with the notion of progress itself, but 'citizens' have gradually been transmuted into 'consumers', so that all human desire and aspiration can be rendered in terms of the products and services that they can choose to consume.

Hamilton himself quotes extensively from a fascinating piece of research (*Yearning for Balance*) commissioned in 1995 by the Merck Family Fund to survey the attitudes of US consumers. Some unambiguous conclusions emerged, with the vast majority of respondents desperate to achieve a better balance between the material and non-material sides of their lives. 'They believe materialism, greed and selfishness increasingly dominate American life, crowding out a more meaningful set of values centred on family, responsibility and community' (Hamilton, 2003). 80 per cent believed that they consume far more than they need to, while recognizing that this lust for material things lies at the root of crime, family breakdown, drug addiction and so on:

> *They can see that materialism is corroding society in themselves, but they are too fearful to change their behaviour in any significant way. They are wedded to 'financial security', even though they understand that non-*

material aspirations are the ones that will give them contented lives. (Hamilton, 2003)

Hamilton goes on to draw his own far-reaching conclusions from this survey, and many other surveys that draw broadly similar pictures of lives lived in the grip of consumer capitalism:

> *The social basis of discontent in modern society is not so much lack of income; it is loneliness, boredom, depression, alienation, self-doubt and the ill health that goes with them. Social exclusion is not so much exclusion from the structures of production and consumption; it is exclusion from social relationships and modes of self-understanding that confer acknowledgement, self-worth and meaning. Most of the problems of modern society are not the result of inadequate incomes; they are the result of social structures, ideologies and cultural forms that prevent people from realizing their potential and leading satisfying lives in their communities.* (Hamilton, 2003)

This goes right to the heart of today's great dilemma. Politicians' near obsessive pursuit of increased growth, year after year, regardless of increasingly negative consequences, might be justifiable (albeit in a somewhat morally defective way) if people were genuinely getting happier – if all that planet-trashing, consumptive economic activity resulted in more and more people feeling more and more content with their lot every year. This is absolutely not happening. Surveys of national wellbeing and satisfaction levels show that when a nation moves from developing to developed status, there is, at first, a significant increase in wellbeing. But once nations reach the level where most or all of their citizens' basic needs are being met, relative affluence beyond that point does not make a difference.

The relationship between economic growth and peoples' quality of life (or 'life satisfaction') has been picked up by senior government advisers in the UK. In a paper published by the Cabinet Office's Strategy Unit in December 2002 ('Life satisfaction: The state of knowledge and implications for government'), Nick Donovan and David Halpern highlight the basic problem contained in the life satisfaction data from the Eurobarometer survey (see Figure 3.2).

Donovan and Halpern then advanced a number of reasons to explain why levels of life satisfaction do not follow increases in national income:

- *the role of hereditary factors might overshadow any effects of income;*
- *while gross domestic product (GDP) may have risen, other trends such as rising crime or divorce rates may have had an offsetting impact upon life satisfaction; and*
- *while an increase in an individual's income may increase their satisfaction, it may also cause envy and reduce that of others (if*

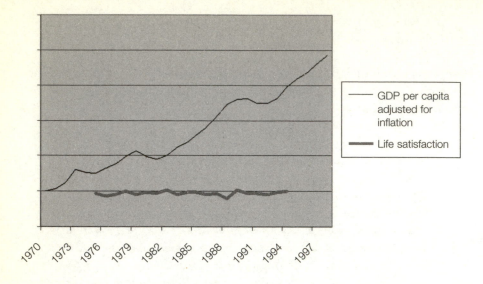

GDP per capita
adjusted for
inflation

Life satisfaction

1970 1973 1976 1979 1982 1985 1988 1991 1994 1997

Source: adapted from Donovan and Halpern (2002)

Figure 3.2 *Life satisfaction*

people's happiness is determined by relative rather than absolute status), or the increase in satisfaction may be temporary (if people adapt to their new circumstances and their aspirations rise). (Donovan and Halpern, 2002)

And that's the nub of it. As Fred Hirsch (1977) so eloquently demonstrated more than 25 years ago in his ground-breaking *Social Limits to Growth*, contentment is not a matter of *absolute* wealth but *relative* wealth. The steady rise in individualistic materialism since World War II has made us all far more preoccupied with status and wealth relative to others. This is sometimes described as the 'Mr Toad syndrome'. In Kenneth Grahame's *Wind in the Willows* (1908), Mr Toad was quite happy with his narrow boat until he set eyes on a passing horse-drawn caravan, and quite happy with his caravan until he saw a car. These days, of course, one car leads inevitably to another (bigger, faster, snazzier) car. As Richard Easterlin (2001) puts it: 'Even though rising income means people can have more goods, the favourable effect of this on welfare is erased by the fact that people want more as they progress.' He refers to this effect as 'the hedonic treadmill' as our desire for more constantly outstrips what we already have.

Not unreasonably, critics of our consumer culture have questioned the degree to which this sense of 'relative dissatisfaction' is, in fact, created (or at least inflated) by the advertising and marketing strategies of those who stand to benefit most from persuading people that they are not quite as happy as they could be – and would be if they bought *x* or *y*. The power of marketing to create demand is, of course, hotly contested; but any parent who's had to watch Saturday morning television with their young children will be deeply unimpressed by the marketing industry's expressions of innocence in this regard. George Monbiot invites us to come to what he sees as an obvious conclusion:

> *Plenty of evidence suggests that as we become richer, we become less content with ourselves. It is incorrect to say that necessity is the mother of invention. In the rich world, invention is the mother of necessity. When people already possess all the goods and services they need, growth can be stimulated only by discovering new needs. Advertising creates gaps in our lives in order to fill them. We buy the products, but the gaps remain.* (Monbiot, 2002)

Ever since the ground-breaking work of Abraham Maslow identifying the 'hierarchy of needs' that people seek to meet, psychologists and alternative economists have set out to demonstrate that far from there being any automatic increase in wellbeing for every increase in levels of consumption, much of our current consumption is turning out to be a very inadequate surrogate for meeting human needs in a more satisfying, durable way. But it may still be playing a very important macro-economic function, as Clive Hamilton points out:

> *Modern consumer capitalism will flourish as long as what people desire outpaces what they have. It is thus vital to the reproduction of the system that individuals are constantly made to feel dissatisfied with what they have. The irony of this should not be missed: while economic growth is said to be the process whereby people's wants are satisfied so that they become happier – and economics is defined as the study of how scarce resources are best used to maximize welfare – in reality, economic growth can be sustained only as long as people remain discontented. Economic growth does not create happiness: unhappiness sustains economic growth. Thus, discontent must be continually fomented if modern consumer capitalism is to survive. This explains the indispensable role of the advertising industry.* (Hamilton, 2003)

Looking at survey figures from around the world, there remains a strong correlation between subjective perceptions of wellbeing and per capita income. But research by Robert Lane, Ed Diener and Ruut Veenhoven clearly demonstrates that, beyond a certain point, the correlation first weakens and then disappears. People may set that threshold at different levels; but it is clear that the law of diminishing returns applies as much here is as in any other area. In *The Loss of Happiness in Market Democracies*, Robert Lane (2000) describes this as 'the waning power of income to yield that ephemeral good utility', and castigates both academics and politicians for being in thrall to that 'economistic fallacy' that, beyond poverty or basic

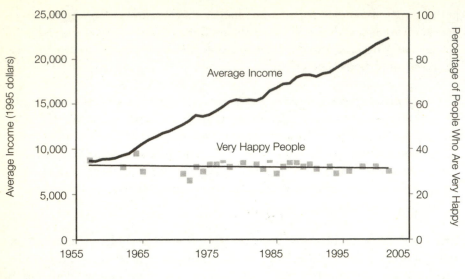

Source: Myers and Diener (2000)

Figure 3.3 *Average income and happiness in the US, 1957–2002*

subsistence levels, higher incomes will automatically increase levels of subjective wellbeing.

This is certainly picked up in the research carried out by David Myers and Ed Diener (2000) in their article 'The American paradox: Spiritual hunger in an age of plenty' (see Figure 3.3).

Worse yet, beyond these relatively manageable levels of dissatisfaction, there is a growing body of evidence which shows that things are actually getting worse in terms of real mental wellbeing. There is a growing consensus among psychiatric researchers that rates of depression, for instance, have been on the increase since the 1950s, especially among the young. In November 2002, a report from the Joseph Rowntree Foundation compared 10,000 people born in 1958 with 10,000 born in 1970. While in their mid 20s, both groups were questioned about their mental health. Among the post-World War II generation, just 7 per cent of those questioned had a tendency to non-clinical depression; among those born in 1970, the figure had doubled to 14 per cent.

Oliver James's hugely revealing *Britain on the Couch* (James, 1998) also points out that suicide rates have increased markedly since 1950, as have levels of violence against the person, alcoholism, drug addiction and substance abuse – all part and parcel of a clear increase in mental illness generally. According to the World Health Organization (WHO), mental health problems are fast becoming the number one health issue of the 21st century, with one in ten people suffering at any point in time, and one in four suffering at some point in their lives. Anthony Stevens and John Price make the necessary connection:

> *It seems likely that the various neuroses, psychopathologies, drug depend-*
> *encies, the occurrence of child and spouse abuse, to say nothing of the ever*
> *rising crime statistics, are not unconnected with Western society's inability*
> *to satisfy the archetypal needs of our kind. The number of people in*
> *whom these basic needs are not met is large and growing, as indeed are*
> *the psychiatric problems which they represent.* (Stevens and Price, 1996)

It is strange how little political salience this seems to have. As a quality-of-life issue, it's difficult to imagine a bigger set of cumulative problems. In 2002, the Institute of Optimum Nutrition surveyed around 22,000 UK citizens, most living in towns and cities, and most below the age of 30. They found that:

- *76 per cent of people are regularly tired.*
- *58 per cent suffer from mood swings.*
- *52 per cent feel apathetic and unmotivated.*
- *50 per cent suffer from anxiety.*
- *47 per cent have difficulty sleeping.*
- *43 per cent have poor memories or struggle to concentrate.*
- *42 per cent suffer from depression.*
  (Institute of Optimum Nutrition, 2002)

Yet we actually spend very little on mental health. In the US, only 7 per cent of health expenditures are targeted at mental illness, and in the UK only 13 per cent. In the UK, only one in five patients suffering from depression is treated by a specialist psychiatrist. Most are simply put on drugs by their GP. Nevertheless, it has been calculated that stress-related illness alone costs the UK around £4 billion a year. But not to worry: the economy, after all, prospers on such chronic levels of anxiety and ill health. The more we spend on the National Health Service (NHS), the bigger our GNP. The more people spend making themselves ill, fat, unhappy and unhealthy in the first place, the more they can then spend trying to make themselves thin, happy and healthy all over again – all of which keeps the wheels of the economy whirring merrily away, even if it is rather difficult to see what this has to do with real progress. Writing in the *RSA Journal* in December 2002, Richard Reeves put it like this:

> *In the last couple of decades, the very idea of progress has lost its mooring.*
> *The principal means through which Western societies have advanced*
> *throughout modern history – economic growth – is faltering: richer no*
> *longer means better. We have lost the philosophical comfort of the Cold*
> *War, which at least provided a clear picture of what we were not. And*
> *science and technology now often appear as handmaidens to scary futures*
> *full of cloned people with microchips in their eyelids, rather than offering*
> *escape routes from disease and want. If we measure our progress in terms*

of our happiness or evaluation of our own wellbeing, we have not advanced for half a century. (Reeves, 2002)

Much of this research is brought together in Richard Layard's (2005) new book *Happiness*. Defining happiness quite simply as 'feeling good', he asks why it is that governments all around the world (with the odd exception such as Bhutan, with its emphasis on gross domestic happiness) more or less refuse to engage in the politics of happiness, to explore the disconnections outlined above, or to address them *explicitly* through different policy interventions. Taking as his mentor the redoubtable 18th-century philosopher Jeremy Bentham ('Create all the happiness you are able to create; remove all the misery you are able to remove'), he goes on to explain the 'greatest happiness' principle: the right action is the one that produces the greatest happiness, and a law is a good law if it increases the happiness of citizens and decreases their misery. He also offers his readers an elegant ten-point exposition as to why happiness matters so much (inadequately summarized here in my words rather than his):

1   Happiness is an *objective* dimension of all our experiences and it can be measured.
2   Human beings are programmed to seek happiness.
3   It should therefore be self-evident that the best society will be the happiest society rather than the richest society.
4   Our society is not likely to become happier unless people explicitly agree that this is what they want to happen.
5   Human beings are deeply social beings; as such, we want to be able to trust each other. Happiness is profoundly affected by levels of trust.
6   Human beings are also very status conscious and are deeply attached to the status quo – they hate loss of any kind.
7   However, extra income increases happiness less and less as people get richer.
8   Human beings are also very adaptable; just because consumption is addictive now does not mean it always will be.
9   Happiness depends upon your inner life as much as upon your outer circumstances.
10 Public policy can more easily remove misery than augment happiness itself.

What makes all of this so interesting is that Professor Layard is an extremely eminent economist, best known for his work on employment issues and inequality. As such, he knows better than most that this is almost taboo territory for orthodox economists, whose focus is predominantly on people's purchasing power, rather than on how happy they are. He has come to the conclusion that the economic model of human nature (which dominates contemporary politics) is far too limited – 'it has to be combined with knowledge from the other social sciences'.

GROWTH AND SUSTAINABLE DEVELOPMENT

And that is precisely where the distinction between economic growth and sustainable development becomes so crucial. As Herman Daly (1996) and others have argued, economic growth is all about *quantitative expansion*, the notionally 'limitless transformation of natural capital into man-made capital'. Sustainable development is about *qualitative improvement*, permitting increased economic activity only in so far as it does not exceed the capacity of the ecosystem. In pursuit of economic growth, conventional economists almost exclusively put the emphasis on the non-physical parameters of the economy (income, choice, distribution, productivity, etc.) and expect the physical variables to be 'adjusted' accordingly. In pursuit of sustainable development, economists must, in future, put the emphasis on the physical parameters (such as resources and the laws of thermodynamics) and accept that the non-physical variables must be adjusted accordingly. Set the physical laws of nature against the vagaries of neo-classical economics and there can only be one winner – and it won't be humankind.

Deep down, more and more economists accept that growth and development are not the same thing, and that there is something here that they just can't go on ignoring. But it is proving hard to give up the old ways:

> *The concept of limits to growth threatens vested interests in power structures; even worse, it threatens value structures in which lives have been invested. Abandonment of belief in perpetual motion was a major step towards recognition of the true human condition. It is significant that mainstream economists never abandoned the belief, and do not accept the relevance to the economic process of the second law of thermodynamics; their position as high priests of the market economy would become untenable did they do so.* (Cook, 1982)

Instead, those 'high priests' of the economics profession keep coming up with all sorts of Houdini-like tricks to escape the laws of nature. We're told that human ingenuity in substituting man-made capital for natural capital will keep pushing those limits away – ignoring the fact (as we will see in Part II) that man-made capital and natural capital are *not* always direct substitutes. Beyond that, we are told that the 'dematerialization' of the economy will indefinitely defer the day of reckoning. Crucial though these responses are (in terms of dramatically reduced biophysical throughput of energy and matter), they do not constitute a panacea for those problems. As Herman Daly (1996) says, 'We can surely eat lower on the food chain, but we cannot eat recipes.'

But the failure to get to grips with the conundrum of economic growth can not just be laid at the feet of conventional economists. Environmental activists (from Europe's green parties through to mainstream environmental organizations all over the world) have done little to encourage a more sophisticated debate by advancing really robust arguments for rethinking the role of growth. After the excessively polarized debate during the 1970s, there has been a marked reluctance to lay claim to a more sensible centre ground, let alone to celebrate the indisputable benefits that economic growth continues to bring people. The rather earnest business of defining exactly what 'ecologically sustainable and socially responsible economic growth' (or 'smart growth', as some have dubbed it) would look like in practice has been somewhat neglected – although the New Economics Foundation in the UK and its sister organizations around the world have done their best to keep that body of work as lively as possible.

What makes this so hard to address is that our single most important indicator of economic prosperity (namely, GNP) obscures the reality of what is actually happening. The standard, aggregated index of GNP is used to capture the sum of all marketed exchanges and government expenditures, and therefore measures the increase in the economic value of overall production – but *not* decoupled from levels of biophysical throughput that generate that increased economic value. So as we eat up our 'natural capital' or degrade the ecosystem's capacity to renew the kind of natural services upon which we depend, we persist in counting all that destructive economic activity as current (benign) income. At the same time, we also count in many so-called 'defensive expenditures', caused by having to deal with some of the externalities of economic growth, be they environmental (such as environmental protection and restoration, and damage compensation) or social (such as car accidents, poor health and rising crime).

As we will see later in Chapter 13, there *are* alternative ways of measuring economic activity, but they are paid only lip service by politicians and are ignored by most mainstream economists. That represents just one facet of the institutionalized denial about the limits to growth that has been going on for decades. As mentioned earlier, this debate almost ground to a halt during the late 1970s when politicians took stock of the consequences to them and their parties if they could no longer fall back on the tried and tested certainties of economic growth. Since then, people have become so accustomed to the notion that 'economic growth solves all' (albeit on the patently inadequate grounds that a bigger overall 'economic cake' means there is more to spread around, or at least more crumbs to trickle down) that to disabuse them of the thermodynamic impossibility of this would exact a heavy political price. Better by far to deny the physically impossible (that biophysical throughput can keep on growing indefinitely) than face the political impossibility of persuading electorates to reduce their expectations.

The latest pernicious attempt to obscure that fundamental reality lies in the self-evident oxymoron of 'sustainable growth' – assuming that we are talking about conventionally determined growth (as above) rather than (to put it somewhat laboriously) growth in levels of welfare derived from growth in economic value decoupled from biophysical throughput. Only when politicians are measured by their success in generating that kind of growth will we have begun to take sustainable development seriously. In that regard, environmentally sustainable growth (or, to be more correct, environmentally and socially sustainable growth) is probably the only intellectually acceptable terminology in this area since it explicitly incorporates proper recognition of environmental and social limits on the growth process.

Elaborating upon the distinction between growth as quantitative increase and sustainable development as qualitative improvement, Herman Daly draws the following crucial distinction:

> *The two processes are distinct – sometimes linked, sometimes not. For example, a child grows and develops simultaneously; a snowball or a cancer grows without developing; the planet Earth develops without growing. Economies frequently grow and develop at the same time, but can do either separately. But since the economy is a subsystem of a finite and non-growing ecosystem, then as growth leads it to incorporate an ever larger fraction of the total system into itself, its behaviour must more and more approximate the behaviour of the total system, which is development without growth. It is precisely the recognition that growth in scale ultimately becomes impossible – and already costs more than it is worth – that gives rise to the urgency of the concept of sustainable development. Sustainable development is development without growth in the scale of the economy beyond some point that is within biospheric carrying capacity.* (Daly, 1996)

'Development without growth' is precisely the kind of talk that sends shivers down the spines of all good capitalists. But the self-inflicted blindness of contemporary capitalism to the laws of thermodynamics is the first and most problematic barrier to reconciling capitalism and sustainability. It is by no means the only barrier.

THE END OF CHEAP OIL

However one reacts to the explosion in economic activity and material prosperity over the last 60 years or so, there is no denying that it has been fuelled predominantly by access to cheap oil and gas. Without that massive and exhilarating infusion of plentiful hydrocarbons, our world today would look *very* different.

They are, by definition, non-renewable resources. They will, inevitably, start running out at some stage in the future. At that point, our lives will change dramatically. Even if we are successful in preparing ourselves for the transition from an oil-rich world to a world largely without oil, the disruptions will still be dramatic and potentially disastrous.

This debate has only just started to warm up again. There is an inevitable sense among politicians of a certain age that they have 'been there and done that'. Most lived through the oil shocks of the 1970s and were exposed to a turbulent debate about the possibility of oil running out in their own lifetime. But just like the debate about economic growth itself, those concerns soon sputtered out. Jimmy Carter's enthusiastic but often ill-directed attempts to get the American people to understand the consequences of their gas-guzzling lifestyles (during which he famously described energy conservation as the 'moral equivalent of war') were swept away by the election of Ronald Reagan in 1980. Right-wing commentators and economists seized the moment to lambaste the doom-and-gloom merchants who had predicted the all-but-instant drying-up of oil supplies, and the high ground occupied by environmentalists concerned about the physical limits to growth was systematically cut away from beneath them.

Looking back over those 30 years, it is clear that this lost opportunity (to set humankind on a more sustainable energy path) represents the single biggest setback for the environment movement during that time. Instead of shifting both public and private sector investments into energy efficiency, renewable technologies and less energy-intensive infrastructure, we have burned our way through billions of barrels of oil with no thought for the future and no thought for the environmental consequences.

Encouragingly, it would appear that this is now beginning to change. The debate about the availability of oil has suddenly livened up again. In March 1998, *Scientific American* published a ground-breaking article by Colin Campbell and Jean Laherrere under the provocative title of 'The end of cheap oil?'. Five years on, Richard Heinberg (*The Party's Over: Oil, War and the Fate of Industrial Societies*, 2003) set out to review all of the conflicting voices commenting on just how long the oil era will last. We know when this 'historic interval' started (with the very first commercial oil well being drilled in Pennsylvania in 1859); but when will it end? The key date for assessing this is the point at which *global* oil production peaks: US production peaked in 1970; UK production peaked in 2000/2001; Saudi Arabian oil is not due to peak until after 2015. But when is the 'big roll-over' likely to come for the world as a whole?

This is no easy calculation, with huge controversy around every aspect of the debate – the size of 'ultimately recoverable reserves'; the growing significance of different extraction techniques; the influence of the price mechanism; the impact of war and security issues, and so on. Geologists involved in the debate tend to incline towards an earlier date (perhaps as soon as 2008), principally on the basis that overall discoveries of oil peaked in the 1960s, with just one new barrel of oil being discovered today for every four that is consumed; economists incline towards a later date (2015/2020), given that there has always been more in the ground than the experts have historically predicted and that extraction techniques just go on getting better and better.

One particularly important issue is the whole question of *net* energy, or energy return on energy invested. It takes a lot of energy to produce energy, and the tougher the terrain, the more energy it takes to get a barrel of oil out of the ground and ready for use. Walter Youngquist, professor of geology at the University of Oregon, explains:

The most significant trend in the US oil industry has been the decline in the amount of energy recovered compared to energy expended. In 1916, the ratio was about 28:1, a very handsome energy return. By 1985, the ratio had dropped to 2:1, and is still dropping. Already, in some situations, energy in the oil found is not equal to the total energy expended. (Youngquist, 1997)

Heinberg's own conclusion about the most likely date for global oil production peaking is as follows:

The global peak of extraction for all fossil-fuel liquids is unlikely to occur earlier than 2006 or later than 2015. If demand for oil decreases due to sluggish or negative economic growth, producers will reduce their rate of extraction, thus delaying the peak. Future economic activity is notoriously difficult to forecast. It is possible to imagine many scenarios. Here are three notable ones:

1 *Robust economy, high demand: in this case, the extraction rates for all fossil-fuel liquids could peak as soon as 2006.*
2 *Global recession: if the global economy limps along at its 2001 rate, with no increase in activity or demand, the peak would be delayed, perhaps until 2010 or 2012.*
3 *Global depression: if the global economy were to nose dive, demand for oil would recede sharply. The extraction peak would then be delayed substantially, perhaps to 2015 or beyond.* (Heinberg, 2003)

Global production peaking is not, of course, the same thing as oil running out. Huge amounts of oil will still be pumped after that point – *but on an inexorably declining basis*. Politicians just seem to be drifting into this hugely challenging new world without so much as a passing recognition of the fact that oil production could be down by as much as 75 per cent within just 30 years. As Colin Campbell (2005) points out in a new collection of articles about the peak oil debate, *The Final Energy Crisis*, we are planning to undertake this transition 'without sight of a substitute energy that comes close to matching the utility, convenience and low cost of oil and gas'.

But is it right to be pressing the panic button at this stage? Long before we see that drop in production of 75 per cent, the price mechanism will, indeed, kick in, and rising prices will extend the period of time that oil remains available for various uses in society – if the worsening consequences of climate change have not already compelled politicians to force all users of hydrocarbon fuels to internalize more of the costs of their use. Many commentators believe not only that these market mechanisms provide the best antidote to today's 'peak oil Cassandras', but that the 'managed volatility' in oil prices in 2004 (exceeding $50 a barrel on a number of occasions) provided proof positive that the system is working quite adequately.

In 2005, however, the analysts began to see things rather differently. Prices in August bumped up against $70 dollars a barrel, and stayed obstinately above the $50 dollar threshold. Goldman Sachs published a report predicting that oil would move to $100 a barrel in a much shorter period of time than anyone was counting on. The debate in the US became much more engaged, with a number of heavy-weight commentators castigating the inertia of the Bush Administration in refusing to do anything to reduce US oil consumption. US motorists suddenly found themselves paying a whole lot more for their petrol, and began to wonder why the big US car companies (particularly Ford and General Motors) seemed to have so little to offer them by way of fuel-efficient cars. Meanwhile, President Bush carried on spending and driving up US debt as if there was no tomorrow, pushing up US consumer demand. The Chinese economy continued to boom on the back of that demand, with China sucking in more and more oil to fuel its astonishing growth. In the Middle East, the situation in Iraq improved somewhat, with their first direct elections in decades; but the prospect of Iraq as a stable, major oil supplier seemed as distant as ever. And the US's threatening noises over Iran and Syria further 'spooked' the oil markets, pushing up prices yet again. Even those who had spent years rubbishing the exponents of the 'peak oil' hypothesis began to acknowledge that something momentous – and really rather scary – was going on.

There are, after all, many different alternatives, including alternative hydro-carbons such as gas, 'clean' coal, tar sands and shale oil. But these all suffer from the same kind of problems: significant environmental impact, accessibility issues, and low net energy returns. So does the answer lie with nuclear power? With the threat of climate change becoming more and more fixed in politicians' minds, a new pro-nuclear bandwagon would seem to be gathering pace. But unless things change significantly over the next few years (for instance, through new reactor designs), the problems with nuclear power remain substantial in terms of excessive costs, disposal of nuclear waste, decommissioning and so on. Two further issues now loom very large indeed: opportunity costs (there is only going to be so much capital available for investments in new generation and infrastructure) and security. The fact that one of the hijacked planes in the 11 September 2001 terrorist outrage was, by all accounts, headed for a nuclear reactor before it crashed has heightened concerns about the vulnerability of nuclear facilities in such an insecure world. For very understandable reasons, governments are keen to ensure that this is not widely debated in the media or beyond; but for those charged with securing these facilities against potential terrorist attacks, this remains a major concern.

That leaves the renewables – wind, solar power, hydroelectricity, tidal and wave power, biomass and bio-fuels, as well as the use of hydrogen *if* the hydrogen can be produced using renewable energy. These undoubtedly offer by far the 'best bet' from a true sustainability perspective, and it is critical that politicians the world over stop flirting with renewables as 'an interesting little niche' and start investing in them as if our very future depended upon them – which, indeed, it does.

But even renewables have their built-in limits – in terms of availability, intermittency, net energy returns, reliability and so on. They will *not* substitute – like for like – for oil and gas in all circumstances.

This is a very challenging prospect for politicians of any persuasion as they seek to keep growing their economies. It means that every facet of our lives will change – and, as we have seen, that change will be upon us in the not too distant future. Heinberg's (2003) own book goes on to explore the detailed implications of some of those changes, building on the work of authors such as David Fleming ('After oil', 2004; see www.geocities.com/davidmdelaney/after-oil-david-fleming.html), Richard Douthwaite (*The Growth Illusion*, 1992) and Richard Duncan ('The peak of world oil production and the road to Olduvai Gorge', 2000). What is remarkable is the failure of politicians to start planning in any way for this *inevitable* transition, or even to start preparing their electorates for its inevitability. There are, of course, all sorts of 'good' reasons for this: the fact that 2015 sounds like another era in political terms; that the credibility of those who first raised this conundrum back in the 1970s took a knock when the wheels didn't instantly drop off our industrial juggernaut; that the current US Administration is violently opposed to any such debate being opened up, as seen in US Vice President Dick Cheney's comment that 'energy conservation may be a sign of personal virtue, but it is not a sufficient basis for a sound, comprehensive energy policy'; and so on.

But the principal reason, I suspect, is that the end of cheap oil means the end of easy economic growth, and the end of that whole 'historic interlude' in which cheap oil fuelled fast growth, high living standards and the kind of 'live for today, live for yourself' lifestyles that have now become so destructive. This will be a crunch point for politicians in every party in every country. Conventional economic growth and cheap oil have marched hand in hand for the best part of 60 years; within just a few years, it will become increasingly apparent that both are on their last legs.

REFERENCES

Beckerman, W. (1974) *In Defence of Economic Growth*, Jonathan Cape, London

Campbell, C. (2005) 'The assessment and importance of oil depletion' in A. McKillop (ed) *The Final Energy Crisis*, Pluto Press, London

Campbell, C. and Laherrere, J. (1998) 'The end of cheap oil?', *Scientific American*, June

Cook, E. (1982) 'The consumer as creator: A criticism of faith in limitless ingenuity', *Energy Exploration and Exploitation*, vol 1, no 3

Daly, H. (1996) *Beyond Growth*, Beacon Press, Boston, MA

Donovan, N. and Halpern, D. (2002) 'Life satisfaction: The state of knowledge and implications for government', Cabinet Office, HMG, London

Douthwaite, R. (1992) *The Growth Illusion: How Economic Growth has Enriched the Few, Impoverished the Many, and Endangered the Planet*, Green Books, Bideford, UK

Duncan, R. (2000) 'The peak of world oil production and the road to the Olduvai Gorge', Pardee Keynote Symposia, Geological Society of America, Summit 2000, Reno, NV, 13 November. Available at www.hubbertpeak.com/duncan/olduvai2000.htm

Easterlin, R. (2001) 'Income and happiness: Towards a unified theory', *Economic Journal*, no 111

Ekins, P. (2000) *Economic Growth and Environmental Sustainability*, Routledge, London

Fleming, D. (2004) 'After oil', *Prospect*, November

Grahame, K. (1908) *The Wind in the Willows*, Methuen, London

Hamilton, C. (2003) *Growth Fetish*, Allen and Unwin, Sydney

Hawken, P. (1993) *The Ecology of Commerce*, Weidenfield and Nicholson, London

Heinberg, R. (2003) *The Party's Over: Oil, War and the Fate of Industrial Societies*, Clairview, Forest Row, UK

Hirsch, F. (1977) *Social Limits to Growth*, Routledge and Kegan Paul, London

Institute for Optimum Nutrition (2002) 'Nutritition and public health', Institute for Optimum Nutrition, London

James, O. (1998) *Britain on the Couch*, Arrow Books, London

Lane, R. (2000) *The Loss of Happiness in Market Democracies*, Yale University Press, New Haven, CT

Layard, R. (2005) *Happiness*, Allen Lane, London

Meadows, D., Meadows, D. and Randers, J. (1992) *Beyond the Limits*, Earthscan, London

Monbiot, G. (2002) 'What do we really want?', *Guardian*, 27 August

MA (2005) *Ecosystems and Human Well-being: Opportunities and Challenges for Business and Industry*, the fourth Millennium Ecosystem Assessment report, available at www.millenniumassessment.org

Myers, D. and Diener, E. (2000) 'The American paradox: Spiritual hunger in an age of plenty', *Scientific American*, May

Randers, J. and Meadows, D. (2005) *Limits to Growth: The 30-Year Update*, Earthscan, London

Reeves, R. (2002) 'The sun sets on the enlightenment', *RSA Journal*, December

Stevens, A. and Price, J. (1996) *Evolutionary Psychiatry*, Routledge, London

Youngquist, W. (1997) *Geodestinies: The Inevitable Control of Earth Resources Over Nations and Individuals*, National Book Company, Portland, OR

4

Unsustainable Capitalism?

INTRODUCTION

Today's optimists are convinced that free markets provide by far the most powerful tool at our disposal in terms of fashioning a sustainable economy. Today's pessimists see free markets (*as they operate today*) as deeply implicated in everything that is unsustainable about today's economy. But the free market (which often isn't free at all) is just one of the defining features of capitalist economies: we must also take into account the pursuit of profit, trade, competitiveness, private property and so on. This chapter takes a whirlwind tour through some of these fundamental characteristics of capitalism to assess whether there is any kind of unavoidable incompatibility in terms of achieving a sustainable society, or whether it is more a question of taming and modifying this particular manifestation of capitalism – variously described by people as 'brute capitalism', 'killer capitalism', 'crony capitalism', 'neo-liberal capitalism' and so on. No easy answers emerge; but this chapter presents enough of a feel for some kind of theoretical compatibility to warrant further investigation in Parts II and III.

CAPITALISM AND SUSTAINABILITY

In mainstream political and business discussions about sustainable development, the key question (are capitalism and sustainability mutually exclusive?) goes largely unasked. In fact, it seems to be almost unaskable. Ours is a capitalist world, with businesses (large and small) creating wealth within the embrace of a capitalist system, and with politicians dedicated to managing those capitalist systems to ensure economic stability and to maximize economic wellbeing. If sustainability as a goal cannot be attained within that broad macro-economic framework, then it is not a goal to which contemporary politicians or business people will want to commit themselves. In those circumstances, the fact that, in the long term, sustainability is a non-negotiable imperative (the only alternative being unsustainability or, in biological terms, extinction) is a truth that will continue to be set aside or actively denied for as long as possible.

But it is a question that *must* be asked. If, as a politically active environmentalist or campaigner for social justice, one's answer to the question is that they are, indeed, mutually exclusive (that capitalism, in whichever manifestation, is in its very essence *inherently* unsustainable), then one's only morally consistent response is to devote one's political activities to the overthrow of capitalism. If one's answer is that they are entirely compatible (that there are no structural, inherent characteristics within a capitalist system that would make sustainability an unattainable goal), then it is morally consistent to pursue sustainable development (as the path that leads to that goal) within and through that capitalist system. And if one's answer is that they are only compatible under certain conditions (it isn't capitalism per se that is at issue here, but which particular model of capitalism), then the transformation of those aspects of contemporary capitalism that are incompatible with the attainment of sustainability becomes both a moral and a political precondition of being an effective environmentalist or campaigner for social justice.

Liberalism and sustainability

From a conventional green perspective, such an enquiry is not uncontroversial. Historically, greens have always veered more to the left than to the right, sometimes explicitly (as with the green parties around the world and various green–red coalitions), and sometimes implicitly (as with those organizations such as Friends of the Earth and Greenpeace who claim strict party-political neutrality, but whose core political sympathies are there for all to see). Over the years, as the range of policy instruments available to governments broadened out to include a much wider variety of market-based mechanisms (taxes, trading schemes, incentives and so on), some greens have adapted with enthusiasm, while others remain suspicious. 'Supping with the devils of capitalism' is a charge that has been brought against all sorts of green activists – including the author of this particular text. The divide still runs deep, as Marcel Wissenburg explains:

> One of the odd aspects of the green critique of economic liberalism is that some see it as the source of most environmental evil, whereas others believe that it is the solution. 'Leftish' greens argue that private ownership and free market conditions, in general, or capitalism and the perpetual quest for economic growth, in particular, are at least barriers for a greener society, often the cause of environmental degradation and according to some even the main cause. On the right, especially in libertarian circles, it is state interference that prevents the free market from developing into a green market. If property and use rights were better defined, individuals would be enabled to defend their rights against polluters and exploiters of nature – and the mechanism of the free market would ensure that no more nor less natural capital than necessary was used for consumption. (Wissenburg, 1998)

The majority of green philosophers and political academics remain convinced that a sustainable society would necessarily be closer to a socialist society than to a liberal, capitalist society. Some of the 'drivers' of capitalism (growth for growth's sake, accumulation, red-in-tooth-and-claw competitiveness, fierce individualism and so on) are seen as major if not irreducible barriers to achieving a sustainable society. Few attempts have been made to interrogate this core assumption, perhaps the most comprehensive of which is Wissenburg's own 'green liberalism'.

After a painstaking comparison between the key tenets of political liberalism and the multifarious 'schools of thought' that make up the global green movement, Wissenburg (1998) identifies a number of significant conflicts between sustainability and liberalism, particularly around the issues of private property and consumption. However, he emerges from his investigations persuaded that there is no fundamental incompatibility between the pursuit of sustainability and political liberalism – a modest but reassuring conclusion to set against a growing number of less well-informed commentators who default so predictably to the canard that a truly sustainable society would have to be a sub-fascist society given the need to constrain human nature and dictate human behaviour. However, faced with a clash between constantly growing wants and needs, on the one hand, and limited natural resources and systems, on the other, Wissenburg reveals the limitations of the liberal position: 'People's needs – for company, children, food, technology, travel and trinkets – are private affairs; control, if possible at all, is impermissible.'

Impermissible! In which case, there is little between where we are now and the ecological abyss that necessarily awaits us if 9 billion people are 'permitted' to acquire trinkets, get obese, travel the world, and own several cars along the lines of the Californian model.

In that context, one thing can be stated with reasonable certainty at this point: capitalism *as we know it today* would, indeed, appear to be incompatible with anything even vaguely resembling sustainability. The continuing (and seemingly inexorable) liquidation of our natural capital throughout the global economy provides ample evidence on this score. And contemporary capitalism's growing social externalities (in terms of widening disparities in wealth, continuing economic exploitation, and the adamantine reality of more than 2 billion people still living on less than $2 a day) compound that physical evidence many times over.

To make such a categorical assertion should not automatically mark one down as an out-and-out anti-capitalist. Indeed, there are many critics of contemporary capitalism whose criticism stems precisely from their strongly held belief that capitalism remains the best and *only* ideological option for enhancing the wellbeing of humankind – but that the flaws in its current form are starting to obscure that reality from less sympathetic critics. As George Soros has said on a number of occasions:

> *Although I have made a fortune in the financial markets, I now fear*
> *that the untrammelled intensification of* laissez-faire *capitalism and the*
> *spread of market values into all areas of life are endangering our open*
> *democratic society. The main enemy of the open society, I believe, is no*
> *longer the communist but the capitalist threat.* (Soros, 1997)

In his coruscating attack on those who continue to defend capitalism in general, by defending this particular manifestation of what he calls 'killer capitalism', Jeff Gates homes in on just one of those problems caused by the growing influence of the 'super-rich' in the US:

> *In 1982, inclusion in the Forbes 400 list of the richest Americans*
> *required personal wealth of $91 million. The list then included 13*
> *billionaires. By 1999, $625 million was required for inclusion on a list*
> *that included 268 billionaires. The combined net worth of the Forbes*
> *400 was $1 trillion in September 1999, an increase from $738 billion*
> *just 12 months earlier. That works out to an average one-year increase*
> *of $655 million each for those who were already the nation's richest.*
>
> *Of this I'm certain: any system that makes it easier for a Bill Gates*
> *to amass another $500 million than it does for a single mother to get*
> *$500 ahead of her bills (while trying to raise the next potential Bill*
> *Gates) is buying a lot of hogwash about the value of the contribution*
> *made to this nation by the super rich. And about the workability of a*
> *democracy that celebrates appropriation of this nation's prosperity by so*
> *few.* (Gates, 2000)

Notwithstanding such strictures, Jeff Gates is still a passionate capitalist, convinced that the malleability of capitalism that has served it so well over 300 years will again rescue it from its current 'unsustainable characteristics', which are causing such serious collateral damage throughout global society.

Inevitably, different people will have different opinions both about the fundamental characteristics of capitalism (those characteristics that are generic in all manifestations of capitalism) and about those characteristics that are 'inherently unsustainable' – and those that are capable of correction. A constant flow of comparative data from different countries shows that alternative models of capitalism will generate very different outcomes on key economic and social concerns. For instance, a major international study on social mobility commissioned by the Sutton Trust from the London School of Economics (LSE) in 2005 demonstrated extreme divergences in performance between the UK and the US, on the one hand, and Germany, Canada and the Scandinavian countries, on the other. Social mobility is a critical indicator of how well any country is managing inequity, holding out the promise that it is possible (through 'equality of opportunity' interventions and targeted education investments for the most disadvantaged) for even the poorest to break out of poverty and secure reasonable material prosperity later in life. The results of this study showed that social mobility in the UK and the US (both of which advocate and practise a much more neo-liberal, free market version of capitalism than all of the other countries in the study) is much lower – and in the case of the UK, still declining even after eight years of a Labour government and huge new investments in education:

> *The expansion of higher education since the late 1980s has so far disproportionately benefited those from more affluent families – during that time, the proportion of people from the poorest 20 per cent of society getting a degree rose from 6 per cent to 9 per cent; but for the wealthiest 20 per cent it rose from 20 per cent to 47 per cent.* (LSE, 2005)

Increased mobility for the already relatively mobile is hardly what one would be looking to a Labour government for, causing many in the UK to question just what kind of capitalism Labour has thrown in its lot with.

With that health warning in mind, what follows is a thumbnail sketch of the sort of analysis that would be required to come up with an answer to the over-arching question about the compatibility/incompatibility of capitalism and sustainability. *Prima facie*, there would appear to be a very strong case for arguing that since market-based economies provide the only economic system that can live side by side with democracy, and that democracy is a necessary precondition of human sustainability, then a sustainable economy must, by definition, be a market-based economy. That is not the same thing as saying that capitalism is the *only* economic system with the potential to deliver a sustainable society in the future: the Bushmen of the Kalahari, or the remnants of what were once thriving indigenous cultures around the world, would give the lie to any such claim.

No attempt is made here to explore the feasibility of non-capitalist economies: this is a pragmatic exploration of the viability of *capitalism* when it comes to delivering sustainability, not of any other system. Nevertheless, it is interesting to note just how little enthusiasm there is today for any hankering after some kind of communist alternative. With the predictable exception of a few remnant green parties in former Eastern European countries, it is now almost universally acknowledged that communism and sustainability are far more incompatible as ideological bedfellows than capitalism and sustainability. It's now nearly 15 years since Murray Feshbach and Alfred Friendly (1992) published their devastating *Ecocide in the USSR: Health and Nature Under Siege*; but all the evidence that has emerged since then has confirmed both the scale and the severity of the damage done under communism to every facet of the environment in Russia and its allies.

The resulting legacy, both in human and financial terms, is truly staggering, and explains why even the harshest critics of today's global capitalism demonstrate zero interest in any communist alternative. In their *Green Alternatives to Globalisation*, for instance, Michael Woodin and Caroline Lucas (2004) look primarily to the *scale* of any market-based economy, pinning their hopes on a wholesale process of 'localization' rather than on any return to nationalization or central planning, let alone communism:

> *The system can and must be replaced by an alternative that challenges its insistence that all economies be contorted to the end goal of international competitiveness, and its emphasis on beggar-your-neighbour reduction of controls on trade and investment. Economic localization is just such an alternative. It involves a better-your-neighbour supportive internationalism, where the flow of ideas, technologies, information, culture, money and goods has, as its end goal, the rebuilding of truly sustainable national and local economies worldwide. Its emphasis is not on competition for the cheapest, but on cooperation for the best.* (Woodin and Lucas, 2004)

I will return to the whole question of scale; but it is first necessary to review some of the defining characteristics of a capitalist system in order to test for any fundamental incompatibilities between capitalism and the attainment of a genuinely sustainable economy: markets, profits, private property and free trade.

Markets

Markets existed long before the emergence of capitalism, and even today can (and do) exist without capitalism. But the opposite is not true: capitalism cannot exist without the marketplace as the principal mechanism for the exchange of goods and services. It is almost universally agreed that markets (though never completely 'free' in the true sense of the word) provide the most effective mechanism for the allocation of resources. It may, indeed, be true that 'markets were never meant to achieve community or integrity, beauty or justice, sustainability or sacredness' (von Weizsacker et al, 1997); but there seems no reason to suppose that properly regulated markets, operating within a genuinely sustainable macro-economic framework, will not continue to be the most effective (and sustainable) mechanism for the allocation of resources. It is also well understood that competition within properly regulated markets is one of the few things that prevents the drift to monopoly which characterizes all capitalist economies.

If one accepts, for instance, that one of the most important characteristics of a genuinely sustainable economy is to squeeze the maximum utility out of the lowest possible throughput of energy and raw materials, then serious thought has to be given to the embedding of 'more-from-less' practices in every facet of the market economy. For all sorts of reasons, it is apparent that command and control regulation cannot achieve that outcome on its own; once an efficiency standard has been mandated, there is no economic incentive to go beyond it, eliminating the possibility of continuous efficiency improvements. But with prices set in such a way as to reflect the *true* cost of the use of energy and resources, competition between producers on a so-called level playing field is not just compatible with the pursuit of sustainability, but a necessary aspect of it. As we will see later on, this is clearly an instance where some of the tools and disciplines of capitalism offer enormous benefits to politicians seeking the right mix of instruments to help transform corporate and personal behaviour.

But 'the market', as a social institution, has taken on an iconic role given its centrality to the neo-liberal revolution over the last 25 years. The market has been promoted not just as an efficient mechanism of exchange and resource allocation, but as an ideological weapon against state socialism and the self-evident horrors of centralized command and control. The idea of the market as the most effective way to reconcile the growing diversity and complexity of human preferences has retained its extraordinary political cachet in capitalist economies long after the wilder extremes of Thatcher/Reagan neo-liberalism are beginning to recede. That still begs all sorts of questions about what we mean by 'properly regulated markets' to secure some kind of 'social purpose': regulated by whom, at what scale of activity, using what mechanisms, and to achieve what sort of social and economic outcomes? But those are *secondary* issues. In and of itself, transacting the exchange of goods and services through a market is *not* the problem as far as the pursuit of sustainability is concerned – as evidenced in practice by the emergence of all sorts of new market-based solutions to today's sustainability crisis, all the way from proposals for a global market for trading carbon through to local schemes, such as farmers' markets and even Local Exchange and Trading Schemes (LETS), which depend both upon market principles and the principles of mutuality and cooperation.

This kind of broad approach features increasingly even in the work of anti-globalization campaigners. Writing in the *Guardian* in April 2001, the environmental campaigner George Monbiot expanded upon the idea that market freedom would become an increasingly important part of the pursuit of sustainability, but only on certain conditions:

> *A genuine free market is surely one which is free for everyone, rather than one in which the powerful are free to squeeze economic life out of everyone else. The prerequisite of freedom, in other words, is effective regulation. This means that in some respects the state will have to become not weaker – as both the anarchists and the neo-liberals insist – but stronger. It must be empowered to force both producers and consumers to carry their own costs, rather than dumping them on to other people or the environment. It must be allowed to distinguish between the protection of workers, consumers and the ecosystem, and trade protectionism. Agreements such as those set by the World Trade Organization, in other words, must be reversed. Rather than setting only maximum standards for the defence of people and the environment, they should set minimum*

> *standards to which multinational companies must subscribe before they are licensed to trade.* (Monbiot, 2001)

Profits

The very purpose of wealth creation in capitalist economies is to generate profits. Production for profit, as opposed to production for human needs, was perhaps the simplest of the old ideological divides between capitalism and communism. Some socialists and radical greens continue to argue that it is 'the profit motive' (the pursuit of profit as the single most important objective in any economic exchange) which still lies at the heart of capitalism's inherently destructive tendencies; many mainstream environmental and community development organizations remain wary of the whole concept of profitability, though less so today than during the 1970s and 1980s. As we saw in Chapter 3, it is the urge to maximize profits that causes some companies to cut corners if they can get away with it and to externalize as high a proportion of their costs as they are legally permitted to do. In *The Corporation*, Joel Bakan (2004) describes the modern corporation as 'an externalizing machine'. Because of its legal status and fiduciary duties to shareholders, it is literally duty bound to maximize profit for those shareholders as long as it stays within the law:

> *The corporation can neither recognize nor act upon moral reasons to refrain from harming others. Nothing in its legal makeup limits what it can do to others in pursuit of its selfish ends, and it is compelled to cause harm where the benefits of doing so outweigh the costs. Only pragmatic concern for its own interests in the laws of the land constrain the corporation's predatory instincts, and often that is not enough to stop it from destroying lives, damaging communities and endangering the planet as a whole. These tend to be viewed as inevitable and acceptable consequences of corporate activity – 'externalities' in the coolly technical jargon of economics.* (Bakan, 2004)

Only governments can systematically force companies to internalize these externalities through proper regulation or through company law. Within a corporate governance framework geared more to sustainability and equity, the concept of *sustainable profitability* should therefore be viable – and perhaps even a necessary condition of making the transition to a sustainable economy as efficiently and painlessly as possible. Excelling in the pursuit of legitimate profitability while simultaneously making continuous progress towards genuine sustainability will become an increasingly important test of real business leadership.

As we will see, however, governments are less and less inclined to introduce, let alone to enforce, new regulations that are invariably opposed by business and their trade associations. Governments in the rich world are not so much the ring-holders between civil society, on the one hand, and corporations intent on making other people pay their bills, on the other; more and more, government and business seem to be working as partners, especially as governments around the world follow in the footsteps of the UK and the US in opening up more and more of the public sector to privatization and market forces.

Even more problematic is the whole question of *accumulation*, with critics of capitalism arguing that its principal purpose is not just to generate profits, but to generate profits with a view to accumulating capital – as much of it as possible, accumulated as fast as possible. Critics further point out that the momentum in favour of unlimited, unsustainable economic growth is, indeed, inherent within capitalism simply because that which is being produced is not so much physical wealth as abstract exchange value.

Profitability has quite simply become the key measure of corporate success in a capitalist system, ensuring frequent and rapid shifts in the productive base of any economy. This process of 'creative destruction' ensures the reallocation of capital and other resources from the less productive to the more productive, however painful such reallocations may be at both the micro and the macro level. And it is those profits that provide the dividends upon which the lives of hundreds of millions of people now depend in terms of their pensions and other investments.

However, it is particularly difficult to make dispassionate judgements about the negative and positive aspects of the pursuit of profit at this particular point in the swing of capitalism's pendulum. We have just come through what must have been one of the most spectacularly debauched periods of unfettered profit maximization since the 19th century, culminating in a sequence of corporate scandals and collapses that has undoubtedly contributed to the pendulum starting to swing back again from its outer neo-liberal extreme.

This is not just a case of the odd rotten apple in the barrel. A report published in 2002 by the US non-governmental organization (NGO) United for a Fair Economy looked at the finances of 23 large US companies under investigation for accounting irregularities. Between 1999 and 2001, the chief executive officers (CEOs) of those companies (including household names such as AOL Time Warner, Bristol Myers Squibb, Enron, Halliburton, Kay-Mart, Lucent Technologies, Tyco, WorldCom and Xerox) took home $1.4 billion between them – at a time when shares in those companies lost $530 billion – roughly 70 per cent of their value. During that time, they earned an average $62 million each, in comparison to CEOs in companies not under investigation earning an average of $36 million.

For many people, this represents the acme of personal greed and corporate fat-cattery; but it is part of a much wider and more pervasive malaise. Board directors in the UK's biggest companies received an average 23 per cent rise in 2002 (seven times as much as average earnings), 17 per cent in 2001 and 28 per cent in 2000. Given the deplorable performance of many of those companies during that time, there can be no conceivable justification for such disproportionate self-advancement. Many business leaders still fail to understand the damage this does to the reputation of the business community as a whole – and, indeed, to the legitimacy of the capitalist system that permits such behaviour. Big share options and other benefits incorporated within pay packages create an utterly perverse incentive for company directors to prioritize short-term profit maximization and share-price inflation over any sense of their company's (and investors') longer-term interest.

Defenders of such an astonishingly powerful accumulative capacity point out that none of this *necessarily* impacts negatively upon those on low incomes in the UK or, in terms of the global economy, upon the world's poorest people. All of that money still has to go somewhere, whether it's in terms of consumption, philanthropy, investment or anything else. There is, therefore, an unavoidable trickle-down effect, regardless of the scale of accumulated wealth. Markets for consumption and investment simply recycle the proceeds. However, it seems impossible to argue that the world is a better place for the concentration of wealth in the hands of so few; by implication, therefore, 'sustainable capitalism' would necessarily need to find ways of limiting the concentration of wealth.

Private property

Not surprisingly, one can find every shade of political opinion about the rights and wrongs of private property within the green movement. Deep ecologists assert that the land belongs to no one and that it is absurd for humans to assume that they have any rights in that respect – either individual or collective. Socialist greens continue (somewhat romantically, it has to be said) to talk up the advantage of collective ownership, while those of a more liberal persuasion see private property rights as all but God-given and a non-negotiable tenet of any effectively functioning market economy.

The traditional justification of the right to own land and other property goes all the way back to the philosopher John Locke (1632–1704) and the prevailing assumption of his time that resources would remain so abundant that one person's private ownership would not constrain anyone else from achieving the same benefits of ownership in due course. The world has got to be a much fuller place since those days! If resources are in short supply rather than abundant, and if they are therefore 'rationed' via the price mechanism, as they are in today's world, then some people will necessarily go without.

But the question for consideration here is a rather different one: is there any fundamental incompatibility between the right to own private property and the pursuit of sustainability? Subject to the same kind of caveats expressed in the preceding section, 'Profits', about the accumulation and concentration of wealth, the *principle* of private ownership itself could surely be managed in such a way as to underpin a genuinely sustainable society. Indeed, there are some critics of contemporary capitalism, such as Jeff Gates, who argue strongly for the rapid extension of private property as one of the most effective ways of combating rather than reinforcing institutionalized inequity: 'With the proper policy environment, humanized ownership of property could do much to advance sustainability across an array of inescapably interdependent domains: economic, social and environmental' (Gates, 1998). From a very different Southern perspective, Hernando de Soto, a passionate advocate for 'capitalizing the poor', has suggested that governments should grant legal title to squatters over their currently illegal huts and shacks. Give them access to capital and to credit, and their prospects for improving their lives will improve dramatically.

Going even further than that, there are many who now believe that the extension of private property rights to those parts of the global commons that are either not managed at all (for example, the atmosphere) or inadequately managed on our behalf by governments or international agencies (such as ocean fisheries) will greatly benefit the pursuit of sustainability. I quote as an extreme but interesting example of this approach an extract from an article in *Nature* by Graciela Chichilnisky and Geoffrey Heal:

> *The environment's services are, without doubt, valuable. The air we breathe, the water we drink and the food we eat are all available only because of services provided by the environment. How can we transform these values into income while conserving resources? We have to 'securitize' (sell shares in the return from) 'natural capital' and environmental goods and services, and enrol market forces in their conservation. This means assigning to corporations – possibly by public–private corporate partnerships – the obligation to manage and conserve natural capital in exchange for the right to the benefits from selling the services provided. Privatizing natural capital and ecosystem services is a vital step as it enlists self-interest and the profit motive in the cause of the environment. Regulation can thus be confined to the more difficult cases.* (Chichilnisky and Heal, 1998)

Such free market zeal is unlikely to win many adherents, not least because it represents a chauvinistic Western point of view that totally ignores countless examples in the rest of the world of extremely successful *common* ownership of common resources. While Garrett Hardin's (1968) much-quoted story of 'The tragedy of the commons' might well apply to the appalling mismanagement of shared resources in the rich world, it does great disservice to all those elsewhere in the world sustaining highly effective systems of resource management and environmental protection without the support of private property or commoditized natural resources. Nonetheless, the notion of 'securitizing natural capital' is a powerful one (see Chapter 7).

Free trade

From the writings of David Ricardo at the start of the 19th century onwards, trade between nations has been considered an essential aspect of capitalism. Economic growth and free trade remain the two driving forces behind the spread of capitalism to every corner of the Earth, and 'opening markets to the benefit of free trade' is still the central ideological tenet of key institutions such as the International Monetary Fund (IMF) and the World Trade Organization (WTO).

Over the last few years the automatic acceptance of the benefits of free trade has been subjected to ever greater scrutiny. Critics have gone back to the work of David Ricardo to remind latter-day free trade apostles that the principle of comparative advantage (enabling capital to be allocated to those areas of enterprise in which a country has natural or acquired advantages in comparison to its trading partners) was premised on the assumption that capital (as well as labour) stayed at home – only the goods were traded internationally.

The mobility of capital changes all that. With capital now more mobile internationally than goods themselves, it is perfectly feasible (and from one perspective, perfectly reasonable) for transnational corporations to capitalize on cheap labour, cheap resources and lower environmental and social standards anywhere in the world that they can find them. In areas of economic production that are not geographically bounded, capital now tends to flow to countries with an 'absolute' advantage in these areas, leading to a standards-lowering competition between nations.

From a sustainability perspective, this is becoming more and more problematic. As we have seen, one fundamental element in moving towards more sustainable economies is the internalization of costs that have historically been 'externalized' on to the environment, other people, future generations and so on. From the earliest social reforms during the 19th century through to the introduction of a raft of environmental measures during the last two decades of the 20th century, legal and fiscal mechanisms have been used to ensure that the price consumers pay for any product or service more accurately reflects the real costs in bringing it to market. 'Footloose capital' can avoid the internalization of those costs by relocating to countries with lower standards; for lack of compensatory tariffs levied on goods at the point of entry into countries with higher standards, competition in the global economy often rewards continuing and perverse cost externalization. I will return to this theme in more detail in the next chapter.

It is worth remembering, however, that this idea of mobile capital (and unregulated currencies) is still a very new phenomenon – and, in reality, one that is still being put to the test. In his *General Theory of Employment, Interests and Money*, John Maynard Keynes (1936) expressed an opinion that is highly unfashionable today, but to which many exponents of the 'new economics' keep returning as they contemplate the consequences of footloose capital:

I would sympathize with those who would minimize rather than those who would maximize economic entanglements between nations. Ideas, knowledge, art, hospitality, travel – these are the things that should of their nature be international. But let goods be home spun wherever it is reasonable and conveniently possible, and above all let finance be primarily national. (Keynes, 1936)

SCALE

Small is Beautiful (the title of Fritz Schumacher's best-known book written in 1973) remains one of the most resonant catchphrases ever thrown up by any green author. It appeals at a deep instinctive level to those keen to keep relationships personal and direct, to retain the closest possible ties of neighbourhood and community, to keep supply chains short, and generally to ensure that things are kept as simple and manageable as possible.

This is not the place to reprise what has been a fiercely controversial debate within the green movement over the last three decades. The proper balance, from a sustainability perspective, in terms of what is best done locally, regionally, nationally, internationally and globally is an extremely complex one. For some, it is almost an article of faith that the more local something is, the more sustainable it is likely to be; pragmatists tend to take a 'horses for courses' approach, looking at the usual trade-offs between environmental, social and economic benefits from things done at different scales. The underlying concern, which permeates the whole of this chapter, is whether there is some dynamic at the heart of capitalism which distorts that kind of balanced approach, which mandates 'getting bigger' as a condition of getting richer, and which unavoidably crushes human scale, diverse cultures and local differentiation.

At the global level, without the kind of systems understanding referred to in Chapter 3, contemporary capitalism has no self-correcting mechanisms when it comes to gauging how big the economy should be, relative both to society and to the biosphere. Bigger is seen quite simply as better and always has been. The world now produces in less than two weeks the equivalent of the entire physical output of the year 1900; total throughput in the global economy doubles every 25 to 30 years. So even though the combination of huge population growth and exploding economies has turned an all but empty world into an all but full world in little more than a couple of centuries, unfettered expansionism is still the name of the game.

One of the best indices of human scale in relation to the biosphere is the percentage of the total product of photosynthesis now appropriated by humankind as the dominant species. Back in 1986, Peter Vitousek and colleagues calculated that 40 per cent of net terrestrial photosynthesis (the total amount of solar energy used by plants, trees, grasses and so on, less the energy used in their own growth and reproduction) was already being appropriated by human beings. If a doubling of the global economy simultaneously entails a doubling in our appropriation of net terrestrial photosynthesis, this would leave just 20 per cent for all other organisms. And since we now know that we cannot survive without the many services nature provides for free, the issue of relative scale is far from academic. Herman Daly has argued:

> *Our manifest inability to centrally plan economies should inspire more humility among the planetary managers who would centrally plan the ecosystem. Humility should argue for the strategy of minimizing the need for planetary management by keeping the human scale sufficiently low so as not to disrupt the automatic functioning of our life-support systems, thereby forcing them into the domain of human management. Those who want to take advantage of the 'invisible hand' of self-managing ecosystems have to recognize that the invisible hand of the market, while wonderful for allocation, is unable to set limits to the scale to the macro-economy.* (Daly, 1996)

And at the heart of the issue of scale lurks the vexed issues of population growth. Cut it which way you will, growing populations necessitate growing economies to provide more food, more houses, more services, more teachers, more doctors and more jobs. Growth-bound economists and politically correct environmentalists conspire to keep the issue of population off the agenda, obscuring the incontrovertible reality that every extra human being makes it just a little bit harder to find ways of living within the Earth's limited carrying capacity. It would, however, seem unreasonable to lay the blame for this uniquely at the door of capitalism. Religion, ignorance, prejudice and political cowardice have at least as much to answer for.

WANTS AND NEEDS

In the erstwhile ideological battle between capitalism and communism, few issues were as stoutly delineated as the question of production for the market versus production for human needs. Although relations between green activists and socialists have often been extremely fractious, the espousal of a steady-state economy by green parties during the 1970s gave some succour to socialists who believed that it would permit a clear hierarchy of production: satisfy all reasonable consumption needs first, and then aim at a 'replacement level' for future production, entirely eliminating any need for capital accumulation. These days, however, the concept of 'production for human needs' would seem to have little currency in the debate about sustainability, and even less in discussions about contemporary capitalism. In those countries where basic needs are met – and for most people in Organisation for Economic Co-operation and Development (OECD) countries, they are – it is seen as the natural by-product of rising economic prosperity. When they are not met (as they are not for more than half of humanity), an enduring faith in the promise of trickle-down economics somehow continues to divert attention from the thorny question of whether they will *ever* be met in today's global economy. Rather than trickling down, many of the benefits of the global economy as it is structured today continue to gush upwards. The United Nations Development Programme's (UNDP's) annual *Human Development Report* continues to offer the most sobering assessment of today's trend: 'Development that perpetuates today's inequalities is neither sustainable nor worth sustaining' (UNDP, 2003).

But is this really as simple, as morally clear-cut, as the 'case against' would seem to indicate? Markets are, indeed, amoral; but governments can (and consistently do) intervene to buttress amoral markets with fiscal and regulatory measures that at any one time may be said to embody a nation's moral precepts – a sense of what is 'owed' to each citizen and what each citizen owes the state. And there is no shortage of eloquent prescriptions regarding how the system could be made to work both more equitably and effectively, all the way from the urbane, market-friendly blueprints of people such as Jean-François Rischard (the World Bank's Vice President for Europe) in *High Noon* (Rischard, 2003) through to uncompromising, NGO-based manifestos that would dramatically rearrange the balance of power between civil society and big business.

Is it right, anyway, to bemoan the fact that capital allocation is not geared to meeting needs, but rather to maximizing rates of return? Would any other generic approach produce the kind of efficiencies in capital allocation that ensure the best use of a scarce resource? Isn't suboptimal capital allocation as much a threat to sustainability as suboptimal resource utilization? Contemporary proponents of ecological sustainability and social justice would seem to be drawing few historical lessons from the grotesquely inefficient, polluting and corrupt economies of the former Soviet bloc countries. Rather than seeking to achieve those fundamental social and environmental outcomes upon which sustainability depends through suboptimal allocation of capital, the trick surely is to ensure that 'optimality' is redefined in order to encompass those fundamental social and environmental concerns?

More problematic is the growing evidence that the kind of economic growth generated by current patterns of capital allocation does not necessarily (let alone automatically) lead to any increase in human welfare. The chronic 'disconnect' between rates of economic growth and increases in human welfare has been highlighted in the UK by the work of the New Economics Foundation and its *Index of Sustainable Economic Welfare*. This brings us back full circle to the issues discussed in Chapter 3 on economic growth, and to which I will return in Chapter 12.

COMPETITION

Within any capitalist system, to be 'uncompetitive' at either the company level or at nation-state level, is to fail. It is a simple as that. Competition for customers, competition for capital, competition for talent, and competition for reputation and brand value: it is competitiveness that sorts out the capitalist sheep from the capitalist goats. Competition has become both dominant and deeply divisive, as pointed out by Tony Stebbing and Gordon Heath:

> *Competition makes economies inherently unstable and leads to the extinction of businesses through dominance and monopoly. The widespread belief that the competitive process must permeate every aspect of life is damaging the global environment since the pace of economic activity exceeds its capacity to assimilate polluting consequences. Competition drives the rate of economic activity towards the maximum energy and resource use. It is unsustainable because there are no intrinsic controls upon the pace of economic activity.* (Stebbing and Heath, 2003)

However, as we have already seen, competition itself need not necessarily pose such a dilemma. In terms of the efficient use of both resources and capital, the challenge to eke out maximum economic value for every unit of energy and raw materials is as critical to sustainability as it should be to commercial success. The problem is not competition per se, but the incorrect valuation of resources and inadequate levels of regulation to create a level playing field conducive to sustainability.

This is probably a judgement that most people would arrive at instinctively anyway. Populist interpretations of evolution, from Herbert Spencer and Thomas Huxley onwards, have accustomed people to the idea of nature being 'red in tooth and claw', with all life forms engaged in endless titanic struggles to ensure 'the survival of the fittest'. So what could be more 'natural' than the history of humankind (both before and after the Industrial Revolution) being cast in the same metaphorical framework? This rationale of social Darwinism has been taken up with unbounded enthusiasm by the politicians and academic economists most centrally involved in the neo-liberal revolution of the last 25 years. When all else fails, it has provided at least some flimsy justification for patterns of irresponsible and uncaring corporate and political behaviour that prioritize competition over everything else, characterized by folksy phrases along the lines of 'It's a jungle out there', 'It's a dog-eat-dog world', 'Let the devil take the hindmost', and so on.

So it often comes as a bit of a blow to them when this interpretation of evolution is revealed as a complete fabrication, a socio-political distortion that tells us much more about Britain during the mid 19th century than about the evolution of life on Earth. What we now know is that individual organisms in a mature ecosystem go to great lengths to avoid competition by specialization or by developing their own differentiated niches. Resources are often shared with frugal efficiency. Territorial animals actually avoid fighting if at all possible, relying upon complex behaviours and rituals that stop short of actual conflict. This has all been formalized by ecologists in what is known as the 'competitive exclusion principle':

the occupant of any niche excludes all others by virtue of specialization, and therefore avoids competition and possible extinction.

Beyond that, the work of scientists such as Lynn Margulis and Janine Benyus has revealed fascinating patterns of mutual interdependence and elegant symbiosis. The great biologist Lewis Thomas is quoted as saying: 'The urge to form partnerships, to link up in collaborative arrangements, is perhaps the oldest, strongest and most fundamental force in Nature. There are no solitary, free-living creatures; every form of life is dependent on other forms' (Thomas, 1980).

This mismatch between how evolution really works and how the majority of people have come to think it works has assumed ever greater significance in the minds of those trying to understand how it is that we permit market economics to destroy so much of what we hold dear. Just before her death in 2001, the renowned environmental activist Donella Meadows wrote a powerful article showing how today's economic 'laws' clash fundamentally with the laws of the planet. Competition is top of that list of clashes:

> *Economics says: compete. Only by pitting yourself against a worthy opponent will you perform efficiently. The reward for successful competition will be growth. The Earth says: compete, yes, but keep your competition in bounds. Don't annihilate. Take only what you need. Leave your competitor enough to live. Wherever possible, don't compete, cooperate. Pollinate each other, create shelter for each other, build firm structures that lift smaller species up to the light. Pass around the nutrients, share the territory. Some kinds of excellence rise out of competition; other kinds rise out of cooperation. You're not in a war, you're in a community.* (Meadows, 2001)

There is, of course, a big difference between how nature does it and how we humans choose to do it: we are able to bring *moral purpose* to bear on the issue. Neo-liberals would have us believe that markets are morally neutral, and that competition within those markets exempts policy-makers from having to choose between different approaches or to make any moral judgements. This moral relativism is now being challenged not just though the predictable swing of capitalism's pendulum away from the excesses of neo-liberalism, but by our increasingly sophisticated understanding of the balance between competition and collaboration in nature.

INEQUALITY

Leading on from that, there's the equally vexed question of whether *inequality* is an inherent and inevitable element in *any* capitalist system. The answer to this must surely be 'yes'. Even with a better balance between competition and collaboration, the dynamism of capitalism depends upon 'winners' making better use of capital and resources than their competitors; and where there are winners, there will inevitably be losers.

Any system that stops short of outright egalitarianism must, by definition, permit the existence of some inequality. Post-war capitalist meritocracies have relied upon varying combinations of the same basic elements to manage that inequality: equality of opportunity (in theory, if rarely in practice); fiscal redistribution to iron out extreme disparities in income and wealth; and a welfare 'net' to catch those who fall through the system. It has worked a great deal better in some countries than in others. As shown in the report from the Real World Coalition, *From Here to Sustainability* (Christie and Warburton, 2001), neither the US nor the UK have yet come close to reconciling the astonishing dynamism of entrepreneurial capitalism with the meeting of basic human needs or social justice. Elsewhere in Europe, particularly in the Scandinavian and Benelux countries, this would appear to be a rather less elusive combination than in the US or the UK. And there is clear evidence, for those who want to see it, that capitalist economies *can* be managed in such a way as to maximize equality of opportunity and to minimize persistent cycles of deprivation and inequality.

The perpetuation of extreme disparities in wealth is becoming increasingly disturbing even for the most zealous defenders of our contemporary model of capitalism. It looks 'inherently unsustainable' for all sorts of pragmatic reasons: just how long do you suppose people will put up with this level of transparent injustice? But social justice has been of little concern to those intent on driving a particular model of US-led globalization, which in country after country has indisputably worsened levels of inequality. This is partly to do with the insupportable levels of debt that many developing countries have accumulated (the cost of servicing that $2.5 trillion worth of debt is around $375 billion a year – more than all developing world spending on education and health combined, and 20 times what they receive annually in terms of foreign aid), and partly to do with the enforced development model that has enriched tiny but hugely powerful elites in most poor countries. The top 1 per cent of households in developing countries account for anywhere between 70 per cent and 90 per cent of all private wealth in those countries.

For most people, these shocking phenomena are still seen as 'unfortunate side effects', the dark side of a process of development and investment in some of the world's poorest countries that they imagine to be largely benign. A growing number of commentators are keen to dispel that illusion, and some have gone so far as to argue that today's inequality is a direct consequence of the way in which the global economy has gradually become a tool of US foreign policy and its hegemonistic intentions. John Perkins, the former 'economic hit man' for American big business, likens their impact upon the world's poor to that of the slave traders:

> *The old-fashioned slave trader told himself that he was dealing with a species that was not entirely human, and that he was offering them the opportunity to become Christianized. He also understood that slaves were*

fundamental to the survival of his own society, that they were the foundation of his economy. The modern slave trader assures himself (or herself) that the desperate people are better off earning $1 dollar a day than no dollars at all, and that they are receiving the opportunity to become integrated into the larger world community. She also understands that these desperate people are fundamental to the survival of her company, that they are the foundation for her own lifestyle. She never stops to think about the larger implications of what she, her lifestyle and the economic system behind them are doing to the world – or of how they may ultimately impact upon her children's future. (Perkins, 2004)

The US itself remains the richest nation on Earth, but also one of the most unequal. The percentage of children living in poverty in the US is the highest in the developed world – one in six. The numbers of so-called 'working poor' (people who work full time without being able to support a family in decent health) have been increasing steadily over the last decade. Household debt as a percentage of income rose from 58 per cent to 85 per cent between 1973 and 1998. Average weekly wages in 1998 were 12 per cent below those for 1973 – and it has got worse since then. The top 1 per cent of Americans now earn more than the bottom 95 per cent (up from 90 per cent just a year earlier). While there are now more than 200 American billionaires, one in seven American adults is functionally illiterate. And while Americans remain more tolerant of this extraordinary economic failure, on the grounds that social mobility in the US is so high that everyone has as good a chance as anyone else to reach those material heights, that is simply no longer true: the chance of American workers in the bottom 20 per cent of the economy moving to the top 60 per cent is less than in any other developed country.

I am indebted to Margaret Legum (2002) for many of those statistics – extracted from her inspiring exposition of what today's alternative economics looks like, *It Doesn't Have to Be Like This*. She also draws a telling comparison between the US economy (still vaunted in most media as the world's most dynamic economy) and the Japanese economy, which is endlessly marked down as 'stagnant' or 'failing'. In fact, the Japanese economy is not only the most egalitarian of all developed countries, it is still among the most successful:

The Japanese have high incomes, more savings, longer lives and better health than Americans. And they work less hard to achieve it. The Japanese also pay lower taxes – less than 12 per cent of their incomes compared to more than 16 per cent. And they get more services. Health-care is virtually free. More Japanese take overseas holidays than Americans. And they still manage to save money. While American workers spent more than they earned in 2000, the average Japanese family put away 13 per cent of its pay cheque in savings. . . Every Japanese household has a colour television, nine in ten have a microwave oven, 85 per cent have

> *a car, 40 per cent a computer and 39 per cent a set of golf clubs. The rate of heart attacks is one third of that in the US; the divorce rate is half the American, the crime rate one third and the homicide rate one sixth. Proportionately, more Japanese 18-year olds go to college than do Americans. Japanese read twice as many books per capita as Americans. There are hardly any homeless Japanese, compared with 700,000 American.* (Legum, 2002)

INHERENT UNSUSTAINABILITY?

The *realpolitik* of all this is clear. Sustainability (at the species level) is a non-negotiable imperative for humankind. Allowing for some increasingly rare exceptions such as Cuba and North Korea, capitalism, in one form or another, is likely to provide the all-encompassing ideological framework for the foreseeable future – as Tom Bentley says: 'The values of individualism, diversity and open exchange, which have been fought over for centuries, have won out in the modern world. They are embodied in the structure of capitalism, which now constitutes the only viable possibility for organizing economies' (Bentley, 2002). Logically, whether we like it or not, sustainability is therefore going to have to be delivered within that all-encompassing capitalist framework. We don't have time to wait for any big-picture ideological successor.

Clearly, each of the different fundamental characteristics of capitalism covered above requires a great deal more analysis from a sustainability-driven perspective before any definitive judgement can be made about the compatibility of capitalism and sustainability. Is there some 'accommodation' that would permit the pursuit of genuine sustainability through a different model of capitalism than that which we have today? Indeed, is there *any* model of capitalism that can accommodate the non-negotiable imperative of achieving biophysical sustainability and the increasingly pressing concerns of global equity and social justice?

This chapter does not pretend to be able to answer that question in one fell swoop; all it seeks to do at this stage is to frame the question and open it up for discussion within the sustainability community. At the very least, based on this kind of analysis, it should be possible to set some of the principal dysfunctionalities of contemporary capitalism against some of the minimum conditions necessary for achieving a sustainable economy – and then explore the political, economic and fiscal reforms that would be required to bridge the gap between the two.

To a certain extent, that is what has been happening when comparisons are made between different models of capitalism, starting with Chris Hampden-Turner and Fons Trompenaars' (1993) magisterial analysis of *The Seven Cultures of Capitalism* through to Will Hutton's (1995) *The State We're In*, and more recent comparisons between stakeholder capitalism and shareholder capitalism. The collapse of Enron and a string of high-level corporate scandals over the last few years have encouraged a far more rigorous scrutiny of today's capitalist paradigm than was available during the 1980s or 1990s. But the 'success criteria' that underpin these comparisons rarely take any proper account of the non-negotiable imperative of securing critical natural capital, and even tend to play down the importance of protecting and building new social capital.

Beyond that kind of economic analysis, it would then be necessary to explore some of the deeper moral and philosophical concerns that many people believe to be at least as important in scrutinizing the 'disconnect' between capitalism and sustainability. Beyond questions about the *feasibility* of continuous economic growth within a capitalist system are questions about its *desirability*.

At a more abstract level, for instance, it is worth bearing in mind that in all variations of capitalism, *money* is the common denominator and the measure of value. Price regulates supply and demand, and is the principal source of information for consumers. For something to have value in such a system, it needs to have a price. Effective markets depend upon the transparent use of the price mechanism. Yet, in giving everything a money value, are we not undermining our capacity to judge what is truly valuable? This continues to raise enormous difficulties for those seeking to protect the environment within decision-making processes (such as planning, development appraisals and cost–benefit analysis) where the choice is often between trying to give that aspect of the environment one is seeking to protect a *monetary* value, however spuriously determined and philosophically corrosive such a valuation might be, or seeing it trashed as 'having no value whatsoever'. The pressure to transmute every aspect of the environment into a commodity that can then be bought and sold like any other commodity is often overwhelming. This would seem to indicate that no capitalist system is likely to value nature properly unless it is framed by a set of deeper, wiser precepts and spiritual values, where the value of something is not exclusively determined by its price.

More than 25 years ago, writers such as E. J. Mishan and Fred Hirsch sought to highlight the less tangible social and moral costs of economic growth, pointing out that when the 18th-century Scottish moral philosopher Adam Smith first started writing about the invisible hand of competition, people could be trusted not to harm the community in pursuing their self-interest – simply because of built-in restraint derived from morality, religion, custom and education. But that is clearly no longer the case in a more secular and relativistic modern world. More recently, Herman Daly has taken this analysis one step further:

> *The forces propelling economic growth are simultaneously eroding the moral foundation of the very social order which gives purpose and direction to that growth. On the demand side of the market, the glorification of self-interest and the pursuit of 'infinite wants' leads to a weakening of moral distinctions between luxury and necessity. Moral limits constraining demand for junk are inconvenient in a growth economy because growth increases when junk sells. So the growth*

economy fosters the erosion of the values upon which it depends, such as honesty, sobriety, trust, etc. On the supply side, the 'infinite' power of science-based technology is thought to be capable of overcoming all biophysical limits. But even if this erroneous proposition were true, the very world view of scientism leads to the debunking of any notion of transcendental value and to undercutting the moral basis of the social cohesion presupposed by market society. (Daly, 1996)

It is this combination of questionable feasibility and doubtful moral desirability that continues to prompt campaigners to predict the demise of capitalism itself. Though such apocalyptic predictions and questions are usually dismissed out of hand by mainstream political parties, the more far-sighted among them are much more nervous than they let on about the increasingly visible 'fault lines' in the system.

REFERENCES

Bakan, J. (2004) *The Corporation*, Constable, London

Bentley, T. (2002) 'Letting go: Complexity, individualism and the left', *Renewal*, vol 10

Chichilnisky, G. and Heal, G. (1998) 'Economic returns from the biosphere', *Nature*, vol 391, February

Christie, I. and Warburton, D. (2001) *From Here to Sustainability*, Real World Coalition/ Earthscan, London

Daly, H. (1996) *Beyond Growth*, Beacon Press, Boston, MA

Feshbach, M. and Friendly, A. (1992) *Ecocide in the USSR: Health and Nature Under Siege*, Aurum Press, London

Gates, J. (1998) *The Ownership Solution*, Penguin, London

Gates, J. (2000) *Democracy at Risk*, Perseus Publishing, Cambridge, MA

Hampden-Turner, C. and Trompenaars, F. (1993) *The Seven Cultures of Capitalism*, Piatkus, London

Hardin. G. (1968) 'The tragedy of the commons', *Science*, vol 162, pp1243–1248

Hutton, W. (1995) *The State We're In*, Vintage, London

Keynes, J. M. (1936) *The General Theory of Employment, Interest and Money*, Harcourt Brace, New York

Legum, M. (2002) *It Doesn't Have to Be Like This*, Wild Goose Publications, Glasgow, UK

LSE (London School of Economics) (2005) *International Perspectives on Social Mobility*, LSE, London

Meadows, D. (2001) 'Economic laws clash with planet's', *Earthlight Magazine*, spring

Monbiot, G. (2001) 'Turn the screw', *Guardian*, 24 April

Perkins, J. (2004) *Confessions of an Economic Hit Man*, Berrett-Koehler, San Francisco, CA

Rischard, J-F. (2003) *High Noon: 20 Global Problems, 20 Years to Solve Them*, Basic Books, New York

Schumacher, E. F. (1973) *Small is Beautiful*, Abacus, London

Soros, G. (1997) 'The capitalist threat', *Atlantic Monthly*, vol 279, no 2, pp 45–58

Stebbing, T. and Heath, G. (2003) 'Competition and the struggle for existence', unpublished article

Thomas, L. (1980) 'On the uncertainty of science', *Phi Beta Kappa Key Reporter*, vol 6, no 1

UNDP (2003) *Human Development Report 2003*, United Nations Development Programme, available at http://hdr.undp.org/reports/global/2003/

von Weizsacker, E., Lovins, A. and Lovins, H. (1997) *Factor Four*, Earthscan, London

Wissenburg, M. (1998) *Green Liberalism*, UCL Press, London

Woodin, M. and Lucas, C. (2004) *Green Alternatives to Globalisation*, Pluto Press, London

5

Through the Global Looking Glass

INTRODUCTION

If it is not capitalism per se causing the problem, is it globalization? Or, at least, the kind of globalization that is extending the influence of free markets and multinational companies into every corner of every country? It turns out, on further investigation, that even the so-called 'anti-globalization movement' is passionate about what they see as the right kind of globalization. These are hotly contested ideological positions; even those archetypal motherhood-and-apple-pie notions of 'freedom' and 'democracy' have been conscripted into the war of words around the war on terrorism. Both *public* institutions – with organizations such as the World Bank and the International Monetary Fund (IMF) representing a 30-year-old Washington Consensus – and *private-sector* multinationals are increasingly under the cosh for accelerating environmental damage and making the lives of the poor even worse – charges which are strenuously denied by both political and business leaders. But does 'sustainable capitalism' mean an end of the huge global companies that have become so powerful over the last 20 years? Or can they, too, be 're-engineered'? Could they really become a genuine 'force for good', as well as a continuing engine of profit generation?

THE PHENOMENON OF GLOBALIZATION

Each and every one of the essential characteristics of capitalism considered in the previous chapters has taken on an additional dimension through the phenomenon of globalization. As international trade and foreign direct investment have multiplied, and more and more business is transacted on a global basis, globalization is alternately eulogized as the solution to the world's problems (and poverty alleviation, in particular) and then demonized as the principal accelerator of all things unsustainable under capitalism. Professor Tom Gladwin summarizes the arguments as follows:

> *The debate is complicated by the distinct worldviews held by those who support and oppose globalization. Supporters have a tendency to manifest*

'technocratic' worldviews. The world is largely empty. Economic growth is the answer to most problems. Technology and human ingenuity are ultimate saviours. The future is cornucopian. All forms of capital are substitutable. Human nature is competitive and human progress is consumption. Liberalism is the true philosophy and ethics are utilitarian. Efficient allocation via free markets is the guiding mechanism. These supporters are generally not neutral observers; rather, they are well connected to those interests that will gain from a more global capitalist system (multinational corporate CEOs, officials of the World Bank, IMF or WTO, investment bankers, business school professors, to name but a few).

On the other side stand a rainbow alliance of anxiety-stricken representatives of environmental organizations, consumer rights groups, family farmers, religious organizations, advocates of democracy and working people. They are all much less connected to the power of internationally mobile capital. In contrast to the technocrats, the critics of economic globalization tend to be 'sustain-centric' in their worldviews. The world is up against the limits set by its carrying capacity – further expansion of resource throughput will produce overshoot and collapse. Precaution is needed. Technology is a mixed blessing. The future is neo-Malthusian. Natural and human-made capital are fundamentally complements and only substitutes at the margin. Human survival demands cooperation and human happiness is not just a function of consumption. Metaphysics are holistic. Time horizons are long. Communitarianism is better than liberalism. We must be equally concerned with social justice and sustainable scale as with allocative efficiency. (Gladwin, 1998)

The caricatures are a little harsh, but the degree of polarization is well captured. As ever, however, description by polar opposite misses out on a lot of critical contextualization. For one thing, globalization is by no means the newly minted economic phenomenon that it is sometimes portrayed as. In the pre-1914 period, for example, international trade and capital flows, both between the rapidly industrializing economies themselves and between these and their various colonial territories, were more important relative to gross domestic product (GDP) levels than they are today.

Secondly, globalization itself is not really the problem. As with capitalism, it's the particular model of globalization that dominates the world economy that is causing the problems. As Naomi Klein says, commenting on the so-called 'anti-globalization' movement:

If this new movement is 'anti' anything, it is anti-corporate, opposing the logic that what is good for business – less regulation, more mobility, more access – will trickle down into good news for everybody else. By focusing on global corporations and their impact around the world, this activist network is fast becoming the most internationally minded, globally linked movement ever seen. When protesters shout about the evils of globalization, most are not calling for a return to narrow nationalism, but for the borders of globalization to be expanded, for trade to be linked to labour rights, environmental protection and democracy. This network is as global as capitalism itself. (Klein, 2002)

The designation of the seemingly inchoate array of concerned organizations and individuals campaigning against poverty, developing world debt, abuses of human rights, corruption, environmental degradation, privatization of the public commons and the unaccountability of multinationals (to name but the most prominent of grievances) as an 'anti-globalization movement' is profoundly misguided. There may well be a very small number of campaigners for whom the only solution to today's converging crises is, indeed, a rapid regression to autarchic, self-sufficient communities; but they are utterly unrepresentative of the vast majority of those campaigning against today's corporate globalization. They are indisputably anti-corporate and a rather smaller number are anti-capitalist; but all would acknowledge that the world is by and large a better place for improved global communications, the internet and improved understanding between nations, and that global problems demand global solutions mediated through accountable global initiatives and institutions.

Beyond that, it's not even correct any longer to argue that this is an exclusively negative movement, eloquent in its denunciation of literally countless abuses of people and planet, but incapable of coming to any kind of agreement as to what it actually stands for – although it *is* true that this is emphatically not a homogenized, unified movement. Phoney consensus is discouraged (at gatherings such as the World Social Forum in Porto Alegre, Brazil), and vibrant diversity and divergence are positively promoted. But the extent of the common ground upon which they *all* stand is becoming clearer and clearer: increased decentralization of power; global and national regulation of large corporations; community-based and local enterprise as a complement to international trade; and a passionate belief in development as freedom rather than development as growth, reverting back to Amartya Sen's (1999) core philosophy.

Interestingly, this is not the first time rich world countries have found themselves at such a turning point. In *The Great Transformation*, Austrian economist Karl Polanyi (1944) highlighted the way in which 19th-century *laissez-faire* economics generated so many negative social costs and inflicted such pain upon so many people that a number of different 'counter movements' sprang up specifically to address these dysfunctionalities. As *Guardian* journalist Larry Elliott puts it:

Put bluntly, the modern world is relearning some of the lessons of the past. Back in the 19th century, there was a similar belief that leaving the forces of supply and demand unencumbered by restrictions and constraints would lead to perfect equilibrium. If only wages could be set by demand and supply, if only all tariffs could be removed, if only entrepreneurs could be encouraged by low taxes, there would be a state of grace. Things didn't quite work out as planned. (Elliott, 2005)

And nor are they working out today as the Hayeks and the Friedmans of 20th-century free market fundamentalism must once have hoped. Counter-movements are again gathering momentum, and governments around the world are beginning to listen. The US Administration appears increasingly isolated in its zealous neo-liberalism, exacerbating tensions resulting from the stand-off between Europe and the US over the Iraq War. And this time round, there is an even more profound driver behind an otherwise familiar ideological divide.

DEMOCRACY AND GLOBALIZATION

For all the confusion, it is actually the defence of democracy and freedom that lies at the heart of the 'anti-globalization' movement, just as the evangelists of increased liberalization claim that it is the defence of democracy and freedom that drives their own passion for free markets and global trade. The neo-liberal rhetoric has always been very strong on the 'democracy through trade' argument, based upon the assumption that free markets create free peoples. As George Bush himself puts it: 'People who operate in open economies eventually demand more open societies.'

There is no denying that US neo-liberals are sincere in their belief that today's pattern of globalization fosters democracy. Such a belief is usually premised on the apparently reasonable extrapolation that since market-based economies are an essential feature of democratic societies, then the bigger those markets are, the more 'open' they are likely to be, and the more global they are, then the greater will be the reinforcement of pro-democratic processes and institutions.

Since 11 September 2001, that has become an even more dogmatic element in the promotion of corporate globalization. Robert Zoellick, US trade representative in George W. Bush's first Administration, was quite explicit in his linkage of the war against terrorism and the need for increased liberalization of world trade. In seeking to persuade the US Congress to give President Bush fast-track powers to negotiate new trade deals which Congress could either accept or reject but not improve, he argued that 'the values at the heart of free trade have become an essential part of the struggle against terrorism: open markets are an antidote to the terrorists' violent rejectionism.' As George Bush spelled out in his second inauguration speech in February 2005, it's now all part of the 'for us or against us' logic that the US first imposed on the rest of the world to secure agreement for what was clearly an illegal and unnecessary war against Iraq. The war against terrorism will be waged as much through the imposed will of the WTO as through the military might of the US, and those who stand opposed to that particular model of globalization must, in the twisted logic of the Bush Administration, be supporters of Al-Qa'eda and apologists for global terror.

There is a strong religious undertone to this analysis: free trade and democracy traditionally thrive in countries buttressed by Christian values and practice; Islamic countries are traditionally undemocratic, often oppressive and remain reluctant to throw in their lot with today's US-dominated global economy. Free trade has therefore been conscripted into a latter-day crusade to open up those closed nations and 'liberate' their people – just as is now being attempted in Afghanistan and Iraq. It is true that the political regimes in some Islamic countries are, indeed, abhorrent – illiberal, anti-women, corrupt, oppressive and usually hostile to any extension of civil rights or political freedoms. The democratization of those countries cannot come too soon. But the idea that the only route to democratization is via the imposition of corporate-led, US-driven globalization is perverse – and extraordinarily dangerous from the perspective of future world peace.

Roger Scruton's *The West and the Rest: Globalization and the Terrorist Threat* (2002) provides some deeply disturbing insights into the potential consequences of this geopolitical stand-off. He argues that Islam and the West have completely diverging views on citizenship, community, law and the role of religion in the lives of both citizens and states. From that perspective, the forward momentum of Western, corporate-led globalization is highly threatening to Islamic values, culture and morality, and the insensitivity of the West to this perceived threat is much resented.

For Scruton, there is additional resonance here in that he personally is persuaded that the Western values which underpin globalization (selfish individualism, moral relativism, progress through increased consumption and materialism, the dominance of individual rights over reciprocal responsibilities, and so on) are, indeed, inimical to the betterment of society and community the world over. While he abominates bin Laden (and the betrayal of the teachings of Islam that bin Laden is responsible for), he can't help but sympathize with the Islamists' horror of the decadence and the corruption at the heart of Western globalization.

The logic of Scruton's thinking leads to one grim conclusion: if we persist with this imposed monolithic pattern of globalization, then a 'clash of civilizations' is all but unavoidable. As we saw in Chapter 2, there are those who believe that none of this is happening by accident, as it were, and that it is all linked to the kind of apocalyptic, religious fundamentalism that now commands such strong support in the US political establishment – all the way up to the White House itself. Tens of millions of Christians in the US have declared their solidarity for the State of Israel (and for the extension of Jewish settlements through the West Bank), and saw the invasion of Iraq as some kind of welcome warm-up act for the big one itself – namely, Armageddon.

The combination of the extreme economic neo-liberalism of the current US Administration and its warped millenarian beliefs is having a dramatic impact both upon social cohesion inside the US itself and upon the diminishing opportunities for improved global security. It is clear that although the US constitution still declares that all people in the US are 'created equal', that is not the view of the religious right who see the world clearly divided by God into the righteous and the wicked. Pre-millennialists even tend to scorn efforts made in the name of religion to correct what is going wrong in society on the grounds that attempting to put in place any kind of programme of social improvement or to turn the energies of the church towards such progressive goals would be to thwart divine purpose and thus delay the advent of Christ.

Ideologically speaking, the US Administration is therefore perfectly comfortable with the extreme inequalities and social division of America today. Michael Northcott (2004) describes this as 'a tragic example of the capacity of perverted religion and secular ideology to distort human lives and relationships and destroy communities', and comments somewhat despairingly upon the malign synergies between neo-conservative economics and pre-millennial fundamentalism:

> For the pre-millennialist, righteous individuals will be mysteriously and suddenly plucked from their beds or workplaces by the divine hand, and so secured from the coming conflagration of Armageddon at the rapture. For the free marketeer, individuals will be redeemed by the invisible hand of market forces. In neither case can collective action decisively affect their fate. It is in the light of the dual effects of these two kinds of fatalism that the increasingly brutal as well as self-interested assertion of American imperial power on every continent in the last few years can be better understood. The US corporate elite increasingly see themselves as engaged in a planetary war for the maintenance of their own prosperity and way of life, and for the directing of all human history to American ends. (Northcott, 2004)

Roger Scruton eschews such apocalyptic analysis, sticking instead to a more conventional but still radical response: reverse the process of globalization, and rebuild national security and social cohesion through smaller-scale, locally based economies. In this prescription, he veers much more towards the precepts of the 'localization not globalization' movements – most effectively captured in Colin Hines's eloquent *Localization: A Global Manifesto* (2000) – and has no truck with the idea of an alternative form of internationalism based upon some kind of emerging 'sustainability consensus' rather than upon today's Washington Consensus. But for many people, there remains something completely unworldly about that kind of return to self-sufficient local communities.

It is a debate that still generates a huge amount of political energy within the international green movement. The September 2003 issue of the *Ecologist* laid on an enlivening exchange between two of the most radical critics of today's pattern of globalization, Helena Norberg-Hodge and George Monbiot. When it comes to alternatives to globalization, Norberg-Hodge is firmly in the localization camp:

> *The essence of localization is to enable communities around the world to diversify their economies so as to provide for as many of their needs as possible from relatively close to home. Economic activity on this scale can be adapted so as not to undermine biological and cultural diversity, and seems essential if we are to avoid further ecological and social breakdown. This does not mean eliminating trade altogether, as some critics like to suggest. It is about finding a more secure and sustainable balance between trade and local production.* (Norberg-Hodge, 2003)

This is a position with which Monbiot would once have found himself in complete agreement. But in his latest book (*Age of Consent: A Manifesto for a New World Order*, 2004), Monbiot appears to have moved full circle in advocating the wholesale reform (but not elimination) of today's international institutions, a huge increase in 'fair trade' to help poorer countries, and even a form of global government.

Confronting the Washington Consensus

Nevertheless, in one area Helena Norberg-Hodge and George Monbiot are still completely united in their views: that the so-called Washington Consensus is an enemy not a friend of democracy. As has now been documented in massive detail, the IMF's Structural Adjustment Programmes (SAPs) have compelled many governments over the last 20 years to set aside their own social and economic priorities and accept the IMF's conditions. As former chief economist to the World Bank, Joseph Stiglitz, says: 'In theory, the IMF supports democratic institutions in the nations it assists. In practice, it undermines the democratic process by imposing its own policies' (Stiglitz, 2002). Both the World Bank and the IMF now intrude ever more deeply into the affairs of sovereign states in ways that go far beyond their original mandates and terms of reference. The IMF's reviled SAPs have now been replaced with poverty reduction strategies; but many campaigners have yet to be persuaded that much has changed in practice.

The World Bank likes to make out that it is now the much friendlier face of those bodies promoting the Washington Consensus. Under the leadership of James Wolfensohn, it tried to recast itself as a global poverty elimination campaign, but with very mixed results. It is reckoned to have paid out $3 to the Western business sector (to help delivery in the developing world) for every $1 received as aid in developing countries. All too often, it has advanced loans to some of the poorest countries in the world for wholly inappropriate mega-projects or to develop export-driven manufacturing or cash-cropping. The fiasco over coffee (in which country after country has been encouraged to make huge new investments in coffee for export, leading to glutted markets and collapsing prices) is a direct consequence of the World Bank's obsession with export-led development. These interventions have often led to severe environmental damage, continued displacement of people in rural areas and the proliferation of dead-end sweatshop jobs. Many Western companies have benefited substantially; but the results for the developing world have often been extraordinarily disappointing. With Paul Wolfowitz now in charge, it seems extremely unlikely that any of these trends will be reversed, and most non-governmental organizations (NGOs) – in both the West and developing countries – anticipate an even cruder imposition of US-led neo-liberal orthodoxy.

National governments fare no better at the hands of the WTO. National ownership of key public services is increasingly interpreted as discrimination against foreign companies; democratic decisions (such as that taken by the EU to ban the import of US beef reared with the help of growth hormones) are fiercely contested and serve as the pretext for yet another trade war; governments may no longer defend higher environmental or social standards if these are seen to represent a non-tariff barrier to trade. At the disastrous WTO meeting in Cancun, Mexico, in 2003, developing countries finally decided that it was time to draw that proverbial line in the sand, after literally decades of hypocritical rhetoric from the rich countries about the importance of opening markets and getting rid of subsidies, and decades doing next to nothing about it in their own backyards. As a result, the meeting fell apart in utter disarray, and it is now hard to see how the WTO is going to be able to transform itself sufficiently so as to become part of the sustainable solution to today's social and economic problems, even if it does cobble together some kind of spurious compromise before the end of 2005.

Outside of the global institutions themselves, some of the world's largest multinational companies unscrupulously use their bargaining power as foreign direct investors to secure exemptions from planning laws, 'special deals' and high-level agreements in which the wishes of local people (or even of the electorate as a whole) are routinely set aside in the interests of a greater economic good. Self-regulation is their demand, and they have secured astonishingly favourable trading conditions as a result. Percy Barnevik, a former CEO of the multinational ABB, defined globalization as 'the freedom for my group to invest where it pleases, when it pleases, in order to produce what it wants by getting supplies and selling wherever it wants, supporting as few constraints as possible regarding workers' right and social conventions'. In the face of all that, as Naomi Klein argues, it seems a bit rich that trade through the global economy is suddenly seen as the great deliverer of freedom and democracy:

> *What I dislike most about the trickle-down democracy argument is the dishonour it pays to all the people who fought, and fight still, for genuine democratic change in their countries, whether for the right to vote, or to have access to land, or to form trade unions. Democracy isn't the work of*

> *the markets and the invisible hand; it is the work of real hands. It is often stated, for instance, that the North American Free Trade Agreement is bringing democracy to Mexico. In fact, workers, students, indigenous groups and radical intellectuals are the ones slowly forcing democratic reforms on Mexico's intransigent elite. NAFTA, by widening the gap between rich and poor, makes their struggle more militant and more difficult to stop.* (Klein, 2002)

Beyond that, it is becoming increasingly obvious that trade liberalization isn't necessarily delivering against its own, much narrower, economic objectives. It is clearly working well in terms of opening up the world to the already rich and powerful, but has failed time after time to provide equal access for poorer countries to the rich world. The United Nations Conference on Trade and Development (UNCTAD) has found that the rapid and extensive trade liberalization undertaken by the poorest countries during the 1990s failed to benefit the poor. In fact, it was associated with rising poverty, with the countries worst affected being those that had liberalized most. Economists have estimated that reducing the worst remaining trade barriers could lead to huge income gains for developing countries – in excess of $100 billion a year. That could be as much as three times the total amount of official development assistance on offer.

This takes us promptly back to Amartya Sen's (1999) critique of 'development as growth' rather than development as freedom. There is little doubt, by analogy, that globalization as growth, mediated through the self-serving expansion of some of the world's largest multinational companies, falls foul of the same strictures. Globalization as freedom, by contrast, offers something very different, as spelled out in the Johannesburg Memo:

> *Broadly speaking, there are currently two concepts of globalization which have gained prominence in recent controversies. Corporate globalization, which aims at transforming the world into a single economic arena, allows corporations to compete freed from constraints in order to increase global wealth and welfare. This particular concept can be traced to the rise of the free trade idea in 18th-century Britain and has come, after many permutations, to dominate world politics in the late 20th century.*
>
> *Democratic globalization, on the other hand, envisages a world that is home to a flourishing plurality of cultures, and that recognizes the fundamental rights for every world citizen. The roots of this concept extend back to the late ancient Greek philosophy and the European enlightenment, with their perception of the world in a cosmopolitan spirit. We believe that the cause of justice and sustainability would be caught in quicksand unless it is elaborated upon in the framework of democratic globalization.* (Johannesburg Memo, 2002)

Importantly, the Memorandum goes on to explore all sorts of ways in which the different institutions involved in promoting the accelerated liberalization of global markets could be reformed or adapted – to secure effective, sustainable, equitable outcomes. This is not the place to go into those details, nor indeed to explore the plethora of constructive public proposals that have emerged from each of the annual World Social Forums, and from literally dozens of NGOs all around the world intent on finding ways of ensuring that globalization really does work for the poor, for the environment and for the future. Suffice it to say for now that these alternatives do, indeed, exist; as John Gray has consistently argued over the last few years, it looks as if 'alternative modernities' are, indeed, available to non-Western cultures, giving the lie to the claim that there is no alternative to today's pattern of globalization in any modernizing view of the world.

It is a debate that can only become sharper. I don't pretend to have given a comprehensively balanced view of what is, after all, a massively complicated and 'protean' phenomenon. Advocates of accelerated globalization – such as Johann Norberg (2001) in his persuasive *In Defence of Global Capitalism* or Martin Wolf's (2004) *Why Globalization Works* – point to a string of statistics about growing prosperity in many parts of the world. It must count for something, after all, that the number of poor people in East Asia as a whole has halved since 1975, and that since China started opening up to the global economy in the 1980s, more than 300 million of its people have been lifted out of poverty. Norberg and Wolf argue passionately that globalization is good for the poor, good for the environment and particularly good for technology transfer. And they are certainly right to point out that China and India are fashioning their own variants of global capitalism without having some standard model imposed upon them.

But with the exception of China and India (very important exceptions, it has to be said), there is little evidence that globalization is producing any significant reduction in relative income disparities, as has always been claimed by conventional economists. Indeed, exactly the opposite would seem to be happening in many parts of the world. By 1960, the income gap between the fifth of the world's people living in the richest countries and the fifth in the poorest countries was 30:1. In 1990, the gap had widened to 60:1. By 1998, it had grown to 78:1. By 2000, it was close to 100:1. Looking at current trends, it is difficult to imagine the point at which this trend will eventually bottom out.

It is, of course, difficult to disentangle cause and effect here. But in a world where the dice are so clearly loaded against the poor, global capitalism *as we know it today* would appear to be inherently incompatible with the pursuit of either ecological sustainability or social justice. Indeed, conceptualizing the journey from where we are today to an ecologically and socially sustainable model of globalization takes a lot of imagination. One of the organizations at the forefront of the 're-conceptualization challenge' is the New Economics Foundation, which over the years has helped to develop a formidable global network of sister organizations. Margaret Legum is the leading light in one of these (South African New Economics), and she has captured the 'before and after' effect of the various campaigns being waged by that network to ensure that the Washington Consensus is succeeded by a very different kind of consensus (see Figures 5.1 and 5.2). I will return to a number of those 'alternative scenarios' in Part III.

Whatever variations there may be in today's different movements against US-led corporate globalization, there is consensus on one point: the role played in the

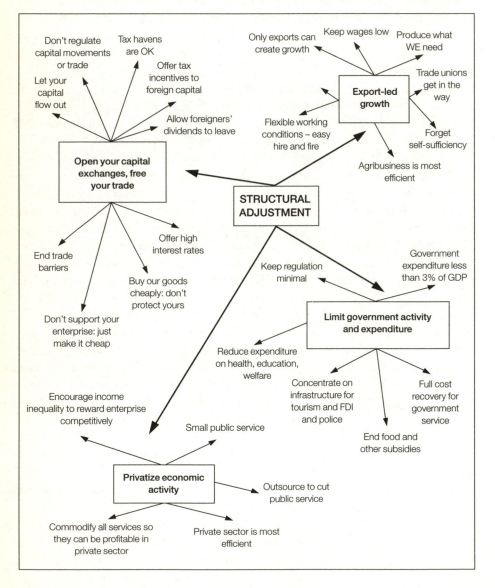

Source: Legum (2002)

Figure 5.1 *The Washington Consensus: how it works*

global economy by multinational companies lies at the very heart of the problem. It is not possible to answer the question about the compatibility of capitalism and sustainability without addressing the contribution made by today's multinationals to our current state – for good or ill – and then addressing the question of what to do about any dysfunctionalities that might be identified.

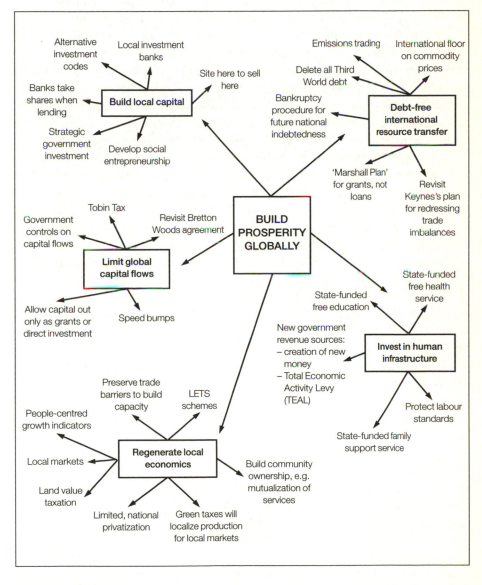

Source: Legum (2002)

Figure 5.2 *An alternative scenario to the Washington Consensus*

ADDRESSING THE MULTINATIONALS

I am always amused by the fact that one of the very first campaigners against multinational corporations was Adam Smith in *The Wealth of Nations* back in 1776, where he warned that managers should not be trusted to steward other people's money, and that only 'negligence and confusion' would result. The corporation as we know it today is essentially a creature of Britain's imperial past, going right back to the establishment of the East India Company in 1600, just one of a series of corporate charters extended first by British monarchs and then by the English parliament to groups of investors. Each charter was slightly different; but essentially they limited the extent of any liabilities or losses suffered by the investors in return for certain obligations designed to serve the public purpose – including any share of profits that would accrue to the Crown. Gradually, these corporations were granted monopoly powers, either over whole territories (as with the East India Company or with the Hudson Bay Company) or whole industries.

During the 17th and 18th century, parliament then passed many new laws to extend these monopoly interests – and it was this slow accretion of power to the corporations that so irked Adam Smith. He saw the emerging nexus of influence between the state and corporations as wholly inimical to the competitive functions of the market. But during the 19th century, the power base of the multinationals shifted to the US as it gradually overcame its hostility to the institution of the corporation, with individual corporations slowly gaining sufficient control over state legislatures basically to rewrite the laws governing their own regulation and the balance of their rights and responsibilities. By the middle of the 19th century, the detailed mechanics of 'limited liability' (limiting the losses an individual investor could incur, in the event of corporate failure, to the amount of money initially invested rather than to the total losses) was finally agreed upon – essentially as a way of attracting the middle classes into the business of buying and selling stocks. And in 1886, the US Supreme Court ruled that a private corporation could be treated as 'natural person' under the US constitution and was therefore entitled to all the protection afforded under the Bill of Rights. As David Korten points out:

> *Thus, corporations finally claimed the full rights enjoyed by individual citizens while being exempted from many of the responsibilities and liabilities of citizenship. The subsequent claim by corporations that they have the same right as any individual to influence the government in their own interest pits the individual citizen against the vast financial and communications resources of the corporation, and mocks the constitutional intent that all citizens have an equal voice in the political debates surrounding important issues.* (Korten, 1995)

This is one of the reasons why many campaigners remain so mistrustful of the concept of 'corporate citizenship'. History tells us that the likes of J. D. Rockerfeller,

Cornelius Vanderbilt, Andrew Carnegie and James Mellon illegitimately arrogated to their enterprises the rights and entitlements of the individual citizen, while simultaneously diminishing the idea of any reciprocal 'public service' obligation on their part. Corporations are *not* citizens, and to abuse the concept of citizenship by attributing it to them is both misleading and unhelpful.

What has all this got to do with multinationals today, as the modern inheritors of all these legal privileges? There is a powerful school of thought which argues that multinationals (particularly over the last 30 years or so) have systematically increased their reach, scope and influence so that they are now *the* dominant social institution anywhere in the world. David Korten's 1995 classic, *When Corporations Rule the World*, lucidly analyses the build-up of corporate power, its progressive 'take-over' of political and legislative systems (particularly in the US, but now everywhere in the world), and the malign consequences of this for effective government, the more equitable distribution of wealth, and any attempt to set the global economy on a genuinely sustainable footing. They behave in this way because we continue to elect governments that continue, in effect, to license multinationals to create wealth often at the expense of people and planet.

According to this kind of radical critique, any reform agenda is seen as a complete waste of time. Multinational corporations have slipped their constitutional leashes, feel that they now owe nothing to society apart from warm words about social responsibility, and are accountable solely to their shareholders in whose interests profits must be maximized at all costs. For one reason or another, enough people are still sufficiently persuaded that this exercise of power predominantly in the interests of a tiny minority of human beings still serves the interests of the vast majority well enough – or, rather, better than anything else on offer. Corporate-dominated media shield them from the reality of what is really happening, and an active propaganda machine seduces people into comatose consumerism as a substitute for real life and active engagement in the world around us.

It is a powerful – and ultimately despairing – hypothesis. But does it really stack up? Of course the interests of shareholders come first: that is the way their legal and fiduciary obligations are currently framed. But it is misleading to argue that this *necessarily* and *automatically* demands corporate practices that degrade the environment, abuse employees and exploit local communities. Indeed, as we will see in Chapter 14, the underlying rationale of the so-called 'business case' for environmentally, socially and ethically responsible behaviour is a great deal stronger than most people allow for.

However, the intensity of the invective still levelled by most campaigners against the multinationals (as if there was still nothing to differentiate a BP from an ExxonMobil, a Unilever from a Nestlé) still comes as something of a surprise to those organizations (such as Forum for the Future) that work alongside such companies to accelerate the many different change processes which are already under way. Over the 11 years that the Prince of Wales's Business and the Environment Programme has been in existence, for instance, we have witnessed a profound shift in both attitudes and behaviours on the part of most of the big multinationals involved. As individuals, the thousand or so senior business people who have been through the Programme's week-long seminar are often as concerned about the state of the world and its people as some of the campaigners lobbing brickbats at them. But they are constrained – by their bosses; by corporate inertia and bureaucracy; by the power of capital markets; by limited consumer and investor enthusiasm for using their purchasing power more sustainably; by muddled, procrastinating politicians.

For all of those reasons, there remains every reason to be extremely cautious about today's unbounded enthusiasm for the notion of corporate social responsibility (CSR). This has little to do with the *Economist's* distaste for anything that seems to imply that contemporary capitalism isn't already doing a near-perfect job, and much more to do with the way in which CSR is interpreted by companies as a ragbag menu of nice-to-do add-ons that never really interrogate their core business model. This is easily demonstrated by the way in which some of the really difficult issues never get on to the menu in the first place.

Taxation and transfer pricing arrangements provide one such example for multinationals today, posing a challenge on both equity and transparency grounds. A narrow interpretation of a company's traditional fiduciary duties to its shareholders means that it should be doing everything in its power, within the law, to reduce the amount of tax it pays to any government and to maximize the financial benefits to be had from juggling prices, revenues and currency exchange across different markets. As a result, companies often end up paying tens of millions of dollars in legal fees to avoid as much of their tax burden as can legally be avoided, all the while talking enthusiastically about their benign influence on poor countries in terms of jobs generated, taxes paid and the 'multiplier effect' they purport to have on local economies. CSR sceptics have rightly pointed out that they could be much more of a 'force for good' if they simply paid over all the taxes owed in any particular country, rather than relying on quasi-philanthropic handouts.

This is likely to become a much bigger issue over the next few years. CSR activists are arguing that taxation policy should now be included as a critical indicator of responsible and ethical business behaviour, and the regulators should insist on far greater transparency in the way in which multinationals account for tax payments and transfer pricing arrangements. Indeed, new disclosure rules were introduced by the UK Inland Revenue in 2004, based on the surprisingly radical rationale that tax avoidance should be seen not just in legal terms, but in terms of morality and corporate responsibility.

There have been a number of moments in the history of the corporation where public pressure of this kind has compelled an overt commitment to interests beyond those of the shareholders; but they have usually been either short-lived (as happened in the US after World War I, when it was even referred to fleetingly as 'the new capitalism') or superficial (as in the Great Depression of the 1930s when corporations were trying to ward off Franklin Roosevelt's 'New Deal' legislation). Joel Bakan emphasizes the need for caution:

> *Business leaders today say that their companies care about more than profit and loss, that they feel responsible to society as a whole, not just to their shareholders. Corporate social responsibility is their new creed, a self-conscious corrective to earlier greed-inspired versions of the corporation. Despite this shift, the corporation itself has not changed. It remains, as it was at the time of its origins as a modern business institution in the middle of the 19th century, a legally designated 'person' designed to valorize self-interest and invalidate moral concern. Most people would find its 'personality' abhorrent, even psychopathic, in a human being; yet curiously we accept it in society's most powerful institution.* (Bakan, 2004)

This kind of anti-corporate rhetoric causes huge offence to large numbers of business people. But critics such as Joel Bakan and David Korten are not talking about individuals in those companies, but about the *corporate persona* as such. By 'psychopathic', Bakan is referring to those traits that psychiatrists would expect to encounter in a psychopathic individual: a readiness to manipulate everything and everybody else; a lack of empathy; an obsession with being 'number one'; a refusal to accept responsibility for their own actions; an inability to feel any guilt or remorse.

If CSR can help, even on the margins, to mitigate those character traits, then we should do nothing to discourage even the most superficial engagement. But it is an illusion to think that responsibility for putting all this to rights lies predominantly with the companies themselves. If society wants companies to rebalance the respective interests of shareholders and other interested stakeholders (employees, local communities, environmental interests and so on), then it is society – through its governments – that must reframe their respective obligations. Governments, not companies, have the democratic mandate to intervene in order to shape market forces. If ministers are persuaded that there is sufficiently widespread public support for raising standards, or encouraging best practice, then they should intervene decisively to secure those public benefits without endlessly passing the buck back to business to do it on our behalf.

No one government can act on its own anyway – hence the call from NGOs (represented most forcefully at the World Summit on Sustainable Development by Friends of the Earth International) for a Global Convention on Corporate Accountability. Although most NGOs acknowledge that multinational companies are already achieving a certain amount through voluntary mechanisms, they do not believe that this can possibly go far enough. A new convention would include mechanisms to obtain redress for any stakeholders adversely affected by the impact of multinationals. Those individuals and organizations should be given legal standing to challenge corporations in their own home country. The convention would identify clear social and environmental duties for corporations, which would include reporting on environmental and social performance in a verifiable fashion, seeking what is called 'prior informed consent' from affected communities, and defining rules for consistently high standards of behaviour wherever corporations are operating anywhere in the world. These rules would be based upon the principles enshrined in international environmental, social and human rights agreements.

There are big questions about whether any such convention could ever be policed; but they usually come couched in a suspiciously self-serving set of excuses and pretexts for inaction. And there is an equally strong view that it is not more legislation that is needed, but the proper implementation of the legislation that already exists, with a readiness on the part of the rich Northern countries to help poorer Southern countries use existing legislative powers (both national and international) to keep multinationals under control. The diversity of views on the 'reformability' of multinationals, as we have seen, covers a very wide span – all the way through from an uncompromising call for their elimination, at one end of the spectrum, to a little bit of incremental tinkering (as favoured by most European governments) at the other, via various shades of moderate or radical reform in between.

Many critics believe that this debate still misses the point and that the real problems lie not so much in the corporate world as in the macro-economic and financial systems within which those corporates have to operate. David Korten again:

> These forces have transformed once beneficial corporations and financial institutions into instruments of a market tyranny that is extending its reach across the planet like a cancer, colonizing ever more of the planet's living spaces, destroying livelihoods, displacing people, rendering democratic institutions impotent and feeding on life in an insatiable quest for money. As our economic system has detached itself from place and gained greater dominance over our democratic institutions, even the world's most powerful corporations have become captives of the forces of a globalized financial system that has de-linked the creation of money from creation of real wealth and rewards extractive, over-productive investment. (Korten, 1995)

Despair in the face of such daunting problems is an understandable reaction. But there are fewer and fewer people who seriously suppose that this particular model of capitalism (dominated by a small number of hugely powerful interests, imposing upon the world a pattern of globalization that alienates millions, impoverishes hundreds of millions, further enriches an already inconceivably wealthy minority, and undermines our life-support systems in the process) can last for very much longer – on ecological grounds alone.

Indeed, there are those who argue, albeit against the run of the last 20 years or so, that the whole crazy edifice is a great deal more vulnerable than might ever be discerned from mainstream media coverage of the already visible cracks and faults in the system. Comparisons with the collapse of Soviet power in Eastern Europe are often made in this context, not least because so few of the pundits and pontificators in the self-same media seemed to have the remotest inkling of what was about to happen as a consequence of the 'velvet revolution' in Eastern European countries back in the 1980s. Even the remote possibility of such a collapse is stirring an ever larger number of enthusiastic capitalists to look far more purposefully to a reform agenda than ever before. But are they looking in the right direction?

Part II, 'A framework for sustainable capitalism', begins to explore what an alternative model of capitalism might look like. As I hope has emerged in the opening five chapters, the principal reason for taking on that challenge is the realization that today's particular model of capitalism simply won't get us to where we need to be: a world in which 9 billion people can live within the Earth's natural limits in a sufficiently equitable, just and healthy society.

The emergence of a sustainable variant of capitalism is not going to happen overnight, jumping instantly from one relatively stable state to another relatively stable state: it will be messy, incremental, controversial and very, very difficult. But that change process is already under way – in terms of our first faltering responses to climate change, the 'Make Poverty History' breakthroughs of 2005 on debt and aid, a growing awareness of our interdependence with all other nations and peoples, a better understanding of the scale of the technological challenges that now confront us, and so on.

What is at stake here is how fast that transition can be driven. I have tried to demonstrate in these first five chapters that we really don't have much alternative, given the state of the life-support systems upon which we depend, and have advanced the tentative hypothesis that there is no absolute 'deal-breaker' in terms of some inherent incompatibility within capitalism that would mean we could *never* arrive at a sustainable society via a capitalist economy. That hypothesis will, no doubt, be torn to shreds by more radical sustainable development activists who are still persuaded that there can be no accommodation whatsoever with capitalism, however 'tamed' and transformed a variant we might end up with.

To help generate that debate is part of the purpose in writing this book. Although I've acknowledged that the environment movement in Europe is not in such a parlous state as would appear to be the case in the US, there is very little room for complacency. Indeed, some harsh commentary comparing the relative success of the Make Poverty History campaign (with its breakthroughs on debt relief and other development issues at the 2005 G8 Summit) with the relative failure of the NGO community to make much impact upon climate change (let alone a host of less prominent sustainability issues) made uncomfortable reading through 2005 for those of us seized with a sense of the extreme urgency in all of this.

This explains the contention that the environment movement is also going to have to raise its game. We have got to get better at presenting the overwhelmingly positive benefits of the proposed transition in terms of new opportunities for entrepreneurs, new sources of economic prosperity and jobs, a higher quality of life for people, safer, more secure communities, a better work–life balance, and so on. In other words, we have got to raise the wellbeing stakes at the same time as we seek to put sustainability itself at the heart of progressive politics. It is only that powerful combination (necessity *and* desirability, sustainability *and* wellbeing) which is likely to drag the politics of sustainable development out of the margins and into the mainstream – a challenge which I seek to address in Part III.

Let me give one concrete example of what that combination might look like. On climate change, the UK has adopted a long-term target of achieving a cut in carbon dioxide (CO_2) emissions of 60 per cent by 2050. At the moment, that means almost nothing to most people – indeed, how could it, when most people have no real sense of where that CO_2 comes from in the first place? So let's get personal about this. When all the calculations are done in terms of concentrations of CO_2 in the atmosphere – stabilized emissions, threshold limits and so on – it all boils down to one simple number: assuming a population of around 9 billion by the middle of the century, each and every one of us will be able to emit the equivalent of approximately 1 tonne of carbon per annum. Welcome to the One Tonne World!

This is what is euphemistically known as a 'stretch target', given that we currently emit the equivalent of a great deal more than that – up to 7 tonnes per person per annum if you are a citizen of the US. At this point, environmentalists usually proffer the sackcloth and ashes, inviting people to contemplate a life of sober reflection, constant sacrifice and greatly reduced material wellbeing – and are a little taken aback when people rapidly decline the invitation. But what if that 'offer' was reworked – promising entry into the One Tonne World on the basis of better value for money, lower electricity and gas bills, better food, less hassle in terms of getting to and from work, improved health, more jobs in the cutting-edge industries of the future, cleaner air, more convivial communities, more time at home or reconnecting with the natural world? One Tonne – real fun!

There is a long way to go before we'll be able to reposition sustainability in that kind of way. And there's an equally long way to go before we get the politics of sustainable development properly sorted out. The case made here is that those interested in the environment must get much more comfortable with some kind of engaged discourse about capitalism itself, and can no longer remain ideologically detached from the cut and thrust of that debate. So, here is my starter question: having made the bold contention that it is theoretically possible to secure a sustainable future for the whole of humankind within the embrace of capitalism, exactly what sort of capitalism will that entail?

References

Bakan, J. (2004) *The Corporation*, Constable, London
Elliott, L. (2005) 'The mistakes of laissez-faire revisited', *Guardian*, 7 February
Gladwin, T. (1998) 'Economic globalization and ecological sustainability' in N. Roome (ed) *Sustainability Strategies for Industry*, Island Press, Washington, DC

Hines, C. (2000) *Localization: A Global Manifesto*, Earthscan, London

Johannesburg Memo (2002) *Fairness in a Fragile World*, Heinrich Böll Foundation, Berlin

Klein, N. (2002) *Fences and Windows*, Flamingo, London

Korten, D. (1995) *When Corporations Rule the World*, Earthscan, London

Legum, M. (2002) *It Doesn't Have to Be Like This*, Wild Goose Publications, Glasgow, UK

Monbiot, G. (2004) *Age of Consent: A Manifesto for a New World Order*, HarperCollins, London

Norberg, J. (2001) *In Defence of Global Capitalism*, Timbro AB, Sweden

Norberg-Hodge, H. (2003) 'Globalization: Use it or lose it', *Ecologist*, September

Northcott, M. (2004) *An Angel Directs the Storm: Apocalyptic Religion and American Empire*, I. B. Tauris, London

Polanyi, K. (1944) *The Great Transformation*, Rinehart, New York

Scruton, R. (2002) *The West and the Rest: Globalization and the Terrorist Threat*, Continuum, London

Sen, A. (1999) *Development as Freedom*, Oxford University Press, Oxford

Smith, A. (1776) *An Inquiry into the Nature and Causes of the Wealth of Nations*, first published in London by W. Strahan and T. Cadell, printers, in 2 volumes. Numerous contemporary editions are available.

Stiglitz, J. (2002) *Globalization and Its Discontents*, Allen Lane, London

Wolf, M. (2004) *Why Globalization Works*, Yale University Press, New Haven, CT

PART II

A FRAMEWORK FOR SUSTAINABLE CAPITALISM

6

The Five Capitals Framework

INTRODUCTION

Behind the notion of *capitalism* lies the notion of *capital* – which economists use to describe a stock of anything (physical or virtual) from which anyone can extract a revenue or yield. Although it is true that many environmentalists and social justice campaigners remain wary of getting sucked too deep into the working practices and language of capitalism, the premise behind the idea of the Five Capitals Framework is that we can't reform capitalism without adopting some of its insights, tools and drivers. But most of today's 'reform agendas' (from the progressive left, for instance) simply refuse to face up to some of the issues covered in Part I of this book, unable to confront the challenge of learning to live within non-negotiable biophysical limits. So much for the theory. This chapter looks at three different levels at which the Five Capitals Framework can be interpreted in practice: as an integrated management system within a particular sector of the economy; as an analytical tool for investors for measuring all-round corporate success; and as a way of framing the massive challenge facing a country such as China as it races towards becoming both the world's largest economy and the world's most terrifying ecological disaster.

GRAPPLING WITH THE CONCEPT OF CAPITAL

Although many critics of today's dominant capitalist paradigm would profoundly disagree with such a position, a viable *hypothesis* emerges from this preliminary analysis that there is no inherent, fixed or non-negotiable aspect of capitalism in general (rather than today's particular form of capitalism) that renders it for all time incompatible with the pursuit of a sustainable society. Moreover, it may well prove to be the case that the protean adaptability of capitalism (that has made it such a resilient and successful cultural phenomenon) will yet again prove to be its 'saving grace' in the face of the ever more pressing challenge of biophysical sustainability.

That makes it possible (intellectually and ethically) to subscribe to what was described earlier as a 'reform from within' strategy: identify those characteristics of today's dominant capitalist paradigm that most damagingly impede progress towards sustainability and set out to change them through the usual levers – government intervention, consumer preference, international diplomacy, education and so on. For those who have already been engaged in just such a reform agenda for the last few decades, that is hardly the most empowering conclusion to have arrived at. But how much worse would it be to be committed to a reform agenda if the system one sought to reform was inherently incapable of accommodating the necessary changes in the first place.

But exactly what kind of 'reform agenda' are we talking about here? There are literally hundreds of manifestos, declarations and high-level statements covering every shade of green or sustainability thinking. On individual causes, campaigns, themes and specific policy areas, the flow of reform proposals from countless organizations and individuals is unceasing. But most, perhaps inevitably, are symptom oriented, dealing with the downstream externalities and impacts of an economic system that simply isn't 'tuned' to the world in which we now live. Few have attempted to address those downstream externalities from a more systematic approach to the economic system itself – capitalism.

As we have seen, capitalism has a number of important characteristics that distinguish it from other economic systems: private ownership of the means of production, reliance upon the market to allocate goods and services, the drive to accumulate capital, and so on. But the core concept of capitalism, from which it derives its very name, is the economic concept of *capital*. Capital is a stock of anything that has the capacity to generate a flow of benefits which are valued by humans. It is this flow – normally of goods and services of benefit to people – that makes the capital stock an asset, and the value of the asset is derived directly from the lifetime value of the flows to which it gives rise.

When people think of capital in this sense, they usually think of some of the more familiar 'stocks' of capital: land, machines and money. But in the description of the Five Capitals Framework that follows, this basic concept of capital (as in *any* stock capable of generating a flow) has been elaborated upon to arrive at a hypothetical model of sustainable capitalism. It entails five separate 'stocks': natural, human, social, manufactured and financial (see Box 6.1).

As we will see, people have different levels of familiarity with these five kinds of capital. We are all familiar with the concept of financial capital as we juggle with our own personal finances; manufactured capital is extremely familiar to business people, acquiring new assets and having to depreciate these through their annual accounts; human capital is in some ways a variation on the more familiar notion of human resources; the concept of social capital has caused a stir of academic interest over the last 20 years or more, but has had relatively little impact upon standard political discourse; and natural capital has been around for a long time as a handy abstraction to describe the uses which we humans make of the natural world.

Such terminology is hardly controversial; but there are many who abhor the terminological reduction of the natural world to natural capital, or of people's unique talents and skills to human capital, or of the intricate pattern of networks,

---

BOX 6.1 THE FIVE CAPITALS

1   *Natural capital* (also referred to as environmental or ecological capital) is any stock or flow of energy and matter that yields valuable goods and services. It falls into several categories: resources, some of which are renewable (timber, grain, fish and water), while others are not (fossil fuels); sinks which absorb, neutralize or recycle waste; and services, such as climate regulation. Natural capital is the basis not only of production but of life itself.

2   *Human capital* consists of health, knowledge, skills and motivation (all of which are required for productive work), as well as an individual's emotional and spiritual capacities. Enhancing human capital (for instance, through investment in education and training) is central to a flourishing economy.

3   *Social capital* takes the form of structures, institutions, networks and relationships which enable individuals to maintain and develop their human capital in partnership with others, and to be more productive when working together than in isolation. It includes families, communities, businesses, trade unions, voluntary organizations, legal/political systems and educational and health bodies.

4   *Manufactured capital* comprises material goods – tools, machines, buildings and other forms of infrastructure – which contribute to the production process but do not become embodied in its output.

5   *Financial capital* plays an important role in our economy by reflecting the productive power of the other types of capital, and enabling them to be owned and traded. However, unlike the other types, it has no *intrinsic* value; whether in shares, bonds or banknotes, its value is purely representative of natural, human, social or manufactured capital.

Source: Forum for the Future

---

institutions and relationships that bind societies together to social capital. They may take some consolation from the fact that the concept of capital can only be used in relation to the fact that we derive a benefit of some kind (tangible or intangible) from a particular service. For example, sand on a beautiful beach is potentially natural capital because it could indirectly help to generate tourist revenues. The same sand in a desert would either not have the same value, or not have any value at all, in which case it cannot be described as capital. However, if technological changes meant that desert sand could be used in semi-conductors, then it would become capital, and its value would be related to the market value of the semi-conductors that it could be used to create.

This will not necessarily allay the concerns of many environmentalists who will see the Five Capitals Framework as further evidence of the inexorable commodification of the world. But if there is any genuinely sustainable variant of capitalism out there, then it will need to work within the conceptual and linguistic conventions that people are now so familiar with. The concept of capital serves not only to explain the productive power of capitalism; it also provides the clearest means of explaining the conditions for its sustainability.

Historically, the first type of capital was undoubtedly natural capital – the capacity of the biosphere to use solar energy to build up and sustain ever more complex life forms and ecosystems. All life forms are totally dependent upon this continuing capacity, and humans are no exception. However, humans responded differently from other species in the use that they have made of the natural world's continuing provision of goods and services. Over the long march of evolution from *Homo Australopithecus* to modern times, humans have developed their own productive powers and, in the process, have become the repository of enormous amounts of human capital. This has many distinct elements, but is best defined as 'the physical, intellectual, emotional and spiritual capacities of any individual'.

With the agricultural revolution some 10,000 years ago, humans began to apply their human capital to the cultivation of natural capital, directing natural flows into crops and animals for human benefit. Well before that, however, humans had applied human capital to natural capital to create *manufactured* capital: artefacts fashioned out of resources which, combined with human skill, could increase human productivity still further.

Even before the creation and use of their earliest tools, humans had become aware, perhaps instinctively, of what was to become one of their greatest developmental strengths: humans are more productive organized in groups than as individuals. Many animals exhibit group behaviour, of course, and in some species it can become quite complex. But humans have taken organization to a quite different level of function and complexity, developing political, legal and financial systems, work patterns that permit ever more specialization and division of labour, and cultural institutions for sports, entertainment and the arts that increase enormously both the quantity and quality of what can be produced. This is *social* capital.

And one particular form of social capital that has acquired more immediate power in modern industrial capitalism than any other is *financial* capital. Money is, of course, a representation of value, rather than having value in itself, and depends for its power in production (or consumption) entirely upon the confidence that is placed in it. However, modern capitalism is now so complex that it could not function at all without a comparably complex financial system that commanded confidence.

These five forms of capital, judiciously combined by entrepreneurs, are the essential ingredients of modern industrial productivity. Natural capital, despite modern sophistications, is still required to maintain a functioning biosphere, supply resources to the economy and dispose of its wastes. Human capital provides the knowledge and skills which create manufactured capital and operate it effectively. Social capital creates the institutions that provide the stable context and conditions within and through which economic activity can take place, and which enable individuals to be vastly more productive. Financial capital provides the lubricant to keep the whole system operating.

All sorts of diagrammatic representations of the Five Capitals Framework present themselves; what matters most is to understand the interconnections and the

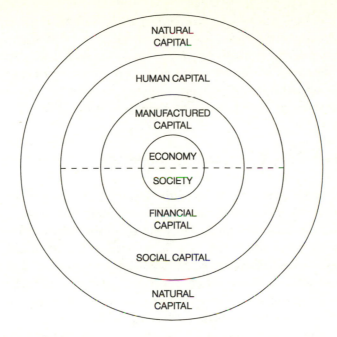

Source: Forum for the Future

Figure 6.1 *The Five Capitals Framework*

interdependencies between the different kinds of capital (see Figure 6.1). Natural and human capital are undoubtedly the primary forms of capital, with social and manufactured capital both derived from natural and human capital. Financial capital is in a rather different category (the word 'economy' is used in Figure 6.1 in its original sense: the management of the home or household – in this context, planet Earth.)

Any illustration must take proper account of what was referred to in Chapter 1 as the preconditionality of natural capital. But within that overarching system, there are no hard lines, especially when it comes to the reciprocal flows between human capital and social capital. All such categorizations are therefore more than a little arbitrary. In reality, there are only two sources of wealth in the world today: the wealth that flows from our use of the world's resources and ecosystems (our natural capital), all powered by incoming solar radiation, and the wealth that flows from the use of our hands, brains and spirits (our human capital). *All* else – money, machines, institutions and so on – is derivative of these two primary sources of wealth.

And to put everything in context, we ourselves are merely an ephemeral subset of that earthly natural capital, which itself is merely a subset of the incalculable material vastness of the whole cosmos!

The rest of this section looks in more detail at each of the five capital stocks. But the connecting rationale is a powerful one:

Sustainability depends upon maintaining and, where possible, increasing stocks of certain kinds of capital so that we learn to live off the flows (the 'income') without depleting the stock of capital itself; if consumption is at the expense of investment, or results in net capital depletion so that the capital stock declines, then such consumption is not sustainable and will be reduced in the future. (Forum for the Future, 2000)

The Five Capitals Framework in practice

It is difficult if not impossible to avoid the descent into economic jargon at this point, and although it's true that you would not find that kind of paragraph in any conventional economic text book, nor would you find many economists who would have any particular objection to it. Spurred on by the likes of Professor David Pearce – whose *Blueprint for a Green Economy* (Pearce et al, 1989) was a complete eye-opener for most environmentalists – and Professor Paul Ekins (2000), there is a growing realization that conventional economics simply has to make a better job of dealing with the challenge of sustainability.

Before engaging with some of the dynamics of each of the five stocks of capital, treated separately in a classically reductionist way, it may be helpful to try and demonstrate up front that the transformative effect of this kind of framework depends upon being deployed in a genuinely integrated way – through three quick examples operating at three very different levels.

First off is an example of this kind of integrated framework being applied to one particular sector of the economy – in this instance, construction and the built environment. Back in 2003, after almost a decade of different initiatives in the UK trying to make sense of the concept of sustainable construction, the New Construction Industry Research and Innovation Strategy Panel asked David Pearce to produce a more authoritative report on 'the social and economic value of construction'. In setting out to answer one deceptively simple question ('exactly what is construction's contribution to sustainable development and the delivery of long-term quality of life improvement?'), the research appraised the role of manufactured capital, human and social capital, and environmental capital as the critical elements in generating sustainable profits for the construction industry as a whole. Its schema for sustainable development is depicted in Figure 6.2.

It's a fascinating report (Pearce, 2003), though I'm not at all sure how much impact it will have had on an industry that is all too often downbeat and defensive about the contribution that it could make to fashioning a genuinely sustainable future for the 9 billion people with whom we will share this planet by the middle of the century.

The impact of the Dow Jones Sustainability Indexes (DJSIs), however, is not in doubt. Launched back in 1999, its Sustainability World Index reviews the social, environmental and ethical performance of over 300 companies from 24 countries,

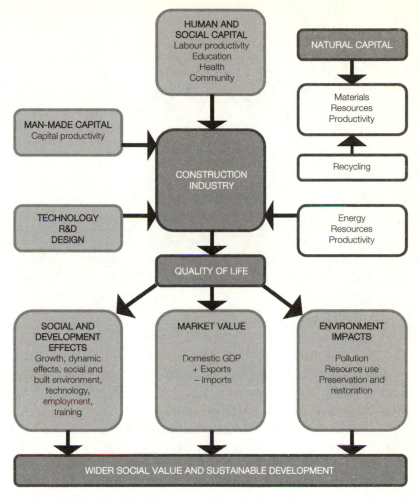

Source: Pearce (2003)

Figure 6.2 *Schema for wider social value and sustainable development in the construction industry*

while the Pan-European Index surveys 167 companies from 12 countries. Despite the fact that all companies are now complaining bitterly about the number of surveys that they have to fill in every year, participation rates in DJSI have increased year on year, covering more than 50 general as well as industry-specific criteria for each sector. Although the criteria are not mapped explicitly against the Five Capitals Framework, there is a surprisingly close fit, not least because their 'best in sector' approach demands that companies have to be performing well in financial terms even to qualify for appraisal.

An index on its own is interesting but of limited value in terms of changing investor behaviour. However, DJSI licenses its research to around 50 asset managers

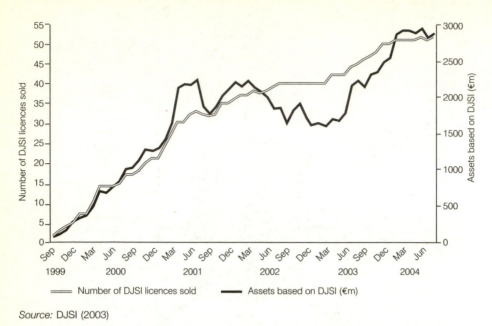

Source: DJSI (2003)

Figure 6.3 *Dow Jones Sustainability Index assets and licences*

in a number of countries to manage a wide range of financial products. As can be seen from Figure 6.3, the scale of these managed funds has reached nearly 3 billion Euros – and is continuing to grow strongly through 2005 (by way of contrast, the total assets in sustainability-driven European retail funds crossed the 19 billion Euro mark in 2004 – an increase of over 50 per cent compared to a year earlier).

All of this means that companies are extremely anxious to perform well in the DJSI – the biggest problem for companies such as BT and Unilever, which have been best in their sector for several years, is their fear of how it would be seen if they lost that top spot!

CHINA'S SUSTAINABILITY DILEMMA

You can be sure of one thing: all of the companies listed in Table 6.1 will either already be established in China or will be thinking of the right point of entry. With a population of 1.3 billion people, around 100 million of whom can already be described as 'middle class', China represents the most enticing market opportunity for future growth to companies the world over. But as many of those companies have already discovered, the risks are proportionately great.

It is a commonplace of sustainable development debates that they often end in the question: 'Well, that's all well and good, but what about China?' And it's the right question. The combined population of China and India in 2050 will be around 3 billion people, approximately one third of total human numbers. Their

Table 6.1 *World asset leaders*

Sector	World sector leaders	European sector leaders
Automobiles	Toyota	Volkswagen
Banks	Westpac Banking Corp	ABN Amro
Basic resources	Alcan	Anglo American
Chemicals	DSM	DSM
Construction	AMEC	AMEC
Cyclical goods and services	Koninklijke (Royal) Philips Electronics	Koninklijke (Royal) Philips Electronics
Energy	Statoil	Statoil
Financial services	British Land	British Land
Food and beverage	Unilever	Unilever
Healthcare	Novozymes	Novozymes
Industrial goods and service	3M	SKF
Insurance	SwissRe	SwissRe
Media	Pearson	Pearson
Non-cyclical goods and services	Proctor & Gamble	Kesko
Retail	Marks & Spencer	Marks & Spencer
Technology	Intel	Nokia
Telecommunications	British Telecom (BT) Group	BT Group
Utilities	Severn Trent	Severn Trent

Source: DJSI (2003)

economies are growing at rates that most mature Organisation for Economic Co-operation and Development (OECD) economies can barely credit (between 7 and 9 per cent per annum), and consumption levels are soaring. By the same token, the sustainability challenges that they face make our challenges in Europe pale into insignificance.

In many ways, China's is the more astonishing story. As the *Economist* puts it:

> *Since Deng Xiaoping launched his 'open door' policy in 1978, China has witnessed probably the most dramatic burst of wealth creation in human history. Its income per head has increased sevenfold in that time; more than 400 million people have been lifted out of severe poverty.* (*Economist*, 2004)

By any standards, this is an extraordinary achievement. In four out of five basic commodities (grain, meat, steel and coal), China now consumes more than the US; the US still burns three times as much oil as China, not least because it has ten times as many cars.

And there have been massive social gains, too. Average life expectancy in China in 1950 was just 35 years; in 2002, this had increased to 71 years. In terms of successful investment strategies, notwithstanding the fact that there are still huge numbers of rural poor in China (more than 60 per cent of the population still live in rural areas), this kind of growth in stocks of both social/human and financial capital is astonishing.

But such growth has come at a truly shocking price in terms of impacts upon stocks of natural capital. By China's own official assessments, 25 years of breakneck growth and resource depletion now threaten ecological meltdown, the early signs of which are already dramatically affecting people's livelihoods and health. Indeed, life expectancy has gone down over the last three years, predominantly because of air and water pollution, and the World Bank has calculated that pollution is costing China an annual 8 to 12 per cent of its $1.4 trillion gross domestic product (GDP) in terms of health bills, disaster relief, lost agricultural productivity and environmental clean-up. President Hu Jintao is on record warning that rates of economic growth will have to be severely curbed to prevent further loss of critical natural capital – 'balanced development', as measured by a brand new 'green GDP indicator', is the new aspiration, though no one is quite certain whether the official goal of quadrupling 2002 GDP by 2020 has been set aside as a result!

It is because of the sheer scale of China, and the sheer speed of its economic development, that this 'growth and sustainability' showdown now looms so large in global terms. The knock-on effect of this for the rest of the world will be profound. China must feed 20 per cent of the world's population on just 7 per cent of the world's arable land. Yet, as appetites grow on account of all the new wealth – according to one study of children in Shanghai, 8 per cent of three- to six-year olds are already obese – total grain production is falling. Last year, China became a net importer of food for the first time in its history. Prime agricultural land was being lost so fast to urban and industrial development (at the rate of 0.6 million hectares a year) that China's leaders had to impose a moratorium on all 'green field developments', as we would call it, in 2004.

Not that this moratorium will do anything to prevent some of China's most fertile land in the north from further drying out after years of drought, rapidly declining water tables and chronic overgrazing. Desertification is a massive problem, with the Gobi Desert now within 240 kilometres of Beijing itself. As a direct consequence of that drought, exacerbated by climate change, huge dust storms regularly sweep through Chinese cities in the north and east and often have a serious impact upon Korea and Japan. In *High Tide*, Mark Lynas (2004) tells the extraordinary story of his visits to inner Mongolia and western China, witnessing at first hand the devastating impact of China's 'red clouds'.

If anything, China's water and energy constraints are even more severe than the constraints on its land. In some parts of northern China, including around Beijing, water tables have shrunk so fast that wells are now having to be drilled to a depth of up to a 1000 metres. The World Bank has predicted 'catastrophic consequences for future generations unless water use and supply can be restored to some kind of balance'. On the energy front, the International Energy Agency calculates that China will be responsible for 40 per cent of all coal burned in the world by 2020, 10 per cent of all oil, 13 per cent of all electricity used – and 20 per cent of all energy-based carbon dioxide (CO_2) emissions. China is already planning to build around 550 coal-fired power stations between now and 2030. In 2002, 1 million new cars were manufactured and sold in China; sales in China up to 2012 will account for 20 per cent of *all* car sales anywhere in the world.

With around $470 billion of foreign reserves stashed away, China can obviously buy its way out of a lot of these resource constraints, and that is exactly what it is doing on energy, food, timber, steel, chemical feed stocks and so on – with a massive impact upon those global markets. But you can't buy fertile topsoil and you can't buy fresh, clean water.

With China's population still growing (at around 10 million a year, predicted to peak in 2030 at 1.46 billion), with its cities burgeoning (around 300 million people will move out of their rural areas into cities by 2020) and the purchasing power of the middle classes soaring, this is a truly titanic struggle. As far as the *Economist* is concerned, it's simply a question of whether China can get rich enough quick enough to curb pollution and have enough money to clean up the mess. For the rest of the world, what's happening in China provides a window on the kind of resource constraints and natural capital dilemmas that we, too, will soon be facing. One can only hope that the Chinese leadership (many of whom are professional engineers) have the skills to balance all their different capital assets in a truly integrated and sustainable way.

MOVING BEYOND TRADE-OFF

It's not just in China that such vastly complicated 'balancing dilemmas' are now being faced up to. Development of the conventional kind (that traded off economic gains for 'acceptable' environmental and social costs) is no longer an available option either for governments or the private sector. In 2003, under growing pressure from non-governmental organizations (NGOs), some of the world's largest financial institutions (including ABN AMRO, Bank of America, Barclays, Citigroup, HSBC, Standard Chartered and the Royal Bank of Scotland) developed a new framework for managing environmental and social impacts in financing new projects with a total capital cost of $50 million or more. The so-called 'Equator Principles' have already had a marked impact upon the way in which foreign direct investment is being managed to secure 'optimized benefits for the long term' rather than short-term economic gains – although it has to be said that many NGOs remain extremely sceptical about the degree to which behaviour has really changed at the end of the day.

Here in the UK, our Department for International Development (DFID) has also been moving to a much more integrated way of assessing the impact of flows of aid, and has adopted the Five Capitals model in developing its Sustainable Livelihoods Framework (see Figure 6.4). Each individual is seen as 'an asset-owning member of a community'; those assets need to be steadily built up to reverse deprivation, and to be protected from seasonal or economic vulnerabilities in such a way that all future development aid can be seen in terms of enhancing the value of all five stocks of capital.

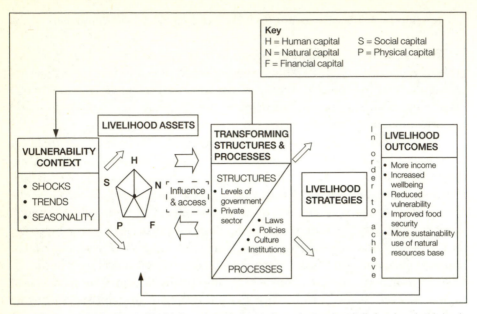

Note: The term 'physical capital' in this figure is equivalent to 'manufactured capital' elsewhere in this book.
Source: DFID

Figure 6.4 *UK Department for International Development's (DFID's)*
Sustainable Livelihoods Framework

As we will see in the following chapters, adopting more integrated approaches of this kind can often be very demanding for decision-makers. But this idea of optimized outcomes (environmental, social and economic) instead of crude trade-off is the great prize available to both politicians and business leaders, the core methodological principle upon which the notion of *sustainable development as opportunity* rather than *sustainable development as constraint* ultimately rests. Before returning to that theme in Part III, we need first to review each of the five sets of capital assets in their own right.

REFERENCES

DJSI (Dow Jones Sustainability Index) (2003) Press Release, 2 September
Economist (2004) 'China's growing pains', *Economist*, 21 August
Ekins, P. (2000) *Economic Growth and Environmental Sustainability*, Routledge, London
Forum for the Future (2000) *Understanding Sustainability*, Forum for the Future, Cheltenham, UK
Lynas, M. (2004) *High Tide*, Flamingo, London
Pearce, D. (2003) *The Social and Economic Value of Construction*, The Construction Industry Research and Innovation Strategy Panel, London
Pearce, D., Markandya, A. and Barbier, E. B. (1989) *Blueprint for a Green Economy*, Earthscan, London

7

Natural Capital

INTRODUCTION

Approximately half of all humans now live in cities; by 2040, it will be 80 per cent. As people move away from the land, they become less and less mindful of the degree to which we are still totally dependent upon the natural world for energy, resources, food, fibre, water and so on. One way of describing that bounty from nature is 'natural capital' – and the way in which we now manage that natural capital is the biggest single determinant of whether a better life awaits us or a very much grimmer one. Unfortunately, most politicians have little understanding of our continuing dependence upon the natural world and have therefore ignored those pioneering economists who have been warning them for decades of the danger of not valuing nature properly. A huge amount of work is now being done to remove these political blinkers (for instance, in terms of assessing the hard-edged economic value of protecting species and habitats), reasserting in the process the critical significance of effective environmental regulation and planning systems that do, indeed, find effective ways of putting nature first.

DEFINING NATURAL CAPITAL

Natural capital (also referred to as environmental or ecological capital) is that part of the natural world which we humans make some use of or derive some benefit from – hence, its definition (in economists' jargon) as any stock or flow of energy and matter that yields valuable goods and services. There are different kinds of natural capital: *resources*, some of which are renewable (timber, grain, fish and water), while others are not (fossil fuels); *sinks* that absorb, neutralize or recycle waste; and *services*, such as climate regulation. Natural capital is therefore not the same as nature, but it is the basis of all production in the human economy and the provider of services without which human society could not sustain itself.

At the heart of the current environmental crisis is the way in which current patterns of consumption and production are unsustainably depleting our natural capital so that its ability to support the projected levels of the human population (let alone at the standard of living of most people in the affluent industrialized countries) is seriously brought into question.

Although the debate about natural capital has become increasingly sophisticated over the last 50 years or so, there is an accessible simplicity about it that must not be lost. The relationship between ourselves and the natural world works at many different levels; but the essence of our evolutionary success as a species has been our ability to transform our natural capital into goods and services that satisfy our needs and improve our wellbeing. This natural capital provides a number of environmental functions which we make use of either directly or indirectly, particularly the flow of natural resources as inputs into our economy, the absorption of the by-products of that economy as wastes, and the provision of a number of critical 'environmental services' that underpin not just the human economy, but the whole of life on Earth. From that perspective, biophysical sustainability has been defined as the maintenance of these key environmental functions, which, in turn, depends upon their resilience and renewability.

Over time, that process of transformation has accelerated dramatically as human numbers and technological productivity have grown, fundamentally altering the relationship between the overall system (the biosphere) and the subsystem of the human economy. One of the reasons why there is still such abiding controversy about environmental issues is that there are very different views about the implications of that shift. The so-called 'contrarians' (such as Bjorn Lomborg and Wilfred Beckerman) argue that the key environmental functions referred to above are still largely unimpaired, and that all evidence to the contrary is either exaggerated or immaterial.

On the other hand, as we have seen, the vast majority of environmental scientists argue that the growth in the human subsystem now threatens the functional viability of the biosphere itself – or, at least, certain aspects of it. This analysis leads on to a further proposition which the contrarians find even more abhorrent: that our species is moving from an era in which man-made capital (human, manufactured, financial) was the limiting factor, to one in which what is left of our natural capital will be the limiting factor. And this has serious implications for the whole area of public policy and sustainable development, as Herman Daly has commented:

> *Economic logic requires that we maximize the productivity of the limiting factor in the short run and invest in increasing its supply in the long run. When the limiting factor changes, then behaviour that used to be economic becomes uneconomic. Economic logic remains the same; but the pattern of scarcity in the world changes, with the result that behaviour must change if it is to remain economic. Instead of maximizing returns to and investing in man-made capital (as was appropriate in an empty world), we must now maximize returns to and invest in natural capital (as is appropriate in a full world). This is not 'new economics', but new behaviour consistent with 'old economics' in a world with a new pattern of scarcities.* (Daly, 1996)

NATURAL ADDED VALUE

In order to understand why we can no longer avoid this reality, we need to return again to the science that lies behind all this. As we saw in Chapter 3, the loss of natural capital should clearly be counted as a cost of economic growth, to be weighed against the benefits of that growth and reflected in our national accounts. That is a relatively easy exercise, although most countries are still failing to achieve even this. More complicatedly, we need to understand that we aren't actually consuming or using up that natural capital as such, merely its quality or its usefulness to us. Alfred Marshall was one of the first economists to understand what this means:

> *Man cannot create material things – his efforts and sacrifices result in changing the form or arrangements of matter to adapt it better for the satisfaction of his wants – as his production of material products is really nothing more than a rearrangement of matter which gives it new utilities, so his consumption of them is nothing more than a disarrangement of matter which destroys its utilities.* (Marshall, 1959)

To use the contemporary jargon, what's being consumed is the 'value added' – the structure that we humans (via our human, manufactured and financial capital) add to the natural capital. This means, of course, that new structure has to be added again before it can be consumed again. It is therefore more than a little surprising that in all their enthusiasm for the concept of 'value added', both economists and business people seem to show very little interest in exactly what it is that value is being added to. In fact, as Herman Daly has pointed out, we don't really appreciate that there are two elements to this added value: the bit that *we* put in, and the bit that *nature* puts in. Atoms of copper, for instance, spread uniformly in the crust of the Earth, are of little economic value to us; concentrated copper ore is much more available for us to start adding our kind of value to the resource. By the same token: 'carbon atoms scattered in the atmosphere can receive value added from us only with the enormous expenditure of energy and other materials; carbon atoms structured in a tree can be rearranged much more easily' (Daly, 1996).

In effect, the more work nature does in advance, the less work we have to do to add that value. Unfortunately, we show nothing but contempt for this contribution from nature, valuing it at zero as some kind of free gift or subsidy, while blithely paying through the nose for the value added by *our* ingenuity, *our* technology and *our* financial resources. Having consumed the added value, we then dump what's left over back into the natural world, giving back (in thermodynamic terms) high entropy matter/energy in return for the low entropy matter/energy to which we added the value in the first place.

So why isn't our civilization overwhelmed by that loss of structure and quality? The answer is simple. While the Earth is a closed system as far as matter is concerned (almost all of the atoms that were here when the Earth was created 4.6 billion years ago are still here, as gravity does not allow matter to escape), it is an open system as far as energy is concerned – with around 10,000 times as much solar energy flowing into the system every year as the total amount of energy used by the whole of humankind.

Through photosynthesis, plants are able to use the solar energy that flows continuously into the Earth's system, gathering dispersed matter and assembling it into new structures. The uniqueness of plants lies in the fact that they obtain their energy from outside the system. Even nature's mechanisms could not function sustainably if the natural cycles were not fuelled by the sun's energy. Over time, nature has evolved to create the necessary conditions to support plants and animals, enabling the development of the living world as we know it today, in a wonderful array of complexity and diversity.

Ultimately, an improved understanding of the importance of natural capital has to cascade all the way through to decisions made by national regulators and local planning authorities. The Five Capitals Framework (see Chapter 6) is one in which a balance can be achieved between potential economic, environmental and social benefits, between the wealthy and the poor (both in this country and between rich and poor nations), and between the interests of this generation and future generations. It is based upon what should be a clear and binding hierarchy for all regulators and planners: first, protect critical natural capital in all circumstances; wherever possible, seek to optimize mutually reinforcing economic, social and environmental benefits over time; where that is not possible, seek to minimize any potential damage to the environment, people and their communities; only then can one trade off potential economic benefits against unavoidable social and environment disbenefits.

As of now, very few countries have really sought to work out what it means 'to optimize mutually reinforcing economic, social and environmental benefits over time'. Cost–benefit methodologies remain crude and are so vulnerable to political abuse (where explicit or implicit 'political assumptions' distort the basis upon which any analysis is carried out) that their credibility has been severely undermined. Worse yet, at exactly the moment when we are beginning to relearn the critical importance to us of natural capital, we are simultaneously going through one of the most aggressively deregulatory periods of modern times. Many governments now eschew straightforward regulatory interventions in favour of voluntary approaches, negotiated covenants or quasi-legal agreements with business. And in the interests of protecting national or regional competitiveness, trade associations and business organizations have become increasingly strident in their denunciation of regulatory cost and burdens.

However, studies in both the US and Europe have exposed the way in which cost estimates prepared by business organizations massively and systematically exaggerate the putative scale of the additional burden. The Confederation of British Industry (CBI) is one of the world's worst inflators of cost estimates; in 2003, for instance, it claimed that the EU Directive on Environmental Liability would cost UK business around £1.8 billion ('and will be the final nail in the coffin of British manufacturing'). In 2005, the UK Government announced that the costs amounted to no more than £50 million.

Most European governments appear to be terminally confused about developing a new strategic approach to environmental regulation. On the one hand, they endlessly parrot the huge value to Europe of the burgeoning world market in environmental goods and services (currently estimated at around $515 billion – comparable with the aerospace and pharmaceutical industries – and forecast to grow to $680 billion by 2010); on the other hand, they unthinkingly default to a much cruder competitiveness agenda to address the ever constant economic threat from China, India and other developing countries.

In some respects, this has become a battle for the heart of Europe itself. The crisis that engulfed Europe in 2005 after both France and The Netherlands rejected the new draft constitution was at least as much about what kind of economy Europe should be pursuing (the more inclusive, interventionist 'social market economy' favoured by the French and Germans, or the 'liberal market economy', with the emphasis on deregulation and competition favoured by the UK) as about the constitution itself. The UK's ideological fervour for 'the privatization, marketization and liberalization of anything that moves' is well reflected in its EU Commissioner Peter Mandelson, whose personal crusade to downgrade the importance of environmental sustainability, social inclusion and better working conditions has caused considerable controversy.

European electorates find themselves on the receiving end of great surges of excitable green rhetoric, only to discover that the self-same politicians are busy watering down regulatory, fiscal and economic interventions that are so badly needed to create those innovative new markets. Here's one such surge from Prime Minister Tony Blair himself:

> *We need to develop the new green industrial revolution that develops the new technologies that can confront and overcome the challenge of climate change. Just as British know-how brought the railways and mass production to the world, so British scientists, innovators and business people can lead the world in ways to grow and develop sustainably. I'm confident business will seize this opportunity. Cutting waste and saving energy could save billions of pounds each year. With about 90 per cent of production materials never becoming part of the final product, and 80 per cent of products discarded after single use, the opportunities are clear.* (Blair, 2004)

These words were uttered at almost exactly the same time as the UK Government was pressing for a higher allocation of carbon credits through the EU's Emissions Trading Scheme to make life easier for the ever-moaning CBI.

This ambivalence is a zero-sum game if ever there was one. From the ground-breaking work of Michael Porter in *The Competitive Advantage of Nations* (1990) – one of the very first works to advance the 'win–win hypothesis' that intelligent and carefully designed environmental regulations may be good for economic competitiveness – all the way through to Adair Turner's *Just Capital: The Liberal Economy* (2001) (as a former director-general of the CBI, Adair Turner's demolition of the 'myths and delusions' that lie behind much of today's defence of national competitiveness is particularly enlightening), the convergence of interest between promoting an innovative and productive economy, on the one hand, and securing a resilient and productive natural world, on the other, has been mapped out in great detail.

Although contemporary politicians have certainly woken up to the importance of environmental issues, it is that deeper understanding of the nature of natural capital that is still wholly absent in the thinking of any Western government today. Even as they address symptoms of that fundamental shift (over-fishing in the North Sea, the need to mitigate the potential impact of climate change, etc.), the systemic reality that lies behind the symptoms remains all but invisible.

There are all sorts of reasons for this, some of which go right back to our evolutionary origins, to our Judaeo-Christian inheritance, and to a model of progress since the onset of the Industrial Revolution which set civilization *against* nature. Latterly, however, it has to be said that mainstream economists have done more to obscure physical reality in this area than any philosophical or historical factors. This is *not* because the concept of sustainability is alien to economists, as many environmental critics have claimed. In fact, the core meaning of sustainability is embedded within one of the 'seminal texts' of contemporary economics – namely, the work of J. R. Hicks in which he coined the definition of income that has been standard since then: 'the maximum amount that a community can consume over some time period and still be as well off at the end of that period as at the beginning' (Hicks, 1946). In that respect, 'as well off' was defined by Hicks as having the same capacity to generate income in the next year – that is, maintaining capital intact.

Unfortunately, economists then proceeded to ignore natural capital (largely on the grounds that it was either not scarce or could not command a market value as it came to us 'for free'), and focused exclusively on the different aspects of man-made capital. Even when it began to dawn on them (at the persistent prompting of pioneers such as Herman Daly and David Pearce) that this was unwise, the key issue of *substitutability* still had to be confronted. Wealth creation is a process that judiciously combines different kinds of capital to produce the goods and services which people want (and therefore value). There is obviously considerable scope for substitution between the different forms of capital as evidenced by our own evolutionary success – converting natural capital into man-made capital. But there is a world of difference between maintaining constant the *sum* of all different kinds of capital, in aggregate, and maintaining each stock of capital constant in its own right. The former position (still dominant in contemporary economics) holds that it is fine to substitute one form of capital for another, and that in most cases there will be no problem, for example, about liquidating natural capital just so long as one invests to create equivalent value in manufactured capital or social capital.

Exponents of the latter position (maintaining each stock of capital in its own right) argue that natural capital and other forms of capital are *complementary but increasingly non-substitutable*, or at least only substitutable at the margins. Here in the UK, for instance, the Government's official advisers on biological diversity (English Nature) define environmental sustainability as 'maintaining the environment's natural qualities and characteristics and its capacity to fulfil its full range of functions'. These functions include the provision of resources, the disposal, recycling and sequestration of wastes, and the maintenance of a diverse, habitable and productive biosphere. English Nature stresses that achieving environmental sustainability often requires the *absolute* protection and conservation of particular components of natural capital, which it calls critical natural capital.

Kerry Turner was one of the first (in 1993) to characterize these different positions as weak sustainability and strong sustainability. He rapidly dismissed both very weak sustainability (which assumes complete substitutability across all capitals) and what he called 'absurdly strong sustainability' (which assumes no substitutability, with all natural capital maintained absolutely intact). There obviously has to be *some* substitution; but controversy still rages around how to define the acceptable limits to that constant trade-off process. This is why the kind of systemic approach adopted by organizations, such as The Natural Step (TNS), is so important, defining strict biophysical limits for all human endeavour (see Chapter 2).

In that regard, it is becoming more commonplace to see environmental sustainability defined as 'the maintenance of critical environmental functions'. As Paul Ekins says:

> . . . the advantage of defining it in this way, rather than as the maintenance of natural capital per se, is that such a definition makes explicit the requirements of manufactured or human capital if they are to be full substitutes for natural capital. Manufactured capital is a substitute for natural capital if it performs the same environmental functions as natural capital. To the extent that manufactured capital and technical change do not fully perform the environmental functions of the natural capital they replace, then substitutability between them has not been complete. (Ekins, 2000)

There is, of course, an important distinction between renewable and non-renewable resources. With regard to renewable resources, the science and economics of sustainable yield management are now much better understood, although inadequately practised wherever one looks. With agriculture, freshwater, forestry, fisheries and so on, maintaining 'cultivated' natural capital of this kind means constraining the annual yield to a level no greater than the annual regeneration capacity of the stock of natural capital concerned – a process that must take account of *all* the different environmental functions that stock of natural capital provides, including the maintenance of fundamental ecological services in that ecosystem from which we ourselves may derive no direct financial return.

As to non-renewable resources, strictly speaking, there is no such thing as sustainable yield management. If there is only a given amount of some mineral or resource to be extracted from the Earth, it will – one day – run out, though as we will see in Chapter 10, there are ways of securing sufficiently high levels of reuse and recycling as to give us (in some cases) all but a sustainable yield. In the meantime, what we should be getting much better at is reinvesting the share of receipts from liquidating our non-renewable natural capital in building up renewable stocks to generate sustainable yields in the future. In this regard, the failure of successive governments in the UK to direct even a small share of the billions of pounds from the exploitation of non-renewable hydrocarbons in the North Sea into renewable sources of energy for the UK (of which we have an astonishing abundance) contrasts starkly with the foresight of places such as Norway and Alaska, which every year set aside a proportion of their hydrocarbon revenues to create a permanent capital fund for the future.

Valuing natural capital

Unfortunately, all of this knowledge about natural systems and the laws of thermodynamics still remains pretty alien for most economists. As already mentioned, David Pearce et al's 1989 *Blueprint for a Green Economy* represented an important breakthrough in promoting different valuation techniques in terms of putting a money value on the use that we make of the natural world. Although it is true that some environmentalists still remain nervous about the whole idea of putting money values on things that are 'beyond price', this approach has, for the most part, greatly strengthened the hand of economists trying to bring 'the environment' closer to the heart of policy-making.

And it has moved on a long way since then. Even the somewhat vague notion of 'environmental services' (the third of the three categories of natural capital referred to at the start of this chapter) is being looked at from the point of view of their economic value to humankind. In 1997, Robert Costanza and colleagues at the Massachusetts Institute of Technology (MIT) set out 'to quantify the global value of ecosystem services consisting of flows of materials, energy and information from natural capital stocks which combine with manufactured and human capital to produce welfare' (Costanza et al, 1997). They identified 17 different services, including pollination, water supply and regulation, the assimilation of wastes, food production from the wild, genetic resources, climate regulation, and even 'cultural and spiritual values that are associated with ecosystems' – for example, eco-tourism, outdoor recreational activities and painting landscapes.

All sorts of valuation techniques were then applied to these 17 ecosystem services (including 'willingness to pay' calculations for some of the benefits derived from these services), and estimates were made of what it would cost to provide man-made substitutes for these services if we didn't get them for free from nature. The bottom line total (which came out at around $33 trillion per annum, with a margin of error of several trillion on either side!) is actually pretty academic: it's the demonstration of our massive dependence upon these ecosystem services that Costanza was trying to establish. This ground-breaking work was powerfully developed in the Millennium Ecosystem Assessment report described in Chapter 1.

Meta-calculations of this sort may not have any direct applicability to most decision-makers, but narrow the focus somewhat and the significance of this kind of approach to valuing natural capital becomes instantly apparent. Andy Balmford at the Department of Zoology in Cambridge has been working away for many years to demonstrate just how good an economic bargain the protection of biodiversity really is. He reckons we already spend around $6 billion a year on conservation, but that we would need to increase that to around $27.5 billion to do the job

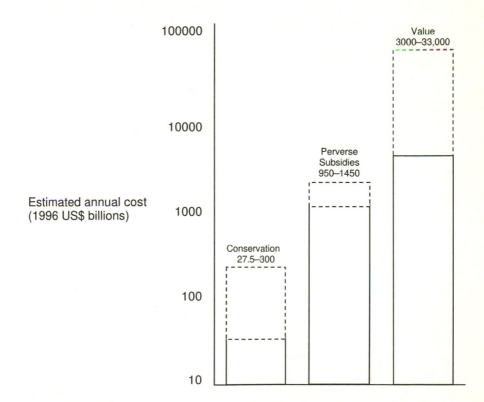

Source: Balmford (2002)

Figure 7.1 *The relative cost of conservation*

properly (with up to 10 per cent of land area strictly protected, with half of that in special reserves) and provide proper compensation for those people 'losing out' in other ways through their land being used essentially for conservation. If we set out beyond that to protect biodiversity properly on farmed land outside of designated nature reserves, the costs rise steeply to a (loosely) estimated $300 billion.

Big numbers – but not that big. Balmford uses a handy little graphic (see Figure 7.1) to demonstrate why we shouldn't be overwhelmed by this, contrasting the potential costs of a properly funded global conservation strategy (between $27.5 billion and $300 billion) with two other related indicators. First, there is the cost to humankind of all the billions of taxpayer dollars we *already* dish out (on subsidies to farmers, energy producers, transportation, fisheries, water consumption and so on), which comes in at an astonishing total of between $950 billion and $1400 billion a year – according to the pioneering work done in this area by Norman Myers (1998). What makes this figure all the more shocking is that the bulk of those subsidies contribute actively to the erosion and outright liquidation of natural capital all around the world. As Balmford and his colleagues say:

> *Implementing a global plan to conserve biodiversity should go hand in hand with the gradual removal of the subsidies. If subsidy reform was linked to investment in environmental protection, a small shift in government spending patterns would accomplish major conservation objectives. An effective global system of nature reserves would cost about 2 per cent of the annual expenditure on environmentally harmful subsidies. A truly comprehensive global conservation programme that incorporated biodiversity within all major natural resource sectors could be launched for only about 20 per cent of the cost of these subsidies.* (Alexander et al, 1999)

Second, the final indicator takes us back to Bob Costanza's meta-calculation of the value to humankind derived from the 17 ecosystem services, set at around $33 trillion. In effect, what this shows us is that we need an annual investment of around $300 billion to secure $33 trillion worth of natural services – not a bad return on investment, all things considered.

If this is still too abstract, we now have literally dozens of powerful examples, backed by hard-edged financial data, showing how investments in natural capital generate real value for money. In 2002, Gretchen Daily and Katherine Ellison published a summary of some of the most striking of these case studies under the arresting title *The New Economy of Nature*:

> *We still think of conservation basically as something to do for moral or aesthetic reasons – not for survival and certainly not for profit. Neverthe- less, the record clearly shows that conservation can't succeed by charity alone. It has a fighting chance, however, with well-designed appeals to*

self-interest. The challenge now is to change the rules of the game so as to produce new incentives for environmental protection, geared to both society's long-term wellbeing and individuals' self-interest. (Daily and Ellison, 2002)

Perhaps the best known example that they use was the decision by New York City in 1997 to invest around $1.5 billion in rehabilitating the city's principal source of freshwater – the Catskill/Delaware watershed – rather than spending even more billions of dollars (around $5 billion) in constructing a new generation of costly, energy-intensive filtration plants to bring the water quality up to the standards set by the US Environmental Protection Agency. The Catskill/Delaware watershed is an area of around 2000 square miles of farmed valleys and forested mountains, with around 50,000 inhabitants. The system had worked fine throughout most of the 20th century, but since the 1980s, growth in tourism and housing started to take off in a big way, while farming systems became ever more intensive and sewage treatment plants struggled to cope. Water quality started to decline.

Given that New York City owns only a small fraction of the total land area, it has proved to be a huge effort bringing everyone on board, persuading them (and paying them) to manage their land and their use of water in ways that keep New York's water pure and fit for use all year round. It is early days still, in terms of evaluating the success of the programme; but it is already inspiring many other towns and cities in the US to think about similar projects. Some experts have calculated that up to 12 per cent of the entire land area in the US could be managed in this way to secure pure, high-quality water for its citizens. But the majority of politicians and economists still can't see the logic in this kind of approach; for them, the best and safest thing to do is to keep on pouring the concrete, relying on costly, high-tech, energy-intensive engineering schemes.

But does all this only work because it is taking place in one of the wealthiest enclaves anywhere in the world, richly endowed with generations of New York dollars and countless individual millionaires? Environmentalists are regularly assaulted with the accusation that 'you have to be rich to be green', and that all 'this environment stuff' means nothing to billions of poor people struggling to improve their material standard of living all around the world with no time to worry about 'the luxury of a clean environment'. Given that the vast majority of these people still depend absolutely upon natural resources, clean water, fertile soils and healthy forests for their livelihoods, this is too absurd a charge to spend much time on. What is much more interesting is the way in which many rural communities in the developing world are starting to think very differently about making better use of their natural heritage. And they are doing that precisely to improve their material standard of living.

One such community is Torra in the remote north-west of Namibia. It is a huge area, with just a few hundred very poor farmers struggling to eke out some kind of livelihood from their herds of cattle and goats. In 1998, with the support of the

World Wide Fund for Nature (WWF), they established a special conservancy based on a very simple deal: the community protects the local wildlife (including a thriving population of black rhino) in return for a share of the revenues earned through tourism and strictly controlled hunting rights. It's not a huge amount of money that they earn; but it is distributed across the whole population, and it's more than enough to underpin new business activity.

This is just one of 70 wildlife conservancies that have been established in Namibia since its independence from South Africa in 1990, based on the robust principles of community-based natural resource management, including formal by-laws to ensure that the conservancies are run democratically at the lowest possible level in the community. More than 250,000 people are now involved, covering around 7 million hectares of land. The journalist Mike McCarthy (of the *Independent* newspaper in the UK) visited Namibia in 2004 to assess what sort of impact this innovative approach was having in one of the world's poorest countries – where there's little to stop desperately poor people mushrooming in numbers and struggling to exist, eating and poaching their wildlife out of existence:

> *Only a truly radical gesture can answer the problem: turn the wildlife over to the people and let them use it. Local people handle their own wildlife; they handle their own money; and, thus, they handle their own future. The farmers of Torra are longing for more tourism, and if you go there you will see the great wild animals of Africa in a setting that you will never forget: a pristine, semi-desert wilderness of harsh but astonishing beauty. But maybe you will see something else too: the hope that Africa's people and its wildlife may live together into the future to the lasting benefit of each other.* (McCarthy, 2004)

There are, of course, 'none so blind as those who will not see'. A basic lack of understanding of how natural systems work lies at the heart of most politicians' and economists' ecological illiteracy, compounded by the fact that disaster (as in widespread ecological meltdown) would until now appear to have been averted. But ecosystems often remain productive even as their resilience continues to decline, masking the inevitability of future collapse unless those systems are allowed to regenerate properly. Although some changes are reversible, many are not. And given our relative ignorance as to the workings of nature, especially when exposed to the impact of exponential economic growth, a much more precautionary approach is clearly advisable. But this is in itself problematic to those intent on maximizing the short-term value to be derived from natural resources.

And 'wonder' may indeed be the missing ingredient as we set about using the natural world and manipulating matter to promote our own material wellbeing. Our whole orientation towards the natural world is deeply instrumental: extractive, abusive and controlling. As Janine Benyus's hugely inspiring *Biomimicry* (1997) keeps on reminding us, such arrogance is unwise:

After 3.8 billion years of research and development, failures are fossils, and what surrounds us is the secret to survival. The more our world looks and functions like this natural world, the more likely we are to be accepted in this home that is ours, but not ours alone. (Benyus, 1997)

Benyus defines biomimicry as 'a new science that studies nature's model, and then imitates or takes inspiration from these designs and processes to solve human problems'. Her book is stuffed full of stories of scientists working away at that particular cutting edge – on photosynthesis, self-sustaining ecosystems, natural medicines, self-assembly processes and so on. She is keen to emphasize the difference between this kind of approach and the way in which so many scientists and industrialists still set about their task of dominating or even 'improving' nature. 'This respectful imitation is a radically new approach, a revolution, really. Unlike the Industrial Revolution, the biomimicry revolution introduces an era based not on what we can extract from nature, but on what we can learn from her' (Benyus, 1997). I will return to this theme in Chapter 10.

Although much of this chapter is about different ways of *valuing* nature, the thrust of this particular philosophical orientation is that we will only benefit from an economic perspective if we completely rethink our relationship with the natural world – if we learn, in E. O. Wilson's words, 'to affiliate with life', in a much more profound way. Our artificially constructed technosphere, however ingenious and powerful it may be, cannot operate independently of the biosphere. It is still embedded deep within that biosphere and is still subject to the laws of nature. Janine Benyus spells that out from the perspective of a working ecologist:

In reality, we haven't escaped the gravity of life at all. We are still beholden to ecological laws, the same as any other life form. The most irrevocable of these laws says that a species cannot occupy a niche that appropriates all resources – there has to be some sharing. Any species that ignores this law winds up destroying its community to support its own expansion. Tragically, this has been our path. We began as a small population in a very large world, and have expanded in number and territory until we are bursting the seams of that world. There are too many of us and our habits are unsustainable. (Benyus, 1997)

But the scale of the 'paradigm shift' required here cannot be underestimated. As Lester Brown puts it:

Transforming our environmentally destructive economy into one that can sustain progress depends on a Copernican shift in our economic mindset, a recognition that the economy is part of the Earth's ecosystem and can sustain progress only if it is restructured so that it is compatible with it. (Brown, 2003)

REFERENCES

Alexander, J., Gaston, K. and Balmford, A. (1999) 'Balancing the Earth's accounts', *Nature*, vol 401, 23 September

Balmford, A. (2002) Presentation to Business and the Environment Programme, Cambridge, UK, March

Benyus, J. (1997) *Biomimicry: Innovation Inspired by Nature*, Quill, William Morrow, New York

Blair, T. (2004) Speech to Prince of Wales's Business and the Environment Programme, London, 14 September

Brown, L. (2003) *Plan B*, W. W. Norton, New York

Costanza, R., Cumberland, J., Daly, H., Goodland, R. and Norgaard, R. (1997) *An Introduction to Ecological Economics*, CRC Press, Boca Raton, FL

Daily, G. and Ellison, K. (2002) *The New Economy of Nature: The Quest to Make Conservation Profitable*, Island Press, Washington, DC

Daly, H. (1996) *Beyond Growth*, Beacon Press, Boston, MA

Ekins, P. (2000) *Economic Growth and Environmental Sustainability*, Routledge, London

Hicks, J. R. (1946) *Value and Capital*, Oxford University Press, Oxford

Marshall, A. (1959) *Principles of Economics*, Macmillan, London

McCarthy, M. (2004) 'Where animals can build a community', *Independent*, 13 December

Myers, N. (1998) 'Lifting the veil on perverse subsidies', *Nature*, vol 392, 26 March

Pearce, D., Markandya, A. and Barbier, E. B. (1989) *Blueprint for a Green Economy*, Earthscan, London

Porter, M. (1990) *The Competitive Advantage of Nations*, Free Press, New York

Turner, A. (2001) *Just Capital: The Liberal Economy*, Macmillan, London

8

Human Capital

INTRODUCTION

There was a time during the late 1990s when the world suddenly woke up to the allure of the 'knowledge economy'. Politicians boldly declared that the future prosperity of their countries would depend far more upon companies' intellectual and human capital than upon their manufacturing and financial capital. It has all died down a bit since then; but the traditional and often undervalued business of managing human resources in any organization gained new stature. As explained in this chapter, the Five Capitals Framework (see Chapter 6) defines human capital in terms of any one individual's physical, intellectual, emotional and spiritual capacities – in other words, what each one of us brings to any working, playing, nurturing or loving relationship. All organizations (for-profit or non-profit) are now keen to find ways of enhancing their human capital, although there's a lively debate as to how best to measure this – or indeed, whether it is worth measuring in the first place.

DEFINING HUMAN CAPITAL

The Five Capitals Framework unhesitatingly asserts the primacy (or 'precondition-ality') of natural capital: after nearly 4 billion years of life on Earth, of which we've been around for just a few tens of thousands of years, that has to be the right way of looking at things.

But the fact that we are the first species (so far as we know) capable of reflecting upon our place in the natural order is just one of the characteristics that makes humankind more than a little special. When it comes down to it, our capacity to create wealth, solve problems, reach for the stars or constantly seek to improve the lot of our fellow human beings depends upon a combination of the natural capital out of which our complex industrial civilization is fashioned and the human capital which generates the designs, systems and assembly processes that make it all happen.

The definition of human capital that we use in the Five Capitals Framework is a simple one: 'the physical, intellectual, emotional and spiritual capacities of any individual'. But human capital has come to mean many different things to different people. Ask an economist, an educationalist, and a human resources professional what the term means to them, and each will have their own slightly different definition and explanation. And as with the concept of natural capital, there are some people for whom the words 'human' and 'capital' just shouldn't be used together – the connotation of even putting a quasi-financial value on each person's head makes them feel uneasy (an issue of *New Internationalist* in 2001 gently mocked the World Bank's use of the term: 'Do the World Bank economists go home at night and tuck up their own units of human capital before reading them a bed-time story?').

In this context, however, thinking about *all* of the different stocks of capital from which we may draw a sustainable flow of services, and in which we need to reinvest to secure that flow over time, it is critically important to integrate human capital within any framework. It is worth a quick look at each of the four capacities, in turn, before reflecting upon the services that flow from them and what it really means 'to invest in our human capital'.

Physical capacities

At the societal level, we can say that stocks of human capital will be greater if we manage to increase healthy lifestyles and healthy life expectancy figures. At the organizational level, investing in the physical wellbeing of employees through offering health education or encouraging sports and physical activity has been shown to improve both productivity and emotional wellbeing. And at an individual level, each of us is able to lead a more fulfilling life if we invest a little time and effort into making our own lifestyle healthier.

This is clearly not the place for a lengthy analysis of the degree to which different societies effectively promote health strategies that nurture this critical aspect of human capital. There is growing awareness of the huge contribution that public health makes to the pursuit of sustainable development and vice versa. As with so many areas of public policy, it means radically changing the paradigm of what healthcare really means:

> *A destructive cycle is one where resources are used in ways that are wasteful and potentially damaging to health and the environment so that, cumulatively, there is more illness and less capacity to provide treatment and care. The virtuous circle is one where patterns of behaviour that promote economic, social and environmental sustainability also have health benefits – directly and indirectly – and where measures to improve health, especially among people who are poor and therefore more vulnerable to ill health, also contribute to sustainable development.*
> (Coote, 2002)

The publication from which this quote is taken (*Claiming the Health Dividend: Unlocking the Benefits of NHS Spending*, from the King's Fund in the UK) amply demonstrates that this is proving to be as frustrating a transition in this country as in most other European nations. Policy-makers, healthcare providers and media commentators seem able to argue at great length about how long people should have to wait for better public health, or how we should finance, structure and manage our 'illness services'. Conventional wisdom about what matters most in health policy is rarely challenged, and political incentives for the health organizations to change their behaviour remain weak.

Yet, this is patently absurd. Thinking in a more integrated way, both public health campaigners and sustainable development activists have long argued that these are just two sides of the same coin. It is clearly possible to achieve improved health outcomes by pursuing less destructive patterns of economic development, and it is clearly possible to achieve a more sustainable (and equitable) society by reducing health inequalities, using corporate resources more efficiently and more strategically, and focusing on preventing illness as far upstream as possible. Anna Coote, Health Commissioner on the UK Sustainable Development Commission, sums it up as follows:

> *The evidence tells us that social isolation, poor education, fear of crime, disrupted family life and unhappiness are bad for health – happy people live, on average, seven years longer than unhappy people. Likewise, poverty, joblessness, powerlessness and economic insecurity are bad for human health. And these, of course, are the social and economic dimensions of sustainable development. Equally, environmental damage is bad for health – air pollution, contaminated water, poor food supplies, heavy road traffic, dislocated neighbourhoods, poorly designed buildings. What's more, these health risks tend to pile up in the lives of the poor and dispossessed in ways that are vividly reflected in health statistics. Poor people get ill more often and die much younger than people who are well off.* (Coote, 2005)

The connection between good health and access to the natural world constantly bubbles along under the surface in all sorts of different ways. The pioneering work by Professor Ulrich in the US demonstrated that patients in hospitals who were able to see green spaces from their windows made a more rapid recovery from surgery than those facing on to a brick courtyard. Here in the UK, the British Trust for Conservation Volunteers has successfully demonstrated that involving people recovering from either physical or mental illness in practical conservation schemes has a marked (and measurable) impact upon recovery rates. Doctors in a growing number of general practices have started to formally prescribe conservation work and outdoor activity as part of their treatment toolkit – building on extensive research carried out by English Nature on the whole question of 'natural and psychological wellbeing'.

This would come as no surprise to Theodore Roszak, whose 1993 book *The Voice of the Earth* outraged the psychotherapy establishment in the US by accusing them of exacerbating the problems of their clients in ignoring the contribution that their alienation from the natural world was making to those problems. The obvious solution is to reconnect people to the natural world as part and parcel of any long-term healing or therapy process:

> *What would it mean to 'prescribe nature' as part of therapy? Therapists, tied to the city by their careers and their bank accounts, cannot be expected to treat their clients anywhere but in the city. The troubled soul locked in a tortured ego will never be coaxed to look out and around at something greater, more lordly, more ennobling: a state of nature that invites the mind to contemplate eternal things. Yet, common experience tells us that a solitary walk by the river or ocean, a few calm hours in the woods, restore the spirit and may produce more insight into our motives and goals than the best labours of the professional analyst. The quiet contemplation of the night sky before one turns to sleep and dreams might do more to touch the mind with a healing grandeur than weeks, months, years of obsessive autobiographical excavation.* (Roszak, 1993)

Lest this sounds like tree-hugging escapism for the pampered middle classes, it is worth bearing in mind that environmental campaigners have struggled long and hard to demonstrate the link between health inequalities in deprived areas and environmental inequalities. There is now a mountain of evidence that people who suffer from environmental injustice (in poor-quality, toxic, polluted, run-down environments) are much more vulnerable to a host of health problems. The upside of this is the increasingly widespread experience that engaging local communities in improving their own local environment can succeed where many other strategies fail.

Those problems, however, pale into insignificance beside those of many developing countries. The scale of the challenge here and the sheer numbers of people suffering from disease or chronic ill health (intoned with a sense of almost fatalistic dread at one global gathering after another) have led some people to conclude that this is just how it is and how it will always be. But as Gro Brundtland (former executive director of the World Health Organization) reminded people in a speech at the 2002 World Summit on Sustainable Development: 'Very small investments (by Western standards) in primary healthcare can make a very big difference, not just to the individuals that benefit directly but to the whole nation.'

INTELLECTUAL CAPACITIES

In 1912 the German psychologist William Stern noticed that even though the gap between mental age and chronological age widens as a child matures, the ratio of mental age to chronological age remains constant. He dubbed this ratio the 'intelligence quotient'; since then, testing of IQ remains one of the most widely used (and controversial) forms of measurement of our intellectual abilities. But our mental powers are more than just a number. Our intellectual abilities include our knowledge, our creativity and our linguistic ability among others. IQ tests, however, measure only a particular kind of intellectual ability – rational, linear intelligence, of the kind best suited to solve particular types of logical problems.

It is to this aspect of human capital that the lion's share of research investment has been dedicated over the last few decades. From a sociological perspective, human capital has come to be associated almost exclusively with the capacity of governments and other organizations to intervene in the lives of individuals to enhance opportunities for learning and education – formal or informal. It is therefore wholly appropriate that efforts to enhance individuals' intellectual capacities through formal education feature prominently in almost all indicator sets designed to demonstrate progress on sustainable development.

From a business perspective, the corollary of this is the capacity for companies to intervene in the lives of their employees to facilitate access to training and other educational opportunities. In particular, there has been much interest of late in the idea of *intellectual capital*. This term was first coined back in 1969 by J. K. Galbraith, but only gained widespread currency during the mid 1990s, when pioneering companies such as Skandia (the Swedish financial services group) and Dow Chemicals started to measure, manage and report on their flows of intellectual capital. Since then, there has been a flood of books and articles on the subject, and many of the large management consultancies still offer specialist services in this area. It should be noted here that the difference between human capital and intellectual capital is that, under most definitions, intellectual capital includes non-human assets, such as brands, patents and computer databases. In the Five Capitals Framework, these are categorized as part of an organization's manufactured capital. There are, as ever, only fuzzy lines between one form of capital and another.

Intellectual capital often accounts for a huge proportion of a company's value and competitive advantage. When investors forced Maurice Saatchi out of Saatchi and Saatchi in 1995, although the company's book value didn't alter, its market value halved. The investors thought that they owned Saatchi and Saatchi. In fact, they owned less than half of it; the rest was embodied in the intellectual capital of Maurice Saatchi and his key staff.

With the growth of the knowledge economy has come an important change in the relationship between employers and employees. Human capital is not owned but rented. In Marxist terms, the means of production are now inside the heads of the workers. As a result, investment in the intellectual capacities of employees is a serious priority for successful companies, not least because of powerful evidence that it generates significant returns. One study by the US Government found that a 10 per cent average increase in the educational level of employees led to an 8.6 per cent gain in total productivity. By contrast, a 10 per cent increase in investment in equipment increased productivity by only 3.4 per cent – suggesting that the marginal value of investing in intellectual capital is three times that of equipment.

EMOTIONAL CAPACITIES

Our emotional abilities include our skills in empathy, conflict management, relationship-building and organizational awareness. Without them, we are less able to participate in the society around us, and less able to function effectively among those with whom we work and live. Emotional abilities are also highly involved in creativity. Musicians, artists and performers show high levels of emotional awareness.

Daniel Goleman is the most high-profile advocate of the theory of emotional intelligence, which came to prominence during the 1990s. He was the first to hypothesize that human emotions are an important factor in human intelligence; if our emotions are healthy and mature, we use whatever IQ we have more effectively. He states that businesses that learn to invest in the emotional abilities of their employees will see greater success since it is our emotional skills which enable us to work effectively in teams and deal with customers in such a way as to secure their loyalty.

Danah Zohar, author of *Spiritual Capital: Wealth We Can Live By*, explains the significance of Goleman's work:

> *The work that Goleman wrote about revolutionized our understanding of intelligence and was quickly seen to have practical application in general life and in the workplace. Unlike IQ, which remains pretty much steady throughout life, EQ (emotional intelligence) can be nurtured and improved. We can* learn *to behave more intelligently with other people or in recognizing and dealing with our own emotions. EQ also broadened out somewhat our notion of strategic thinking because it became evident that people pursue emotional strategies as well as rational ones, or at least that there is often an emotional contribution to the strategies we form.* (Zohar, 2004)

Emotional abilities are particularly key to leadership; the most successful leaders use their emotional intelligence to create a working climate that nurtures employees and encourages them to give their best. In the UK, a study of 42 schools found more positive teacher attitudes and higher pupil exam grades in the schools with head teachers with greater emotional abilities, and underperformance at the schools where the head teachers relied upon lesser emotional abilities. In a study of US insurance companies, companies whose chief executive officers (CEOs) exhibited more emotional competencies showed better financial results as measured by both profit and growth.

It sounds so obvious, from a company perspective, that one wonders how (under the current shareholder model of capitalism) the critical importance of nurturing both intellectual and emotional capacities among employees could have been so consistently and damagingly devalued by such a large number of companies. Interestingly, it is often those companies that have made the clearest commitment to sustainable development that have withstood shareholder pressures to abuse their employees' human capital. At Dow Chemicals, for instance, the very first commitment within the Sustainable Development Operating Plan is 'the implementation of a comprehensive people strategy'. And this is far more than a standard human resources plan – it is a comprehensive strategy that articulates priorities around developing the workforce, defining the obligations of both Dow and its employees. As Michael Parker, former chief executive officer of Dow Chemicals, put it:

> *Let us, once and for all, deflate the myth that shareholder and employee interests are somehow mutually exclusive. Using a business model rooted in sustainable development – with its triple bottom line of economic prosperity, environmental stewardship and corporate social responsibility – we now have a framework that validates the intuitive notion that employees' 'intellectual capital' is as essential to an enterprise's success as shareholders' invested capital.* (Parker, 2002)

SPIRITUAL CAPACITIES

Although there are many for whom the very idea of spiritual capacity will trigger intellectual disdain or outright hostility, others have suggested that the Five Capitals Framework should really be a *six* capitals framework – with spiritual capital or moral capital designated as a separate capital stock of its own. That is very much the line taken in works such as Stephen Young's *Moral Capitalism* (2003) or Peter Heslem's *Globalization and the Good* (2004), where moral capital is defined as the norms, values, and ethics ('often formed by religion') that underpin any community or society:

> *What is needed, therefore, is a new kind of capitalism (if that is what we still want to call it) that places value on the largest stocks of capital it employs – the natural resources and living systems of natural capital, and the relational, cultural, ethical and spiritual aspects of life that are the basis of human, social and moral capital. It would be a type of capitalism in which the fortunes of these types of capital would take priority over the maximization of financial return.* (Heslem, 2004)

The decision of Forum for the Future to treat this whole area of human experience as a subset of human capital rather than as a separate stock of capital in its own right may well reflect higher than usual levels of scepticism about such an approach here in the predominantly secular society of the UK. That does not alter the fact that the vast majority of humankind still subscribes to one form of religious belief system or another; empirically, such beliefs constitute a critical part of what it is that makes us human. In talking about spiritual capital, however, it is important to stress that the word 'spirituality' has no formal connection with institutionalized religion. Many people might feel themselves to be highly spiritual in their approach to life (or be perceived by others to be well endowed with spiritual capital), but to have absolutely no involvement or even interest in mainstream religion. By the same token, some very religious people often appear to have no discernible spirituality about them at all. In that context, I have much sympathy with Danah Zohar's understanding of spirituality as an enhancement of our daily lives, based on the Latin *spiritus*, that which breathes life or vitality into a system:

> *Spiritual capital adds the dimension of our shared meanings and values and ultimate purposes. It addresses those concerns we have about what it means to be human and the ultimate meaning and purpose of human life. It is the cultivation and sharing of our truly ultimate concerns that acts as the real glue in society. It is only when our notion of capitalism includes spiritual capital's wealth of meaning, values, purpose and higher motivation that we can have sustainable capitalism and a sustainable society.* (Zohar, 2004)

For advocates of sustainable development, there is a deeper resonance here. In the past, Max Weber's (1864–1920) idea of the Protestant work ethic described the primary drivers for people to use their God-given talents along the lines of 'I work so that I might go to heaven.' For the average rich world citizen today, the consumer work ethic of the late 20th century has replaced the Protestant work ethic with 'I work so that I might buy more.' While this might be in the interest of businesses trying to sell more and more, it will clearly prove to be environmentally and socially unsustainable in the near future. So for sustainable development, what motivates us as individuals to use our own human capital is key, and for some, a spiritually inspired work ethic will be an important instrument of change.

Take just two of today's most pressing sustainability challenges: how to counter the all-but-universal seduction of consumerism (a theme which I return to in Chapter 15) and the need for people to go beyond rational respect for the natural systems upon which we depend by developing a much more humble, reverential ethos. There are few sources of authority (let alone wisdom) in addressing these two challenges that are not derived from religious or spiritual sources. Yet, that critical inheritance is deemed illegitimate by many of those who continue, quite forlornly, to exhort people to 'respect nature' and 'consume responsibly' from the stony ground of self-indulgent, secular materialism. In *Natural Alien: Humankind and the Environment*, Neil Evernden wrote:

> *Although they seldom recognize it, environmentalists are protesting not at the stripping of natural resources, but at the stripping of earthly meaning. I have suggested elsewhere that environmentalism, like romanticism in a previous century, actually constitutes a defence of values. I am now asserting an even more fundamental role for environmentalism – namely, the defence of meaning. We call people 'environmentalists' because they are moved to defend what we call the environment; but at the bottom, their action is actually a defence of the cosmos, not of scenery.* (Evernden, 1993)

What we are talking about here are some of the 'ultimate ends' that give meaning and purpose to the lives of billions of people. In Figure 8.1, the relationships between means and ends (as originally conceptualized by Herman Daly, 1996) and the links with the Five Capitals Framework are schematically represented. In the bottom square are the 'ultimate means' – the life-support systems that provide the physical requirements for human society; the intermediate means are the key inputs into the productive economy; and the intermediate ends are the macro-goals that the politicians aspire to deliver, deploying a range of economic instruments and policy interventions to secure 'the greatest good for the greatest number'. As to the 'ultimate ends', in the top box, although these clearly differ in different nations, cultures and communities, there is a surprising commonality that informs all societies.

For more and more people, the business of nurturing our spiritual capacity is now a serious priority. At the heart of this endeavour is the idea of finding 'a new story', enabling us to reconnect with our evolutionary origins going back over 14 billion years of unfolding life, to understand better our place in creation, and to experience that sense of interconnectedness and interdependence with the rest of life on Earth – the loss of which now imperils our very future. As Thomas Berry (1999) says: 'The historical mission of our times is to reinvent the human, at the species level, with critical reflection, within the community of life systems in a time-developed context, by means of story and shared dream experience.'

That 'story' can be construed either in a completely secular way or from a spiritual/religious perspective. In that respect, it is genuinely 'universal', though an atheistic geologist will obviously be getting something rather different out of it than a pantheistic tree-hugger! There can be no race, creed or culture that would find this story exclusive or incompatible with its own beliefs – with the exception of a small number of 'creationists' who continue to deny the hard-edged scientific reality of evolution. But the spirit of it will move different people in different ways, according to their own beliefs and value systems.

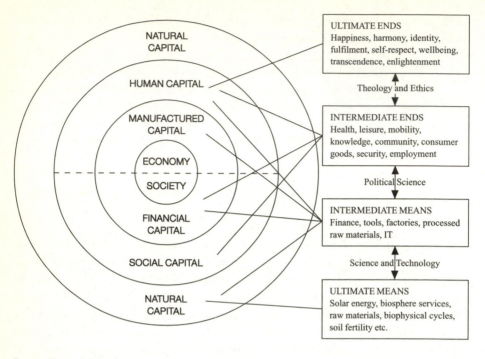

Source: Forum for the Future

Figure 8.1 *Spirituality and the Five Capitals Framework*

VALUING HUMAN CAPITAL

It may seem strange to end a brief examination of our spiritual capacities by talking of the potential for building some kind of universal common ground between people of different faiths and religions. Historically, there has been no greater source of schism, war, oppression and exploitation than the world's major religions. It requires an heroic 'act of faith' to assume that it will be different in the future.

In this as in every other respect, human capital is a morally neutral concept. The uses people make of their individual capacities may or may not be benign in societal and environmental terms. Intelligence can be used for purely selfish reasons to harm others, or to accelerate environmental degradation; spiritual capacities can be deployed to worsen religious intolerance and social divides; even good health, in terms of superior physical strength, can be used to abuse women, bully children or dominate 'weaker' colleagues.

But it is, of course, the benign 'flows' from our net stock of human capital that the focus should be on in any model of sustainable capitalism: good health that liberates people to fulfil their own and other people's aspirations; parenting skills; providing caring, nurturing, emotional support; creativity, works of art, novels and poetry; productive work of every kind; spiritual practice, compassion, humanitarian devotion; new ideas, design, innovations; the capacity for empathy. When thinking about the flow of benefits and 'free gifts' from people's human capital in such broad terms, it is clear that it cannot possibly be measured in financial terms. Indeed, in most instances, it's not even possible to quantify it in any serious way.

During the 1990s, however, companies such as Skandia (a large Swedish financial service company) devoted considerable resources to developing appropriate intellectual capital metrics (see Figure 8.2). For several years, it produced comprehensive annual reports to demonstrate the value to shareholders of its intellectual capital, defined as 'the sum of a company's intangible assets or, more simply, the difference between a company's net worth and its market value' (Skandia, 1997). In *Intellectual Capital: The New Wealth of Nations*, Thomas Stewart (1997) defined intellectual capital as 'the sum of everything everybody in a company knows that gives it a competitive edge'.

This was, of course, the period when people who really should have known better were getting almost hysterically overexcited about the dot.com boom – or dot.com bubble, as we now know it to have been. Politicians and business people waxed equally lyrical about the knowledge economy and the importance of being able to quantify 'the rental value of any individual's intellectual capacities'. For most companies, however, the biggest use of intellectual capital was not for external reporting purposes, but for management and decision-making inside the company, using a combination of qualitative indicators (motivation or empowerment indexes, staff satisfaction surveys, and so on) and standard quantitative indicators (turnover, average years of service, training costs per employee, etc.).

And there is, of course, a completely different way of looking at human capital inside a company, drawing far more upon the moral and spiritual capabilities of employees, seeing business as a 'vocation' to serve humankind as well as a means of creating wealth and generating profits for shareholders. Although many individual business people will feel distinctly ill at ease about such a 'touchy-feely' way of looking at the role of business in the world today, it is important to bear in mind that the current, somewhat brutal and reductionist view of what makes for business success may not reign supreme for ever. Danah Zohar likes to challenge her business clients by inviting them to think of themselves as 'servant leaders' in signing up to the following 'credo':

> *I believe that global business has the money and the power to make a significant difference in today's troubled world, and that by making that difference it can help itself as well as others. I envision business raising its sights above the bottom line. I envisage business becoming a vocation, like the higher professions. To make this possible, I believe that business must add a moral dimension, becoming more service- and value-oriented, and largely eliminating the assumed natural distinction between private enterprise and public institution. I envisage business taking responsibility for the world in which it operates and from which*

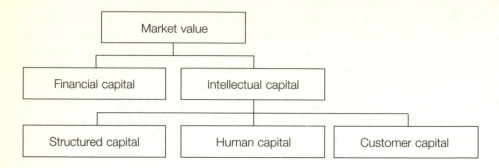

Notes: *Structured capital:* the infrastructure of human capital, including the organizational capabilities to meet market requirements. Infrastructure includes the quality and reach of information technology systems, company images, databases, organizational concept and documentation.
Human capital: the capabilities of the company's employees necessary to provide solutions to customers, to innovate and to renew. In addition to individual capabilities, human capital includes the dynamics of an intelligent (learning) organization in a changing competitive environment, its creativity and innovativeness.
Customer capital: the relationships with people with whom a company does business. Although this usually means clients and customers, it can also mean suppliers. It has also been referred to as *relationship capital*.
Source: Skandia (1997)

Figure 8.2 *Skandia's model of intellectual capital*

it creates its wealth. And I envisage myself becoming one of those business leaders who are 'servant leaders' – leaders who serve not just stockholders, colleagues, employees, products and customers, but leaders who also serve the community, the planet, humanity, the future and life itself. (Zohar, 2004)

For many non-profit organizations, by the same token, there is something inherently suspicious in deploying too heavy-handed a set of metrics, implying as they do a readiness to reduce each individual to a value-generating coefficient instead of taking a more balanced approach to weighing the value of intellectual capital against other essential and desirable employee attributes – not least emotional intelligence! In Forum for the Future, a small educational charity employing around 70 people, we went to some lengths to get to grips with understanding the dynamics of our own human/intellectual capital as part and parcel of our integrated sustainability management system (see Figure 8.3). But ours is definitely a qualitative rather than a quantitative approach!

Outside of the controlled work environment, it is even harder to track, let alone measure, what is happening to people's stocks of human capital. Unfortunately, it's a great deal easier to see when things are going wrong with the stock of human capital: when stress-related illnesses proliferate, when more people become addicted to drugs or alcohol, when the incidence of child abuse or crimes of violence increases, or when neglected, unloved children go on to become neglectful, unloving parents. As we will see in the next chapter, all of these things have a

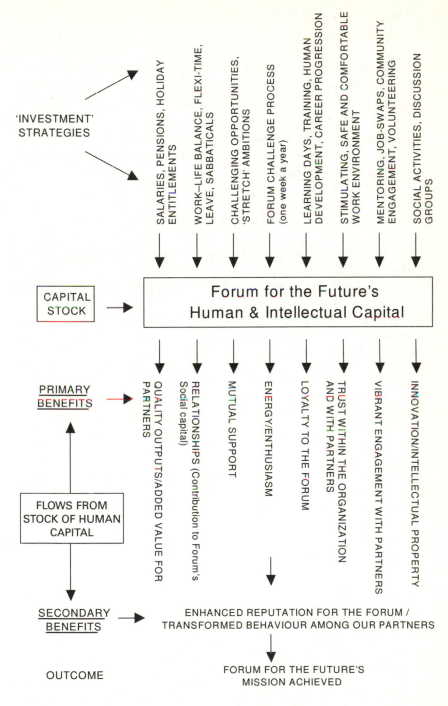

Source: Forum for the Future

Figure 8.3 *Forum for the Future's human and intellectual capital*

damaging impact upon stocks of social capital; but they originate in the failure to create the conditions in which each individual can fulfil his or her own potentiality to the full.

The quite proper focus for government and international bodies is therefore to create those conditions, starting with measures to ensure minimum standards of healthcare, nutrition, education and material wellbeing. Governments can't make people happy, healthy or rich – but they can invest in those institutions, systems and services that best enable individuals to make the most of their life chances. They can systematically build up social capital that nurtures and underpins each individual's human capital.

REFERENCES

Berry, T. (1999) 'The legal foundation for Earth survival', unpublished paper for Gaia Foundation, London

Coote, A. (2002) *Claiming the Health Dividend: Unlocking the Benefits of NHS Spending*, King's Fund, London

Coote, A. (2005) 'Public health and sustainable development', unpublished speech, Sustainable Development Commission, London

Daly, H. (1996) *Beyond Growth*, Beacon Press, Boston, MA

Evernden, N. (1993) *Natural Alien: Humankind and the Environment*, Oxford University Press, Oxford

Heslem, P. (2004) *Globalization and the Good*, SPCK, London

New Internationalist (2001) 'Enduring terrors', *New Internationalist*, November

Parker, M, (2002) 'The shareholder–employee balance: Beyond the rhetoric', *New Academy Review*, vol 1, no 2

Roszak, T. (1993) *The Voice of the Earth*, Bantam Press, London

Skandia (1997) *Skandia Annual Report*. Available at www.skandia.com/en/ir/orderprintfin info.jsp

Stewart, T. A. (1997) *Intellectual Capital: The New Wealth of Nations*, Nicholas Brealey, London

Young, S. (2003) *Moral Capitalism: Reconciling Private Interest with the Public Good*, Berrett-Koehler, San Francisco, CA

Zohar, D. (2004) *Spiritual Capital: Wealth We Can Live By*, Bloomsbury, London

9

Social Capital

INTRODUCTION

QUESTION: *When does one person's stock of human capital become a community's stock of social capital?*
ANSWER: *It doesn't really matter, as long as they are mutually reinforcing and help to secure a better quality of life for the greatest number of people in any particular area.*

Although the concept of social capital is beginning to receive real traction in both policy-making and business circles, it is still struggling somewhat to cast off its aura of academic theorizing about what it is that binds communities and societies together. This is unfortunate; in many ways, social capital lends itself far more to the development of concrete, measurable interventions by business than the aggravatingly elusive determinants of corporate social responsibility (CSR). In essence, it all comes down to things that we are all very familiar with in both our personal and working lives: good networks, trust, shared initiatives and solidarity – the 'social glue' that keeps things bound together, often in the teeth of increasingly 'atomized' lifestyles, with each individual going his or her own way regardless of the impacts upon society, community or family.

COMMUNITY AND CIVIC ORGANIZATIONS

The links between human capital and social capital are clearly very strong; but in recent years there has been a far greater emphasis in public policy on the importance of the latter rather than the former. Leading politicians talk passionately about the importance of community. Sociologists stress the role of 'friendship networks' for getting jobs. More and more funding for regenerating run-down neighbourhoods supports community groups, as well as invests in new infrastructure. International institutions such as the World Bank are increasingly promoting community groups, non-governmental organizations (NGOs) and the 'building blocks' of civic society as crucial to economic and social development.

Why such interest in community and civic organizations? Advocates argue that they make two important contributions to a sustainable economy and society. First, friends, family and mutual groups can provide people with practical support, from looking after children and old people, to lending money or providing informal counselling. During an era in which state resources continue to be tight and trust in state institutions is often low, many commentators see such informal support as increasingly important.

Second, broad social networks and civic organizations are perceived to foster cooperation between people. They increase trust, which, in turn, helps people to enjoy a higher quality of life and entrepreneurs to do business. They provide structures for discussing and agreeing ways to overcome shared challenges, such as how to run a school, reduce crime or protect the environment. In contrast, a socially fragmented society finds it difficult to engage in the kind of debate that is essential for democratic government.

Advocates argue that such mutual support, trust and the ability to work together to solve common problems contribute as much to a country's success as do its material resources (physical capital) or the skills of its population (human capital). Consequently, they have dubbed these attributes *social capital*.

BRIDGING AND BONDING

Although the first usage of 'social capital' has been traced back to 1916, contemporary usage of the term owes much to the work of three thinkers: Pierre Bourdieu, James Coleman and Robert Putnam. Of these, it is Robert Putnam who is responsible for popularizing the concept and bringing it into mainstream political debate. Putnam's book *Bowling Alone* (2000) takes bowling clubs as a defining example of activities that previously helped to sustain the social fabric of life in the US, but which are now in decline. He draws on a vast body of data and research to show that the past 40 years have seen a dramatic decline in participation in social structures, from the church and political parties to parent–teacher associations and bowling leagues.

Putnam defines social capital as the 'features of social life – networks, norms and trust – that enable participants to act together more effectively to pursue shared objectives'. Other 'features' often referred to in the literature are institutions, relationships, values, levels of participation, reciprocity and community cohesion – though it is important to point out that there is far more to the concept of social capital than is captured in the notion of community. To develop a more nuanced understanding of the different dynamics within social capital, Putnam distinguishes between two types:

1   *Bridging* (or inclusive) social capital: this is outward looking and encompasses people from different social groups. Examples include the civil rights movement and ecumenical religious organizations.

2   *Bonding* (or exclusive) social capital: this is inward looking and tends to reinforce exclusive identities. Examples include urban gangs, church-based women's reading groups and fashionable country clubs.

Bonding social capital creates in-group loyalty and solidarity, and offers strong support for less fortunate community members. Bridging networks tend to be more useful for accessing external assets and contacts. Putnam summarizes the differences as follows: 'Bonding social capital constitutes a kind of sociological superglue, whereas bridging social capital provides a sociological WD-40' (Putnam, 2000).

A third category – 'linking capital' – has now been added to bridging and bonding capital by some social commentators. This is used to refer to connections between those with different levels of influence or status in society (for instance, the connection between political elites and the general public, or between individuals from different social classes).

All commentators on social capital are quick to point out that this too, just like human capital, is a 'value-neutral term'. All forms of social capital can produce negative effects as well as positive effects, and the academic literature identifies a wide range of possible downsides to social capital. As one critic pointed out: 'Wouldn't it be better if Timothy McVeigh *had* gone bowling alone?', since McVeigh, whose bomb in Oklahoma killed 168 people, gained valuable advice from the network of friends he used to go bowling with. Putnam acknowledges that the positive consequences of social capital – mutual support, cooperation and trust – can often be matched by negative consequences, such as sectarianism (dividing rather than uniting communities or societies), ethnocentrism, corruption, and creating barriers to social inclusion and social mobility.

Indeed, there is a substantial body of academic work in the US which supports one of Robert Putnam's more controversial hypotheses that geographical areas with high levels of ethnic and social diversity will display *lower* levels of social capital over a wide range of indicators – including trust and civic engagement. The work of Costa and Kahn, for instance, suggests that the more ethnically homogenous an areas is, the higher its trust levels are likely to be. By contrast, some recent research by the Home Office in the UK, arising out of its 2003 Citizenship Survey, challenges these findings, demonstrating *no* simple relationship between ethnic diversity, levels of trust and community participation.

This kind of rich but often inconclusive batting back and forth of rival theories seems to go with the social capital territory! Despite a growing body of academic work (much of it reflected in a recent collection of perspectives on social capital edited by Stephen Baron, John Field and Tom Schuller, 2000), it still remains a fairly nebulous term, difficult to pin down and even harder to implement. In *Bowling Alone*, Robert Putnam uses 14 principal indicators of community networks and social trust:

- *Measures of community organizational life:*
  1 *percentage served on committee of some local organization during last year;*
  2 *percentage served as officer of some club or organization during last year;*
  3 *civic and social organizations per 1000 population;*
  4 *mean number of club meetings attended during last year;*
  5 *mean number of group memberships;*
- *Measures of engagement in public affairs:*
  6 *turnout in presidential elections, 1988 and 1992;*
  7 *percentage attended public meeting on town or school affairs during last year;*
- *Measures of community voluntarism:*
  8 *number of non-profit organizations per 1000 population;*
  9 *mean number of times worked on community project during last year;*
  10 *mean number of times engaged in volunteer work during last year;*
- *Measures of informal sociability:*
  11 *agree that 'I spend a lot of time visiting friends';*
  12 *mean number of times entertained at home during last year;*
- *Measures of social trust:*
  13 *agree that 'most people can be trusted';*
  14 *agree that 'most people are honest'.* (Putnam, 2000)

By way of a summary, commentators have gone on to suggest that a society can be said to have high stocks of social capital if it has:

- high levels of trust between people;
- high membership of civic organizations;
- high levels of volunteering and charitable giving;
- high levels of participation in politics, including membership of political parties;
- high levels of participation in religious groups; and
- high levels of informal socializing.

These should all help people to give each other mutual support, cooperate to solve common problems, establish a system of good government and do business together. Societies with high membership of civic organizations also tend to have higher trust, more informal socializing and political participation. This is why we can talk about some societies having more or less social capital.

Connectedness can also vary depending upon the scale of society we look at. A society might have lots of local social capital, but few connections at a national level. One hundred years ago, Britain arguably had greater social capital in many local areas: churches acted as local social and political hubs, people knew more of their neighbours, and local mutual associations such as local guilds were stronger. Yet, the connections between these different communities were lower than today. For example, there were fewer national and international interest groups. People's social networks were often more restricted by geography and class.

The evidence to back up the importance of social networks and civic organizations is fairly strong. States in America whose residents have high levels of informal socializing, volunteering, community groups and trust of others tend to have lower crime and relatively good schools, health facilities and government. Individuals with good social connections tend to prosper. There is also some evidence that countries and regions with low social trust have relatively poor economies.

Robert Putnam (2000) has attempted to pick out the factors that accounted for the decline in social capital over the last four decades in the US. He tentatively estimates that changing patterns of work account for 10 per cent of the decline; suburbanization accounts for another 10 per cent decline because people live further away from each other and their work, and spend more time commuting. Television accounts for a quarter of the decline because it provides a more isolated form of entertainment. The majority of the rest of the decline he attributes to a rather vague change in the cultures of different generations. For example, those who lived through World War II appear to have established patterns of political and social engagement which their children never learned.

Other researchers agree with Putnam that Americans are becoming more socially isolated and less civically engaged; but they suggest different root causes. Amitai Etzioni, an influential sociologist, argues that communities have been undermined in Western countries because governments have given people too many individual rights. Individualism has become rampant, he claims, because everyone has been given rights to free healthcare, education, a minimum income, privacy, divorce, compensation for almost any wrong and so on, without any corresponding duties and responsibilities.

William Julius Wilson, one of the leading writers on ghetto culture, claims that poor urban areas in the US have suffered a breakdown in community. Trust has declined, civic organizations have withered. Those social groups which thrive – such as gangs – are very exclusive and contribute little to cooperation between all residents. But he attributes the root cause of this not to the time pressures of work, nor a culture of individual rights, but to the economic dislocation caused by the flight of stable employment from such neighbourhoods.

While these analysts look to underlying social, political and economic factors to account for social and civic engagement, others such as Samuel Huntington focus on the more immediate capacity of civic institutions. Huntington argues that political participation is not falling because people are less interested in politics, but because political institutions are failing to represent people's opinions, are dominated by corporate finances, and have done a pretty bad job at improving the economy and skills over the last three decades.

Building social capital

As interest has increased in social capital, numerous questions have been asked about how it can be fostered. How can trust be developed, community groups supported and networks expanded? This institutional focus has also been the basis of most attempts to stimulate social capital over the last decade. Governments are increasingly funding programmes that aim to strengthen the *capacity* of civic organizations – for example, by giving their members training. Internationally, much of the support given to emerging democracies in Eastern Europe has been to help them develop civic institutions, from funding small community centres upwards. Even those such as Robert Putnam, who attribute the decline in social capital to economic, cultural and technological factors, believe that the way to foster social capital is to create new community and civic institutions.

In April 2002, the UK Prime Minister's Strategy Unit carried out an intriguing review (Cabinet Office Strategy Unit, 2002) of the many different ways in which the concept of social capital is permeating political discourse in the UK and elsewhere. In seeking to answer the question 'why is social capital important?', it advanced six potential areas of economic and social benefit – in the terminology of the Five Capitals Framework, these represent hypothetical flows from the stock of social capital from which the whole of society (as well as many individuals) benefits.

1   Social capital is important because it may facilitate higher levels of GDP

> *The efficient functioning of markets requires clear definition of property rights, the ability easily or cheaply to enforce contracts or other negotiated agreements, low transaction costs and good information.* (Fukuyama, 1995)

This was the principal thesis of Francis Fukuyama in his article 'Social capital and the global economy' (1995). Robert Putnam (2000) argues that there is now detailed empirical evidence from Tanzania to Sri Lanka to Italy which demonstrates that economic development can be, and often has been, boosted by enhanced stocks of social capital. In one small but intriguing manifestation of this, the 1997 World Values Survey shows that countries where trust of strangers is high also tend to be countries with high gross domestic product (GDP). All of these correlations have proved to be particularly important in explaining variations in economic development in developing nations.

2 Social capital is important because it may facilitate the more efficient functioning of job markets

> *The level and duration of unemployment is partly a function of search costs. The networks and contacts that make up social capital can provide highly cost-effective mechanisms for facilitating job search.* (Cabinet Office Strategy Unit, 2002)

The evidence here is strong. Those who live in particularly disadvantaged neighbourhoods are even less likely to get jobs and break out of any poverty cycle than individuals with similar qualification and characteristics living in better neighbourhoods – a conclusion reinforced by studies that show more unemployed people find jobs through friends and personal contacts than through any other route.

3 Social capital is important because it may facilitate educational attainment

> *At the individual level, there is a strong positive association between levels of social capital, measured by the size and diversity of social networks, community engagement and social trust, and levels of educational attainment.* (Cabinet Office Strategy Unit, 2002)

Figure 9.1 demonstrates the different sources of social capital influencing educational attainment in individuals, with a balance of both formal and informal learning sources.

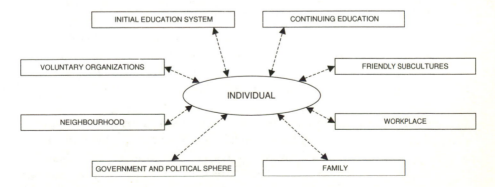

Source: adapted from Baron et al (2000)

Figure 9.1 *Sources of social capital that influence the attainment of education*

4 Social capital is important because it may contribute to lower levels of crime

> *Within criminology, this is sometimes known as 'social control theory' – social networks and bonds to mainstream society are what prevent people from offending – and has been impressively demonstrated by longitudinal studies at both the individual and neighbourhood level.* (Cabinet Office Strategy Unit, 2002)

For many people living in the cities of both rich and poor countries, crime (or fear of crime) is one of the most significant factors in a reduced quality of life. Higher levels of social capital acting both as a deterrent (before any crime is committed) and a support network (after a crime is committed) can make an enormous difference to people's levels of wellbeing.

Indeed, financial support by either local or central government for initiatives along the lines of Neighbourhood Watch may well prove to be an extremely cost-effective way of making a real difference in people's lives. There are therefore few more disturbing manifestations of low levels of trust and social capital in urban areas than the emergence of 'gated communities', with more and more wealthy individuals choosing to withdraw behind various kinds of physical barrier to put themselves as far beyond the reach of criminal or anti-social elements as possible.

Although the *State of the World Report* (Worldwatch Institute, 2004) is somewhat more tentative in drawing any conclusions here, it talks of social capital fostering 'virtue among the citizenry', making citizens more community oriented, more law abiding, cooperative with the state and willing to pay taxes.

5 Social capital is important because it may lead to better health

> *Wider social relationships may have an impact on health through their impact on individuals' perceptions of their social status; stress; the strength of social affiliations; 'daily hassles'; and more general feelings of safety and fear. Social capital provides tangible assistance and care, and also creates a sense of wellbeing and belonging, whereas its absence leads to isolation and depression.* (Cabinet Office Strategy Unit, 2002)

Sociologists have demonstrated time after time the importance of bonding relationships on health – particularly in childhood and in old age. Even when they are well cared for in orphanages (with a good diet, comfortable facilities and so on), children's development can be badly affected by the lack of love and trust provided in normal family relationships.

The Worldwatch Institute's 2004 *State of the World Report* comments on just how significant this can be when assessing ways of securing a better quality of life for people:

*People who are socially connected tend to be healthier — often signifi-
cantly so. More than a dozen long-term studies in Japan, Scandinavia,
and the US show that the chances of dying in a given year, no matter
the cause, is two to five times greater for people who are isolated than for
socially connected people. For example, one study found that in 1234
heart attack patients, the rate of a recurring attack within six months
was nearly double for those living alone. And a Harvard study of health
and mistrust in the United States concluded that moving to a state with
a high level of social connections from a state where the level is low would
improve a person's health almost as much as quitting smoking.* (Worldwatch Institute, 2004)

6 Social capital is important because it may improve the effectiveness of institutions of government

The report would appear significantly to underestimate the importance of this
dimension of social capital. Governments and politicians nowadays are widely
distrusted and ignored. In many European countries politicians at all levels of
government command the outright trust of less than one tenth of the population.
Well over half of young people do not bother to vote in any elections. Democratic
legitimacy is diminishing rapidly all over the Western world. Revitalizing systems
of governance is a critical part of the challenge of sustainable development, and it
is clear that investments in social capital can do much to help achieve this purpose.

The report concludes that there is an array of *possible* policy interventions for 'positively stimulating the creation of social capital', some of which are already in place,
with many more under consideration.

From a sustainability perspective, the concept of social capital offers an exciting
new way of thinking about and measuring the social dimensions of sustainability.
But despite the wealth of research on natural capital and environmental sustainability, there have been surprisingly few attempts to explore the links between social
capital and social sustainability.

Yet there are some hints of convergence. In a paper in 2001, Ismail Seregaldin
and Christiaan Grootaert of the World Bank argue that social capital 'is best studied
in the context of the contribution it makes to sustainable development'. They set
social capital alongside natural, human and manufactured capital, and explore ways
of measuring the stocks and flows of all these capital types. Using a 'back of the
envelope' calculation, they estimate that in 192 countries, human and social capital
equals or exceeds natural capital and manufactured assets combined (the only
exception to this rule being a few large exporters of raw materials). Manufactured
capital represents only 16 to 20 per cent of the wealth of most countries; but, as

they rightly point out, it is this small slice of the cake that nearly all economic policy is focused upon.

Environmentalists may take issue with the rather low valuations that Seregaldin and Grootaert place on natural capital; but most would agree with their conclusion – that an overhaul of economic policy and the introduction of more sophisticated metrics for valuing different capital types will be critical if we are to achieve sustainable development. There are the beginnings here of a powerful synthesis, and academics and practitioners in both areas should endeavour to strengthen the intellectual and political links between their work.

Beyond this, there is growing interest in assessing the degree to which investments in natural capital simultaneously enhance the conditions for social sustainability. Research conducted by The Natural Step has been seeking to assess the degree to which our understanding of how natural systems work can inform our understanding of how social systems work. Starting with the somewhat understated wording of The Natural Step's fourth System Condition ('in a sustainable society, people are not subject to conditions that systematically undermine their capacity to meet their needs'), three key 'success criteria' underpinning sustainable *natural* systems have emerged as being equally critical components of any sustainable society:

1   *self-organization* (creating the conditions in which all individuals are able to meet their needs and fulfil their aspirations through education, basic human rights, equitable access to resources and so on);
2   *diversity* (upholding the entitlements of divergent traditions and beliefs, protecting the cultures and economies, promoting tolerance and so on); and
3   *interdependence* (acknowledging not just 'connectedness' but 'mutual dependency' in a world where rights are balanced by obligations, and where cooperation and reciprocity count for as much as competition and self-interest).

It is the interplay between these three success criteria that is particularly interesting. Self-organization and diversity need to be acknowledged for what they are – essential elements in any vibrant society that should be celebrated for the way in which they enhance our capacity to lead creative, colourful and interesting lives. But the exercise of self-organizing power which then denies others the opportunity to use their own capacity to meet their needs (for example, through domestic violence, organized crime and trafficking of human beings) can never be part of a sustainable society. For any society to achieve true sustainability, these two success criteria must simultaneously be shaped by mutual acceptance of the interdependent nature of each and every one of us, and by recognition of the fact that the purpose of society is to translate those mutual dependencies into effective relationships.

The thrust of this chapter has been to look at ways in which governments can both conceptualize social capital and bring forward specific initiatives to help build social capital at different levels in society. Beyond that, there are equally important opportunities for the *private sector* to re-conceptualize what is now a rather soft and even flabby CSR agenda in terms of social capital, taking a much more rigorous approach to understanding the stocks of social capital for which it is responsible (and from which it derives considerable benefits) and the most effective ways of securing constant value from those stocks of social capital. Companies are often unaware that they may be involved in building or depleting social capital as the terminology is rarely used in business or management literature, or by CSR practitioners. For many business people, the definition used in this chapter would need to be reworked to give it a much more grounded relevance – something along the lines of social capital being seen as 'the sum of social channels, networks and norms which expedite action on the part of any company pursuing its legitimate business interests'.

I will be returning to this specific theme in Chapter 14 as part of a broader analysis of what leading companies are doing to implement as much of the Five Capitals Framework as is now available to them under current company law and other legislation. However, it is worth commenting at this stage that there are already a substantial number of case studies exploring both the business and societal value of corporate engagement on social capital issues – particularly with reference to the role of big multinationals in developing countries where some of the socio-economic challenges are a great deal more pressing than conventional environmental issues. For instance, an interesting article appeared in the *New Academy Review* in June 2004, appraising the contribution of a number of multinationals to building social capital in South Africa, which many now see as a critical 'laboratory' for bringing forward innovative approaches to CSR/sustainable development. It focuses in particular on GlaxoSmithKline, through its involvement in the International Partnership against AIDS in Africa, and BHP Billiton.

A lot of this is reflected in the World Bank's thinking on social capital, seeing it as a class of assets that yield a stream of benefits useful for economic development of every kind. The Worldwatch Institute's 2004 *State of the World Report* describes why this has become so important to them:

> *Stephen Knack of the World Bank warns that low levels of societal trust may lock countries in a 'poverty trap,' in which the vicious circle of mistrust, low investment and poverty is difficult to break. Knack and his colleagues tested the relationship between trust and economic performance in 29 countries included in the World Values Survey. They found that each 12-point rise in the survey's measure of trust was associated with a 1 per cent increase in annual income growth, and that each 7-point rise in trust corresponded to a 1 per cent increase in investment's share of GDP.* (Worldwatch Institute, 2004)

The simple truth of it is that, without high and stable levels of social capital, no society can achieve its collective aspirations, companies and entrepreneurs find it much harder to transact their day-to-day business, and fewer individuals have the opportunity to develop to their full potential.

REFERENCES

Baron, S., Field, J. and Schuller, T. (eds) (2000) *Social Capital: Critical Perspectives*, Oxford University Press, Oxford

Cabinet Office Strategy Unit (2002) *Social Capital: A Discussion Paper*, Cabinet Office Strategy Unit, London

Fukuyama, F. (1995) 'Social capital and the global economy', *Foreign Affairs*, vol 74, no 5, September/October

Putnam, R. (2000) *Bowling Alone: The Collapse and Revival of American Community*, Simon and Schuster, New York

Worldwatch Institute (2004) *State of the World 2004: Progress Towards a Sustainable Society*, Earthscan, London

10

Manufactured Capital

INTRODUCTION

Ever since the publication of *Limits to Growth* (Meadows et al, 1972), sustainable development pragmatists have convincingly argued that the best hope of averting ecological meltdown is pervasive technological innovation: keep on driving down the environmental and social impacts of each unit of production, in whatever sector, through incremental improvements in resource efficiency. This, after all, is going to be a lot easier than trying to get on top of the population challenge (in the shape of around 80 million new citizens arriving on planet Earth every year), or trying to persuade consumers to reduce their levels of personal consumption. Eco-efficiency and eco-innovation have been the response. However, not only are governments *not* driving the resource productivity challenge with sufficient clarity or purposefulness, but even if they did, efficiency gains would barely keep up with burgeoning increases in consumption all around the world. A much more radical approach can be found in concepts such as 'biomimicry' or 'cradle-to-cradle wealth creation' – all of which depend upon a profound transformation in the way in which we see ourselves as embedded absolutely at the heart of the natural world, rather than somewhat detached observers of it from afar. Technology alone can't get us out of a hole: we have to re-engineer our mindsets at the same time.

DEFINING MANUFACTURED CAPITAL

The two remaining stocks of capital (manufactured and financial) are probably the most familiar to people. Levels of technical understanding (from an economist's point of view) may be low; but most people would have a 'working knowledge' of what both represent – particularly those working in business.

However, manufactured capital is not quite as simple a concept as it sounds. It is made up of material goods that contribute to the production process, but do not become embodied in the output of that process. The main components of manufactured capital include buildings (the built environment of villages, towns and cities); infrastructure (the physical fabric supporting social and economic life, including transport networks; schools; hospitals; media and communications;

energy; and sewerage and water systems); and technologies (the means by which goods and services are produced, from simple tools and machines to information technology, biotechnology and engineering). Just to make things even more confusing, this list of components also includes software and chemical formulae, blueprints, instruction manuals and so on.

But the underlying 'story' is much easier to grasp. Children the world over are brought up on the same evolutionary account: that it was humankind's capacity to use tools that first helped us to establish our ecological niche, and that this slowly evolved into an increasingly powerful ability to assemble raw materials extracted from nature into objects, machines, buildings and so on. For most of our short history, this conversion process (from natural capital into manufactured capital) was relatively modest, localized and mostly low-impact as far as the environment was concerned. But from the mid 18th century onwards, the Industrial Revolution transformed the balance of that relationship between the biosphere and the technosphere. The availability of cheap fossil fuels from the middle of the 20th century onwards has further increased the dependence of human beings upon countless different sources of manufactured capital.

SUSTAINABLE TECHNOLOGY?

It's within the broad concept of manufactured capital that the whole debate about the role of technology and sustainability has been subsumed. This is certainly not the place to attempt a résumé of one of the most important areas of intellectual divergence within green thinking over the last 40 years, but before launching into any analysis of the *potential* contribution that manufactured capital may make to achieving a just and sustainable society, it's important to remember that for some environmentalists, it is technology itself that is the problem. As far back as 1971, the eminent American activist Barry Commoner pointed the finger of blame at 'the sweeping transformation of production technologies since World War II', and argued that this transformation would have to be 'redone in order to bring the nation's productive technology much more closely into harmony with the inescapable demands of the ecosystem' (Commoner, 1971).

Perhaps the most consistent articulation of this perspective over four decades has been Teddy Goldsmith's plaintive laments in the *Ecologist* magazine at the usurpation of the biosphere by the technosphere, leaving humanity stripped of any proper connectedness with the natural world, and leaving society rushing headlong into an increasingly destructive frenzy of exploitation and consumption. Such voices have always been in a minority – an influential minority (especially in terms of the image that people may now have of environmentalists' overall attitude to technology as a result), but a minority for all that. Over the last decade, it is much closer to the truth to say that the dominant intellectual force in this debate has been fundamentally pro-technology and increasingly focused on the benign potential for technological transformation. Indeed, some of the most eloquent and powerful advocates of sustainable development today (Lester Brown, Paul Hawken, Amory and Hunter Lovins, Bill McDonough, Ernst von Weizsacker, Paul Ekins and many more) start from the premise that the only way of achieving sustainability is through a 'second Industrial Revolution', entailing the wholesale transformation of the way in which we think about manufactured capital.

Put at its simplest, this all goes back to the equation first promulgated by Paul Ehrlich in the 1960s to encapsulate the sustainability dilemma: $I = P \times C \times T$, where I represents total environmental impact, P is population, C is per capita consumption, and T is the technological efficiency with which that consumption is generated (impact per unit of consumption).

For a host of different reasons, most contemporary politicians have proved themselves incapable of addressing population issues (however blindingly obvious it may be that the more people there are on Earth, the harder it is going to be to fashion a genuinely sustainable future for each and every one of us), and remain extremely reluctant to engage in any debate about consumption – other than to subscribe (implicitly or explicitly) to the horribly flawed notion that the more people consume, the happier they must be. The consequences of these two variables – lower population and reduced consumption – effectively being ruled 'off-limits', as far as contemporary political debate is concerned, has had a huge impact upon the way in which people have addressed today's sustainability challenges, with a quite disproportionate emphasis on the third variable – technology.

With global population rising to around 9 billion in the second half of this century, and per capita consumption likely to go on rising (especially in today's poorer developing countries), the challenge of getting more (in terms of economic value) out of less (in terms of the throughput of energy and raw materials) becomes all important – which explains the current wave of enthusiasm for concepts such as eco-innovation, resource efficiency, zero waste or zero emissions, carbon neutrality and so on.

How much more we can squeeze out remains a moot point. Calculations by Paul Ekins (2000) in his *Economic Growth and Environmental Sustainability* demonstrate that environmental impact per unit of consumption would need to fall by at least 90 per cent to achieve genuine environmental sustainability – the much talked-about 'Factor 10' improvement in resource productivity. Others argue that this is the absolute minimum required. As Lester Brown points out:

> *If China were to have a car in every garage, American style, it would need 80 million barrels of oil a day – more than the world currently produces. If paper consumption per person in China were to reach the US level, China would need more paper than the world produces. There go the world's forests. If the fossil fuel-based, automobile-centred, throwaway economic model will not work for China, it will not work for the other 3 billion people in the developing world – and it will not work for the rest of the world.* (Brown, 2003)

However, advocates of a new 'green industrial revolution' believe that this kind of efficiency transformation is perfectly viable. In sector after sector, scenarios are now bandied about showing how our existing stocks of manufactured capital must be replaced as soon as possible with buildings, infrastructure, investments and new technologies that will enable an efficiency revolution of this kind. In *Natural Capitalism*, for instance, Paul Hawken and colleagues balance their inevitable anger and frustration at the continuing blindness and denial on the part of the world's ruling elites to today's converging crises with hugely optimistic accounts of technological breakthroughs already available to us or just around the corner (Hawken, 1999).

Over and above the imperative of 'radically increased resource productivity', the authors stress two further trends, both of which will have a significant impact upon our understanding of manufactured capital in the future. The first is the shift from products to services – from the acquisition of goods as a measure of affluence to an economy where the continuous receipt of service, quality, utility and performance is what is seen to promote real wellbeing. Although the number of cases where this shift is happening in practice still remains very small, there is now increased attention to the potential for substantial sustainability gains in this area.

BIOMIMICRY

The second trend is the growing interest in biomimicry, defined by Janine Benyus (1997) – author of the influential *Biomimicry: Innovation Inspired by Nature* – as a:

> ... *new science that studies nature's models and then imitates or takes inspiration from these designs and processes to solve human problems. A new way of viewing and valuing nature, it introduces an era based not on what we can extract from the natural world but on what we can learn from it.* (Benyus, 1997)

Biomimicry provides one of the most visionary approaches to meeting the overarching challenge of aligning humankind's model of progress and growth with nature's systems and processes (about which, as we have said, we have no choice). But, once again, one has to take stock of the scale of the transformation required to effect such an alignment. In Table 10.1, Janine Benyus's 'canon of nature's laws, strategies and principles' (on the left) is juxtaposed with countervailing generalizations about our human way of doing things (on the right).

Two important questions remain regarding the likelihood of this kind of transformation in our stocks of manufactured capital. How viable is it economically? How likely is it politically? Opinions differ enormously on economic viability. The optimists look to a sequence of win–win technological transitions that both help to reduce environmental damage and generate economic growth in the

Table 10.1 *Nature versus human nature*

Nature's laws, strategies and principles	Common human responses
Nature runs on sunlight	Humankind runs on fossil fuels
Nature uses only the energy it needs	Humankind wastes massive amounts of energy
Nature fits form to function	Humankind forces Nature's form to fit its own functions
Nature recycles everything	Humankind recycles next to nothing
Nature rewards cooperation	Humankind idolises competition
Nature banks on diversity	Humankind opts for monoculture, destroys diversity
Nature demands local expertise	Increasingly, the local is lost in a global economy
Nature curbs excesses from within	Humankind celebrates excess: greed is good
Nature taps the power of limits	There are no limits, says humankind

Source: adapted from Benyus (1997)

process. The wholesale shift from hydrocarbons to solar/renewable technologies is perhaps the most likely place where this may happen. By contrast, pessimists view such a scenario as improbable:

> *Saving the environment without causing a rise in prices and subsequent check on production growth is only possible if a technology is invented that is sufficiently clean, reduces the use of space sufficiently, leaves the soil intact, does not deplete energy and resources,* and *is cheaper than current technology. This is barely imaginable for our whole range of current activities. From the above, it follows that saving the environment will certainly check production growth and probably lead to lower levels of national income.* (Green Alliance, 2002)

This is obviously a key area of debate. But, ultimately, given that there is no real choice, we will have to pay whatever price it takes to get humankind on to a genuinely sustainable path. However much this may cost, it will be a great deal less costly than carrying on regardless.

As to political feasibility, optimism does not come easily here either. Levels of ecological illiteracy remain so deep as to beggar belief after 40 years of accumulating evidence that all is not well with our dominant model of progress. Symptoms, not systems, remain the political order of the day. There is little, if any, applied understanding among politicians of how natural systems work; the laws of thermodynamics obtain only in engineering textbooks; and frontier mentalities (based on an atavistic assumption that there are no real limits to what the human species can aspire to do) have proved astonishingly resilient.

This is precisely the kind of challenge that some of the world's most progressive companies are facing as they seek to reduce the overall impact of their products – to really work the 'T' variable in the I = P × C × T equation in order to get us closer to something resembling sustainable production systems. One of the most popular tools used by companies to achieve these efficiency gains is life-cycle analysis, assessing the impact of a product from manufacture through to final disposal, reuse or recycling. It sounds simple; but I suspect few people understand the complexity of the kind of analysis that has to be done to work out how best to make those gains.

Back in 2003, the electronics giant Matsushita came up with its 'Factor X' initiative to demonstrate to consumers what has to be done both to improve the quality of life (through its products) and reduce their environmental impact. It uses three environmental benchmarks or 'factors': reduction in greenhouse gases (or GHGs), resource efficiency, and the elimination of toxic and persistent chemicals. The GHG factor is calculated by comparing the GHG efficiency of the old product versus the new (lower-impact) product, and the resource factor by comparing the resource efficiency of the old product versus the new (lower-impact) product. The higher the factor, the greater the contribution to the development of more sustainable lifestyles.

It sounds relatively simple; in practice, it's anything but simple. Figures 10.1 and 10.2 reveal the complexities of using detailed life-cycle analysis of this kind, as far as companies such as Matsushita are concerned. The first reveals the overall approach to reducing the emission of greenhouse gases from the use of any standard electrical product (in this instance, the television). The second diagram shows the detailed calculation of the improvement in performance (in terms of a reduction in greenhouse gases emitted) of moving from an old model to a new model. On top of that, there's an equally complex calculation of improvements in resource efficiency.

But even with companies such as Matsushita beginning to take a real lead in applying comprehensive life-cycle techniques of this kind, it's proving a lot harder to move society towards a better understanding of what is now required. Linear models of resource use – *make, use and dispose* – are still dominant (see Figure 10.3). Unlike the cyclical resource flows of natural systems, which result in no net accumulation of waste, human-induced linear resource flows *inevitably* lead to an accumulation of waste and to a build-up of entropy. Statistics that bear out the scale of this systems dilemma provide even more telling illustrations: if Americans had recycled the 32 billion cans of fizzy drinks they threw away in 2002, for example, they would have saved 435,000 tonnes of aluminium – enough to rebuild the world's entire commercial air fleet more than 1.5 times.

The scale of the problem is extraordinary. More than 90 per cent of all the materials extracted to manufacture ordinary consumer products ends up as waste; only 10 per cent – and sometimes a lot less – ends up in the product itself. And given the success that some manufacturers have had in ensuring that their products don't last very long (through built-in obsolescence), the lifetime of many of those products is very short before they are rejected and replaced.

By contrast, Figure 10.4 highlights what would need to happen to move us towards the sustainable use of material resources. This vision is *not* a more eco-

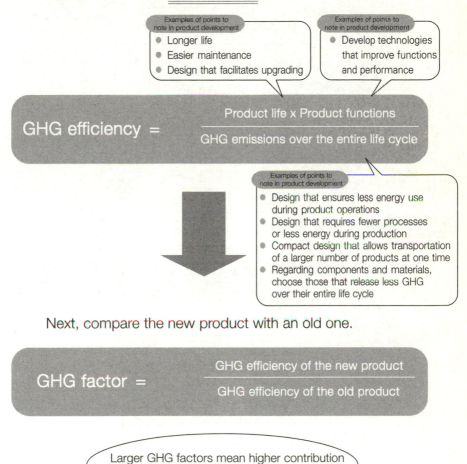

Figure 10.1 *Improving performance in the greenhouse gas (GHG) factor*

efficient version of today's inherently unsustainable resource-use patterns. It is much more radical than that. It reflects the pressing need to adapt the production and use of materials to match the sustainable and cyclical patterns of resource flows in the natural world. Nevertheless, governments throughout the world have, as yet,

TV

● **Data of compared products**

	New model	Old model
Product	36" BS digital high-definition TV	36" high-definition TV
Produced in	2000	1993
Product no.	TH-36D10	TH-36HV10
Weight	78.7 kg	91.0 kg
Power consumption during operation	228 W	410 W
Annual power consumption	260 kWh/year	630 kWh/year
Power consumption during standby	0.2 W	5 W
Product life	8 years	
Operation/hour	4.5 hrs/day	
Standby mode/hour	19.5 hrs/day	

GHG factor evaluation results

		New model		Old model	
		FY2000 model		FY1993 model	
		GHG emissions	Unit	GHG emissions	Unit
Produce	Material production	25.76	kg/unit	50.55	kg/unit
	Electronic component production	499.02	kg/unit	738.14	kg/unit
	Packaging material production	6.09	kg/unit	6.99	kg/unit
	Production process	14.74	kg/unit	14.74	kg/unit
Transport	Transportation	12.11	kg/unit	14.13	kg/unit
Operate	Power consumption during operation	883.10	kg/unit	2030.06	kg/unit
	Power consumption during standby	4.86	kg/unit	121.54	kg/unit
	Consumable material (battery)	0.00	kg/unit	0.00	kg/unit
Return/ Circulate	Recycling/disposal	0.91	kg/unit	0.94	kg/unit
Total	GHG emissions over the entire lifecycle	1446.58	kg/unit	2977.09	kg/unit

Product life	8 years	8 years	
Product functions: Assumed to be the same	1	1	
GHG efficiency	0.0055	0.0027	
GHG factor	**2.1**		

● **Reduction of the standby power consumption (5W → 0.2W) by**
developing a microprocessor specialized for the standby mode
  ● **Reduction of the power consumption during operation (410W → 228W) by**
improving efficiency of the high-tension defection circuit and the power transformer

Source: Matsushita Electric Industrial Co.

Figure 10.2 *Reducing the greenhouse gas (GHG) factor in the television*

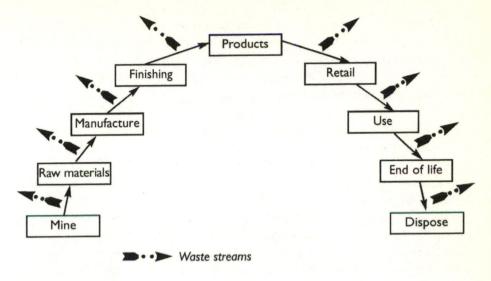

Source: The Natural Step

Figure 10.3 *Linear resource use*

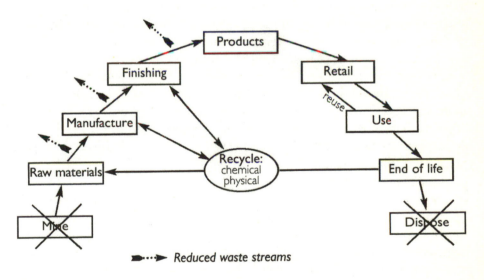

Source: The Natural Step

Figure 10.4 *Cyclical resource use*

made little effort to shift the basis of their productive economy towards such a vision.

For the reasons referred to earlier, there are many who do not subscribe to the view that even the most systematic re-engineering of our manufactured capital over a 20- to 30-year period will deliver a genuinely sustainable economy for humankind. But given that this is the most practical, deliverable and economically manageable way of getting us at least some way down that track, not to engage urgently in that process as our number one sustainability priority represents a shameful lack of political leadership and vision.

It's clear that there remains a big problem in the way in which we frame this whole question of waste and resource management. The lion's share of the work that goes into the crafting of new policy or new economic instruments has, as its principal objective, 'the reduction of waste'. Because this in itself is hard enough (in an age where simply chucking things away regardless has become standard human behaviour in far too many countries), no attempt is made to think that challenge through in terms of total resource flows, compatibility with natural systems and so on. So we tend to get very worked up about levels of recycling as the sole benchmark of success in this area without necessarily asking the more difficult questions about whether or not recycling makes much sense in either economic or thermodynamic terms. Sometimes it does, but sometimes it doesn't.

This, of course, gets very problematic for both politicians and the citizens whom they are seeking to influence on waste and recycling issues – or, indeed, on any other sustainable development issue for that matter. Try telling people that recycling can sometimes be 'bad for the environment' and there's a serious risk that people will just want to give up on the whole thing. That is why it is so misleading to think about resource flows, eco-efficiency and manufactured capital in a technocratic vacuum all of its own: all of these issues have to be seen in a much more holistic way and be embedded much more deeply in our educational systems – both formal and informal. Without a basic level of what might be called 'sustainability literacy', it's going to be extraordinarily difficult to start making the kind of lifestyle changes that are now so urgently required. Forum for the Future's Education and Learning Programme has worked hard to define exactly what sustainability literacy might look like (see Box 10.1).

One of the most stimulating voices in this debate is that of Bill McDonough, an American architect and visionary who is less and less tolerant of conventional environmental thinking. Together with Michael Braungart, he wrote a book called *Cradle to Cradle* (McDonough and Braungart, 2002), the subtext of which is 'why being less bad is actually no good', given the scale of the challenge we now face, and why our current 'cradle-to-grave' thinking is leading us down a very dangerous blind alley. He also takes a serious swipe at the World Business Council for Sustainable Development's most treasured concept – namely, eco-efficiency:

> *Eco-efficiency is an outwardly admirable, even noble, concept; but it is not a strategy for success over the long term because it does not reach deep enough. It presents little more than an illusion of change. We do not mean to lambaste those who are working with good intentions to create and enforce laws meant to protect the public good. In a world where designs*

Box 10.1 Sustainability literacy

Expressed at the highest level, a sustainability-literate person would be expected to:

- understand the need for change to a sustainable way of doing things, individually and collectively;
- have sufficient knowledge and skills to decide and act in a way that favours sustainable development; and
- be able to recognize and reward other people's decisions and actions that favour sustainable development.

Understand the need for change to a sustainable way of doing things, individually and collectively

Most people do have some understanding of what sustainable development means. However, a sustainability-literate person will have sufficient knowledge and understanding to talk to others in a positive and engaging way about matters relating to sustainable development. They will need to be able to make a coherent argument for why change in behaviour is needed and how it might happen in practice, drawing examples from their own sphere of influence and operation and linking that to their own values and to the wider context in which they live. They will be able to make links between the social, environmental and economic aspects of sustainability and make connections between their neighbourhood, their workplace and what is happening globally.

Have sufficient knowledge and skills to decide and act in a way that favours sustainable development

A sustainability-literate person will be equipped with a number of intellectual and practical tools that enable them to take decisions and act in a way that is likely to contribute positively to sustainable development. They will be able to make decisions on specific matters, such as advising on financial investment, buying food or writing new policy for prisons, by applying the 'at the same time' rule – that is, taking environmental, social and economic considerations into account simultaneously, not separately.

Be able to recognize and reward other people's decisions and actions that favour sustainable development

A key principle of reinforcing good practice or behaviour is to recognize when it is taking place and to acknowledge, if not reward, it. A sustainability-literate person will know the importance of encouraging and reinforcing behaviour that favours sustainable development.

Source: adapted from Forum for the Future's Education and Learning Programme

are unintelligent and destructive, regulations can reduce immediate deleterious effects. But, ultimately, regulation is a signal of design failure. In fact, it is what we call 'a licence to harm': a permit issued by a government to an industry so that it may dispense sickness, destruction and death at an 'acceptable' rate. But as we shall see, good design can require no regulation at all. (McDonough and Braungart, 2002)

The challenge, then, has to be articulated not in terms of being 'less unsustainable' but 'genuinely sustainable', in every particular. In advancing the alternative concept of 'eco-effectiveness', McDonough and Braungart remind us that we have to become as effective as nature in imitating the cradle-to-cradle systems of nutrient and resource flows upon which the entire system depends. 'To eliminate the concept of waste means to design things – products, packaging and systems – from the very beginning in the understanding that waste does not exist', or must cease to exist if the metabolism of the human species is eventually to align with the metabolism of the natural world. So they put their minds to coming up with the following outcomes from the design and architecture process:

- *buildings that, like trees, produce more energy than they consume and purify their own waste water;*
- *factories that produce effluents that can be used as drinking water;*
- *products that, when their useful life is over, do not become useless waste but can be tossed on to the ground to decompose and become food for plants and animals and nutrients for soil; or, alternatively, that can be returned to industrial cycles to supply high-quality raw materials for new products;*
- *billions, even trillions, of dollars' worth of materials that accrue for human and natural purposes each year;*
- *transportation that improves the quality of life while delivering goods and services;*
- *a world of abundance, not one of limits, pollution and waste.* (McDonough and Braungart, 2002)

And just in case you're starting to think that no serious text on sustainable wealth creation should provide a platform for such deranged dreamers and tree-huggers, it's worth bearing in mind that Bill McDonough's architectural firm is highly successful and is much sought after by some of the largest companies in the world – even by the Chinese Government as they develop comprehensive master plans for a whole new generation of sustainable cities.

What connects Bill McDonough and Janine Benyus is their deep understanding that the only way in which the biosphere and the technosphere can co-exist is for the technosphere to become biologically compatible with the rest of life on Earth. Our economies are ecosystems in themselves and, like any ecosystem, take in energy and materials and transform them into products. The problem is that we do it by way of linear transformation, whereas nature's transformation is cyclical.

Our economy/ecosystem is also at a very immature stage of development – what is referred to by ecologists as the 'colonizing' or 'pioneer' phase in any organism's evolution. Acting on the twin assumptions that there were no limits to our use of the natural world, and that we could lay claim to as much of its productivity and resource flow as we saw fit, the human species has opportunistically set out to colonize all but the most inhospitable habitats on Earth. In that process, we have behaved as if we were just passing through, grabbing anything we could get our hands on in the short term without any particular concern for what happens next.

We have now reached the outer limits of that ecosystem, having pretty much filled up the world in the process, and are now having to think very differently given that we've got nowhere else to move on to – which means 'living on the Earth as if we intended to stay here'. Or, as ecologists would put it, we have to evolve out of being a pioneer species into a mature species by learning to be 'self-renewing right where we are'. Again, Janine Benyus has found a compelling way of capturing what it would mean for the human species to mimic nature in that very broad systems approach:

> *Over billions of years, natural selections come up with winning strategies adopted by all complex mature ecosystems. The strategies in the following list are tried-and-true approaches to the mystery of surviving in place. Think of them as the ten commandments of the Redwood clan. Organisms in a mature ecosystem:*
>
> *1   use waste as a resource;*
> *2   diversify and cooperate to fully use the habitat;*
> *3   gather and use energy efficiently;*
> *4   optimize rather than maximize;*
> *5   use materials sparingly;*
> *6   don't foul their nests;*
> *7   don't draw down resources;*
> *8   remain in balance with the biosphere;*
> *9   run on information;*
> *10   shop locally.* (Benyus, 1997)

As we will see in Chapter 14, there are now a large number of companies intent on internalizing at least some of these ten commandments in the way that they deploy their manufactured capital. But as with the Matsushita example in this chapter, it doesn't come without a substantial investment of human and intellectual capital, backed by an equally substantial financial involvement. It is to that final stock of capital that we must now turn.

REFERENCES

Benyus, J. (1997) *Biomimicry: Innovation Inspired by Nature*, Quill, William Morrow, New York

Brown, L. (2003) *Plan B*, W. W. Norton, New York

Commoner, B. (1971) *The Closing Circle: Nature, Man, and Technology*, Random House, London

Ekins, P. (2000) *Economic Growth and Environmental Sustainability*, Routledge, London

Green Alliance (2002) *Building a Bright Green Economy*, Green Alliance, London

Hawken, P., Lovins, A. and Lovins, L. H. (1999) *Natural Capitalism*, Earthscan, London

McDonough, W. and Braungart, M. (2002) *Cradle to Cradle*, North Point Press, New York

Meadows, D., Meadows, D., Randers, J. and Behrens III, W. W. (1972) *Limits to Growth*, Universe Books, New York

11

Financial Capital

INTRODUCTION

Economists will tell you that financial capital shouldn't really be included in any model of this kind since it's not a capital stock in its own right, but just a means of exchange between other kinds of capital. That may be so, but the uses to which financial capital are put have a huge impact upon the prospects of us ever achieving a genuinely sustainable society – from the role money plays in our own lives, all the way through to the way today's capital markets operate, with their increasingly destructive emphasis on short-term profit maximization in the service of disloyal and footloose investors. That makes it all the harder for companies to balance the interests of other stakeholders, even if (as we will explore in much greater detail in Chapter 14) there now exists a robust and persuasive 'business case' for companies getting themselves sorted on their key social, environmental and ethical responsibilities. And there are still those, of course, who believe that money is indeed the root of all evil – the principal source of psychological alienation and unsustainable lifestyles in today's consumer capitalism.

DEFINING FINANCIAL CAPITAL

The role of financial capital is perhaps the least understood of all the categories of capital now seen as essential to a sustainable economic system. Indeed, it is usually excluded from such models on the grounds that financial capital has no intrinsic value, is not *essential* for the production of goods and services, and simply provides a means of exchange for the fruits of other categories of capital. Paper assets that make up the stocks of money, bonds and equities have no value in themselves, but are simply derivatives of the underlying manufactured, natural, social or human capital stocks. In that fundamental sense, financial capital is *not* a separate category to the other capital stocks, but, as will be explained in this chapter, an aspect of social capital.

FINANCIAL STOCKS AND FLOWS

But that's not the whole story. In a world where all businesses and consumers have perfect information and foresight, exchange in the marketplace would be a simple matter. Businesses seeking to invest in new manufactured capital would know who had surplus funds, and the saver or lender would know that the borrower would be able to repay the loan in the future. There would be no transaction costs associated with combining the right amounts of manufactured, human and natural capital to produce the goods and services desired. There would be no need for banks to attract and agglomerate surplus funds, or to select and monitor the projects or businesses to which they might lend. In fact, there would be no need even for the paper assets of money, bond or equity since investors would know who has surplus human or natural capital to construct the new bit of machinery required. The reason that this is not the way the world works is information or, rather, its imperfections. Imperfect information gives economic and social value to the paper assets, markets, institutions and, most importantly, social conventions that make up the stock of financial capital.

As a result of imperfect information, the paper assets of money are necessary to reduce the substantial time and effort costs of carrying out a transaction in a barter economy. Barter does still take place. (Pepsi Cola, for example, used to ship profits from Russia in the 1990s in the form of vodka, which it then sold in the US and Europe for cash). However, in mature economies, these transactions will always remain the exception because of the difficulties of satisfying the 'double coincidence of wants'. Money is the lubricant of the exchange economy.

As well as facilitating exchange, the imperfections of information mean that there is an important role for financial capital to play in the production of goods and services. That comes from the role financial markets and institutions play in allocating funds between different businesses and individual borrowers. It also derives from the social conventions that enable the paper assets, financial markets and institutions to function. Recall Putnam's (2000) definition of social capital as being 'networks', 'norms' and 'trust'. Financial markets and institutions are networks with built-in norms; and 'trust' forms a key element of financial capital. Financial markets are therefore 'network capital' in the same sense as those networks described in Chapter 9 on social capital.

They are also different from ordinary markets, which involve the contemporaneous trade of commodities. What is exchanged is money today for a promise (often vague – as with equities) of money in the future. This 'inter-temporal' trade and the risk associated with it (loans may not be repaid) are the essence of financial markets. With other markets, there is no need to select and monitor projects as the product or service just goes to the highest bidder.

Institutions such as retail and commercial banks, investment banks, asset managers and insurers provide the stocks of specialist information and expertise. They have accumulated organizational and individual knowledge on how to attract

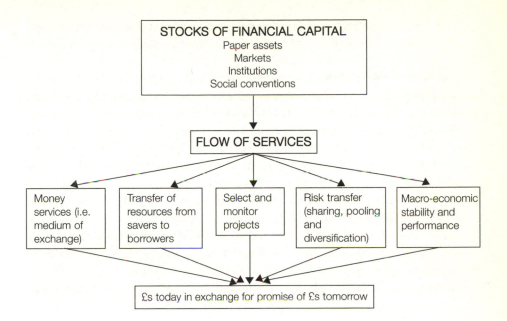

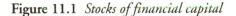

Source: Forum for the Future

Figure 11.1 *Stocks of financial capital*

the resources from savers to provide to borrowers, on how to select and monitor projects or businesses to lend to, and on how to transfer, share, pool or diversify the risks inherent in making a loan that may not be repaid (see Figure 11.1).

Social conventions are the final facet of financial capital. As with trust and norms in relation to social capital, these are also an important (if not the most important) aspect of financial capital. Dogs' teeth in the Admiralty Islands, seashells in parts of Africa, gold during the 19th century, token (notes and coins) and IOU (bank deposits) money today, internet money, time dollars in the US – all are examples of money. What matters is not the physical commodity, but the social convention or norm that it will be accepted without question as a means of payment.

The same is true with the role of financial capital in the production process. Flows of information between people and between institutions are better and higher if there are closer social relationships. Such information flows include the creditworthiness of individuals and projects. The success of micro-credit in some developing countries is a prime example of how social relationships (in selecting and monitoring projects and enforcing repayment) underpin the way in which financial capital is created and sustained.

There are a number of economic functions or services that flow from the stock of financial capital:

- *Running the medium of exchange (money).* Banks, in particular, can be thought of as running the medium of exchange, including activities such as cheque clearing.
- *Transferring resources from savers to borrowers.* In any capitalist economy, there is never a perfect coincidence between those who have funds and those who can make use of those funds. As a result, financial markets and institutions have a vital role to play in the production process by transferring resources from savers to the borrowers or investors. Banks and private equity providers are the main conduits of finance for new projects. Equity markets in the US and the UK are used mostly to trade existing paper assets rather than to raise new capital.
- *Selecting and monitoring projects.* There are always more individuals and businesses who claim to have good uses for resources than there are funds available. With perfect information, there is simply no problem with selecting and monitoring projects; in the real world, this is one of the most important functions of financial markets and institutions. For example, asset managers running socially responsible investment funds will use environmental and social screens to select and monitor equities for their investor clients.
- *Risk transfer, sharing, pooling and diversification.* Asset managers running unit trusts or mutual funds provide risk diversification services. For instance, weather-derivative markets are already providing the means for insurers to transfer the risk of losses from extreme weather events from the insurance book.
- *Macro-economic stability and performance.* As well as allocating finance between businesses and individuals, financial institutions and markets play an important role at the macro-economic level. The failure of one bank can lead to a run on the whole banking system. The Asian banking crisis of 1997 was one of the most recent examples, where poorly managed financial capital caused enormous damage to the rest of the economy.

Financial capital, like all other forms of capital, depreciates as it is used and can be degraded if abused. It needs investment and good stewardship to continue to provide the flow of services required at the same rate and quality. This involves governments, financial institutions and borrowers:

- Government financial regulation can prevent systemic collapse and 'moral hazard'. The government or central bank must stand as lender of last resort to an ailing financial institution in order to maintain the trust which forms such an important part of the fabric that makes up financial capital.
- Financial institutions can back (financially and with capacity-building) new financial intermediaries such as micro-credit and mini-enterprise lending. This extends the reach of financial capital into developing economies and the poorer regions of the developed economies.
- Borrowers can provide new information to offset some of the imperfections that give financial capital its value (and raise the cost of borrowing). By providing information and taking action in the following areas, borrowers should be able

to reduce their cost of borrowing: corporate governance structures; performance measurement (including green accounting, etc.); and transparency and accountability.

The role of governments in shaping financial markets should never be under-estimated, whatever the prevailing deregulatory rhetoric may seem to imply. Above all, incentives need to be designed in such a way that private self-interest is not incompatible with securing socially beneficial outcomes. As Stephen Young says:

> *For incentives to be properly aligned, governments must do their part. Title to property and a marketable interest, such as ownership of inventions, must be secure; contracts must be enforced; currencies must be stable; corruption must be prevented; bankruptcy laws must permit smooth realignment of interests after misjudgements have brought on business failure; information necessary for accurate valuation of assets and correct pricing must be provided openly; and financial institutions must be prevented from funding speculative bubbles.* (Young, 2003)

GOVERNANCE FAILURES

So much for the basics, in terms of understanding the role of financial capital in today's global economy. But this is not the value-free, depoliticized terrain that many would have us believe; issues regarding both the ownership and the use of financial capital go right to the heart of what sustainability means, and to the prospects of fashioning a genuinely sustainable future for humankind. As suggested in Part I, there are many aspects of contemporary capitalism that are in direct conflict with the pursuit of sustainability. There is still considerable debate as to whether these incompatibilities are structural and permanent (that is, inherent, unavoidable elements in all models of capitalism) or temporary, aberrant pheno-mena that can be transformed into a different set of system characteristics that *would* be compatible with the pursuit of sustainability. The working hypothesis in this book is that compatibility is *theoretically* available to us, even though the political and economic challenges in engineering that convergence are daunting.

In the *Divine Right of Capital*, for instance, Marjorie Kelly (2001) challenges the dominant model of contemporary shareholder capitalism in an attempt to develop a new consensus. For her, many of the fundamental attributes of capitalism (supply and demand, competition, profit, self-interest, private property and free trade) are, indeed, fine – 'sturdy, healthy and well worth keeping'. But the whole complex edifice of capitalism is for her threatened by the contemporary obsession with maximizing returns to shareholders:

> *To judge by the current arrangement in corporate America, one might suppose capital creates wealth – which is strange, because a pile of private*

> *capital sitting there creates nothing. Yet capital providers – stockholders*
> *– lay claim to most of the wealth the public corporations generate.*
> *Corporations are believed to exist to maximize returns to shareholders.*
> *This is the law of the land, much as the divine right of kings was once*
> *the law of the land. In the dominant paradigm of business, it is not in*
> *the least controversial. Though it should be.* (Kelly, 2001)

Part of Kelly's analysis as to why this approach to investment has become so dysfunctional depends upon scotching the myth that it is shareholders who create wealth through the investment they make in companies. According to figures from the Federal Reserve in the US, about $1 in $100 trading on Wall Street actually reaches companies. The other $99 are all speculatively invested. In 1999, the value of new stock sold was $106 billion; the value of all shares traded was $20.4 trillion. By the time stock buy-backs are taken into account, as well as dividends paid by companies to shareholders, an extraordinary picture emerges:

> *New equity sales were a negative source of funding in 15 out of the 20*
> *years from 1981 to 2000. In other words, when you look back over two*
> *decades, you can't find any net stockholder money going in – it's all going*
> *out. The net outflow since 1981 for new equity issues was negative $540*
> *billion. Rather than capitalizing companies, the stock market has been*
> *de-capitalizing them. Stockholders for decades have been an immense*
> *cash drain on corporations. They are the deadest of dead wood. It's*
> *inaccurate even to speak of stockholders as 'investors', for more truthfully*
> *they are 'extractors'. When we buy stock, we are not contributing capital:*
> *we are buying the right to extract wealth.* (Kelly, 2001)

This analysis has been powerfully re-enforced by Henry Mintzberg in a 'Memo to CEOs', written for *Fast Company* in June 2002. Reminding chief executive officers (CEOs) of the origins of corporations and the initial rationale behind granting them their charters – to serve society – he suggests that shareholders have essentially 'muscled out' all other stakeholders whom a company must deal with, and that CEOs have been complicit in this (inadvertently or not) given that their own remuneration over the last decade has become more and more closely tied to share price and shareholder return through stock options and other performance incentives.

There might be some justification for this approach if the majority of shareholders had any long-term commitment to the companies in which they invest – of which they are the 'theoretical' owners. In fact, investment markets today are dominated by huge funds that buy and sell millions of shares on a daily basis following a variety of tracker indexes, or by day-traders out for tiny shifts in share price. Boards of directors are in thrall to institutions and individuals who have no concern for their companies, their products and services, let alone their employees or the communities in which they are based.

As many commentators have pointed out since the collapse of Enron and other huge US companies, this servitude to detached and indifferent shareholders (mediated through hugely influential market analysts) has led to a pattern of self-serving, irresponsible and illegal behaviour that would beggar belief if it was not such a logical consequence of everything that's been going on over the last 20 years. In terms of the balance between different kinds of capital (particularly financial capital and human capital), this makes it a great deal harder to deploy capital to secure equitable and genuinely sustainable outcomes. As Henry Mintzberg says:

> *Shareholder value thus drives a wedge between those who create the economic performance and those who harvest its benefits. It is a wedge of disengagement, both between the two groups and within each. Those who create the benefits are disengaged from the ownership of their efforts and treated as dispensable, while those who own the enterprise treat that ownership as dispensable and so disengage themselves from its activities. Can we have healthy corporations, and a healthy society, without commitment?* (Mintzberg, 2002)

In effect, it's becoming clearer and clearer that we've wasted the best part of 20 years pursuing to the point of utter exhaustion a model of capitalism that can only succeed by liquidating the life-support systems that sustain us and systematically widening the 'inequity gaps' upon which any kind of social cohesion depends in the long run. It seems impossible to imagine that people will be prepared to condone such a system for very much longer; but it is a sobering thought that it's now at least 20 years since a generation of eminent economists (such as J. K. Galbraith, Robert Heilbroner and Fred Hirsch) flagged the inevitability of this particular model's failure.

These chronic dysfunctionalities now cast such a pall over the workings of the world's capital markets as to prejudice the efforts of all those working to secure a more sustainable utilization of capital within the existing system. It is an extraordinary irony that at exactly the same time as a large number of deeply immoral corporate executives were doing everything they could to line their own pockets, often at the expense of their companies and the entire system of wealth creation that supported them, a quite different group of people (made up of other business leaders, academics and progressive non-governmental organizations, or NGOs) has been seeking a radically different business model for more sustainable wealth creation.

THE BUSINESS CASE

As we will see in more detail in Chapter 14, the evolution of the so-called 'business case for sustainable development' represents an interesting shift towards 'a more successful capitalism', generating a growing amount of coverage over the last few years. At the heart of this business case is a simple but powerful proposition: if it can be demonstrated that the interests of shareholders, over time, are best served by companies that seek radically to improve their social, environment and ethical performance, then capital could be allocated against a different set of criteria, and short-term profit maximization would cease to be the driving force behind an inherently destructive model of capitalism. This, it has to be said, makes the business case for sustainable development a rather more interesting concept than those who see it primarily in terms of saving small amounts of money by installing a few energy-efficient light bulbs.

It's possible to be cautiously optimistic about such an hypothesis. In a piece of research commissioned by the Co-operative Insurance Society in 2002 (titled *Sustainability Pays*) Forum for the Future's Centre for Sustainable Investment found that the majority of academic studies carried out from the 1970s to the 1990s were able to demonstrate evidence of a positive correlation between environmentally and socially responsible business practices and financial performance. By the same token, however, there is no evidence that being green and socially responsible *always* pays. What really emerges is this: sustainable development and corporate social responsibility (CSR) *can* create shareholder value for some issues, in some industries, with some firms and for some management strategies. The question is not 'does CSR pay', but 'when does CSR pay?'

This is not as definitive and substantive a correlation as many people are looking for. But for those who can remember the days in which any environmental investment or any decision to practice more socially responsible business behaviours was dismissed as anti-business and a constraint upon improved competitiveness, such findings (confirmed by a large number of studies over the last three years) are certainly significant.

There is, of course, a conundrum here. If the business case for sustainable development is already that strong in the eyes of those companies which have started to embrace both its principles and its practice, why is there still so much inertia and indifference within the majority of large companies around the world? If a reconciliation between the pursuit of profitability and the achievement of genuine sustainability seems at least potentially feasible, looking at this collective experience, why are politicians so slow to drive those policy measures that would accelerate such a convergence? And if there would appear to be no threat to the paramount interests of shareholders (with investments in those pioneering companies generating at least average returns and possibly even some small additional premium), why are the world's capital markets still so slow to ensure that capital is being allocated in such a way as to reflect the desirability of securing the Earth's life-support systems even as we secure a good return on our investments?

Paul Gilding and his colleagues at the Ecos Corporation suggest that the answer to this problem lies in the flawed advocacy of those promoting the business case, with an overdependence on moral imperatives and an inappropriate appeal to values and ethics. For him, the primary focus should be on the financial *value* to be had in designing and implementing corporate sustainability strategies:

> *Put simply, we believe a focus on value drives change more effectively and therefore drives more change. The logic of this has three key elements:*
>
> 1 *If a business focuses on value creation when undertaking action and initiatives in the name of sustainability, it is far more likely to create value.*
> 2 *If companies consistently create, measure and report value from sustainability, then financial markets are far more likely to recognize and reward the company.*
> 3 *If investor recognition occurs, it will create a positive, self-perpetuating loop encouraging more business action on sustainability, in turn making it more likely that corporate sustainability itself will succeed in the long term.* (Gilding, 2002)

As we will see in Chapter 14, there are, indeed, many companies intent on pursuing that hard-nosed approach to defining a competitive business case for their shareholders. For other companies, that just doesn't work, culturally, in terms of the values through which they run the business. Matsushita, for instance, whose use of life-cycle analysis we looked at in Chapter 10, still follows the precept of its founder Konosuke Matsushita, embodying the notion that a company is a 'public entity of society'. Its basic management objective – 'Recognizing our responsibilities as industrialists, we will devote ourselves to the progress and development of society and the wellbeing of people through our business activities, thereby enhancing the quality of life throughout the world' – doesn't even mention shareholders. In refreshing contrast to most companies' stodgy corporate responsibility/sustainable development reports, Matsushita is quite happy to wear its heart on its sleeve in terms of its ambitions to relieve world poverty and achieve 'material and spiritual prosperity'.

One way or another, most companies are seeking out a balance between the interests/demands of their shareholders and their responsibilities to other stakeholders. Few have thought as systematically about those responsibilities as the Danish healthcare and pharmaceuticals company Novo Nordisk. In its 2002 sustainability report, it summarizes why this kind of strategic approach now works so well for them (see Figures 11.2 and 11.3).

Interestingly, Novo Nordisk is one of the few global companies to have tried to tease out the difference between its financial performance and its broader economic performance. As mentioned in Chapter 2, far too many companies have interpreted the financial element of their triple bottom line accounting in very narrow terms: profits, net present value, productivity, return on investment, and so on. But economic performance is *not* the same thing as financial performance,

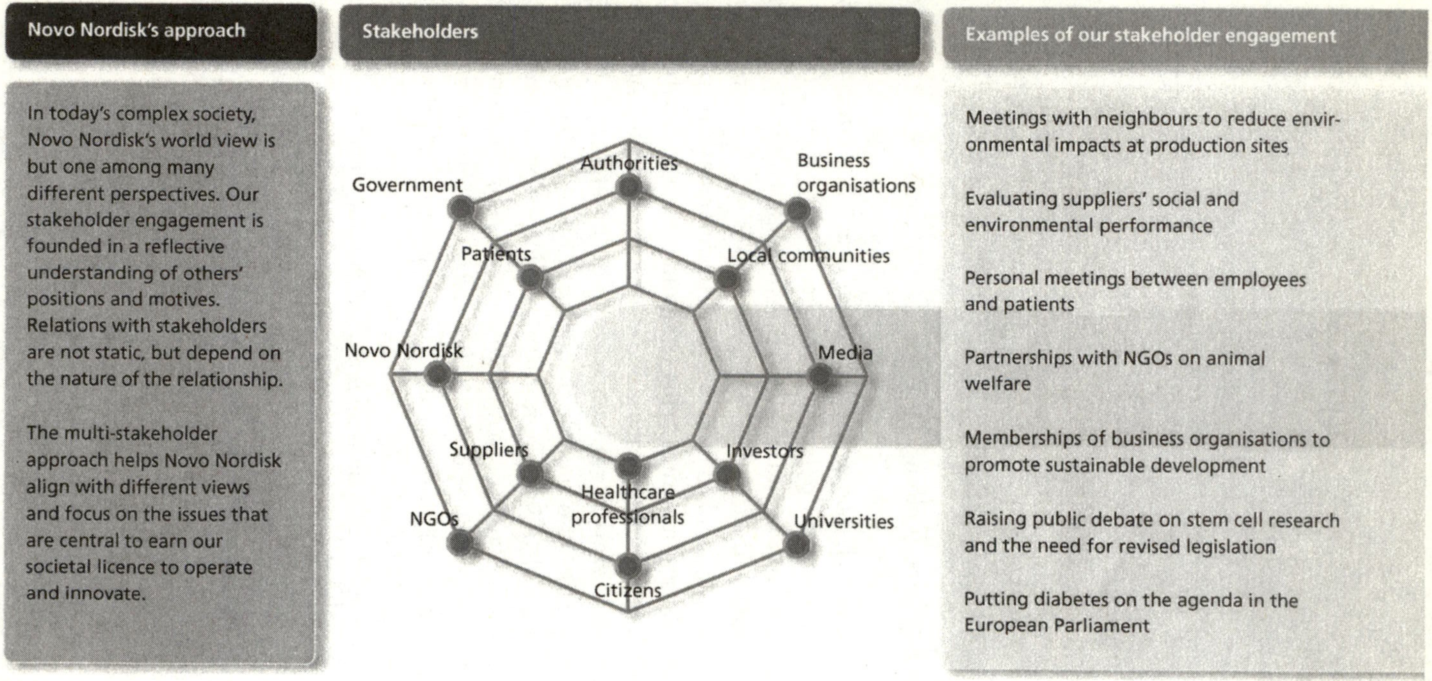

Novo Nordisk's approach	Stakeholders	Examples of our stakeholder engagement

Novo Nordisk's approach

In today's complex society, Novo Nordisk's world view is but one among many different perspectives. Our stakeholder engagement is founded in a reflective understanding of others' positions and motives. Relations with stakeholders are not static, but depend on the nature of the relationship.

The multi-stakeholder approach helps Novo Nordisk align with different views and focus on the issues that are central to earn our societal licence to operate and innovate.

Stakeholders

Business organisations
Local communities
Media
Investors
Universities
Authorities
Healthcare professionals
Citizens
Government
Patients
Novo Nordisk
Suppliers
NGOs

Examples of our stakeholder engagement

Meetings with neighbours to reduce environmental impacts at production sites

Evaluating suppliers' social and environmental performance

Personal meetings between employees and patients

Partnerships with NGOs on animal welfare

Memberships of business organisations to promote sustainable development

Raising public debate on stem cell research and the need for revised legislation

Putting diabetes on the agenda in the European Parliament

Figure 11.2 *Novo Nordisk's engagement with its stakeholders*

Source: Novo Nordisk Sustainability Report (2002)

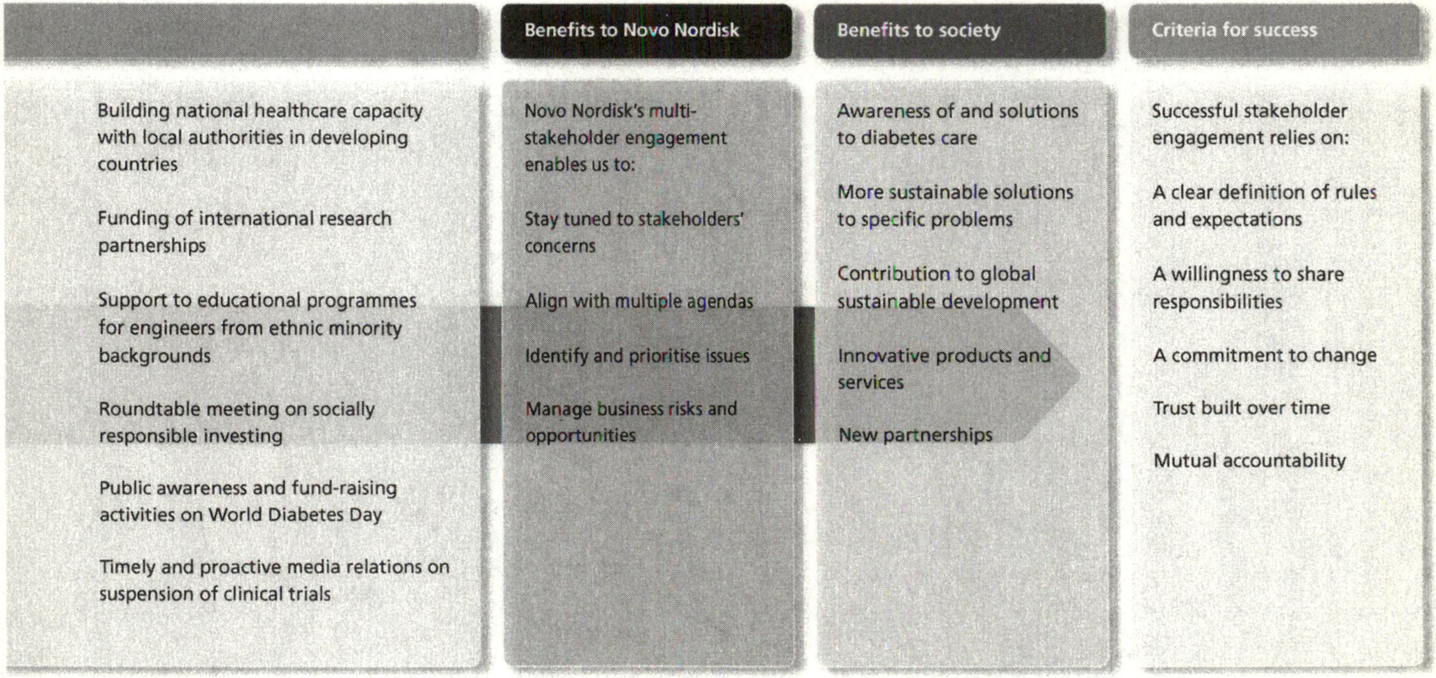

Benefits to Novo Nordisk

Novo Nordisk's multi-stakeholder engagement enables us to:

Stay tuned to stakeholders' concerns

Align with multiple agendas

Identify and prioritise issues

Manage business risks and opportunities

Building national healthcare capacity with local authorities in developing countries

Funding of international research partnerships

Support to educational programmes for engineers from ethnic minority backgrounds

Roundtable meeting on socially responsible investing

Public awareness and fund-raising activities on World Diabetes Day

Timely and proactive media relations on suspension of clinical trials

Benefits to society

Awareness of and solutions to diabetes care

More sustainable solutions to specific problems

Contribution to global sustainable development

Innovative products and services

New partnerships

Criteria for success

Successful stakeholder engagement relies on:

A clear definition of rules and expectations

A willingness to share responsibilities

A commitment to change

Trust built over time

Mutual accountability

Figure 11.3 *Novo Nordisk's strategic approach to sustainability*

Source: Novo Nordisk Sustainability Report (2002)

as is now much more clearly laid out in the latest version of the Global Reporting Initiative's *Sustainability Reporting Guidelines*. Companies are now expected to provide information on where they generate their income, on taxes paid, on how different stakeholders benefit from their activities and other 'economic multipliers'. To assist in that process, the Novo Nordisk economic stakeholder model (as represented in its 2002 sustainability report) demonstrates the kind of progressive thinking that will soon become part and parcel of all leading companies' perform- ance assessment (see Figure 11.4).

It also provides an annual breakdown of exactly how the income it generates is used in terms of payments to suppliers, salaries for employees, dividends for share- holders, taxes for local and national governments, and research and development investments to secure the future prosperity of the company. Again, measures of this kind are gradually becoming more common throughout the world's leading companies. This recognition of the importance of addressing *all* externalities (social, economic and environmental – both positive and negative) will clearly allow companies to give a much better account of the way in which they are managing their financial capital.

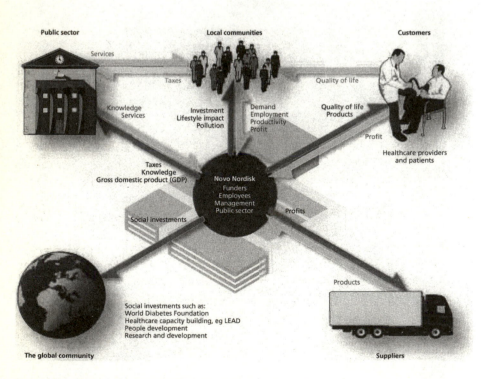

Source: Novo Nordisk Sustainability Report (2002)

Figure 11.4 *Novo Nordisk's economic stakeholder model*

Measured against Alfred Rappaport's *Creating Shareholder Value* (1998) (which analyses shareholder value in terms of sales growth rate, profit margins, fixed capital investment, working capital investment, competitive advantage period, cost of capital and taxation levels), there is no doubt these days that corporate sustainability can and does create value. In some areas, these benefits are tangible (in terms of monetary value) and, in other areas, more intangible. But all ultimately translate into conventional financial performance, and that is where they will need to be judged: in their capacity to increase margins, grow revenue, reduce risk and increase capital efficiency.

But how best to determine which actions will most powerfully reinforce such a business case? From the perspective of natural capital, we have already suggested that The Natural Step framework offers one of the few authoritative ways of assessing whether or not any proposed new investment will be working to maintain or enhance stocks of natural capital. From a financial perspective, there are familiar techniques that are just as relevant here as with any other investment decision. Some of these are briefly explored in *To Whose Benefit: Building a Business Case for Sustainability*, co-sponsored by the World Wide Fund for Nature (WWF) and Cable and Wireless (2001). These include return on capital employed; economic value added; weighted average cost of capital; and discounted cash flow. As the report says:

> *The application of standard business evaluation and assessment tools may help companies to communicate their proposed strategies to financial stakeholders, using standard business terms. The application of financial performance tools will also provide a consistent framework for monitoring progress during the implementation phase of the business case. Such actions may, in turn, serve to prompt equity market managers to take wider consideration of the potential opportunities and threats associated with sustainability issues.* (WWF and Cable and Wireless, 2001)

There has been much discussion about the business case for sustainable development over the last few years, but very few hard-edged attempts at measuring it in any serious way. The Co-op Bank and BT (see Chapter 14) have made notable efforts at measuring the value to their shareholders of their ethical and CSR policies. However, the numbers revealed are usually small. The response of analysts whom they are trying to impress has usually been 'So what? This tells me nothing of what is really driving the success of your company.' A huge opportunity is being missed by the concentration on eco-efficiency, cost savings and 'green premiums' by most valuation efforts to date. The real *business* value of sustainability must come from the added value it generates for that particular company, for the ways in which it protects and develops that company's strategic assets, and the competitive advantage that flows from the responsible use of all five stocks of capital.

Bringing financial capital down to Earth

All of this is genuinely encouraging in terms of promoting more environmentally and socially responsible behaviour within the existing economic and financial structures. But if those structures are themselves dysfunctional and incapable of delivering genuine sustainability, then what we're really talking about here is damage limitation rather than transformation. This means that we cannot any longer put off the need for far more radical proposals regarding the way in which financial capital is created, distributed, owned and used. David Korten doesn't beat around the bush in identifying the root cause of our current problems:

> The problem is this: a predatory global financial system, driven by the single imperative of making ever more money for those who already have lots of it, is rapidly depleting the real capital – the human, social, natural and even physical capital – upon which our wellbeing depends. Pathology enters the economic system when money, once convenient as a means of facilitating commerce, comes to define the life purpose of individuals and society. The truly troubling part is that so many of us have become willing accomplices to what is best described as a war of money against life. It starts, in part, from our failure to recognize that money is not wealth. In our confusion, we concentrate on the money to the neglect of those things that actually sustain a good life. (Korten, 1997)

But what can we do about it? Some, as we saw in Chapter 8, prescribe a decade-long process of 'metaphysical reconstruction' (as Fritz Schumacher described it) to restore a proper sense of value and balance in people's lives; others, as we've seen, dream of a great global movement gathering enough momentum to compel politicians to dethrone both the elites and the redundant economic orthodoxies that still dominate out lives; most campaigners chip away at the edges, looking for the occasional opening that allows the breadth of more radical reform to enter into what they see as a seriously corrupted system. But it is extremely difficult for most people to get a sense of the ferment of ideas that is going on out there given that our mainstream media rarely, if ever, reach out beyond the completely safe confines of financial orthodoxy.

Why is it, for instance, that we are never invited to think more creatively about the question of monetary reform and the impact that today's monetary system has upon the pursuit of sustainability? Social justice campaigners are understandably focused on questions of debt, aid and trade in their tireless efforts to find a more equitable set of global financial arrangements – but rarely question the monetary system itself. Environmental campaigners focus on taxation issues, perverse subsidies, improved accounting systems and so on, but are about as interested in monetary reform as they are in the issue of population.

James Robertson has been proposing radical ideas ever since his ground-breaking book *The Sane Alternative* in 1978. His most recent publication is *Monetary Reform: Making it Happen*, co-authored with John M. Bunzl (2003), focusing on the utterly perverse way in which money supply is managed in almost all countries. For instance, about 97 per cent of the UK's money supply is created by commercial banks more or less out of thin air as interest-bearing (profit-making) loans; the remaining 3 per cent is created debt-free by the Bank of England and the Royal Mint as bank notes and coins. The banks in the UK make about £20 billion a year in interest from this arrangement.

It is pretty much the same situation all around the world, and one wonders quite how we've allowed ourselves to get into that situation – as J. K. Galbraith himself put it: 'The process by which banks create money is so simple the mind is repelled . . . where something so important is involved, a deeper mystery seems only decent' (Galbraith, 1975). The money supply created in this way is not linked to real resource use or to the amount of goods and services in the national economy – it is based entirely upon the banks' commercial judgement about the ability of an individual or an enterprise to repay their loans. The more money there is, the more debt there is; as the money supply increases, so does a nation's indebtedness.

Robertson's proposal (backed by a growing number of experts in this area) is a simple but comprehensive one: take away this power from the commercial banks and transfer it to the Bank of England, which can then give the money debt free to the government to spend into circulation. In one fell swoop, taxation can either be substantially reduced or public spending substantially increased; a debt-free money supply will help reduce levels of public and private debt; the economy will become more stable; the Bank of England will be better able to control inflation; and, lastly, environmental stress will be reduced. When, as now, almost all of the money we use is debt, people have to produce and sell more things in order to service and repay debt than they would if money were put into circulation debt free.

Many now believe that without that kind of monetary reform, we are unlikely to sort out the huge problems that confront benefits and welfare systems throughout the rich world. Over the last few decades, there have been all sorts of proposals to replace the UK's intensely complicated, costly and fundamentally unfair benefits system with some kind of 'citizens' income' – also known as the basic income, social dividend or negative income tax. One stalwart in these debates is Clive Lord, whose short primer (*A Citizens' Income: A Foundation for a Sustainable World*, 2003) on this neglected yet critical area of radical reform raises a profound challenge for mainstream political parties in the UK:

> *The citizens' income is the principle that every man, woman and child should receive a weekly sum sufficient to cover the basic needs of food, fuel, clothing and accommodation. It will be tax-free, paid to individuals and unconditional. So everyone will keep it whether they are working or not, or even whether they need it or not. The citizens' income*

will replace all existing social security benefits and income tax allowances for the able bodied. In short, the citizens' income is the unconditional provision of basic necessities for all from a common fund, provided by members of the community as a whole according to their ability to pay.
(Lord, 2003)

Again, this is not something that most environmentalists (or even, it has to be said, most campaigners for a more equitable economy) have paid much attention to. It just doesn't seem to command the same level of political engagement, even though, over the years, a surprising number of eminent economists have ended up acknowledging just how significant a reform this could be – including those polar opposites of Milton Friedman, on the one hand, and J. K. Galbraith on the other. As Margaret Legum (2002) points out in *It Doesn't Have to Be Like This* (which includes one of the best expositions of the benefits of a citizens' income or basic income), there are now groups actively involved in researching or promulgating similar approaches in Holland, Ireland, Spain, Sweden, France, Germany, New Zealand, Australia, Brazil, Canada and the US – as well as the UK. By her reckoning, 'Brazil is out in front. Some municipalities are already paying something like a basic income grant as a monthly payment to households, not individuals. Research already shows that where the household grant is in place, employment rises and crime drops' (Legum, 2002).

On the whole question of ownership, we would appear yet again to be stuck in some very predictable tramlines. If private property is one of those fundamental characteristics of capitalism (as briefly explored in Chapter 4), then a constant examination of the ease with which people can get access to the ownership of land and other assets, or the use of credit, is obviously critical. I have already mentioned the work of the Peruvian economist Hernando de Soto, whose hugely stimulating book *The Other Path* (1989) documents in great detail how lack of secure title for poor people in developing countries seriously inhibits economic development. As one concrete example of what a difference this can make, he cites a study showing that investment in home improvements increased ninefold when squatters in townships around Lima gained title to their homes. Throughout South America, land on which there is no secure title is often overexploited by peasant farmers who have no expectation of settled residence; 'land stewardship' becomes a meaningless nonsense without that kind of security.

Closer to home, the American lawyer and activist Jeff Gates has campaigned strenuously to show how extending access to various ownership opportunities can work directly for a more sustainable economy. *The Ownership Solution* (Gates, 1998) is an extraordinary book that starts from the premise that the real problem with capitalism today is that there are so few practising capitalists! Ownership of assets is restricted to such a tiny number of people that the momentum towards increased inequity and injustice is all but unstoppable. Starting with the already familiar (employee share-ownership schemes, for instance, or co-operatives), he then reviews a battery of different ways in which 'a pragmatic ownership strategy could weave a broader web of personal, economic and civic participation'.

Some of the alternatives are already quietly getting on with things out of the public eye. Perhaps the best known of these in the UK is the John Lewis Partnership, or United Airlines in the US, which is 55 per cent employee owned. One of my favourites is the Scott Bader Commonwealth, a successful chemical company founded in 1921 and reconstituted as a charitable trust in 1951. Its founder, Ernest Bader, believed passionately that 'a world where capital employs labour is not sustainable, and that labour should employ capital, acknowledging the quality of everyone as individuals'. Membership of the Commonwealth, and with it, co-ownership of the various operating companies, is open to all employees once they have worked for the company for a specific period of time. It remains a successful enterprise – and a hugely inspiring example that it really is possible to do things differently.

But there is so much more that could be done in this area, especially by those who are concerned for the future of capitalism itself. As Jeff Gates says:

> Today's capitalism embodies a curious and dangerous inconsistency. It extols the necessity of private ownership. Yet, while the capital is there and so is the capitalism, what's missing are people who can rightly be called capitalists. The reason for this is poorly understood: contemporary capitalism is not designed to create capitalists, but to finance capital. Without political will those dramatically different goals will never be combined. A more participatory capitalism could gradually displace today's exclusive, detached and socially corrosive ownership patterns. (Gates, 1998)

Many people have commented on the arrogance of the capitalist establishments in the Western world, particularly in New York and London, with their constant barrage of propaganda about the ineffable superiority of their particular model of capitalism. In fact, we might have just as much to learn from other countries as they do from us, and the inspiring example of the Grameen Bank in Bangladesh provides an excellent example of that kind of reverse flow of intellectual capital. One of the pioneers of today's micro-credit movement, the Grameen Bank makes small loans available to groups of women who don't meet conventional loan criteria simply because they don't have enough collateral. The bonds between the women in each group provide the critical social capital, based upon informal networks and trust as well as the final sanction that the members of the group accept joint responsibility for repayment. The success of the Grameen Bank has had a huge impact, as the Worldwatch Institute points out:

> The economic payoff of these types of social connectedness has made micro-credit successful in many parts of the world. The Grameen Bank

claims that 98 per cent of its micro-credit loans are repaid, a better record than in most commercial banks. Grameen has inspired the spread of micro-credit globally. An initiative known as the Micro-credit Summit Campaign has set a goal of enrolling 100 million people in micro-credit programmes by 2005. By the end of 2002, they were more than halfway there, with 68 million people participating. (Worldwatch Institute, 2004)

In the following chapters, we look at what all of this means in more operational terms.

REFERENCES

de Soto, H. (1989) *The Other Path,* Harper & Row, New York, NY

Galbraith, J. K. (1975) *Money: Whence It Came, Where It Went,* Houghton Mifflin, Boston, MA

Gates, J. (1998) *The Ownership Solution,* Penguin, London

Gilding, P. (2002) *Sustaining Economic Value,* Ecos Corporation, Sydney, Australia

Kelly, M. (2001) *The Divine Right of Capital,* Berrett-Koehler, San Francisco

Korten, D. (1997) 'Money versus wealth', *Yes! A Journal of Positive Futures,* spring, www.hackvan.com/pub/stig/articles/yes-magazine-money-issue/Korten.html

Legum, M. (2002) *It Doesn't Have to Be Like This,* Wild Goose Publications, Glasgow, UK

Lord, C. (2003) *A Citizens' Income: A Foundation for a Sustainable World,* Jon Carpenter Publishing, Charlbury, UK

Mintzberg, H. (2002) 'Memo to CEOs', *Fast Company,* June

Novo Nordisk (2002) 'Sustainability report 2002', available at http://susrep2002.novonordisk.com/sustainability/default.asp

Putnam, R. (2000) *Bowling Alone: The Collapse and Revival of American Community,* Simon and Schuster, New York

Rappaport, A. (1998) *Creating Shareholder Value,* Free Press, New York

Robertson, J. (1978) *The Sane Alternative,* James Robertson, Cholsey, UK

Robertson, J. and Bunzl, J. M. (2003) *Monetary Reform: Making it Happen,* International Simultaneous Policy Organization, London

Worldwatch Institute (2004) *State of the World 2004: Progress Towards a Sustainable Society,* Earthscan, London

WWF (World Wide Fund for Nature) and Cable and Wireless (2001) *To Whose Benefit: Building a Business Case for Sustainability,* WWF, Gland, Switzerland

Young, S. (2003) Moral Capitalism: Reconciling Private Interest with the Public Good, Berrett-Koehler, San Francisco, CA

PART III

BETTER LIVES IN A BETTER WORLD

12

Confronting Denial

INTRODUCTION

Sticking with the hypothesis that it's theoretically possible to transform the workings of contemporary capitalism in order to achieve a sustainable economy, you have then got to ask why it is proving so difficult to address that transformative challenge – bringing us back to the uncomfortable but pervasive phenomenon of *denial*. As we saw in Chapter 1, it's all but impossible to ignore the accelerating decline in our life-support systems; yet politicians seem paralysed by the immensity of the changes required. What this means is that we have to completely rethink our understanding of *security*. The billions of dollars we currently spend on arms and military security (not least on the increasingly costly 'war against terror') are systematically undermining the ecological and social conditions upon which our long-term security actually depends. The continuing dependence of the US upon wholly unsustainable supplies of oil, particularly in the Middle East, inflicts massive direct and indirect costs on both its own citizens and the rest of the world, hampering efforts to address issues of chronic poverty in developing countries and equally pressing issues of collapsing natural systems. But why is it that environmentalists have failed to make a more compelling case for change?

THE CAPACITY FOR DENIAL

The Five Capitals Framework presented in Part II draws upon ideas from many different disciplines: economics, ecology, sociology, psychology and so on. This does not as yet constitute a fully worked-up reform agenda for capitalism; but what it does seek to do is provide the context within which that all-important question about the compatibility between capitalism and sustainability can be pursued.

That still won't make it appealing to mainstream politicians. Their capacity for denial remains extraordinary, not so much in terms of denial of the empirical environmental and social data (which is by now largely undeniable), but rather denial of the implications of that data. In *Seeing Green* (Porritt, 1984), I wrote about the 'Faustian bargain' that people in the developed world had implicitly signed up to through the post-World War II period, during which environmental quality and social justice were increasingly traded off against growing prosperity and consumption (unknowingly traded off, to begin with, as the data about the impact of this particular model of progress on the planet and its people was largely unavailable before the mid 1980s). These days, it's very different. The data is now amassed by official government scientists, independent academics and international agencies all around the world. It tells them pretty much the same story, establishing a far-reaching consensus which is not fundamentally undermined by the views of dissenting contrarians, even though people's confidence in that consensus may be weakened as a consequence of never quite knowing who to trust.

As to the ways in which people interpret that data, it's a different story. For most, the basic model of progress (achieved through unfettered growth in an increasingly global economy) still remains sound, requiring only a little bit of market-based corrective action for the environment and more concerted efforts to address poverty in the world's poorest countries. A few, however, are beginning to question and even lose faith in the model itself; and one particular aspect of our Faustian bargain (that it is acceptable to trash the planet for a better life today) looks increasingly suspect.

ECOLOGICAL DECLINE REVISITED

It is still the case, however, that the debate about the scale and speed of today's ecological crisis is not an easy one to track, and because it has been rumbling on for more that three decades – albeit episodically and inadequately – there is an understandable assumption across society that so much worrying away at something *must* have got it all sorted out by now. As we saw in Chapter 1, some things do, indeed, get sorted – such as the gradual recovery of the protective ozone layer after prompt action was taken more than 15 years ago to eliminate the use of most ozone-depleting chemicals. However, the fact that it will take at least 40 years to restore the ozone layer to its proper state is a cautionary aspect of this success story that all too often gets overlooked. Indeed, recent evidence from the United Nations Environment Programme (UNEP) on the scale of smuggling in ozone-depleting chemicals demonstrates that even this isn't quite the 'done deal' that it is customarily portrayed as.

Beyond that, in the developed world at least, the consequence of at least 30 years' worth of environmental regulation has ensured significant improvements in the quality of our drinking water and bathing waters, a reduction in the use of toxic chemicals, improvements in local air quality (in most, if not all, places) and so on.

There are, therefore, enough success stories to encourage the so-called 'cornucopians' (those who trust in the 'limitless bounty' of the Earth and in its capacity for self-healing) to continue to dismiss environmentalists as an irritating swarm of whining Cassandras and Jeremiahs with nothing better to do than promise imminent doom. The latest in a long line of these cornucopian contrarians is Bjorn

Lomborg, whose book *The Skeptical Environmentalist* (2001) created an absolute furore about the degree to which the natural world was or wasn't falling to pieces.

Lomborg was a gift for most countries' predominantly right-wing media, allowing them to vent their accumulated spleen at a global environment movement that has consistently chipped away at their own complacency and subservience to big business. Unfortunately for them, their star contrarian flew a bit too close to the sun and plummeted Icarus-like to Earth when the Danish Committee on Scientific Dishonesty came to the conclusion that his book was 'clearly contrary to the standards of good scientific practice. Objectively speaking, the publication of the work under consideration is deemed to fall within the concept of scientific dishonesty.' This won't necessarily deter future media-savvy contrarians. They know only too well how easy it is to play to the media's love of engineering a good debate: now that there is almost universal consensus about the seriousness of today's ecological crisis, the dissenters inevitably become much more interesting even as they become more extreme and more detached from the data.

However, it may just be that the seriousness of climate change has at last fixed itself in the minds of enough decision-makers to warrant more of a sense of urgency about the need for change. The extraordinary climatic events that we see more and more of every year can just about be dismissed as 'extreme but still entirely natural phenomena, the like of which have been seen many times before'; but as we saw in Chapter 1, it's getting harder and harder to get away with this kind of denial. The World Meteorological Organization (a deeply cautious and even conservative organization) issued an uncompromising warning to politicians in July 2003 that events of this kind were getting more frequent, more serious and much more costly. Sir John Houghton (the UK's most eminent climate scientist) hit the headlines in 2003 with a trenchant attack on the supine response of world leaders, contrasting their paralysis in the face of climate change to their resolve in dispatching Saddam Hussein:

> *If political leaders have one duty above all others, it is to protect the security of their people. Thus it was, according to the prime minister, to protect Britain's security against Saddam Hussein's weapons of mass destruction that this country went to war in Iraq. And yet, our long-term security is threatened by a problem at least as dangerous as chemical, nuclear or biological weapons, or indeed international terrorism: human-induced climate change. I have no hesitation in describing it as a 'weapon of mass destruction'.* (Houghton, 2003)

Climate change is now very high on the international agenda, notwithstanding the intransigence of George Bush and his oil-corrupted administration. But many other issues are not on the agenda. It is clear, for instance, from reports coming in from all over the world and particularly from Indonesia and other countries in South-East Asia, that the world's tropical forests are being destroyed at as fast a rate today as when Friends of the Earth first forced this issue on to the global agenda during the mid 1980s. Twenty years on, and the forests are still coming down. Unfortunately, that's true of all too many global issues, as the Earthwatch Institute's authoritative *State of the World* reports make clear year after year. We may have slowed the rate of decline, but almost *all* of the principal indicators of planetary wellbeing are still heading in the wrong direction.

In *Collapse*, Jared Diamond (2005) explores the phenomenon of denial in relation to earlier societies and civilizations (such as the Maya civilization) which disappeared off the face of the earth because of a failure to manage natural resources properly. His most lovingly developed case study is Easter Island ('the clearest example of a society that destroyed itself by overexploiting its own resources'), which he invites the reader to see as a 'metaphor, a worst-case scenario for what may lie ahead of us in our own future'. How could this particular collapse have happened? Or, as one of Diamond's own students put it to him, 'What do you suppose the islander who cut down the last tree on Easter Island said to himself as he was doing it?' Given that in this instance there was no extreme shift in the island's climate at that time and no hostile invaders, why would any group of people commit 'ecocide' in such a dramatic fashion?

Diamond advances a number of potential explanations to that question (in relation to *all* of the different collapses and near collapses that he explores). And a number of these explanations have direct relevance to our own ecological crisis: a failure to anticipate future consequences; an inability to read trends or see behind the phenomenon of 'creeping normalcy', with each year things getting just a little bit worse than the year before, but never bad enough for anyone to get too agitated; and the disproportionate power of detached elites, particularly when they condone or even positively promote what Diamond describes as 'rational bad behaviour' on the part of those who manage or use natural resources.

In Chapter 14, I will be focusing on the more benign influence of multi-nationals in promoting a more sustainable world. But their role as 'rational bad actors' over the last 40 years or more cannot go un-remarked, not least because of the horrifying legacy (environmental, social and economic) that their activities have left behind (on a continuing basis) in literally dozens of developing countries which they purported to be assisting. Much of this goes back to the phenomenon of 'licensed cost externalization', where governments set standards so low (and consumers have correspondingly low expectations) that companies can quite legally pollute, degrade, exploit and cause irreversible ecological damage and lasting social misery.

There are now many accounts of this kind of 'rational' bad behaviour. I've already commented on Robert F. Kennedy's extraordinary book *Crimes Against Nature* (2004), which lays bare a litany of corporate greed and malpractice. But John Perkins's *Confessions of an Economic Hit Man* (2004) digs even deeper into the warped psychology of the individuals involved in this asset-stripping 'corpora-tocracy', revealing in extraordinary detail the conjunction of interests between an imperialistic US and large American companies securing massive development and infrastructure contracts all around the world – with America's 'national interest' top of the list of priorities:

> The 'corporatocracy' is not a conspiracy, but its members do endorse common values and goals. One of the corporatocracy's most important functions is to perpetuate and continually expand and strengthen the system. The lives of those who 'make it' and their accoutrements – their mansions, yachts and private jets – are presented as models to inspire us all to consume, consume, consume. Every opportunity is taken to convince us that purchasing things is our civic duty, that pillaging the Earth is good for the economy and therefore serves our higher interest. (Perkins, 2004)

This is, indeed, at one level, perfectly rational behaviour on the part of the individuals and the corporations involved. At an individual level, most would consider such behaviour to be deeply immoral, however rational it might be. But as we have seen, denial of this kind depends, in part, on maintaining the myth of the *amoral* corporation and on the 'separation of functions' which allows the same person to behave one way in his/her business life and quite differently as a mother or father or 'pillar of the local community'. The irrationality usually lies elsewhere – in those who license such behaviour for perverted ideological reasons (such as the neo-conservative empire-builders in Washington today), notwithstanding the growing body of evidence that this particular model of economic warfare is entirely unsustainable in both ecological and social terms, and in those who continue to elect such governments even as they turn a blind eye to the symptoms of chronic failure all around them.

Having reviewed a wide range of collapses and near collapses, Jared Diamond spends an equal amount of time dissecting those 'irrational' manifestations of denial. The often irreconcilable clash between the pursuit of short-term gratification and the defence of future generations' long-term interests features prominently in many of his collapse case studies – the concept of 'intergenerational justice' was clearly no more compelling to some of these long-gone societies than it is for us today. What's more, the greater the level of change required to a society's core values, the easier it becomes to lapse into systematic and falsely reassuring denial. Anticipating a wide range of rebuttals to his central hypothesis (that the kind of collapse experienced by many cultures and civilizations during the past could easily happen to modern-day societies), he reminds people that we are *already* witnessing the conditions for collapse in a number of different countries:

> Just as in the past, countries that are environmentally stressed, overpopulated or both become at risk of getting politically stressed, and of their governments collapsing. When people are desperate, undernourished and

without hope, they blame their governments, which they see as responsible
for or unable to solve their problems. They try to emigrate at any cost.
They fight each other over land. They kill each other. They start civil
wars. They figure that they have nothing to lose, so they become terrorists,
or they support or tolerate terrorism. (Diamond, 2005)

Many of us can more or less recognize this from afar, somewhat murkily, and can instinctively recognize that this is a highly probable set of generic consequences that have been set in train by policies and events stretching back over many decades. The sight of more than 1 million people marching through the streets of London (and millions more around the world) in opposition to the war in Iraq in 2003 provided powerful testimony that very large numbers of people remain entirely unpersuaded by the geopolitical game plan being played out by Washington and its more compliant allies. But there is still enough residual comfort in 'better the devil you know than the devil you don't' mindsets to ensure that the alternatives often command little mainstream support.

This same combination of constant but low-level ill ease, compounded by a somewhat fatalistic sense of there not being very much that anyone can do about it, can be seen to be operating at the personal level as well as the geopolitical level. Surveys across the world (in rich and poor countries) demonstrate that people do, indeed, care about the state of the environment, particularly in terms of their own local environment. Where once environmental damage was accepted as the inevitable price to be paid for economic progress, there is now far less willingness to accept this as an unavoidable trade-off: why can't we have both economic progress and a secure, healthy environment?

However, there is also a school of thought (predominantly but not exclusively associated with the more extreme fringes of today's neo-conservative ideology) that this kind of meta-trade-off – humankind prospering, planet degrading – is rational, legitimate and not immoral. For such people, the concept of intergenerational justice (what one generation owes future generations) is philosophically flawed and a dangerous irrelevance; if people today are that concerned about the future, then they should reflect this in their own behaviour as an individual consumer and not expect governments to 'distort' markets today in the forlorn hope of protecting the interests of people tomorrow. In these terms, politics is quite simply about the maximization of short-term individual gratification – a somewhat dispiriting reflection on that Enlightenment ideal of the perfectibility of humankind.

There is a deeply disturbing religious aspect to this, which I've touched on a number of times during this work. Understandably, much of the commentary today is about the potential 'clash of civilizations' between Christianity, on the one hand, and Islam, on the other. But in many respects, it's 'the clash of Christianities' that is at least as important, with liberal, progressive Christians fighting on two fronts: against the absolutist 'moral' intolerance of the Catholic Church against women and responsible family planning (is it really possible that a new 21st-century

Pope will perpetuate the incomprehensibly cruel dogma of his predecessor in decreeing that the use of condoms cannot even be condoned within a conjugal relationship where one partner has contracted HIV/AIDS and the other has not?), and against the millenarian madness of huge numbers of Christian fundamentalists in the US.

The fact that UK Prime Minister Tony Blair, himself a profound and genuine Christian, should find himself so closely aligned politically with an American administration so powerfully influenced by millenarian fundamentalism is a source of continuing bemusement to those who see him as a strong, moral and decent man. Are his security advisers briefing him properly on the Project for the New American Century, on the implications of the influence of pre-millenarian fundamentalism on US foreign policy, and on the views of Dick Cheney, Paul Wolfowitz and President Bush himself? Michael Northcott brings forward a powerful indictment on that score:

> *Political economists who describe modern government in terms of rational constitutions, social contracts and the 'laws' of supply and demand disable a proper understanding of the apocalyptic spirit that drives the politics of American empire, the civil religion that sacralizes it and the idolatrous rituals of consumerism which it sustains. Like so many of the emperors and monarchs of what came to be known as Christendom, Bush and his speech writers use a distortion of Christian apocalyptic, combined with American civil religion, to legitimate and sacralize imperial violence.*
>
> *That Christian ethics can be put to such use is perhaps the greatest indictment of Christianity for many secular humanists in the first decade of the third millennium. Were more Christians in America, Britain and beyond to recover the radical Christianity of the founder, then the abuse of religion by political leaders and by terrorists to sacralize their wars, and their apocalyptic divisions of humanity into the wicked and the righteous, would be undermined.* (Northcott, 2004)

PRIORITIZING POVERTY

Against that kind of bizarre background, it has often been difficult to unpick today's 'rational bad behaviour' from such irrational bad behaviour in the world's most powerful nation. Whatever the source of that bad behaviour, the impact of it upon the rest of the world has been enormous, particularly on the 2 or 3 billion people who have yet to see any real improvement in their material circumstances notwithstanding the astonishing increase in the sum of wealth created through the global economy.

It's not hard to feel overwhelmed at the sheer scale and persistence of poverty in so many parts of the world. But one of the great things about the Make Poverty History campaign, and all the new energy brought to bear on debt relief and trade issues through 2005, was the constant refrain that there really is something we can do about this. Over the last few years, far too many people have settled into a somewhat fatalistic state of mind about this state of affairs: such poverty is certainly unfortunate and disturbing, but probably inevitable; a lot of it is 'their own fault' anyway – because of endemic corruption, political incompetence and a continuing failure to get on top of the problem of rising populations – so does it really make much difference what we do when we can do so little?

Development organizations and developing world charities have to struggle against this downbeat and often deliberately distorted worldview. In seeking to demonstrate both the effectiveness of international aid and the readiness of the political leadership of the world's poorest countries to deploy that international aid equitably and transparently, they have often ended up downgrading the importance of corruption – which remains one of the most serious barriers to eliminating poverty in literally dozens of countries. Denying the seriousness of this issue has damaged the credibility of many development organizations, providing powerful ammunition to those on the right who despise the very idea of international aid. But even once one takes corruption more fully into account than is usually the case, the balance sheet of the international development movement is not a brilliant one 60 years on from that extraordinary moment in human history when world leaders came together in the aftermath of World War II to fashion a new international order that (it was hoped) would eliminate poverty and keep all conflicts in check:

> *Half a century is enough for the system to have proved itself, and while there are a few well-publicized success stories, there has been no general gain in prosperity or security. We still live in a world scarred by absolute poverty (with 1.3 billion people living on less than $1 a day), rising inequality both within and between countries, and continuing ethnic conflict. Foreign aid is declining almost everywhere, assailed by critics from across the ideological spectrum. The end of the Cold War has not revitalized international cooperation, as many had hoped, and support for military intervention in conflict zones has fallen away since the debacles in Somalia and the Balkans. The United Nations and other international bureaucracies are under constant threat: and even support for NGOs – the darlings of the development world – seems to have peaked. The international business of helping is in serious trouble.*
> (Edwards, 1999)

That summary is taken from *Future Positive: International Co-operation in the 21st Century*, a lively and insightful account of development issues by Michael Edwards. Since its publication in 1999, some of those trends have undoubtedly improved;

foreign aid is increasing again (having dropped from $73 billion in 1992 to $57 billion in 2002), with a growing number of countries reconfirming their determination to hit the UN target figure of 0.7 per cent of gross domestic product (GDP). Edwards himself is optimistic about the potential for making a real difference in the lives of the world's poorest people in the future – but *only* if the governance arrangements (through the UN, bilateral agreements, trade rules, flows of aid and so on) are transformed. The chances of that, unfortunately, seem slim. The Bush Administration in the US clearly abhors the whole UN system (as evidenced by the enforced appointment of John Bolton in the summer of 2005), and remains intent on imposing its own unilateralist solutions across the world. The rest of the rich world often seems to have too much else on its plate, with the Millennium Development Goals (MDGs) – to which they all signed up at the Millennium Summit in 2000 – remaining a relatively low political priority.

BOX 12.1 GOALS AND TARGETS AGREED AT THE UNITED NATIONS MILLENNIUM SUMMIT

- Halve the number of people living on less than $1 per day, currently 1.2 billion, by 2015.
- Achieve universal primary education, including the 113 million children with no access to primary schools.
- Eliminate all gender disparities by 2015 – for example, by narrowing the gap between genders in literacy, refugees and employment.
- Reduce by two-thirds the number of children dying before their fifth birthday, currently 11 million a year, by 2015.
- Reduce by two-thirds the ratio of women dying in childbirth (today the risk is 1 in 48 in developing nations).
- Halt and begin to reverse the spread of HIV, combat malaria and other diseases.
- Reverse the loss of environmental resources by 2015, including halving the population without access to safe drinking water.
- Develop a global partnership for development, including an open trading and financial system that includes a commitment to good governance, development and poverty reduction, tackling debt problems, provision of work for youth and access to affordable essential drugs in developing countries, and make available the benefits of new technologies – especially information and communications technologies.

Source: UN (2000)

Here again, however, 2005 is turning out to be a much more uplifting year in terms of efforts to address international poverty. The 2005 Millennium Development Summit (to review progress on the Millennium Development Goals) was less of a cynical talk shop than many people had feared, and undoubtedly helped to secure renewed commitment on the part of a large number of countries. Jacques Chirac led an increasingly influential campaign to raise substantial sums of new money for development investments from imposing a levy on international financial transactions (the so-called Tobin Tax), or, as an alternative, on international air travel – much to the irritation of the US and the UK! Gordon Brown's debt forgiveness campaign for the world's poorest countries, combined with a new International Finance Facility, secured the support of the majority of G8 nations, raising the prospect of a real and lasting improvement in the lives of millions of people. In the UK, the Make Poverty History campaign has re-energized a development movement that appeared to have got somewhat stuck in a very deep rut. The hundreds of millions raised in the UK for the survivors of the Indian Ocean tsunami was, indeed, an extraordinary reminder of people's latent capacity for a deeply empathetic engagement with the world's poor.

It is still the case, of course, that many of the world's richest nations have their own anti-poverty battles to fight. Here in the UK, after 18 years of the Tories conducting their neo-liberal experiments at the expense of the less well-off, it has proved a long, slow haul for Labour righting some of these wrongs since 1997. With poverty defined as 'living on less than half the average income', there are still around 12 per cent of people in the UK living in poverty. And even the Government's commendable determination to make an absolute priority of eliminating child poverty over the course of the next decade would seem to depend upon what would be a seismic shift in public attitudes on taxation.

This has been a fiercely anti-tax age. As the Fabian Society's ongoing campaign to reassert 'the social value of fair and proportionate taxation' has shown, the legacy of more than 25 years of vitriolic condemnation of the business of raising and spending taxes has taken a serious intellectual toll. Even now, the UK Prime Minister's lack of enthusiasm for overtly redistributive policies is compounded by unremitting anti-tax propaganda from the UK's predominantly right-wing media; there are mighty few politicians or economists prepared to make the case for higher levels of taxation in the face of such public hostility. Yet it's a mystery to many political commentators how anybody imagines that this country can go on improving its health and education services, restore its transport infrastructure, improve the state of both the natural and the built environment, let alone do more to help developing countries, protect the global environment and create the necessary conditions for lasting security in countries currently ravaged by war and conflict, without higher taxes.

Perhaps the swing of capitalism's pendulum to which I have referred elsewhere will make it easier to argue the case for maintaining and enhancing social, human and natural capital through fair and proportionate taxation. And if the moral case for a more equitable society (or family of nations) doesn't do it for electorates, then the appeal to 'enlightened self-interest' would appear to be getting more powerful by the day. This is the line consistently elaborated in *From Here to Sustainability*, the most recent publication from the Real World Coalition:

*Extreme inequalities threaten the whole economy in the long term as a
large proportion of society loses any connection with the assets and
organizations that generate wealth. Social cohesion is undermined by
excessive wealth and poverty, and there is growing evidence that narrowing income inequality in a society adds to the overall social quality of
life. In societies where the income distribution is narrow, there is greater
social cohesion, less violence and crime.* (Christie and Warburton,
2001)

RETHINKING SECURITY

On the international stage, this kind of appeal to enlightened self-interest has also
started to resonate somewhat more persuasively, albeit against the less than
propitious backdrop of the 'war against terror'. In November 2001, with memories
of 11 September and its 3000 victims still very fresh in people's minds, the *New
Internationalist* (2001) provocatively set out to remind its readers of how hard it is
to get any proper perspective on such events, first by quoting from Mark Twain
about the French Revolution and then by drawing a series of somewhat poignant
comparisons (see Box 12.2)

As we saw in Chapter 5, the rich world's standard response to these enduring
and truly terrible problems is to work towards an accelerated process of market
liberalization and the promotion of Western values. This has clearly brought some
benefits to some people in some countries; but as a universal model for addressing
these 'enduring terrors', it is, at best, hopelessly inadequate and, at worst, a form of
economic medicine that often makes things worse. As Roger Scruton so powerfully
argues in *The West and the Rest: Globalization and the Terrorist Threat* (2002), it is
precisely the imposition of that corporate globalization that fuels the fires of Islamic
extremism and pretty much guarantees an eventual 'clash of civilizations' *unless* the
current model of globalization is radically reformed.

It is in this context that the synergistic convergence of some of the 'radical
discontinuities' referred to in earlier chapters becomes so threatening, a theme that
Forum for the Future has already pursued through a publishing programme
spearheaded by Martin Wright, editor of the Forum's magazine, *Green Futures*. Our
addiction to oil, for instance, is not only environmentally unsustainable, but – as
with any addictive habit – inevitably leads to rash and potentially violent actions
in an effort to satisfy our cravings. It may be unfair to ascribe the whole of Western
strategy on Iraq to no more than a thirst for oil; but you would have to have your
head buried deep in the sands of Saudi Arabia not to spot a certain confluence of
interests. And whatever people think of Vice President Dick Cheney, the man
certainly deserves points for honesty for having argued *openly* as long ago as 1998
(together with the likes of Paul Wolfowitz and John Bolton) for the overthrow of
Saddam as a means of boosting American oil supplies.

BOX 12.2 THE WAR AGAINST TERROR IN CONTEXT

There were two 'Reigns of Terror', if we could but remember and consider it: the one wrought murder in hot passions, the other in heartless cold blood; the one lasted mere months, the other had lasted 1000 years; the one inflicted death upon 1000 persons, the other upon 100 million; but our shudders are all for the 'horrors' of the momentary Terror, so to speak; whereas, what is the horror of swift death by the axe compared with lifelong death from hunger, cold, insult, cruelty and heartbreak? A city cemetery could contain the coffins filled by the brief Terror which we have all been so diligently taught to shiver at and mourn over; but all France could hardly contain the coffins filled by that older and real Terror – that unspeakable bitter and awful Terror which none of us has been taught to see in its vastness or pity as it deserves.

(from *A Connecticut Yankee in King Arthur's Court*, Mark Twain)

ENDURING TERRORS

- Number of people who died in attacks on the Twin Towers, 11 September 2001: 3000.

- Number of people who died of hunger on 11 September 2001:* 24,000.
- Number of children killed by diarrhoea on 11 September 2001:* 6020.
- Number of children killed by measles on 11 September 2001:* 2700.
- Number of malnourished children in developing countries: 149 million.
- Number of people without access to safe drinking water: 1100 million.
- Number of people without access to adequate sanitation: 2400 million.
- Number of people living on less than $1 a day: 1200 million.
- Number of African children under 15 living with HIV: 1.1 million.
- Number of children without access to basic education: 100 million.
- Number of illiterate adults: 875 million.
- Number of women who die each year in pregnancy and childbirth: 515,000.
- Annual average number of people killed by drought and famine 1972–1996: 73,606.
- Annual average number of children killed in conflict, 1990–2000: 200,000.
- Annual average number of children made homeless by conflict, 1990–2000: 1.2 million.

Note: * Assuming annual deaths were evenly spread across the year.
Source: New Internationalist (2001)

Both Europe and America are set to become increasingly dependent upon imported oil and gas supplies – much of them from politically volatile regions with little reason to love the West. Indeed, despite enthusiastically pursuing the development of what's left of its own reserves in Alaska and elsewhere, the US is expected to rely upon the Middle East for no less than 70 per cent of its oil by 2020. That reliance, of course, is the prime reason for US military presence in Saudi Arabia and Iraq – a presence which provides Osama bin Laden with the strongest possible pretext for continuing to wage war (in his terms) on US imperialists. Our need for oil makes us insecure.

So we might be forgiven for seeking some crumbs of comfort from President Bush's announcement of billions of dollars' worth of research into hydrogen fuel cells as one means of pursuing 'energy independence'. That is a relative drop in the ocean, of course, when set against the US Administration's unbridled enthusiasm for Big Oil, but it's a start. And it's not beyond hope that, sooner rather than later, we might all wake up to the realization that true independence means a decisive shift away from fossil fuels in favour of a combination of renewables and improved efficiency – both of which offer huge scope for progress. Energy guru Amory Lovins calls efficiency gains 'the rapid deployment energy resource': it takes years to discover and develop a new oil field, but just months to make sufficient efficiency savings to make it redundant before it even starts pumping.

In *Winning the Oil Endgame*, Lovins (2005) gives us a comprehensive account of the way in which US dependence on oil imperils not only its own national security, but inflicts on US taxpayers a huge bill in terms of both direct and indirect costs. If ever there was a time for the US Administration to free itself of that dependency, it has to be now: the imported proportion of US oil will rise from around 50 per cent today to around 70 per cent by 2025 (compared to 66 per cent in the European Union), and policy-makers are well aware that even today's figure is *twice* the level of imports in 1973 at the time of the first Organization of the Petroleum Exporting Countries (OPEC) oil shock. In 2000, these imports cost $109 billion, accounting for a full 25 per cent of the US trade deficit, which has become such a major headache that it is eroding the value of the dollar – which, in turn, boosts the price of oil. As Alan Greenspan has often pointed out: 'All economic downturns in the US since 1973 have been preceded by sharp increases in the price of oil.'

But Lovins (2005) emphasizes that the *indirect* costs are, if anything, more of a problem than the direct costs. A quarter of US imports come from OPEC countries and one seventh from Arab OPEC countries. Reliance upon such unstable sources means huge costs in terms of having to protect access and maintain a substantial US presence throughout the Middle East. By analysing US Department of Defense figures, Lovins comes to the conclusion that the annual cost to US taxpayers through the 1990s was anywhere between $54 billion and $86 billion dollars, which means 'the US pays two to three times as much to maintain military forces poised to intervene in the Gulf as it pays to buy oil from the Gulf'.

Mind you, even those huge sums have to be set against *global* military spending, which has been rising rapidly since the onset of the war on terror: $956 billion in 2003 and in excess of $1 trillion in 2004. Military expert Chris Langley reminds us of the devastating implications of that kind of chronic misallocation of capital:

> *The economic, social and environmental cost to the world of this military procurement and development is immense. Much of it is borne by poorer countries in Africa, the Middle East and Latin America, where most of*

> *the world's wars are taking place and many of the weapons are concen-*
> *trated. These three regions spend $22 billion a year on arms, many of*
> *which are supplied by the G8 countries, such as the US and the UK.*
> *The result, inevitably, is instability – a consequence the arms-supplying*
> *nations seem to have ignored. Noticeably lacking from most of the*
> *military–research partnerships are conflict-resolution or peace-building*
> *strategies. In 2004, only 6 per cent of the UK Ministry of Defence's*
> *budget went towards conflict resolution.* (Langley, 2005)

Perhaps we might all feel better about this level of expenditure if there was any sense that it was actually increasing global security. But even US security experts have been compelled to admit that the occupation of Iraq has dramatically accelerated the radicalization of many Islamic countries, while re-energizing the Al-Qa'eda network in literally dozens of countries. On top of that, there's the full opportunity cost to be borne in mind. The Worldwatch Institute's 2005 *State of the World Report* is devoted entirely to the linkage between security issues (as conventionally understood) and today's converging environmental, resource and social issues. It summarizes the full extent of those costs:

> *Surprisingly modest investments in health, education and environmental*
> *protection could tap the vast human potential now shackled by poverty*
> *and break the vicious circles that are destabilizing large areas of our*
> *planet. Estimates suggest that programmes to provide clean water and*
> *sewage systems would cost roughly $37 billion annually; to cut world*
> *hunger in half, $24 billion; to prevent soil erosion, another $24 billion;*
> *to provide reproductive healthcare for all women, $12 billion; to*
> *eradicate illiteracy, $5 billion; and to provide immunization for every*
> *child in the developing world, $3 billion. Spending just $10 billion a*
> *year on the global HIV/AIDS programme, and $3 billion or so to control*
> *malaria in sub-Saharan Africa, would save millions of lives. All this adds*
> *up to a little more than half the $211 billion likely to be appropriated*
> *for the Iraq War by the end of 2004.* (Worldwatch Institute, 2005)

Environmental degradation and social injustice are increasingly feeding off each other. You don't need a degree in environmental management to spot that the refugee camps of the Gaza Strip, for example, are an object lesson in unbearable unsustainability, or to conclude that people who are forced out of their rural homelands and into squalid urban squatter camps due to water shortages, soil erosion, climate change and civil conflict – the sort of runaway environmental and social breakdown that is happening right across Africa and Asia – will make a ready audience for fundamentalist firebrands. In Maoist terms, it's those pressures which fill up the 'sea of sympathy' in which the fish of Al-Qa'eda and the like can swim. And you can't dry out that sea by force of arms. Military might can kill individual terrorists; it rarely saps their support. For proof, look at Palestine, where decades of Israeli *force majeure* have only fed increasingly violent uprisings. If we are to drain that sea of sympathy, we have to address the root causes of injustice and degradation with a resolve which we have sadly lacked to date.

And therein lies another searing irony: while the fruits of the global economy are far from equitably distributed, the hype about its supposed benefits increasingly is. The world's refugee camps and squatter homes are increasingly alive with the flickering seduction of television images portraying Western consumerism in all its elusive, bloated glory; the streets of developing world cities are lined with hoardings holding out the promise of the same. For several years through the 1990s, the most watched TV programme across the world was 'Baywatch'. And for the vast majority, the gulf between their daily reality and the astonishing wealth on display is unimaginably huge, a distant, shimmering dream jealously guarded by the military and financial muscle of America and its allies. So should we really be surprised if the world's 2 billion people surviving on less than $2 a day end up responding with a mix of anger, envy and intense bitterness? Or that some adopt ideologies which wholly reject Western values, and, *in extremis*, end up as conscripts in the extremists' *jihad*? As James Wolfensohn, president of the World Bank, puts it: 'The idea that a rich world and a poor world can co-exist without dramatic implications collapsed along with the Twin Towers on 11 September.'

In short, we cannot divorce our own physical security from that of the world's poor. If we want a long-term future that is safe, we shouldn't just be worrying about the threat from rogue states, but about the yawning gulf between the over-indulged world and the dispossessed. If we want to feel more secure ourselves, we should start by improving the security of the poorest. And doing that simultaneously means doing right by the environment: tackling climate change which, unchecked, is helping to cause the droughts and storms which destroy poor peoples' chances of making a living on the margins; investing in clean water supplies and decent sanitation, and in non-polluting, small-scale renewable energy, all of which can make it possible for vulnerable communities to stay on their land and earn a living from it, rather than join the drift to the city slums. As Martin Wright, the author of a new Demos/Forum for the Future pamphlet puts it:

> *Growing competition over resources such as oil, water, timber and minerals, many of them sourced in the world's more volatile regions, is increasing political tension and triggering conflicts across the globe. Soil erosion, plunging water tables and forest destruction are threatening to bring about the collapse of rural societies, sending millions into already overburdened cities. Climate change is already destabilizing agriculture worldwide and threatening far more chaotic consequences in the years ahead.* (Wright, 2005)

Seen in this light, reducing our ecological footprint is not some feel-good gesture: it is one of the most persuasive tools of international diplomacy. Applying basic standards of social justice to decisions over international business is not a fad for fans of fair trade: it's our best insurance policy against fanaticism. And that means a less frenzied promotion of commercial interconnectedness and a more conciliatory acknowledgement of global interdependence. To quote former EU Commissioner Chris Patten in his 1999 Forum for the Future Lecture: 'The investment we make in sustainable development is as much a part of our global security as the investment we make in our armed forces. And it should offer much better value for money.'

Such sustainability-related concerns about global security are matched in equal measure by concerns about some of the technologies that have been developed over recent decades. It's not just environmentalists who are sounding the alarm bells these days, but many of those who have been working at the very heart of these cutting-edge innovations. Perhaps the most pessimistic of these is Bill Joy, co-founder of Sun Microsytems, whose article in *Wired* in 2000 ('Why the future doesn't need us') fast-forwarded several decades to look at some of the implications of that troika of technologies that will shake the very foundations of the 21st century: genetics, robotics and nanotechnology. Just as some climatologists have flagged the possibility of 'runaway climate change' (where natural feedback mechanisms combine to accelerate processes in ways that simply can't be foreseen), Bill Joy focuses on the 'runaway potential' of computers and robots surpassing human control to the point where they actually take us over. Michael Crichton's fictional account of self-replicating 'nanobots' threatening to reduce all life on Earth to a 'grey goo' (in Eric Drexler's words) has provided for many a 'working model' of Bill Joy's theoretical concerns, however dreadful a novel it may be.

For me, however, the pessimism of Sir Martin Rees, Astronomer Royal and most eminent of contemporary cosmologists, hits home a lot harder. His book *Our Final Century* (Rees, 2003) speculates about every conceivable kind of meltdown or Doomsday scenario for humankind, from the illicit use of plutonium or enriched uranium from the former Soviet Union through to asteroid impacts and comets, from climate change through to catastrophic disasters caused by experiments in today's particle accelerators. But by far the most worrying sections of the book focus on the likelihood of what he calls 'bio-error or bio-terror' – the accidental or deliberate release of micro-organisms, pathogens, 'designer viruses' or other biological agents that could have a devastating effect on humankind. In June 2002, the US National Academy of Sciences reminded politicians just how high the stakes are at this stage in human history:

> *Just a few individuals with specialized skills and access to a laboratory could inexpensively and easily produce a panoply of lethal biological weapons that might seriously threaten the US population. Moreover, they could manufacture such biological agents with commercially availably*

equipment – that is, equipment that could also be used to make chemicals, pharmaceuticals, food or beer – and therefore remain inconspicuous. The deciphering of the human genome sequence and the complete elucidation of numerous pathogen genomes allow science to be misused to create new agents of mass destruction. (US National Academy of Sciences, 2002)

And that's the nub of it. The self-same techniques that are so enthusiastically promoted by both big business and government as promising huge benefits (in terms of agriculture, health, waste management and so on) inevitably become available to those for whom the advancement of humankind is a pathetic irrelevance. Within just a few years, the genetic blueprints of large numbers of species (including bacteria and viruses) will be as easily available via the internet to latter-day Dr Strangeloves as to the likes of John Sulston and others who worked so tirelessly to unlock the secrets of the human genome for the betterment of the human species.

All of this should give us additional reason to think again as to the vulnerability of some of our other environmentally dubious habits. Almost without exception, technologies which are more sustainable are less prone to being hijacked, in any sense of the word, by those intent on inflicting harm. No terrorist is going to make governments tremble by threatening to bomb a wind turbine or release clouds of compost over our cities. Compare that to the destructive potential of nuclear power and toxic chemicals. A more sustainable world is, indeed, a safer world.

And if bio-error or bio-terror don't get us, then the measures taken to try and ward off such horrors very well may. We have already seen the first signs of what this might mean. The response to the events of 11 September 2001 has already seriously eroded civil liberties in the US, the UK and many other countries; constitutional and legal 'niceties' have been unceremoniously set to one side in the interests of national security. But to what end? As Martin Rees points out:

An organized network of Al-Qa'eda-type terrorists would not be required: just a fanatical social misfit with the mindset of those who now design computer viruses. There are people with such propensities in every country – very few, to be sure, but bio- and cyber-technologies will become so powerful that even one could well be too many. (Rees, 2003)

So is there anything that can be done about this seemingly inexorable slide into terror met with oppression met with terror and so on? Martin Rees reviews the various possibilities in terms of slowing the speed of technological advance in these areas – through more regulation, voluntary moratoria and increasingly intrusive surveillance. But none seems feasible. This may well account for the fact that he once staked $1000 on a bet 'that by the year 2020 an incidence of bio-error or bio-terror will have killed 1 million people'.

In these circumstances, it makes little sense dumping total responsibility for this nightmarish vision on today's rudderless world leaders, weakened as they so clearly are by the unmanageability and complexity of both society and technology. But whenever I hear world leaders telling us that 'we have no choice', in the interests of economic growth and international competitiveness, but to push on ever faster and ever more furiously with genetic research, biotech, nanotech or whatever the next 'tech' may be, I wince at the sheer scale of tribute that the great god of economic growth now demands of us. I am not suggesting that 'genies' such as these can be put back into their bottles; indeed, why would we want to, given that humankind will undoubtedly benefit greatly from some of the uses to which these technologies will be put? But I do believe that today's obsessive pursuit of economic growth at all costs makes those genies much less controllable than they might otherwise be.

All of this draws us back yet again to the critical notion of *interdependence*. This means acknowledging the degree to which security for any one country or community can only be achieved by making others more secure in their countries and communities, not just by reinforcing commercial and cultural interconnected-ness, but by stressing mutual dependency. In advocating a rapid shift to 'the politics of resilience', Martin Wright makes the point in a suitably provocative way:

> *The emphasis in the future should be on a more integrated agenda of positive security and shared resilience. This recognizes the links between areas such as resource conflicts, energy policy and climate change, on the one hand, and our approaches to issues like failed states, terrorism, global governance and poverty relief, on the other. And, crucially, it identifies ways in which these can be tackled simultaneously. It shows how a community wind farm on a Welsh hill side is, in its way, as much a part of a counter-terrorist strategy as an ID card; how a shift to sourcing hospital food in the UK from local farms can help bring about a more secure future for African villages; how a scheme to tackle obesity among school children can cut our dependence on oil from the Gulf.* (Wright, 2005)

CONSPIRACY OR COWARDICE?

All in all, this chapter does not offer us a happy global prospect. It is one rendered harder to confront by the continuing fragility in the world economy, with Japan in semi-permanent deflation, most European economies stalled, and the US remain-ing buoyant and dynamic only by virtue of building up an unprecedentedly massive budget deficit. 'Don't rock the boat' may sound wise advice against such a backdrop. But there's rocking and there's rocking. Cast your mind back over the communiqués of the last half dozen G8 meetings, or EU summits, or World Trade conferences, or even the Johannesburg Plan of Implementation from the 2002 World Summit on Sustainable Development, and the level of denial involved beggars belief.

So what's going on? The worst possibility, of course, is that a significant proportion of Western leaders are now so thoroughly co-opted by a tiny but hugely powerful business and political elite that they couldn't start to question the paradigm that serves that elite so well even if they wanted to. Berlusconi's Italy provides the living embodiment of that malign convergence. In the US, the Bush Administration makes no secret of its unyielding allegiance to such an elite, as evidenced both by its devotion to the deepest of pork-barrel politics and by its continuing tax cuts that serve only to enrich the already very rich.

But once the conspiracy theories are put to one side, the principal reasons offered for the phenomenon of this continuing, utterly perverse denial on the part of politicians are these: ignorance (however improbable that may seem for any politician, business person, community leader or media commentator able to see the world as it really is); dogmatic adherence to the 'revealed truth' of post-World War II materialism (certainly a powerful contributory factor, as covered in Chapter 3); and the hypothesis that the challenge of governance itself in a demanding, complex, interconnected and increasingly individualistic society has become all but impossible. Tom Bentley of Demos puts it as follows:

> *A defining characteristic of the manifold changes taking place in this wider environment is complexity. The claim is not new; it crops up regularly in the history of social thought, often in response to the disruption of technological change. However, the combination of rapid increases in the volume and complexity of formal knowledge, especially in science, and the flowering of new, network-based forms of communication and interdependence, or 'connexity', provides good reason for thinking that the current period of change is special, if not completely unprecedented. Identity and social allegiance are more fluid, diverse and difficult to predict. Globalization of economic exchange, communications and culture through interconnected technology networks further contributes to the complexity of the phenomena with which governments wrestle, from migration flows to tax receipts, drug distribution to demand for child care, media ownership and urban regeneration.*
> (Bentley, 2002)

Such analysis commands a growing following in contemporary political circles. But what if a substantial slice of that unmanageable complexity is, in essence, a *consequence* of the failure of politicians to realize that the dominant paradigm of progress through exponential economic growth, at almost any cost, is now generating as many disbenefits as genuine benefits? Were that to be the case (as many advocates of sustainable development now believe it to be), then no amount of 'modernization' in the way policy is implemented is likely to make all that much difference if the 'meta-narrative' of contemporary politics remains unchanged. At that level, politicians of all mainstream parties continue to subscribe, with varying degrees of enthusiasm or reluctance, to the suffocating embrace of 'There Is No Alternative'.

Even to contextualize an alternative approach within a pro-market, democracy-enhancing, reforming framework looks, at best, subversive and highly risky (as in former Chancellor Kohl's charge that all green ideas are like tomatoes: 'they may start out green, but they all end up the deepest red') and, at worst, revolutionary. We are back, it seems, to the apparent impossibility of looking at economic growth and development in a very different way. But are such fears justified? Is the level of political pain and electoral risk really so high if one focuses in the near term on some of the most important *transitional strategies* that present themselves pretty much as no-brainers for anyone still intent on reconciling the non-negotiable long-term imperative of biophysical sustainability with the highly desirable short-term dynamism and creativity of capitalism? Politicians certainly think it is, and environmentalists have had relatively little success over the last 25 years in persuading them to change their minds.

The fate of Europe's green parties reflects this *realpolitik* all too clearly. In 2000, green parties were involved in coalition governments in 5 out of 15 EU states; in 2005, that had shrunk back to just 1 – namely, Germany, with every likelihood that the latest election will see the ruling Social Democratic–Green coalition ousted from power. Environmentalists like to reassure themselves by seeing things in terms of gently rising curves of environmental awareness and action, incrementally moving nation states towards a greener, safer way of living. That's simply not the case. In many places things are moving rapidly backwards – in the US, for instance, in the EU, as a whole, and particularly in Germany where a resurgent CDU–CSU coalition has promised, if elected, to bring back nuclear power, work more closely with big business, stop spending so much money on renewables, rethink Germany's opposition to genetically modified crops and so on.

And it's here we must confront denial of a different kind, not on the part of politicians, big business, the world's major religions or the general public, but on the part of the environmental movement itself. Our denial lies in the simple fact that we have done very little over the last few years to change our conventional ways of campaigning and lobbying, despite 'the evidence of relative failure' being all around us. The most recent example of this was the 2005 general election in the UK, where environmental issues (including climate change) received as close to zero attention as it's possible to get. Although public support for environmental issues is very broad, it is also very shallow. Politicians have learned that they can get away with doing as little as is necessary, while deferring, downgrading and diluting the range of interventions open to them, in the sure knowledge that consistent underperformance in this area will not bring people out on to the streets or even affect their electoral chances. Only small minorities vote in elections because of their environmental concerns, as evidenced by the difficulties of the European green parties to extend their supporter base much beyond a hard core of 5 to 10 per cent of voters.

Only rarely do European environmentalists ask themselves how much of this failure can be attributed to our own underperformance rather than to the failure of everyone else. There is always just enough going on (in terms, for example, of new EU processes, occasional 'victories' and incremental policy shifts) to justify the kind of 'stick to the knitting, do what we do best' tactics that have served environmental organizations reasonably well over so many years. This makes for a very muted and ineffective kind of debate.

THE DEATH OF ENVIRONMENTALISM

Not so in the US. As already discussed in Chapter 2, the 'death of environmentalism' debate has been exercising the leadership of environmental non-governmental organizations (NGOs) since Michael Shellenberger and Ted Norhaus first published their devastatingly self-critical article. Their sense that US environmentalists were losing the war (particularly on climate change) was heightened by an Environics survey showing that the number of Americans who agree with the statement 'to preserve people's jobs in this country, we must accept higher levels of pollution in the future' increased from 17 per cent in 1996 to 26 per cent in 2000. And the number of Americans who agree that 'most of the people actively involved in environmental groups are extremists, not reasonable people' leapt from 32 per cent in 1996 to 41 per cent in 2000. This led the authors of 'The death of environmentalism' to the following conclusion:

> Of the hundreds of millions of dollars we have poured into the global warming issue, only a small fraction has gone to engage Americans as the proud, moral people they are, willing to sacrifice for the right cause. It would be dishonest to lay all the blame on the media, politicians or the oil industry for the public's disengagement from the issue that, more than any other, will define our future. Those of us who call ourselves environmentalists have a responsibility to examine our role and close the gap between the problems we know and the solutions we propose. (Schellenberger and Norhaus, 2005)

Their analysis of the principal obstacles to making progress on big issues such as climate change is very different from that of conventional environmental thinking – though much closer to the broad approach adopted in this book. The list poses quite a challenge to conventional environmental and conservation organizations:

- *our failure to articulate an inspiring and positive vision;*
- *our inability to craft legislative proposals that shape the debate around core American values;*

- *the radical right's control of all three branches of the US Government;*
- *trade policies that undermine environmental protection;*
- *the influence of money in American politics;*
- *poverty;*
- *overpopulation;*
- *old assumptions about what the problem is and what it isn't.*

By 'old assumptions', Shellenberger and Norhaus are referring to the fact that the standard approach of US environmentalists has not changed much in 40 years since the publication of Rachel Carson's *Silent Spring* (1962): first, define a problem as specifically 'environmental'; then work up a whole set of technical policy solutions to that specific environmental problem; and then persuade legislators to adopt those policies. Their contention is that although this worked really well for 25 years or so, it's brought very little success at all since the neo-conservatives started out on their crusade to be seen as the defenders of core US values and virtues. By allowing the environment to be seen as just another special interest, to be ranked alongside every other special interest vying for public attention, environmentalists have boxed themselves into a very narrow corner from which it is proving extremely difficult to escape:

> *The marriage between vision, values and policy has proved elusive for environmentalists. Most environmental leaders, even the most vision oriented, are struggling to articulate proposals that have coherence. This is a crisis because environmentalism will never be able to muster the strength it needs to deal with the global warming problem as long as it is seen as a 'special interest'. And it will continue to be seen as a special interest as long as it narrowly defines the problem as 'environmental' and the solutions as technical.* (Schellenberger and Norhaus, 2005)

I will return to this question of the balance between vision, values and policy in Chapter 16. Although it simply isn't true (in Europe, anyway) that environmentalists have always put 'the technical policy cart before the vision-and-values horse', the naivety of some environmentalists regarding the scale of the culture war and the ideological battles that they are engaged in has been a problem for a very long time. In a strange sort of way, over-reliance on the assumed power of evidence and on the rational consideration of long-term, collective self-interest to shift political systems has proved to be something of a mistake.

The alternative that is now being pushed much more actively in the US entails the building of a much broader coalition of interests, including trade unionists, industrialists and economists, to crack climate change by creating new jobs in renewables and energy efficiency (rather than appearing to threaten old jobs), and reducing energy costs in the long run by securing much greater energy security. As referred to before, this has been Amory Lovins's crusade for more than two decades, and the subtitle of his latest book makes no bones about his game plan: 'innovation for profits, jobs and security'. He provides a stirring vision:

> Our energy future is choice, not fate. Oil dependence is a problem we need no longer have – and it's cheaper not to. US oil dependence can be eliminated by proven and attractive technologies that create wealth, enhance choice and strengthen common security. This could be achieved only about as far in the future as the 1973 Arab oil embargo is in the past. When the US last paid attention to oil, in 1977–1985, it cut its oil use 17 per cent while GDP grew 27 per cent. Oil imports fell 50 per cent and imports from the Persian Gulf by 87 per cent in just eight years. That exercise of dominant market power – from the demand side – broke OPEC's ability to set world oil prices for a decade. Today we can rerun that play, only better. The obstacles are less important than the opportunities if we replace ignorance with insight, inattention with foresight, and inaction with mobilization. American business can lead the nation and the world into the post-petroleum era, a vibrant economy and lasting security – if we just realize that we are the people we have been waiting for. (Lovins, 2005)

Amory Lovins puts enormous emphasis on the role of the business community. And it's certainly true that engineering the transition to a more sustainable world will require the best efforts of business people, professionals, religious and spiritual leaders, NGOs, educationists, the media and so on. But it is clearly politicians who have to make the most decisive interventions to enable others to play a fuller part in that transition. It's governments that win democratic mandates from electorates; it's governments that frame the legal and constitutional boundaries within which individual citizens and corporate entities must operate; it's governments that set the macro-economic framework through the use of fiscal and economic instruments; and it's governments (by and large) that set the tone for public debate and that can take the lead on controversial and potentially divisive issues.

Yet that kind of government-first hierarchy is distinctly out of fashion – for all sorts of reasons. All nation states, for instance, have already ceded a certain amount of national sovereignty to supranational bodies – to the EU, to the UN and to global markets. Many governments are now predisposed against decisive interventions in the marketplace, look on regulation 'as the policy instrument of last resort', and greatly prefer the use of voluntary instruments or old-fashioned exhortation to try to change individual or corporate behaviour. What's more, governments have become adept at shedding both risk and responsibility – on to businesses, quangos, arm's length executive agencies, community bodies, citizens and, of course, 'the market' itself.

This is particularly true in the realm of promoting environmentally and socially responsible behaviour in the corporate world. The increasingly authoritative 'business case' for companies voluntarily to reduce their negative environmental and social externalities has come as manna from heaven to today's business-friendly, deregulation-inclined governments. If it can be shown that companies really do end up doing better (for example, by way of market share, performance and shareholder return) by championing corporate responsibility, why shouldn't governments just sit on the sidelines cheering them all on, doing a bit of 'naming and shaming' to encourage the others, and setting up catchy but invariably ineffective initiatives such as the UK Government's shiny new Corporate Social Responsibility Academy?

Unfortunately, the *current* approach to corporate responsibility simply isn't up to the task in hand. In *Just Values* (BT and Forum for the Future, 2003; a co-publication with BT) and *Government's Business* (Cowe and Porritt, 2002; a co-publication with former *Guardian* correspondent Roger Cowe), Forum for the Future has mapped out both the powerful drivers that the business case for sustainable development *can* provide *and* the very clear limits to the effectiveness of that business case:

> There are many aspects of sustainable development that cannot be addressed by companies acting individually, either because they would be put at a competitive disadvantage or because market conditions need to change. Voluntary agreements across industry sectors have delivered some benefits; but they are time consuming to conclude, dogged by the 'lowest common denominator' effect, and vulnerable to inadequate monitoring and sanctions for non-performance.
>
> At a higher level, many requirements for sustainable development depend on changes in market conditions – framework conditions, as they are sometimes known – which cannot be delivered even by corporates cooperating across an industry. For example, renewable energy is unlikely to be adopted by most consumers while it continues to be more expensive; in order to thrive, developing country farmers need tariff reductions in the developed world; and transport costs need to reflect each mode's different environmental impacts. (Cowe and Porritt, 2002)

Although responsibility for bringing about the necessary changes is, indeed, shared between different parties, the *primary* responsibility for making it all happen still lies with government – and that's where our attention must now turn to investigate the scope for bringing forward some short-term but still effective measures to get the transition to a more sustainable economy properly under way.

REFERENCES

Bentley, T. (2002) 'Letting go: Complexity, individualism and the left', *Renewal*, vol 10
BT and Forum for the Future (2003) *Just Values*, Forum for the Future, London. Available at www.forumforthefuture.org.uk/publications/JustValuesPublication_page760.aspx

Carson, R. (1962) *Silent Spring*, Houghton Mifflin, Boston, MA

Christie, I. and Warburton, D. (2001) *From Here to Sustainability*, Real World Coalition/ Earthscan, London

Cowe, R. and Porritt, J. (2002) *Government's Business: Enabling Corporate Sustainability*, Forum for the Future, London. Available at www.forumforthefuture.org.uk/publications/ governmentsbusiness_page55.aspx

Diamond, J. (2005) *Collapse: How Societies Choose to Fail or Succeed*, Allen Lane, London

Edwards, M. (1999) *Future Positive: International Co-operation in the 21st Century*, Earthscan, London

Houghton, J. (2003) 'Climate change: Weapon of mass destruction', *Guardian*, 28 July

Joy, B. (2000) 'Why the future doesn't need us', *Wired*, April

Kennedy, R. F. (2004) *Crimes Against Nature*, Penguin, London

Langley, C. (2005) 'The best defence', *New Scientist*, 22 January

Lomborg, B. (2001) *The Skeptical Environmentalist: Measuring the Real State of the World*, Cambridge University Press, Cambridge, UK

Lovins, A. (2005) *Winning the Oil Endgame: Innovation for Profits, Jobs and Security*, Rocky Mountain Institute, Snowmass, CO

New Internationalist (2001) 'Enduring terrors', *New Internationalist*, November

Northcott, M. (2004) *An Angel Directs the Storm: Apocalyptic Religion and American Empire*, I. B. Tauris, London

Perkins, J. (2004) *Confessions of an Economic Hit Man*, Berrett-Koehler, San Francisco, CA

Porritt, J. (1984) *Seeing Green*, Blackwell, Oxford

Rees, M (2003) *Our Final Century*, William Heinemann, London

Schellenburger, M. and Norhaus, T. (2005) 'The death of environmentalism: Global warming politics in a post-environmental world', *Grist Magazine*, www.grist.org

Scruton, R. (2002) *The West and the Rest: Globalization and the Terrorist Threat*, Continuum, London

UN (2000) The Millennium Assembly of the United Nations, 6–8 September 2000. Further details available at www.un.org/millennium/summit.htm

US National Academy of Sciences (2002) *Biological Weapons*, National Academy of Sciences, June, Washington, DC

Worldwatch Institute (2005) *State of the World 2005: Global Security*, Earthscan, London

Wright, M. (2005) *Positive Security: A New Politics of Resilience*, Forum for the Future, London

13

Changing the Metrics

INTRODUCTION

One of the best ways of overcoming denial is to show people more clearly exactly what's going on in terms of the constant trade-off between economic progress and environmental damage. Gross domestic product (GDP) just doesn't do that – indeed, it wasn't designed to do that. So we need to develop parallel measures of economic success and quality of life, and to move well beyond our total reliance upon economic metrics by taking proper account of individual wellbeing. In due course, when we start to get really serious about climate change, we will need to become as conscious about carbon as we are about cost, measuring and even trading in the amounts of carbon dioxide (CO_2) that each and every one of us causes to be emitted as we go about our daily lives. But it's *price* that remains the most powerful source of information in a market economy, and politicians will need to think far more systematically about 'ecological tax reform' and other interventions to start penalizing the things we want less of (waste, CO_2 emissions and so on), while reducing the tax burden on things we want more of – jobs, livelihoods, new business start-ups and so on. There has been a lot of talk about this over the years; but politicians never quite seem to find the courage to make it stick in practice.

GROSS DOMESTIC PRODUCT (GDP)

In Chapter 3, I reviewed some of the critical concerns that economists and activists alike have about the use of GDP as our principal indicator of economic success. Ed Crooks (*Financial Times* correspondent and a former member of the UK Sustainable Development Commission) puts it like this:

> *In his foreword to the Government's first Sustainable Development Strategy in May 1999, the Prime Minister made a straightforward but often neglected distinction: 'Real progress cannot be measured by money alone. We must ensure that economic growth contributes to our quality of life, rather than degrading it.' From the first day of any undergraduate course to the most sophisticated current research, the inadequacies of the*

current definitions of gross domestic product (GDP) and economic growth as yardsticks for wellbeing are staples of academic economics. Yet, economic policy still seems to be designed as though maximizing GDP was its sole objective.

The Treasury defines its aim as 'to raise the rate of sustainable growth, and achieve rising prosperity, through creating economic and employment opportunities for all'. By 'sustainable', the Treasury has said it means 'growth must be both stable and environmentally sustainable. Quality of growth matters, not just quantity'. But in practice, policy decisions generally leave out of the picture critically important considerations of fairness and resource use. Although many (perhaps most) economists would agree that the limitations of the basic utility-maximizing models are very important, few people in government seem to act as though they believe it. (Crooks, 2003)

Exactly. So why is it that the amount of political will available to address this lamentable state of affairs is all but non-existent? The United Nations, for example, has a high-level working party looking at ways for governments to prepare their national accounts differently in order to reflect some of those concerns. It has been at it for nearly 20 years now without being able to come up with any serious recommendations. Here in the UK, the Labour Government boldly produced some 'satellite accounts' in 1998, essentially designed to see what would happen if they deducted the depletion of non-renewable natural capital from GDP. It did that for two years, but then gave up, claiming it was a lot more complicated than it had at first thought. And that's the last that's been heard of this initiative since then.

To be fair, one has to admit it's *not* all that easy. Campaigners' favoured alternative to GDP is the Index of Sustainable Economic Welfare (ISEW); many others, however, are not entirely persuaded that any single aggregated index can do the job. At this stage, we probably need a much more pluralistic approach, developing a number of different metrics to get people used to the fact that there's more to national success than GDP.

GDP still has an important role to play. Given all the concerns about the wrong kind of economic growth, it might be imagined that the best prospects for an environmentally sustainable economy would be provided by a no-growth economy. That was the underlying thrust of the debate during the 1970s, and is a view still espoused by a small minority of radical greens today. However, the vast majority of alternative economists have acknowledged that capitalist economies need growth of some description if they are not to be thrown into massive social hardship. All the evidence suggests that a capitalist economy that is not growing at all may not be economically viable. Nor is it necessarily even environmentally benign. This suggests that 'no growth' under capitalism would not further the cause of environmental sustainability as such, but would, in fact, be more likely to put it further beyond reach.

In the broad sweep of human history, it seems most improbable that capitalism will prove to be the last word in humanity's organization of its economic affairs. But it is all that is credibly on offer at present, and if capitalism needs economic growth, then the only chance for economic and environmental sustainability in the coming decades is to make that growth consistent with sustainability, rather than conjuring fanciful visions of how to do without it. This is the principal challenge that stands at the core of the concept of sustainable development and the principal problem behind the idea of just 'getting rid of GDP'. As any child psychologist would point out, it is very unwise for parents forcibly to separate their child from his/her security blanket: better by far to divert that child's attention with other compellingly interesting toys or activities.

ADJUSTED GDP

The inadequacy of GDP stems, in part, from the failure of accounting systems to fully account for 'natural capital'. As we saw in Chapter 7, natural capital can be thought of as the exploitable resources of the Earth's ecosystems – its oceans, forests, mountains and plains – that provide the raw material inputs, resources and flows of energy into our production processes. It also consists of a range of 'ecosystem services', as described in Chapter 1. These services include the maintenance of a stable climate, a protective ozone layer, and the absorptive capacities to disperse, neutralize and recycle the material outputs and pollution generated in ever-increasing quantities from our global economy. While some account is taken of the depletion of resources in the calculation of GDP, no account is taken of the degradation of what has been described as 'critical natural capital', the essential ecosystem services without which our lives would look very different.

Evidence of this incomplete accounting is abundant. For example, while governments may account for the timber which is extracted from its forests, they do not account for the ecosystem services provided by that forest. These include water storage, soil stability, habitat maintenance, and the regulation of the atmosphere and climate. Unfortunately, the costs of losing these essential ecosystem services only become apparent when they start to break down. In China's Yangtze Basin in 1998, for example, deforestation triggered flooding that killed 3700 people, inundated 24 million hectares of farmland and disrupted the lives of 225 million people. This $30 billion disaster forced a logging moratorium and a $12 billion emergency reforestation programme.

The logic for adjusting our national income calculations to take account of such factors is unanswerable. National income is defined as the amount that may be consumed during the accounting period while leaving the consumer (a nation, in the case of national income) no worse off at the end than at the beginning of the period. Income, therefore, represents a quantity which is, by definition, sustainable precisely because its consumption has not affected the capital stock from which it is derived. However, national income will only faithfully reflect this inherent sustainability of income if the deductions from GDP for capital consumption are an adequate approximation of the *total* consumption of capital that has taken place. At the moment, national income is computed by subtracting capital depreciation from gross income, or GDP. Given that natural capital, in exactly the same way as manufactured capital, makes a significant contribution to the production of GDP, the negative effects on it from that production should, in principle, be subtracted from GDP in exactly the same way as depreciation is subtracted.

When it comes to calculating what should be subtracted (in terms of depleted natural capital), there are a number of different methodologies. Paul Ekins, associate director of Forum for the Future, has advocated a number of techniques for assessing what he calls 'the sustainability gap'. Having determined the necessary conditions that need to be complied with for ecological sustainability to be achieved (using agreed international standards as the best proxy for measuring critical natural capital available to us to today), a 'sustainability gap' for all key environmental functions can be defined and measured. That gap can then be related to the national accounts by allocating the environmental impacts that comprise it to the various sectors responsible for them, and by giving the gap a monetary valuation that reflects the cost of what it would cost to reduce the gap to zero. The size of this monetary sustainability gap provides a macro-economic aggregate that can then be subtracted from GDP.

Of course, it's not perfect. Calculations would inevitably be very rudimentary to start with. But as any finance director or accountant will tell you, calculations of depreciation on manufactured capital are not exactly 'state of the art' either.

INDEX OF SUSTAINABLE ECONOMIC WELFARE (ISEW)

In 1989, Herman Daly and John Cobb came up with what has since become the favoured alternative among many critics of the status quo: the Index of Sustainable Economic Welfare. With regard to the US, their conclusion was stark:

> *Despite the year-to-year variations in ISEW, it indicates a long-term trend from the late 1970s to the present that is, indeed, bleak. Economic welfare has been deteriorating for at least a decade, largely as a result of growing income inequality, the exhaustion of resources and the failure to invest adequately to sustain the economy in the future.* (Daly and Cobb, 1989)

In 1994, this work was replicated here in the UK by Professor Tim Jackson, coming to much the same conclusion as Daly and Cobb. The research was then taken up in a big way by the New Economics Foundation, which has done much to popularize the value of the index as a full-blown alternative to GDP. As well as adjusting for the loss of natural capital, the ISEW is also seeking to provide a better measure of *welfare* than GDP by adding to it some measures of un-traded benefits (such as unpaid domestic work), by subtracting the value of activities which are traded but do not contribute to human welfare (such as the treatment of pollution-related illnesses) and by correcting for income inequality. ISEWs calculated for several other developed countries all show the same overall pattern of levelling off and decline. This overall shape is robust over a wide range of weightings of the contributory factors – a partial answer to valid criticisms that ISEW is something of a methodological mongrel, made by arbitrarily aggregating incommensurable (and often individually questionable) indicators of very different kinds of things.

Unfortunately, it's hard to validate the ISEW conclusions against comprehensive studies of perceptions of quality of life since few surveys have been done that measure changes in people's views of their own wellbeing. However, the accumulated data from many theoretical, quantitative and qualitative studies that have examined aspects of quality of life *do*, indeed, suggest that the ISEW's picture of a sizeable gap between GDP per capita measures of welfare and 'real life' welfare is on the right lines.

In international terms, perhaps the best known and simplest of alternative indicators is the United Nations Development Programme's (UNDP's) Human Development Index (HDI), which has some similarities with the Index of Sustainable Economic Welfare. The HDI is calculated annually for the UNDP's *Human Development Report* to allow simple comparisons to be made between different countries. It is based on three essential dimensions: longevity (as measured by life expectancy at birth); knowledge (as measured by adult literacy and enrolment ratios at primary, secondary and tertiary levels); and prosperity – as measured by GDP per capita.

RESOURCE EFFICIENCY INDEX

From the point of view of biophysical sustainability, the key measure is how much economic value we can derive from ever lower levels of material throughput. And from an international perspective, that should, *indeed*, be *the* principal comparator of relative economic success and competitiveness, rather than GDP, if we are going to start getting serious about resource efficiency.

Given global population growth and current aspirations for increased material prosperity, Paul Ekins and others have calculated that to achieve environmental sustainability in an affluent industrial country would require a reduction in the environmental intensity of consumption (the environmental impact per unit of consumption) by a factor of about ten (that is, a 90 per cent reduction) by about 2050. Thereafter, if economic growth continues, the environmental intensity of consumption will have to continue to decrease, at least at the rate of economic growth for those impacts that are at the threshold of sustainability.

It has to be said that the current picture on *overall* resource consumption in industrialized countries is reasonably encouraging. For instance, a 2002 comparison of European Union (EU) countries rated the UK as one of the top five in terms of resource use efficiency. Research by the Wuppertal Institute in Germany showed that the UK's 'total material requirement' grew by just 12 per cent between 1970 and 1999, while GDP increased by 88 per cent during the same time, a 'decoupling' of economic growth and resource use that has surprised many commentators given the enormous difficulties that the UK has had in implementing effective waste policies. Much of the decoupling effect can be attributed to the shift from manufacturing to services, which tend to have a far lower environmental impact per unit of GDP.

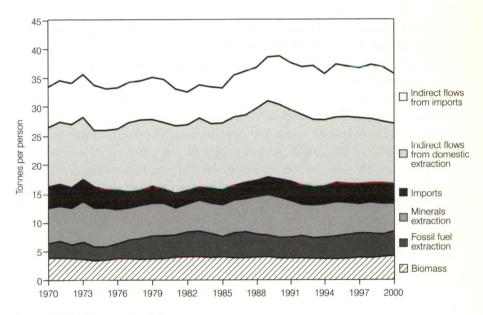

Source: DEFRA/Wuppertal Institute

Figure 13.1 *The components of total material requirement*

But governments around the world are going to have to get much more serious about 'decoupling' GDP from resource consumption, over and above more conventional measures of economic success such as growth per se, jobs, productivity and so on. There are all sorts of different ways in which this can be measured:

• decoupling economic growth from emissions of greenhouse gases;
• decoupling economic growth from emissions of nitrogen oxide and sulphur dioxide;
• decoupling economic growth from its impact upon river quality;

- decoupling economic growth from the generation of solid waste;
- decoupling economic growth from the use of natural resources;
- decoupling economic growth from the use of water resources;
- decoupling economic growth from the use of undeveloped land;
- decoupling electricity use from environmental impacts of electricity generation;
- decoupling road transport use from harmful environmental impacts;
- decoupling agricultural production from harmful environmental impacts;
- decoupling manufacturing industry from harmful environmental impacts; and
- decoupling household consumption from harmful environmental impacts.

AND WHAT ABOUT WELLBEING?

Lastly, any consideration of metrics must address the vexed issue of how people are feeling about all this – their 'life satisfaction', level of contentment, happiness, call it what you will. For a long time, alternative economists have pointed out just how important it is to look at whether or not people are actually getting any happier as a consequence of all this astonishing economic growth and increased prosperity, and the disturbing reality (described in Chapter 3) would appear to be that we are not. Policy-makers in rich countries are, in effect, confronted with a double dilemma: increased economic growth is generating more and more negative externalities that threaten to overwhelm the life-support systems upon which we depend; yet, at the same time, increased economic growth isn't necessarily making people any happier.

All sorts of efforts have been made to construct a specific 'wellbeing index' to take a nation's pulse, as it were, in terms of levels of contentment and people's general satisfaction with their work, personal life, achievements and so on. Apart from Bhutan's measure of 'gross domestic happiness' as a direct alternative to gross domestic product, most of these are similar to the Index of Sustainable Economic Welfare, focusing on national, social and economic indicators. The Osberg-Sharpe Index of Wellbeing, for example, concentrates on consumption flows and stocks of wealth, as well as measures of equality and economic security; the Fordham Index of Social Health is a composite index looking at 16 health indicators affecting different age groups; the Weighted Index of Social Progress uses no less than 46 indicators; and Robert Prescott-Allen's Wellbeing Index uses a full 87 indicators to measure human and ecological wellbeing. Governments can use the Wellbeing Index to identify 'quality-of-life gaps' and Prescott-Allen has himself standardized the data and summed them into a single score for comparison across 180 different countries.

What is still missing, of course, is the much more subjective, impressionistic feelings that individuals experience year on year, such as those captured in the surveys referred to in Chapter 3. It's questionable, however, whether there is any real value in trying to quantify subjective perceptions of that kind in any way other

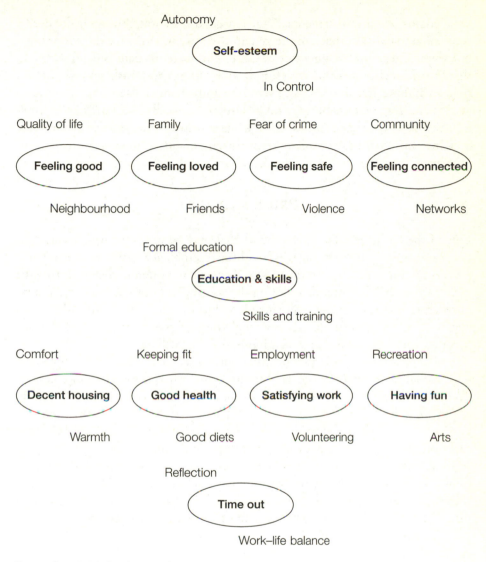

Source: Sustainable Development Commission

Figure 13.2 *The components of wellbeing*

than by big picture generalization – along the lines of 'more or less happy/content' at any particular moment. Quantification often obscures the subtlety of all the different factors involved in making us feel up or down about our lives. Professor Tim O'Riordan and I, for instance, have been exploring a 'wellbeing map' for use by UK local authorities as they develop their sustainable community strategies, showing the principal influences on a cluster of key determinants (see Figure 13.2). But imagine what it would take, first, to measure each of those influencing factors in its own right, and then to aggregate them into a single indicator!

Perhaps this already represents 'index overload' anyway? But we badly need a short, sharp statistical shock to the system if we are to challenge the continuing, but wholly illegitimate, supremacy of GDP. 'Surfacing the data' is the first step in this transitional process; interpreting it and using it to transform government policies and practices is obviously even more important. This is sometimes called 'mainstreaming sustainability', and although it's hardly the stuff of headline-grabbing news coverage, it probably has a bigger impact upon changing the culture and institutions of government than dozens of one-off, *ad-hoc*, 'just do it' initiatives.

PRICE SIGNALS

One of the few economic developments that may be predicted with certainty is that the economy in the future will bear little resemblance to that of today. There is every reason to believe that the pace and extent of economic change during the next 50 years will be faster than during the last 50. It is not, therefore, a question of whether structural change will take place, but in which direction; and it is not a question of whether completely new industries will provide the next generation's incomes and livelihoods, but which industries they will be.

Market economies bring about structural changes of this kind all the time, and with globalization, may be expected to do so more frequently and more rapidly. To move towards environmental sustainability, capitalist economies will need to ensure that they use the forces of structural change to shift away from environmentally intensive sectors and develop new, comparative advantages and capabilities in technologies and sectors with low environmental impact – or, even better, in technologies and sectors concerned with environmental restoration and improvement. Such an economy will earn incomes and sustain livelihoods even as it improves environmental performance, one of the great win–win opportunities offered by the new imperative of achieving biophysical sustainability.

The principal responsibility for government is, therefore, to stimulate structural and technological change within the economy away from those environmentally damaging sectors towards those that are positively beneficial. And *prices* are the key to this transformation. Prices are fundamental both with regard to the present allocation of resources and in influencing the direction of economic development in the future. But as we have seen, prices today rarely reflect full environmental costs. For markets to operate efficiently, we need environmental taxes to help internalize those costs. As Paul Ekins (1997) points out, environmental taxes also have a far more fundamental role in moving an economy towards environmental sustainability and keeping it there:

- *By charging for the use or depletion of resources, they signal the end of 'environmental free goods', whether the goods in question are water, air (as a dump for pollutants) or soil. Where it is clear that the charges will be escalating, they give the clearest possible signals to markets of future environmental scarcity (in economic terms). Perceptions of scarcity are among the strongest motivations in markets for the development of substitutes and of more efficient technologies.*

- *An escalating price signal not only weakens or removes the rebound effect, it strengthens incentives for further efficiency gains. In a growing economy, an escalating price is also necessary to maintain the cost of using the environment relative to incomes. Without such escalation, income growth will inevitably lead to increased environmental damage and resource use.*

- *Charging for use of the environment stimulates structural change away from environmentally intensive sectors towards those that are less damaging. Exempting environmentally intensive sectors from environmental taxes, as is common, cancels out this stimulus to structural change, which was, or should have been, one of the rationales for the tax in the first place.*

- *Environmental taxes raise revenues which, even when they are successful in dampening demand for the object of the taxation, can remain substantial. This allows other taxes, in particular taxes on labour, to be reduced. This stimulates employment. Over time the economy will evolve towards technologies and patterns of production that use more labour and fewer environmental resources: more jobs and less environmental destruction. Another win–win outcome for the environment and economy will be the result.* (Ekins, 1997)

The role of prices in markets is so fundamental that it is most unlikely that any market economy could move systematically towards environmental sustainability until rising prices across *all* the sensitive dimensions of the environment are in place. Uniquely, such price signals would simultaneously stimulate continuous technological change, reinforce consumers' environmental awareness, counteract any rebound effect, strengthen incentives for increased environmental efficiency, offset the income effect of economic growth, and change the structure of the economy in favour of environmentally neutral or beneficial sectors. It may confidently be predicted that a fiscal shift of this sort will be an essential element of any transition by capitalism to biophysical sustainability, and it is now one of the highest priorities of all those organizations around the world seeking to promote a new economic paradigm (see Box 13.1).

TAX REFORM

In political terms, however, it's not quite that simple! Seeking increased environmental efficiency simply by raising the price of key resources will, where these resources provide for basic needs, be likely to be regressive – that is, the poor will pay

BOX 13.1 NEW ECONOMIC APPROACHES TO TAXATION

Taxes should be about two things. Government revenue is only one. The other should be to use the price mechanism which incorporates taxes in order to encourage the activities and conditions that we want and to discourage those we do not want.

Taxes should *encourage*:

- social inclusion;
- social equity;
- economic efficiency;
- environmental sustainability.

Taxes should *discourage*:

- use of non-renewable resources;
- monopoly of God-given common resources;
- pollution and waste.

Therefore, *we should not tax the value that people add,* as we do now through:

- value-added tax (VAT);
- personal income tax;
- company tax.

We should tax the value that they subtract – for example, through:

- green taxes;
- taxes on value created by society;
- site value taxation on land;
- taxes on speculative currency transaction.

Existing taxes are perverse. They:

- reduce employment by taxing employment and value added;
- reduce employment by subsidizing capital-intensive production and energy to increase competitiveness;
- encourage polluting and waste because the state funds measures to restore health and cope with waste;
- encourage inefficient land use and speculation;
- encourage currency speculation;
- encourage inefficient use of resources and pollution by subsidizing long-distance transport using fossil fuels;
- deepen social exclusion by means testing benefits;
- fall most heavily on poor people, especially VAT;
- create poverty and welfare traps.

New Economics taxation would replace income, company and value-added taxes with taxes that encourage the activities we want and discourage those that cause damage. They do that not by clumsy regulations but by using the price mechanism. Taxation has the power to make some things relatively cheaper and some things more expensive, and that is the way consumption patterns can be influenced. Some of these taxes are broadly known as green taxes because a major feature is that they protect and promote the natural environment. Global market forces, left to themselves, destroy it.

Source: Legum (2002)

a higher proportion of their income in meeting that tax than the rich. That is politically unacceptable. However, this does *not* mean that the price mechanism should have a diminished role in the allocation of resources given that regressive effects can always be removed by complementary measures if there is the political will. And there is more than one equity issue at work here. When the present generation's unwillingness to face up to these issues causes it to fail to pay the full environmental costs of its own activities, these costs are simply shifted to future generations, which is, in effect, as inequitable as failing to remove regressive effects in the present.

Environmental policy, especially when implemented through environmental taxes, does not need to be regressive. When raising revenue from the relatively rich as well as from the poor, there is always enough money from the tax to give rebates to the latter so that regressivity is removed. Achieving this through the social security system may be complex and may require imagination; but addressing the issue in this way is both feasible and preferable to simply passing on the costs to the next generation. Alternatively, regressivity may be removed by exempting from the tax an initial *tranche* of use of the resource – a minimum entitlement, as it were, to ensure that basic needs are properly met in all households. This is done with water in some parts of Portugal and with domestic energy in The Netherlands.

Policies to remove any regressivity in environmental policy are not an optional extra, but a prerequisite for successful policy-making. Environmental policy that bears harder on the poor than the well-off in order to generate benefits for, or fulfil obligations to, future generations makes no sense in terms of social justice and is obviously completely 'unsellable' in today's political climate. If policies to achieve and maintain environmental sustainability are to be implemented, they must both be socially just *and* be seen to be socially just. This means that regressive effects from environmental policy must always be meticulously analysed before the measure is introduced, and removed through complementary or compensating measures if necessary.

Given the overarching significance of pursuing this process of 'ecological tax reform', it is disappointing that progress is currently so slow in so many countries. If there was one thing that the UK Government could do to kick-start the transition to a more sustainable economy, it would be to get serious about eco-taxation. *Guarantee* fiscal neutrality (so that eco-taxes are not seen as cynical revenue-raisers for governments that care little about the state of the environment), map the scale of the changes required, give business plenty of time to gear their investment decisions to the new fiscal environment, disregard the whingeing of narrow, backward-looking business interests (as we saw in Chapter 7, research going back over the last 30 years shows that the *real* costs to business of environmental improvements and higher standards is a fraction of the *projected* costs that business organizations invent to keep such improvements at bay), and get on with it.

In November 2002, the UK Treasury published its *Tax and Environment: Using Economic Instruments* (UK Treasury, 2002) to serve as a five-year progress report on its 1997 *Statement of Intent on Environmental Taxation* (UK Treasury, 1997). That early document had boldly stated:

> *Over time, the Government will aim to reform the tax system to increase incentives to reduce environmental damage. That will shift the burden of tax from 'goods' to 'bads'; encourage innovation in meeting higher environmental standards; and deliver a more dynamic economy and a cleaner environment to the benefit of everyone. This is very much in line with the Treasury's own Public Service Agreement 'to protect and improve the environment by using instruments that will deliver efficient and sustainable outcomes through evidence-based policies'.* (UK Treasury, 1997)

In some areas, decisive action *is* being taken in the UK: landfill tax, for instance, will increase by £3 per tonne per annum (from 2005 onwards) until it reaches the rate of £35 a tonne – still much less than in many other European countries, but a clear enough signal of the need for dramatic changes in our waste management strategy. In other areas (such as pesticide reduction or ending the anomaly that no taxes are paid on aviation fuel), it is all talk still, with no real intent to get to grips with the different problems. The Department for Transport (DfT) has successfully warded off the imposition of any charges or taxes on aviation, on many different occasions, effectively undermining the Government's own climate change programme.

The astonishing increases in air travel over the last few years have stimulated intense debate not just about national (or European) measures to compel at least partial internalization of the environmental costs of flying, but about a global scheme to levy a charge on *all* international flights to generate additional income for international aid – at the kind of scale that is now required. However, with oil prices now hovering around $60 dollars a barrel, the impact upon airlines of increased fuel charges is already severe, and there currently seems little prospect of this particular idea making much headway.

By contrast, the other well-known idea for a new global tax (the so-called Tobin Tax) on the value of all foreign exchange transactions continues to command substantial support, with the Canadian Government formally committed to such a measure and many European countries actively investigating the feasibility of it. Professor Tobin (a Nobel laureate for economics) first came up with the idea during the late 1970s, with the dual intention of reining in market volatility and raising revenue for international development. Since then, the problems associated with foreign exchange transactions have intensified. In 1983, the *daily* volume of foreign exchange trading was around $550 billion; now it is over $2 trillion and growing by around 20 per cent a year – whereas real physical trade grows by little more than 5 per cent per annum. Of that $2 trillion, as much as 95 per cent is purely speculative, moving from one trader to another in a virtual economy all of its own. Margaret Legum describes how such a tax would work:

The rate recommended by the international movement for a Tobin Tax is 0.25 per cent, which would discourage all speculation at profits of less than 0.3 per cent. It would therefore have a relatively calming effect. Even this small tax would raise, on the current daily transactions of around $2 trillion, some $250 billion every year. Compare this with the $160 billion that Jubilee 2000 reckons to be the cost of wiping out the un-payable debt of Southern countries. It could also address the $80 million the UNDP estimates would be needed to eliminate the worst forms of poverty. A Tobin Tax would net that amount each year. If the tax served the purpose of reducing speculative transactions, then the take from the tax would, of course, decline. This could be offset by raising the tax depending on the relative expectations from it. (Legum, 2002)

There's still a very long way to go before this proposal makes further progress, with countries such as the UK and the US predictably hostile. The situation is rather more encouraging on other reform issues – there are, for instance, at least eight European countries that have introduced a carbon tax of one kind or another. However, on the equally pressing issue of eliminating the wide range of 'perverse subsidies' that still dog so many economies, progress is still very slow. As Norman Myers has argued, these perverse subsidies are particularly damaging (in terms of the environment) in six main sectors: fossil fuels (exacerbating acid rain, urban smog and global warming); road transportation (causing local and national air pollution, and contributing to congestion and road accidents); agriculture (promoting unnecessary production and causing every conceivable kind of environmental impact, from soil erosion to loss of biodiversity); forestry (supporting over-logging in every corner of the world); water use (encouraging inefficiency in agriculture and industry, and reducing already scarce supplies); and fisheries, (with numerous fish species now on the verge of commercial if not biological extinction) at a cost to taxpayers of around $20 billion a year (Myers, 2002). As Myers points out, this borders on the insane:

If perverse subsidies were to be reduced, there would be a double dividend. First, there would be an end to the formidable obstacles imposed by such subsidies on sustainable development. Second, there would be a huge stock of funds available to give an entirely new push to sustainable development – funds on a scale unlikely to become available through any other source. In the case of the United States, for instance, they would amount to $550 billion. An American pays taxes of at least $2000 a year to fund perverse subsidies, and then pays another $1000 through increased costs for marketplace goods and through environmental degradation. (Myers, 2002)

The principal reason for this kind of backsliding, as we saw in earlier chapters, is that taking cost internalization and resource productivity seriously (that is, systematically driving down resource and energy consumption across the entire economy) is not as pain free as it first appears. There are losers as well as winners, and unavoidable political consequences. However disconcerting it may be for relatively affluent, well-educated environmentalists, most people not only enjoy the benefits of a cheap-energy, consumer-driven economy, but would appear to be relatively unconcerned about the impact of this upon future generations. They are undoubtedly *not* out dancing in the streets at the news that such an economy's days are numbered in the interests of intergenerational equity!

However, it is equally misguided to underestimate the huge economic benefits that will accompany many of the necessary shifts. The single most important requirement for structural change required for biophysical sustainability is a shift from fossil fuels to renewable energy sources. The EU has estimated that the renewables business in the EU by 2010 will be valued at 37 billion Euros, with a further 17 billion Euros from exports in the expanding world markets. The World Energy Council has projected that cumulative global investments in renewables from 2000–2010 will be in the range of £150 billion to £400 billion. This makes renewables likely to be the biggest single market opportunity to emerge in this field (or, indeed, in any other) through to the middle of this century. It suggests that while the shift to renewables may, indeed, be an absolute prerequisite for capitalism to become more environmentally sustainable, it also provides an unparalleled opportunity for the kind of entrepreneur-driven technological change in the generation of which capitalism excels.

There will be many other opportunities. Today's technology optimists draw attention to a dazzling array of possibilities across the whole range of environmental impacts, which could serve to reduce these impacts by the amounts required for environmental sustainability. Some of the possibilities are already available and only require that businesses become aware of them and governments stimulate their introduction for them to become fully competitive in the marketplace. Others still need development. However, over time and given a favourable framework of public policy, there seems to be no reason why these should not quite naturally become part of the next generation of infrastructure and industrial production. Closed-loop production processes with zero emissions, producer responsibility for material flows through to the end of the life of all products, and full recyclability of these products could cause today's problems of waste disposal and toxic pollution to be viewed from the vantage point of 2020 in the same light as urban pollution from horse manure in the 1880s or the London smogs of the 1950s.

But technological change is, by its very nature, uncertain. From the almost infinite range of technological possibilities, bringing about the systematic selection, development and diffusion of those that cause minimum environmental impact will require a level of sustained focus in government, and awareness and commitment in consumers, that cannot be taken for granted. For capitalism to become environmentally sustainable, it will have to find a way to institutionalize the achievement of technical change for *continuous* environmental improvement, especially in the most environmentally intensive sectors, in order to counteract the adverse environmental effects that are likely to result from the growth of those sectors and, to a lesser extent, from that of the economy as a whole.

For this reason, a growing number of commentators have been advocating a much more radical approach, especially in the face of growing concern about the impacts of climate change. One of the most interesting of these is the idea of 'domestic tradable quotas' for carbon, with each individual above a certain age being allocated an annual carbon quota to cover all personal consumption. Everyone would receive exactly the same quota, regardless of income, and as the quota was gradually brought down (in response to the need to reduce global emissions), individuals could either sell whatever fraction of their quota they didn't need, or buy the extra allocation they required to make possible a more carbon-intensive lifestyle.

For a radical new idea to work in today's highly controversial climate change debates, it has got to work on many different levels. This one does. Internationally, the arguments have already started regarding what is going to come after 2012 – the final year covered by the current Kyoto Protocol agreement. Some countries favour a relatively straightforward reworking of Kyoto, with much tougher targets for Organisation for Economic Co-operation and Development (OECD) countries, and first-time targets for developing countries (that currently are not included). Others have already written off this kind of process on the grounds that the US will never have anything to do with it, now or in the future, and are exploring an 'equal rights for all' approach. Each person on Earth would have an equal right to emit a given amount of carbon dioxide equivalent (in effect, an equal share of the capacity of the atmosphere to absorb those greenhouse gases), with each country's national allocation calculated according to its population.

The assiduous campaigning over the last decade by the Global Commons Institute (based on its idea of 'contract and converge', under which the rich nations undertake to reduce emissions even as developing nations are permitted to grow their emissions until such time as per capita emissions converge at the same level) has given this kind of approach some real credibility. So, too, has the readiness of developing countries such as China, Brazil, Indonesia and Argentina to accept emissions targets for their own counties – not least because they are already beginning to feel the impacts of climate change.

The real strength of this approach is that it is based upon a trading system, with rich nations needing to purchase additional carbon credits from poorer nations. This appeals a lot to those campaigning for global economic justice: a global trading system in carbon would begin to shift substantial resources from rich countries to poor countries as nations with wasteful, carbon-intensive lifestyles had to purchase additional carbon credits from nations with low-carbon economies. However, the politics of all this is no easier than the politics of the Kyoto Protocol:

it would still be countries such as the US, Canada, Australia and much of Europe that would 'lose out', and it will take a very brave US president to bite that particular bullet.

But one of the indirect benefits of personalizing it in this way (through individual quotas) is that it makes transparent what is currently completely hidden from most people – that we are all, in one way or another, complicit in the growing emissions that are contributing to climate change. The reality is that carbon is going to have to become almost as important a measure of value as money, with people instinctively taking account not just of the cost of something, but of its carbon intensity – the amount of carbon embedded in any product or service. Such parallel 'carbon metrics' will be quite a stretch for people brought up in an age where the environment counted for literally nothing in the pursuit of an ever higher material standard of living, but will rapidly become second nature for young people more and more alert to the implications of climate change in terms of their own future prospects. Indeed, I wager that it won't be long before the latest mobile phone comes fully equipped with its very own 'carbon calculator' to give young people an instant take on the amount of carbon 'embedded' in a particular pair of jeans or CD!

Carbon quotas would clearly have a huge impact upon the business community, directing companies into ever more ingenious ways of getting the carbon out of whatever it is that they are selling. As with any initiative to create a genuinely

Table 13.1 *Balance sheet of a low-carbon economy*

Winners	Losers
Manufacturers of efficient appliances, lights, cars, etc.	Manufacturers of inefficient appliances, lights, cars, etc.
Construction industry, other than the transport sector	Construction industry for the transport sector
Renewable energy manufacturers – for example, of wind turbines and solar water heating	Manufacturers and suppliers of fossil-fuel energy stations
Bio-fuel companies	Fossil-fuel companies
Bus and bicycle manufacturers	Car manufacturers
Organic and other UK farmers	Energy-intensive agriculture
Domestic tourism	Overseas tourism
Bicycle repair shops	Garages and petrol stations
Local shops and businesses	Regional shopping centres
Service and knowledge economy	Short-life goods economy
International communication systems	Airlines
Businesses offering low energy/carbon solutions – for example, zero-energy homes	Businesses selling high-energy systems – for example, domestic air conditioning
New technologies such as micro-combined heat and power (CHP), electric heat pumps, hybrid cars and airships	Old technologies such as direct heating

Source: Hillman (2005)

transparent and fair market by eliminating historical distortions caused by the refusal of previous governments to come down hard on systematic cost externalization, there will be the usual fallout in terms of winners and losers. In *How We Can Save the Planet* Mayer Hillman (2005) presents a balance sheet under a low-carbon economy (see Table 13.1). Mayer Hillman prefers to talk about 'carbon rationing' as a less mealy-mouthed way of getting people to understand what's really going on:

> *In comparison with food rationing, carbon rationing would, in some respects, be less prescriptive and intrusive in everyday life. People could select from a range of ways in which to adjust their lifestyles and energy use in order to reduce their personal carbon dioxide emissions. However, the need for carbon limitation is likely to be less clearly felt than the need for food rationing. This was necessary to ensure that populations remained well fed at a time of national crisis and restricted food supplies. Education has a key role to play so that the public understands why rationing is being introduced and for that reason supports it as the only fair and realistic way of responding to climate change.* (Hillman, 2005)

Hillman is right to bring it all back to education and to the complex psychology of transforming people's attitudes and lifestyles. As the American economist Lester Thurow has written: 'The proper role of government in capitalist societies is to represent the interests of the future to the present.' Yet, in many ways that gets harder and harder in a world seemingly obsessed with instant gratification and short-term profit maximization – which puts the pressure not just on governments to act today 'in the interests of the future', but on those who create the wealth that enriches the lives of so many hundreds of millions of people.

REFERENCES

Crooks, E. (2003) 'Redefining prosperity', unpublished paper, Sustainable Development Commission, London

Daly, H. and Cobb, J. (1989) *For the Common Good*, Beacon Press, Boston, MA

Ekins, P. (1997) 'Sustainability: The challenge for capitalism in the new century', unpublished paper for Forum for the Future

Hillman, M. (2005) *How We Can Save the Planet*, Penguin, London

Legum, M. (2002) *It Doesn't Have to Be Like This*, Wild Goose Publications, Glasgow, UK

Myers, N. (2002) 'Sustainable development: Tackling problems – or sources of problems?' in H. van Ginkel and B. Barrett (eds) *Human Development and the Environment*, United Nations University Press, Tokyo

UK Treasury (1997) *Statement of Intent on Environmental Taxation*, HMSO, London

UK Treasury (2002) *Tax and Environment: Using Economic Instruments*, HMSO, London

14

Business Excellence

INTRODUCTION

Companies started to come under pressure from governments to reduce their impacts upon the environment and society more than 30 years ago, giving rise to a continuing swathe of regulation to oblige them to internalize more and more of the costs they once imposed upon society. But all of today's progressive companies have now moved way beyond the regulated minimum, and are voluntarily seeking out a more durable convergence between their shareholders' interests and broader societal interests. Some of this is serious; some is still in the green-wash mode – or 'blue-wash' in the case of the United Nations Global Compact. Recent initiatives, all underpinned by a strong business case, have stimulated more creative partnerships to help fashion sustainable livelihoods for some of the world's poorest people. The real test, however, is to gauge just how successful companies have been in 'mainstreaming' these sustainability behaviours through more integrated management practices and better metrics and accounting. This is hardly the high point in today's sustainable development debates – but crucial in understanding what's really happening in practice.

REVIEWING THE BUSINESS CASE FOR SUSTAINABLE DEVELOPMENT

I would argue that the kind of opportunity-driven agenda outlined in Chapter 13 gives the lie to right-wing commentators, conservative think tanks and defensive trade associations that sustainable development must, by definition, be anti-business and anti-prosperity. What one suspects that they don't like is the idea that the self-same market forces which they venerate may well turn out to be the most powerful driver of change in our inevitable transition to a sustainable economy.

So, is the role of business just to sit back and wait for government and international bodies to change the rules of the game, restructure markets and rebalance the short-term interests of profit-maximizing shareholders with the longer-term concerns of other stakeholders? In the strictest sense, as explained in Chapters 12 and 13, the answer to that question could be 'yes': only governments

Table 14.1 *The business benefits of sustainable development*

Eco-efficiency	1	Reduced costs
	2	Costs avoided (design for environment, eco-innovation)
	3	Optimal investment strategies
Quality management	4	Better risk management
	5	Greater responsiveness in volatile markets
	6	Staff motivations/commitment
	7	Enhanced intellectual capital
Licence to operate	8	Reduced costs of compliance/planning permits/licences
	9	Enhanced reputation with all key stakeholders
	10	Influence with regulator/government, etc.,
Market advantage	11	Stronger brands
	12	Customer preference/loyalty
	13	Lower costs of capital
	14	New products/processes/services
	15	Attracting the right talent
Sustainable profits	16	Option creation
	17	New business/increased market share
	18	Enhanced shareholder value

Source: Prince of Wales's Business and the Environment Programme

have the democratic mandate to re-engineer the macro-economic framework in that sort of way. However, the onus is increasingly on companies to be proactive rather than reactive, to anticipate inevitable change, to fill the space available to them for much more environmentally and socially responsible actions, and to lobby Government *for* faster change, rather than oppose it at every turn.

The idea of there being a specific business case for sustainable development (one that is framed and articulated in terms of business priorities and using business-friendly language) goes back to the creation of the World Business Council for Sustainable Development in the run-up to the 1992 Earth Summit in Rio de Janeiro. Looking back on that early documentation, one can see just how crude a concept it was at that time, with almost all of the emphasis on 'savings to the bottom line through eco-efficiency', or the importance of 'earning the licence to operate in society'. As the Table 14.1 shows (this is now the standard potential benefits list we use in both Forum for the Future and the Prince of Wales's Business and the Environment Programme), things have moved on a long way since then.

All sorts of companies have found their own way of assessing their own particular business case, drawing on a combination of different benefits to demonstrate the clear convergence between shareholder interests and increased environmental and social responsibility. And an ever wider range of academics and business consultancies have sought to provide some coherent intellectual underpinning to what has been, in effect, a pretty pragmatic process of promoting changed behaviour. One of the most persuasive of these is the 'shareholder value model' developed by Stuart Hart (see Figure 14.1).

Source: Hart (2005)

Figure 14.1 *The shareholder value model*

With the warning that 'firms must perform well in all four quadrants of the model if they are to continuously generate shareholder value over time' (and those two little words 'over time' are very important in the context of the debate about short-term profit maximization and building long-term shareholder value), Hart proceeds to fill out the different boxes in the model (see Figure 14.2).

Looking at models such as these, one gets the distinct feeling that we are on the very edge of a sea-change in corporate behaviour. What counts as corporate social responsibility (CSR) today will soon be seen as the palest imitation of genuinely sustainable behaviour. And those in the CSR industry who prosper by peddling superficial add-on palliatives to inherently unsustainable business models need to check out their own business model if they have their own sustainability in mind.

THE SEDUCTIVE ILLUSION OF CORPORATE SOCIAL RESPONSIBILITY (CSR)

When it comes to 'filling the space available' to companies (the territory between the regulated minimum and the point where shareholder interests are jeopardized by behaving uncompetitively or too riskily), the difference between today's prevailing band-aid CSR and an integrated, strategic commitment to becoming genuinely sustainable, over time, couldn't be greater. The very fact that the majority

Figure 14.2 *The second shareholder value model*

of companies still opt for CSR (or, increasingly, just 'CR' without the 'S') as the self-contained box into which to pack all their 'good stuff', while they continue to pursue their core business (quite legally and, indeed, quite logically, given the failure of politicians to change the rules) without the remotest likelihood that they or their products/services will ever become genuinely sustainable, reveals all one really needs to know about the empty, seductive illusion that is CSR.

That may be a bit harsh. Like its predecessor, the triple bottom line, CSR may well help to raise awareness, to enable people to reach the first base camp along the road to sustainability. And there is certainly no denying the fact that countless good deeds are done in the name of CSR, by an ever-growing army of companies, and that the world is a marginally better place for it – but *only* if it paves the way for a much more serious analysis on the part of business leaders of the challenge the for-profit sector now faces in today's increasingly unsustainable world.

There are now serious questions about the efficacy of many of today's voluntary efforts to promote CSR. Perhaps the grandest of these is the United Nations Global Compact, personally brokered by Secretary-General Kofi Annan back in 1999 to help create 'a more sustainable and inclusive global economy by fostering a more beneficial relationship between business and societies'. Drawing on some of the 'landmark' international agreements, such as the Universal Declaration of Human Rights, the Compact asks its signatory companies 'to embrace, support and enact a set of core values' in the following areas:

- Support and respect the protection of internationally proclaimed human rights.
- Avoid complicity in human rights abuses.
- Uphold freedom of association and the effective recognition of the right to collective bargaining.
- Eliminate all forms of forced and compulsory labour.
- Effectively abolish child labour.
- Eliminate discrimination with respect to employment and occupation.
- Support a precautionary approach to environmental challenges.
- Promote greater environmental responsibility.
- Promote development and diffusion of environmentally friendly technologies.
- Businesses should work against all forms of corruption, including extortion and bribery.

There are currently hundreds of signatories to the Global Compact from all around the world. But as non-governmental organizations (NGOs) have pointed out, there are no mechanisms for assessing the degree to which any one of them is complying with those principles *in practice*, leading to the inevitable (and not excessively cynical) conclusion that many of those signatories are just in it for the UN badge – the phenomenon known as 'blue-washing' as contrasted with the more conventional 'green-washing'. That is certainly the prevailing view in a country such as Spain, where there has been little historical engagement in corporate responsibility or sustainable development, only to see a large number of companies suddenly signing up when a new (and much more progressive) government was elected in 2004.

There are many who believe that the bar should now be raised on all such voluntary initiatives. Here in the UK, the Co-op Bank is actively campaigning for all participants in the well-established Corporate Responsibility Index of Business in the Community (BITC) to publish the self-assessments upon which the rankings in the index are based – and has led the way on that score itself. Few have followed the lead. The concerns of the Co-op Bank were amplified early in 2005, when one of BITC's most progressive members (the small brewer Adnams, which won BITC's Small Company of the Year Award in 2003) resigned on the grounds that not enough was being done to challenge *in public* poor performing members of BITC, and to strip away the 'public relations fig leaf' that so many companies have come to wear so elegantly.

That's a tough call for Business in the Community, which would pretty soon find itself in an uncomfortable financial position if it started taking some of its 700 members to task in public. But Adnams is right about one thing: companies very rarely break ranks to criticize poor performance in their sector or industry. 'There but for the grace of God go we' seems to be the dominant, risk-averse mindset, ensuring that the general public rarely gets a chance to understand that there are substantial divergences (ideological as well as tactical) among business leaders today, including very different ways of articulating what it is that business owes to society for its continuing licence to operate in our midst.

This takes us promptly back to the Five Capitals Framework. Forum for the Future finds itself in a privileged, trust-based position with a number of leading companies in the UK with whom it has collaborated to develop the framework. Companies such as BAA and Wessex Water have engaged seriously in matching the Five Capitals Framework against their own long-term visions – not always with total consensus emerging as the end result, but always with improved understanding. The framework can be used both conceptually (to help envision what a genuinely sustainable company in a particular sector would look like) and practically (to help prioritize 'indicative strategies' in terms of changed policy and practice).

However, addressing the business case for sustainable development in isolation can be both limiting and illusory. It is true that NGOs working with the business community have no option currently but to 'sell in' sustainability on the back of such a business-friendly approach; but it's important to realize that this is, in essence, no more than a tactical ploy; the non-negotiable *imperative* of sustainability sometimes makes such devices appear pretty banal. It must therefore be possible to demonstrate the closest possible correlation between the increasingly familiar business case for sustainable development and what might be described as the 'societal case for sustainable development'. In an ideal world, *all* actions taken by a company to enhance its own commercial success should simultaneously generate benefits for society *over and above* those that come directly through the use of that company's products and services.

UNPACKING THE LICENCE TO OPERATE

We are, of course, a very long way away from that kind of reciprocity, given the degree to which the interests of shareholders have been systematically prioritized by governments over the interests of all other stakeholders. Crude trade-off remains the name of the game in far too many instances. However, as Tables 14.2 and 14.3 demonstrate, the Five Capitals Framework at least makes it possible to envisage a business environment (in which governments could regulate or motivate investment strategies for a company) which did, indeed, generate both direct and indirect benefits for society.

And this really wouldn't be as risky and uncompetitive – to use the language of the current debate in the European Union (EU) – as most Organisation for Economic Co-operation and Development (OECD) governments would have their electorates believe. As many commentators have pointed out, no less an authority than the redoubtable Joseph Schumpeter constantly reminded politicians that the real driving force of capitalism is *disequilibrium*, based on new combinations of technology, opportunity, information and shifting demand. He described this phenomenon as 'creative destruction' and urged governments not to intervene in markets to protect sectors or individual companies that were being overwhelmed

Table 14.2 *The Five Capitals Framework: benefits for business*

Five Capitals	Business Strategies	Direct Business Benefits →	← Indirect Business Benefits	Aggregate Benefits
Natural Capital	Eco-efficiency Climate Change Strategy Design for Sustainable Development Biodiversity Action Plans Product Stewardship	• Lower costs • Future costs avoided • Stimulate increased innovation	• Reputation enhanced • Regulatory impact avoided • Better risk management • Take advantage of government incentives	Enhanced Reputation
Social Capital	Corporate Community Investment Communications for Sustainability Proactive Stakeholder Engagement Human Rights Policy	• Reduced cost of compliance • Local business links • Community goodwill • Reduced costs of getting planning permission	• Long term "licence to operate"/"licence to grow' • Enhanced reputation with Government/Regulators • Lower transaction costs • Favourable communications	Stronger Brands Customer Preference
Human/ Intellectual Capital	Employee Rights and Entitlements Process Innovation Quality Management Values-led Leadership Personal & Professional Development	• Loyalty/staff motivation • Easier to recruit top talent • Staff productivity • Retention of key staff • Improved Health & Safety record	• New products and services • Enhanced knowledge networks • Improved customer services	**Market Advantage**
Manufactured/ Technological Capital	Eco-Innovation Reduced Energy Intensity Dematerialization Closed Loop Process Virtualization (move from Product to Service)	• Constant refinement of product range • Minimize impact of new taxes/charges etc • Innovation flourishes • Creativity brings its own reward	• New products and services • Business opportunities identified early	Risk Reduction Option Creation (Responsiveness to changing world)
Financial Capital	Performance Measurement Transparency & Accountability Best Practice Corporate Governance Green Accounting/Cost Internalization Investment Criteria (Pension Funds etc)	• Reduced cost of capital • Improved cost controls • Reduced insurance costs	• Better risk management • High standing with Socially Responsible Investment analysts • 'Future proofing' • Lower transaction costs	

Source: Forum for the Future

Table 14.3 *The Five Capitals Framework: societal benefits*

Five Capitals	Business Strategies	Direct Societal Benefits →	← Indirect Societal Benefits	Aggregate Benefits
Natural Capital	Eco-efficiency Climate Change Strategy Design for Sustainable Development Biodiversity Action Plans Product Stewardship	• Cleaner, safer environments • Reductions in mortality/morbidity • Improved air & water quality	• Life support systems protected • Aesthetic recreational benefits • Obligations to the future met	Social/Environmental Security
Social Capital	Corporate Community Investment Communications for Sustainability Proactive Stakeholder Engagement Human Rights Policy	• Participation/engagement • Human/civil rights reinforced • Inequalities diminished • Local economic multipliers	• Companies have to earn their 'licence to operate' • Companies acting as 'Good Neighbours' • Enhanced community spirit • Cultural diversity honoured	Community Cohesion
Human/ Intellectual Capital	Employee Rights and Entitlements Process Innovation Quality Management Values-led Leadership Personal & Professional Development	• Employees' rights/ entitlements protected • Access to training/ learning opportunities • Improved working environment • Opportunities for more challenging/rewarding work	• Better work/life balance • Life-long learning • Better educated workforce/ society	**Improved Quality of Life**
Manufactured/ Technological Capital	Eco-Innovation Reduced Energy Intensity Dematerialization Closed Loop Process Virtualization (move from Product to Service)	• Better value for money from goods & services • Reduction in unforeseen risk • Easier to reuse & recycle • 'Smarter' products & services	• Extended range of options • Easier to act as responsible consumers • Reduced environmental/ social footprint	Greater Access to Economic Opportunities
Financial Capital	Performance Measurement Transparency & Accountability Best Practice Corporate Governance Green Accounting/Cost Internalization Investment Criteria (Pension Funds etc)	• Prices internalize their full social/environmental costs • Better informed consumers/ investors	• Economic/employment opportunities spread more widely • Increased opportunities for Socially Responsible Investment • Greater trust between companies and their stakeholders	Personal Needs/ Aspirations Met

Source: Forum for the Future

by the transformative power of capitalism seeking out the next best way of generating better returns. As we know, this process of creative destruction can be very
painful, especially as older industrialized economies (which are often very labour
intensive) give way to different (more capital-intensive) models of creating value.

As Stuart Hart (2005) has pointed out in *Capitalism at the Crossroads*, this
debate about creative destruction has a direct bearing on the way in which different
companies are responding to the respective threats and opportunities posed by
today's sustainability challenge. On the one hand, there's a cautious, modest process
of continuous improvement under way (formalized in management systems such
as ISO 14001), providing plenty of reassurance and comfort for those companies
whose core business models evolved in an era of cheap energy, abundant raw
materials and no sense of physical limits. On the other hand, one can now identify
a growing number of new entrepreneurs more interested in bringing on 'disruptive'
technologies or processes with a view to making those old business models entirely
redundant – however much incremental 'greening' they may go in for. Hart draws
an interesting analogy here:

> *Just as nature enables some species to out-compete others through a process
> of natural selection and succession, so the sustainability revolution will
> enable those firms with more sustainable strategies to outperform – and,
> ultimately, replace – those with outmoded strategies and damaging
> technologies. No amount of greening will save firms from the gales of
> creative destruction that are likely to ensue in the coming decades.
> Greening perpetuates the current industry structure; it fosters continuous
> improvement rather than reinvention or fundamental innovation.
> Given the velocity of technological change and the growing significance
> of sustainability, this no longer appears to be a viable strategy: creative
> destruction appears to hold the key not only to the growth industries of
> the future, but to corporate survival.* (Hart, 2005)

A classic example of this dilemma can be seen with today's chemicals industry. In
2003, I found myself as the sole representative of 'civil society' on the UK
Chemistry Leadership Council – a body set up by the UK Department for Trade
and Industry (DTI) to lift the sights of the chemicals industry by pressing the case
for much smarter innovation, better training and a serious commitment to the
notion of sustainable chemicals. The game plan was to reach out beyond the
industry's own trade associations to engage with big users of chemicals and
chemistry (pharmaceutical companies, car manufacturers, retailers and so on), as
well as the industry's wider stakeholders. It has proved to be an extraordinary
challenge, working against a backdrop of depressed industry expectations, rising
NGO and consumer demands, big problems in recruiting high-quality staff, and
intense competitive pressures as more and more of the production of bulk
commodity chemicals shifts to China or the Middle East.

All of this has resulted in the dominance of highly defensive, reactive mindsets throughout large parts of the industry. Spokespeople for the industry feel that it has already 'cleaned up its act'; indeed, as a consequence of those external pressures, the industry has, bit by tortuous bit, improved its social and environmental performance, built better relationships with the communities in which its plants are based, and become far more transparent in both data management and reporting. Classic incremental greening, best represented in the global industry by the Responsible Care programme, a 15-year-old voluntary initiative that has had a big impact upon all large chemical companies. Within a limited framework, Responsible Care has worked: it has helped to reduce the industry's collective environmental and social externalities, and helped to present a 'better case' to its respective stakeholders. But it has *not* helped the industry to focus on *genuine sustainability* in that it has not asked what changes are now required to ensure that the use of chemicals in society, at every level, can be secured within nature's limits.

The Chemistry Leadership Council took on that challenge, and produced a vision for the industry (or, rather, for the much wider chemistry-using supply chain) based upon the Five Capitals Framework and looking at a very different pattern of creating wealth through chemistry:

> *These trends are pushing the industry towards adding value in very different ways, with many companies becoming smaller, faster, more consumer-oriented and more flexible as they focus on the 'knowledge content' of products and processes. This is being accelerated by the convergence between different scientific disciplines as biologists, biochemists, chemists, chemical engineers, geneticists, systems engineers and IT and computer specialists combine forces in a sometimes bewildering array of new research and product development configurations. Achieving sustainability will mean that those who have responsibility for specifying materials or designing products will need to have a much fuller understanding of the need for radical 'dematerialization' and the far more efficient use of materials and energy.* (Chemistry Leadership Council, 2005)

This presents a real quandary for governments, currently evidenced in the intense debate about the right way of regulating for the use of chemicals through the EU. The European chemicals industry has argued that the EU's new regulatory proposals are far too onerous and costly – and have deployed the combined fire power of Prime Ministers Blair, Schroeder and Chirac to help 'defend the competitiveness of one of the EU's core industries'. By contrast, NGOs and European parliamentarians have argued that the proposals do not go far enough, in that they will not encourage the industry to move as fast as it now needs to in order to meet the social and environmental challenges of sustainability. It's all very well to argue (as we do through the Chemistry Leadership Council) that it is utterly impossible to envisage a sustainable future for humankind without chemicals (or, rather, without a dramatically different and smarter use of chemistry) to help meet the needs and aspirations of 9 billion people; but governments have got to do far more here than default to crude defence strategies in the name of competitiveness.

For governments to start thinking in this way will strengthen the general case that sustainable development is fundamentally not about trade-offs: it is first and foremost about win–win outcomes, in a real sense, and only then about unavoidable trade-offs. Moreover, the alignment that is proposed here is not so much the conventional triple bottom line alignment, but the aligning of business ('private') interest with societal ('common') interests in a far more challenging interdependence. In that respect, such an approach to the business case would, in essence, re-present the case first made by Adam Smith, and more recently by Herman Daly and John Cobb (1989) in *For the Common Good*, that wealth creation should be so organized as to simultaneously optimize both profit *and* social wellbeing. It does not, however, go as far as Paul Hawken (1993) who has argued that the *primary* purpose of business is to increase social wellbeing, with profit playing a secondary role. That seems an ideological bridge too far at this point in the evolution of our capitalist systems.

It is interesting how reluctant business leaders are to publicly engage in this kind of debate. They effortlessly fall back on the old 'division of labour argument': that this isn't really legitimate territory for them since it is up to governments using their democratic mandate to regulate the social, environmental and economic framework within which business then creates the wealth that society needs. Yet it is not disputed that all large multinational companies are lobbying away furiously to persuade governments that you couldn't put a cigarette paper between their interests and the interests of society as a whole – even though this is transparently not proven in the majority of cases. The very concept of 'corporate citizenship' (which seems to imply the same kind of balance between rights and obligations for a company as for an individual citizen) turns to ashes when one contemplates close up some of the flagrant abuses of 'citizenship' carried out by some of today's least responsible multinational companies.

As we have seen, many business leaders (particularly in the US) do, indeed, see sustainable development as a serious threat to today's neo-liberal, corporate-led economy, not least because any serious rebalancing of the interest of shareholders and other stakeholders would have a marked impact upon their own financial prospects. But few of them any longer speak out about this in public. Lecturing at Boston College's Chief Executives Club in March 2005, Peter Brabeck-Letmathe, chief executive of Nestlé, gave rare voice to what one suspects many chief executives may still feel in private: 'What the hell have we taken away from society by being a successful company that employs a lot of people?' He went on to pour scorn on the notion of any company having any additional obligations to a community over and above creating jobs and profits, and to argue that any 'charitable work' a company engages in should be geared exclusively to helping make more money for investors. Such an unyielding approach may explain why, for many environmental and social justice campaigners, Nestlé remains one of the most criticized and heavily targeted multinationals in the world today.

It may also explain why Stephen Viederman, president of the Jessie Smith Noyes Foundation, argues that 'corporations and sustainable development are simply incompatible since these corporations have no commitment to community or place, to future generations, to democracy, to equity or to alleviating poverty'. I don't accept that irreconcilable incompatibility, as I have already made clear in Chapter 5; but he's certainly right in pointing out that multinational companies have a very partial perspective on corporate responsibility, especially on issues such as corporate governance, taxation and even macro-economic concerns such as overall levels of employment.

In this respect, there remains an extraordinary mismatch between the power of multinationals and their contribution to global employment. The top 300 corporations own an estimated 25 per cent of the world's productive assets; the top 500 account for 75 per cent of all commodities traded. Despite that, the world's top 200 corporations (accounting for 28 per cent of global economic activity) employ less than 0.25 per cent of the global workforce. Estimates vary; but the whole lot of them employ less than 1 per cent of the global workforce – a figure which has not increased for more than two decades. Yet, for most people in the developed world (and increasingly in the developing countries), access to a job is still the principal mechanism for improving one's material standard of living. For many people, the fact that multinational companies play such a minute role in creating direct job opportunities while controlling such a huge share of total productive assets raises a serious question mark over their so-called 'licence to operate'. As we have seen elsewhere, there are many who believe that they are simply not paying enough for that licence.

ENGAGING WITH THE BASE OF THE PYRAMID

World class companies are increasingly aware of the way in which societal expectations are rising on issues of this kind. Ever since C. K. Prahalad and Stuart Hart published their influential article 'The fortune at the bottom of the pyramid' in 2002, growing attention has been paid to the challenge of addressing the needs of the poorest 4 billion people in the world today. This strategic thrust has been championed by the World Business Council for Sustainable Development (WBCSD), which brought out an excellent booklet in 2004 (*Doing Business with the Poor: A Field Guide*) demonstrating the different ways in which multinational companies are already trying to 'blend financial and social value'. It is clear that a number of global trends are now encouraging companies to start thinking far more proactively about engaging with 'the base of the pyramid' to help promote sustainable livelihoods:

- Many companies now see a need to break out of mature markets with their near-glutted profile and seek new opportunities in emerging, more dynamic markets.
- Enabling conditions in many developing countries are improving in terms of legal structures, investment conditions, less corruption and so on.
- Global communications are improving all the time, making the world a smaller and easier place for businesses to operate in.
- It's getting easier to find the right kind of partners to experiment with more innovative, cross-sectoral approaches.
- Many more countries now see foreign direct investment as an important way of helping to address poverty, reinforcing aid flows rather than undermining them.
- There is a much clearer realization that business can make a genuine difference, and that it badly needs to; as the WBCSD puts it: 'Business cannot succeed in a society that fails.'

What emerges from the WBCSD's *Field Guide* (2004) is an array of interesting 'hybrids' involving more than 20 companies (see the Vodacom Community Services Programme in Box 14.1). They are not philanthropic, nor are they necessarily securing the same rate of return as those which companies would expect for investments in developed markets. But to be sustainable, such ventures do, indeed, have to be quasi-commercial to start with, with a clear expectation of financial sustainability being achieved in due course:

> *This report may strike the wrong note with some, as we insist on the commercial character of sustainable livelihoods. But this is what is new and potentially revolutionary. Business, working in a spirit of 'enlightened self-interest', can improve the developmental path of billions of people by facilitating their access to the marketplace, by finding new ways to address the needs of the poor and helping them into mainstream economic activity. A growing body of evidence indicates that intelligent engagement will also result in new revenue and profits.* (WBCSD, 2004)

I have to admit that I was somewhat sceptical about this 'base-of-the-pyramid' stuff. It seemed to me that a lot of it was flimsy and was much more about coming up with smart new ways of flogging more things to more people than about addressing real poverty or sustainability issues. But Stuart Hart's latest book *Capitalism at the Crossroads* (2005) has caused me to rethink that scepticism in that he's come up with a far more compelling and inspirational rationale for base-of-the-pyramid strategies than anything I've seen before:

> *Over the past few years, it has become apparent that there is a large prospective market to be served in the base of the pyramid. It has also become clear that the prospect transcends mere market potential: The opportunity is to use commerce as a driving force for human betterment*

BOX 14.1 VODACOM COMMUNITY SERVICES PROGRAMME

The Vodacom Community Services Programme in South Africa shows how a technology company can learn to operate profitably in a lower-income market segment. Vodacom is a joint venture between Vodafone and Telkom South Africa, and has developed a shared service model for providing telecommunications services to poor communities. It began with a government mandate (to have 22,000 lines in operation within five years in order to provide affordable cellular communications to under-serviced areas – a required precondition for serving more lucrative market segments), but turned into an important source of learning and an opportunity for future profitable growth.

The basic approach has been to set up stationary phone shops or kiosks with multiple lines, all connected to Vodacom's existing infrastructure through a wireless link. To identify local entrepreneurs to run the phone kiosks, the company looked at the phone-use patterns of its existing customers. They realized that those who appeared to be using their phones a great deal were probably renting them call-by-call to friends and neighbours. This allowed Vodacom to identify the natural village entrepreneurs and to hire them and train them to manage the mobile kiosks. Vodacom used a franchise model to promote local entrepreneurship and to reduce start-up capital requirements.

Vodacom found that each mobile phone shop spawned five new jobs and unquantifiable spin-off economic gains. Benefits to the community of having telecommunication services available include allowing families with a migrant worker to keep in touch and manage family affairs, helping people to conduct their businesses more effectively, and allowing delivery drivers to keep in touch with headquarters.

The cost of setting up a phone shop is equivalent to about $7400. Vodacom pays about $3950 to purchase and modify shipping containers to turn them into phone shops. The individual owners are responsible for purchasing the internal equipment and paying to transport the container to its final site. The franchisee's total investment is approximately $3450. There are now more than 23,000 phone lines at approximately 5000 sites. Total revenue (to Vodacom) in 2003 was $129.5 million. Vodacom is paid two-thirds of total revenue, while the phone shop owner keeps the other one third, so each shop brings in an average of $38,800 per year in gross revenues.

Source: WBCSD (2004)

and environmental restoration – to literally raise the base of the pyramid. Attempts to adapt the top of the pyramid model for use at the base, however, appear destined to fail. Only through a concerted focus on the base of the pyramid will it be possible for large corporations to combine a humanitarian, even activist, orientation with the conventional motivations of growth and profitability. (Hart, 2005)

The case studies that Stuart Hart uses to demonstrate that this kind of shift is already manifesting itself in all sorts of different ways are also very motivational. Although the critics of multinationals quoted elsewhere in this book would still be inclined to dismiss all such case studies as a 'green veneer' on an otherwise unreconstructed and fundamentally unsustainable business model, a more positive approach (especially for governments trying to work out their own role in promoting more socially and environmentally responsible business engagement) would be to distil critical success criteria from these case studies and to work hard to promote them elsewhere – as is already happening through today's Base of the Pyramid Learning Laboratory. The story of Cemex, for example, a Mexican cement company, demonstrates important aspects of this new approach, even as critics around the world would point out that Cemex is by no means a paragon of virtue on many sustainability issues (see Box 14.2).

One of the most interesting aspects of Stuart Hart's argument is that the base of the pyramid is likely to prove a far more welcoming test bed for some of the bolder, disruptive technologies upon which our sustainable future depends. Mature OECD economies are often so fixed in their ways, so deeply trapped in fixed infrastructures and decades' worth of sunk capital investments, that the prospective losers in any 'disruptive transition' towards a more sustainable economy fight like fury to protect their own (and their shareholders') vested interests. In many base-of-the-pyramid contexts, such vested interests do not command such blocking rights, opening up opportunities for far more radical market creation strategies.

One particularly important example of this relates to the emergence of a host of new technologies designed to generate electricity at the point of use – the home, the office, the hospital, school or factory. These so-called 'distributed generation' or micro-generation technologies (including mini-wind turbines, mini-CHP (combined heat and power) plants, photovoltaic (PV) fuel cells, biomass boilers and biogas digesters) are not dependent upon grid connection, and could make a huge difference in terms of securing reliable and low-carbon supplies of energy. Indeed, in Schumpeterian terms, it's hard to imagine a more necessary process of 'creative destruction' than this one. Not surprisingly, the principal power-brokers in today's energy industries have been less than enthusiastic about investing in the research and development required to bring these alternatives to market. Obstacles confront pioneers of distributed energy systems at every turn. So why not look elsewhere, suggests Stuart Hart:

> *Distributed generation faces few of these obstacles among the rural poor in the developing world. It may be decades before the electrical grid system is extended to provide service to those who currently lack access to dependable electric power. As a consequence, the rural poor spend a significant portion of their income – as much as $10 per month – on candles, kerosene and batteries to have access to lighting at night and periodic electrical service. Furthermore, generating electricity using kerosene and batteries is expensive, costing $5 to $10 or more per kilowatt hour. If offered a viable substitute, these people might abandon these dangerous, polluting and expensive technologies in favour of clean, efficient and renewable electric power. Yet few producers of distributed generation have targeted the rural poor at the base of the pyramid as their*

BOX 14.2 CEMEX: A MEXICAN CEMENT COMPANY

Cemex, Mexico's largest cement company, provides a glimpse into how to go about constraint identification as a vehicle for reaching the BOP (base of the pyramid). The 1994 financial crisis in Mexico was a major blow to the company's domestic business, which constituted nearly half of Cemex's cement sales at the time. . . However, Cemex executives noted that whereas revenues from upper- and middle-class customers dropped by half, cement sales to the poorest tier of the population were hardly affected. . . Given that cement sales to the poor constituted 40 per cent of Cemex's Mexican business and that the company knew little about this customer segment, corporate leadership decided that it was worthy of further investigation.

In 1998, a team of Cemex employees began to explore this issue in greater depth. They began by issuing a Declaration of Ignorance, an open admission that the company knew virtually nothing about 40 per cent of its Mexican market. They then resolved to learn all they could about the needs and problems of the people in the urban slums and shantytowns where demand for the company's cement was the strongest. To accomplish this, the team lived in the shantytown for six months. Their mission was to better understand the context in the BOP, not to sell more cement.

At first glance, the shantytowns appeared to be chaotic assemblages of half-built squatter homes stretching as far as the eye can see. . . But after spending several months living in this context, the team came to realize that the people were doing the best possible job that could be done, given the constraints and the circumstances. Poor, do-it-yourself homebuilders in the shantytowns, they learned, often take 4 years to complete just one room and 13 years to finish a small four-room house. The reason is that banks and other businesses will not engage with poor residents of informal settlements where the legal status of their property ownership is murky. Haphazard design, combined with material theft and spoilage, conspire to make home construction a costly and risky proposition. Vendors prey upon the poor, selling them off-quality goods in quantities that are inappropriate because they have little bargaining power or ability to complain. The Cemex team came to realize that if these constraints could be removed, it might be possible for the poor to build much better-quality homes in less time, while also saving money on material in the process. And, yes, they might also grow the cement business as well.

To accomplish this end, the team created a new business model. Through its programme called *Patrimonio Hoy*, which, roughly translated, means Equity Today, Cemex formed savings clubs that allowed aspiring homebuilders to make weekly savings payments. In exchange, Cemex provided material storage and architectural support so that homes could be well designed and built in sensible stages. Given its clout as a major buyer, Cemex could negotiate with material suppliers for the best possible prices and quality, something that the shantytown dwellers themselves were unable to do. Participants in the programme built their houses three times faster, with higher-quality materials and designs, and at two-thirds the cost. *Patrimonio Hoy* has been growing at a rate of 250 per cent per year and has enrolled more than 20,000 poor families since its inception. The goal is to reach 1 million families in Mexico in five years.

Source: Hart (2005)

early market for these technologies, despite the fact that the market is potentially huge and is populated by people who would be delighted with technologies that cannot compete along the metrics used in developed markets. (Hart, 2005)

DISRUPTIVE PARTNERSHIPS

It goes without saying that any such vision would depend upon developing a completely different kind of stakeholder strategy; it is not just disruptive technologies that this business model requires, but disruptive processes – particularly when it comes to new patterns of partnership. Some of the most creative partnerships these days are cross-sectoral, particularly when it's a question of negotiating management of community assets or biological diversity. And this can be very difficult territory. The business of providing clean water and sanitation services in developing countries, for instance, has caused intense controversy over the last decade or more as Western countries and multilateral institutions have sought to advance privatization as the solution to all such problems. The scale of the problems, as recognized in the Millennium Development Goals (MDGs), is not in dispute: at least 1 billion people (one person in five) lack access to safe water. Twice as many lack access to improved sanitation. Every year, 2 million people die because of the unclean water they are forced to drink – that is nearly four people for every minute of every day. But the solution to these problems certainly *is* in dispute.

In February 2005, the World Development Movement (WDM) brought out its latest report in this area, *Dirty Aid, Dirty Water*, fiercely criticizing the UK Government for continuing to champion the privatization of water services in the teeth of growing evidence that it simply isn't working in one country after another. Privatization schemes often fail to extend water and sewerage networks to the poorest communities (on the grounds that they can't afford them), or alternatively end up with the poor facing substantial price hikes. Yet the Department for International Development (DFID) in the UK perseveres:

> *Through the Department for International Development, millions of pounds of aid have been spent employing consultants, often UK companies, to 'advise' developing country governments to hand management of their water to foreign companies. And despite the many costs of privatization to the poor, the UK is leading international efforts to create mechanisms to fund privatization consultants. Aid money for the much needed restructuring of water and sanitation provision in poor countries is then only forthcoming if the consultant's privatization plan is accepted. The UK is also taking an international lead in finding ways to subsidize multinational companies' involvement in providing this service.* (WDM, 2005)

In fact, most multinational water companies have become equally wary about making huge new investments in developing countries. Many of them have had their fingers very badly burned, with poor returns, inadequate regulatory enforcement and high political risk. It was partly because of that gloomy prospect that Thames Water (now part of the German RWE Group) decided to try something very different, convening an international consortium made up of itself, Halcrow, Unilever, Care International, the World Wide Fund for Nature (WWF) and WaterAid, to establish the Water and Sanitation for the Urban Poor (WSUP) project. The basic idea is to use international aid funding and contributions in kind from the members of the consortium to identify and develop projects in conjunction with local community organizations and local authorities.

Although it's early days, it is hoped that the areas where assistance will really be brought to bear will include project management of infrastructure works, as well as assistance in the development of sustainable, locally managed arrangements for operating and maintaining the system. Emphasis will be on building the capacity of the local service authority staff and on the sustainability of that service. Local people will fill key positions, and external assistance will only be provided when and where necessary. None of the organizations involved in the different project consortia will seek long-term commercial involvement in the project locations, thereby opening up opportunities for the local private sector. And once the consortium has achieved its purpose, which it is assumed will generally take three to five years, it will hand over the project to the local service provider or community.

The first WSUP project is under way in Bangalore to provide 70,000 residents of urban slums with safe water and effective sanitation. That, of course, is just a drop in the proverbial ocean of need in developing countries; but at least WSUP is trying to break out of the deadlock over water privatization that has bedevilled innovative thinking in this area for more than a decade. And the principal victims of the deadlock have been poor people themselves. As C. K. Prahalad and Al Hammond (2002) have so convincingly demonstrated, the urban poor often end up paying anywhere between twice to 20 times as much for water (and, indeed, other basic services) as consumers 'at the top of the pyramid'. Exploitative local vendors, corrupt local government officials and utterly ruthless local moneylenders often combine forces to deprive some of the world's poorest and most vulnerable people of basic services. Any major initiative that begins to combat that nexus of exploitation has to be an important step forward.

A key characteristic that many of these case studies has in common is a much less risk-averse approach to finding the right partners for any project. The concept of 'coalitions of the willing' emerged from the World Summit on Sustainable Development in Johannesburg in 2002 as a way of overcoming some of the usual barriers to progress; many companies are, indeed, much more willing to pool both learning and risk by taking forward new ideas in conjunction with others, especially in areas of particular controversy.

The Business Leaders Initiative on Human Rights (BLIHR) is a case in point, bringing together seven global companies (ABB, Barclays PLC, The Body Shop International, MTV Networks Europe, National Grid Transco, Novartis and Novo Nordisk) to help embed good practice on human rights issues in a more profound way than has happened up until now. In 2004, the United Nations Human Rights Sub-Commission approved 'Norms on the Responsibilities of Transnational Corporations and other Business Enterprises with Regard to Human Rights'. Not surprisingly, these norms have already proved to be controversial, with a number of companies (and, more particularly, their trade associations) claiming that compliance with them would jeopardize competitiveness in establishing new businesses in developing countries. The role of the BLIHR is to work through that kind of dilemma, in practice, which it does by exploring with its members a continuum of potential corporate behaviours, from 'non-negotiable essentials' (compliance with minimum obligations such as existing labour, environmental tax and other laws, with requirements of market regulators and licence granters, and with government requirements on health and safety, corporate reporting and so on) at one end, through to 'expected behaviours' (such as public reporting, public statements on social and environmental issues, internal processes that support such policies, monitoring and audit programmes), and, at the other end, the category of 'desirable behaviours', including strategic philanthropy and social investment, public policy dialogue, assistance to disadvantaged groups, and creating positive multipliers along a company's supply chain.

TOWARDS A MORE BALANCED SCORECARD

Nevertheless, it is easy to get seduced by the allure of the individual project, ignoring the fact that such projects are often unrepresentative (in that they do not necessarily reflect core business behaviour or affect the dominant business model) and ephemeral – failure rates are high. Though it's much less 'sexy' in media terms, and therefore far less visible to the outside world, the real test of a company's intentions in this area can only be gauged by scrutinizing in detail the management systems and practices by which it seeks to mainstream sustainable development/ corporate responsibility into the *whole* of the company. To what extent are companies developing a more sophisticated, balanced scorecard to take proper account of these complex societal and ethical issues?

To test this out, the Five Capitals Framework has been adapted to provide just such a 'balanced scorecard' in a project called SIGMA (Sustainability Integrated Guidelines for Management), initiated by Forum for the Future, co-developed with the British Standards Institution (BSI) and an NGO in this area called AccountAbility, and paid for by the Department for Trade and Industry in the UK. The purpose of SIGMA was to test the feasibility of an integrated management standard covering the whole range of sustainability issues in response to companies becoming increasingly anxious about the multiplicity of management standards and voluntary codes being promoted in this area – such as International Organization for Standardization (ISO) 14001, the Eco-management and Audit Scheme (EMAS), Investors in People, ISO 9000, AcountAbility (AA) 1000 and the Global Reporting Initiative (GRI).

The interim outcome of the SIGMA Project is a set of integrated guidelines to help organizations more effectively meet the challenges posed by social, environmental and economic dilemmas, threats and opportunities, and to become architects in their own sector of a sustainable future. These guidelines comprise a set of principles (based on the maintenance and enhancement of the Five Capitals); a management framework using the classic four-stage process (Leadership and Vision; Planning; Delivery; and Monitor, Review and Report) to help embed sustainability thinking and practice within core organizational processes; and a toolkit stuffed to the gills with practical tools to get all that done – benchmark audits, stakeholder dialogues, environmental accounting, sustainability scorecards (a more sustainable version of the balanced business scorecard) and so on (see Figure 14.3).

Such detail is important: not only is sustainability capable of rigorous scientific definition and interpretation (as explained in Part I); so, too, is it capable of strategic mainstreaming and detailed implementation in *any* organization. We are no longer marooned in a sea of well-meaning theory and intellectual abstraction; as demonstrated by the 21 supporting organizations involved in SIGMA (including 15 blue-chip companies), this is starting to happen in an applied way to improve performance across the whole range of areas of concern. This process will, no doubt, accelerate rapidly as the British Standards Institution now takes SIGMA forward with a view to it being accredited as an international standard. And this is just one of a large number of 'mainstreaming initiatives' that are now being pioneered by different companies.

A lot of this comes back to the old adage that 'what can't be measured can't be managed'. Because so many business impacts upon the environment and society have remained obstinately outside any 'measure it to manage it' framework, most companies still don't know the degree to which their notional end-of-year profits are, in part, inflated by their ability to go on externalizing costs and drawing large subsidies from the natural world or the 'social capital' upon which they depend.

Hence the critical importance of environmental accounting – and the more innovative and integrated approach embodied in sustainability accounting. In September 2002, the UK's Chartered Institute of Management Accountants (CIMA) published its *Environmental Accounting: An Introduction and Practical Guide*. Basically, environmental accounting is an attempt to put a monetary value on the cost to companies of avoiding external environmental impacts. This allows companies to internalize these costs in order to help them improve both environmental and economic performance (see Box 14.3). Several leading companies are already using this methodology. These include AWG (formerly Anglian Water),

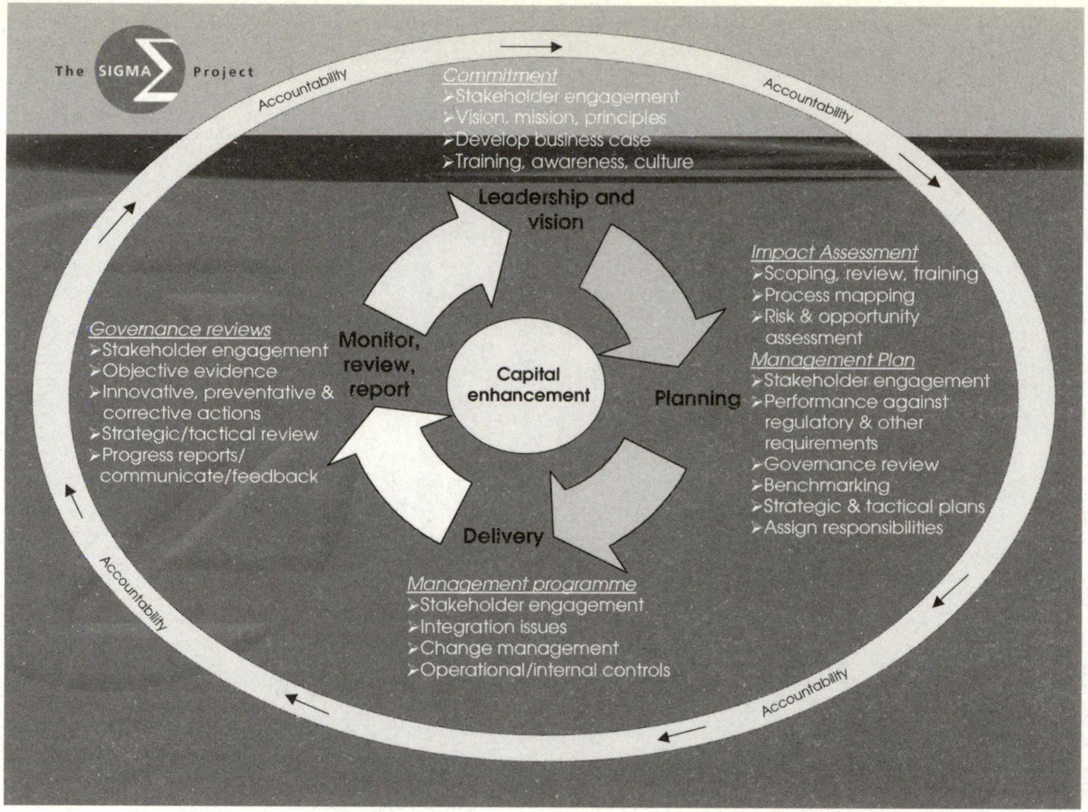
The SIGMA Project
Accountability
Accountability
Accountability
Accountability
Commitment
➢Stakeholder engagement
➢Vision, mission, principles
➢Develop business case
➢Training, awareness, culture
Leadership and vision
Planning
Delivery
Monitor, review, report
Capital enhancement
Impact Assessment
➢Scoping, review, training
➢Process mapping
➢Risk & opportunity assessment
Management Plan
➢Stakeholder engagement
➢Performance against regulatory & other requirements
➢Governance review
➢Benchmarking
➢Strategic & tactical plans
➢Assign responsibilities
Management programme
➢Stakeholder engagement
➢Integration issues
➢Change management
➢Operational/internal controls
Governance reviews
➢Stakeholder engagement
➢Objective evidence
➢Innovative, preventative & corrective actions
➢Strategic/tactical review
➢Progress reports/ communicate/feedback

Source: The SIGMA Project

Figure 14.3 *The SIGMA Project*

BOX 14.3 WHAT IS ENVIRONMENTAL ACCOUNTING?

Using an accounting approach anchors sustainability considerations in data that goes far beyond simple indicators. By converting environmental – and, eventually, social – benefits and costs into monetized values, a company can account for its contribution to sustainability in a way that is consistent with other business activities. Financial environmental accounting can help to make the link between financial and environmental performance and therefore give management the information they need to come up with win–win decisions.

Environmental accounting has three different faces:

1 *Tracking the benefits and costs to the company of its initiatives*. The costs of environmental activities are all too prominent, but the benefits are often hidden. Many projects have environmental and financial benefits: avoiding fines, creating cost efficiencies or leading to new sources of revenue while increasing resource productivity and reducing waste. More intangible benefits come from motivating employees and enhancing a company's reputation. Unless these benefits are brought to management's attention, environmental activities only look like a cost centre. Bringing the costs and benefits of environmental activities together allows companies to build the business case.

2 *Measuring the externalities created*. An externality is the cost borne by other people, now and in the future, from an activity which was not included in the transaction price. It is now possible to calculate the externality a company is creating; but because externalities are by definition outside of the market's price-setting process, any valuation is judgemental.

3 *Calculating the cost and benefit to the company of avoiding its environmental impacts*. A company needs to know the financial exposure of having to internalize its externalities. Companies can be quickly asked to reduce their environmental impacts – either through regulation and taxes (such as the Climate Change Levy or Landfill Tax) or from changes in stakeholder expectations (disposal of oil rigs such as the Brent Spar). With an account of how much it would cost the company to avoid or restore its main environmental impacts, a company can move to limit its exposure, improve its decision-making and report progress to stakeholders.

Forum for the Future has worked with a number of partners to develop a technique to account for the cost of avoiding or restoring environmental impacts. The results of our work were published with the Chartered Institute of Management Accounting (CIMA) in *Environmental Cost Accounting: An Introduction and Practical Guide* (2002). The guide sets out four steps:

1 identification of the most significant/major environmental impacts resulting from the company's activities and operations;
2 estimation/determination of what a sustainable level of emissions/impacts may be – that is, the determination of relevant sustainability targets or the 'sustainability gap';
3 valuation of the cost of closing the sustainability gap through market-based avoidance and restoration costs;
4 estimation of the company's sustainability cost and 'environmentally sustainable profits'.

This approach links monetized corporate environmental data to the company's financial accounts in order to arrive at an *environmentally adjusted profit level*. Roger Adams, technical director of the Association of Chartered Certified Accountants (ACCA), a leading accounting institute, said that:

> The Holy Grail of sustainability accounting is to see it developed to a stage where it is sufficiently robust to be accepted for mainstream financial reporting and tax calculation purposes. Hopefully the work of Forum for the Future will one day be able to tell us where the Grail is hidden.

Our partners are using a number of techniques: assessing risk exposure; deciding between different capital investment projects; and reporting sustainability performance to stakeholders.

The next stage is to move from environmental into social and economic issues, something we have begun to do with the social cost of alcohol and the social return on community investment programmes. To be useful in decision-making, sustainability accounting must provide tools to assess different strategic options for their impact upon the company and wider society.

Source: Forum for the Future

Wessex Water, Bulmers, Carillion, Marks and Spencer and Interface Europe. Some are also reporting the results; for the third year running, Wessex Water has published its full external cost accounts, alongside its conventional financial statements, within its main annual report and accounts. Similarly, AWG has reported the impact of its sustainability cost estimates upon their reported profits for the last six years in a row.

The CIMA publication was just the latest in a series of outputs, many from other accounting bodies. These include *Full Cost Accounting: An Agenda For Action* from the Association of Chartered Certified Accountants (ACCA, 2001), and a recent publication from Envirowise (a UK government programme) to help companies increase their profitability through improved resource productivity: *Using Environmental Management Accounting to Increase Profits* (Envirowise, 2004). In 2004, the Institute of Chartered Accountants of England and Wales (ICAEW) published its *Sustainability: The Role of Accountants*, another encouraging sign that the accountancy profession is becoming increasingly engaged in helping to facilitate the transition to a more sustainable economy.

There is no reason why sustainability accounting shouldn't become a standard procedure for any well-managed company. It provides a mechanism to unlock 'hidden value', and to reduce impacts and enhance profits through more complete and transparent accounting for aspects of an organization's environmental performance. These eco-efficiency savings can be significant. Baxter Healthcare, for example, has reported that environmental investments instituted as early as 1992 have yielded approximately $86 million per annum in savings and cost avoidance.

In December 2003, Sir John Browne, chief executive of BP, updated shareholders on BP's own emissions reduction programme: 'Within the first three years, we added $650 million of value, for an investment of around $20 million.' Examples of this kind (and there are many) clearly provide a very powerful signal to boards of directors to initiate further sustainability investments and to replicate identified good practice across the organization.

Sustainability accounting can also help companies to develop strategies to reduce and manage external environmental and social risks. Recent legislative developments across most OECD countries (together with a number of voluntary initiatives and guidelines on reporting and public disclosure) have dramatically increased the pressure on all companies to manage and report the non-financial risks associated with their business. Here in the UK, these include legislative changes arising from the recent Company Law Review, the new combined code, and the Turnbull Report on internal controls. Together with the earlier Pensions Act disclosure requirements, several of these initiatives promote active institutional investor engagement in relation to companies' environmental, social and ethical performance. Finance directors and investor relations departments increasingly have to incorporate a review of these issues to reduce risk and add value in their communications with their financial stakeholders, and the new Operating and Financial Review (OFR) will further accelerate that process. Environmental and social issues will need to be disclosed in company OFRs 'to the extent necessary' for investors to make an informed judgement about future strategies and their chances of success.

Eco-efficiency savings and risk management are just two aspects of the overall business case for sustainable development. For some companies, more value is likely to be derived from the *intangible* benefits associated with greater social and environmental responsibility. These include the impact upon brand value and reputation, the ability to attract and retain the best people, higher productivity from a motivated and inspired workforce and access to new markets (and maintenance of existing markets (see Table 14.1 for the intangible benefits associated with the business case for sustainable development). Innovative work by the Co-op Bank, for example, investigates the link between their ethical policies and the bank's overall profitability. Table 14.4 shows how they reported the results in their *2005 Partnership Report.*

For some time, the Co-operative Bank has been recognized as a leading proponent of the Sustainable Development Business Model. Research strongly indicates that while 'ethics' is a major determining factor for customers of the Co-operative Bank (24 per cent cite ethics as being influential in opening an account and this is by far the most frequently specified reason), it is only rarely specified by customers of other banks (fewer than 1 per cent of customers cite ethics as being influential in opening an account). The bank's co-operative, ethical and sustainability positioning contributes to the bank's profitability. In 2004, 34 per cent of bank profits can be attributed to customers who cite these as important factors

Table 14.4 *The Co-operative Bank's ethical and sustainability positioning (percentage pre-tax profit)*

	Profitability contribution made by customers who state that ethics is the most important factor	Profitability contribution made by customers who state that ethics is an important factor
2001[i]	14%	25%
2002[ii]	13%	24%
2003[iii]	17%	29%
2004[iv]	20%	34%

Notes: i Profit before tax as reported in the Co-operative Bank's interim results to 28 July 2001: £60.2 million.
ii Profit before tax as reported in the Co-operative Bank's full year results: £122.5 million.
iii Profit before tax as reported in the Co-operative Bank's full year results: £130.1 million.
iv Profit before tax as reported in the Co-operative Bank's full year results: £132.0 million.
Source: CFS (2005)

(2003: 29 per cent), and 20 per cent to customers who cite these as the most important factors (2003: 17 per cent) (CFS, 2005).

Sceptics may point out that it's a great deal easier for the Co-operative Bank (and its other half, the Co-operative Insurance Society) to adopt such an approach than it is for 'mainstream' banks given that it is so much smaller and that its whole marketing approach is based upon this kind of ethical appeal. True enough, but so what? The real point is to keep track of the way in which the kind of vanguard positioning pursued by the Co-operative Bank over the last ten years or more is subsequently taken up by mainstream players; it is this 'multiplier effect' that really matters and which completely justifies the Bank's claims to consistent and inspirational leadership in this area.

Interestingly, very few companies commit to doing the hard graft involved in working out exactly what the financial benefits accruing from serious engagement in social, ethical and environmental behaviour amount to. BT's analysis of the contribution to customer satisfaction of maintaining an excellent reputation with customers is one of the few examples in the public domain (see Figure 14.4).

All of this points to the urgent need to evolve the techniques of environmental accounting into a more integrated sustainability accounting framework, capturing monetized data on a full array of environmental and social impacts. Work on this is already under way in Forum for the Future, collaborating with the construction industry and with companies such as Carillion and Bulmers.

Suffice it to say, in conclusion, that there is a lot going on in the business world, which is genuine (*not* driven by public relations), substantive and long term. As evidence of this, one only has to take account of the proliferation of new books published over the last four or five years analysing the impact of sustainable development/corporate responsibility thinking on the business community, highlighting the progress that is being made, and exemplifying that progress

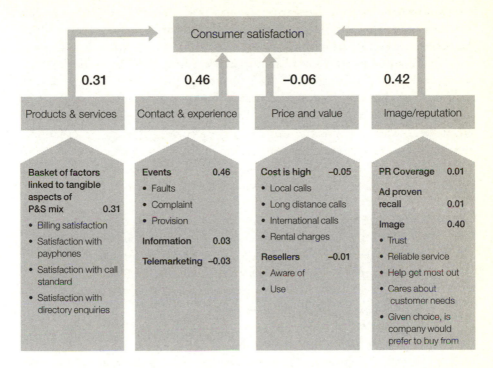

Note: Under each of the four main column headings in this figure is a list of the detailed measures we have data on – for example, customer satisfaction with our billing processes, the number of complaints we receive, the cost of our calls relative to our competitors, the balance between positive and negative media coverage on BT, and survey data on what the UK general public feels about our company.

The numbers at the head of each column are the cause and effect modulation factors for each of the four main drivers of customer satisfaction. They are best explained by example. If BT's overall image and reputation goes up by, say, 2 per cent, then we would expect to see a (2 x 0.42) 0.84 per cent increase in our customer satisfaction rating. Or if people perceive that our prices have increased by 10 per cent, then we would expect to see a (10 x –0.06) 0.6 per cent fall in our customer satisfaction rating.

The customer satisfaction model is a critical part in understanding, at the fundamental level, how we deliver business success within the enlightened stakeholder approach. But the big surprise that came out of this work was the criticality of BT's overall image and reputation as a major determinant of customer satisfaction.

Source: Danon (2001)

Figure 14.4 *British Telecom's analysis of consumer satisfaction*

through literally dozens of case studies on every conceivable area of concern. One of the most authoritative and accessible of these hands-on tracts is the World Business Council for Sustainable Development's *Walking the Talk: The Business Case for Sustainable Development* (WBCSD, 2002), which is still highly relevant for those trying to track down what is actually happening in practice.

And there is further encouragement from a new generation of business leaders who are prepared to speak out much more trenchantly on the need for more effective government–business relations to advance better policy-making. In a speech that UK Prime Minister Tony Blair gave in September 2004 to mark the tenth anniversary of the Prince of Wales's Business and the Environment Programme, he challenged the business community to start thinking more proactively about its role in getting serious on climate change. I suspect he may well have been somewhat taken aback when a consortium of 13 chief executives of major international companies (convened as the Business and the Environment Programme's Corporate Leaders Group) came right back at him with a response in June 2005, in effect offering a new kind of partnership between business and the UK Government:

> At present, we believe that the private sector and governments are caught in a 'Catch 22' situation with regard to tackling climate change. Governments tend to feel limited in their ability to introduce new policies for reducing emissions because they fear business resistance, while companies are unable to take their investments in low-carbon solutions to scale because of lack of long-term policies.
>
> In order to break this impasse, we are proposing to work in partnership with the government in order to:
>
> * support the development of a world-leading climate change policy framework capable of enabling a step change in private-sector investment in low-carbon technology in the UK;
> * significantly increase support for action on climate change from UK businesses, the public and other governments and businesses internationally;
> * dramatically scale up investment in low-carbon technologies and processes by our companies and others in response to a new policy.
>
> (Prince of Wales's Business and the Environment Programme, 2005)

There is nothing too dramatic in all of this, it's true; but compare this kind of positioning with that of the Confederation of British Industry (CBI), and a different kind of business leadership begins to emerge. However, the combined effect of all these examples of business engagement has yet to win over many critics of the role of multinationals in today's global economy. As we saw in Chapter 5, only a much more fundamental downsizing and reconfiguring of the limited liability corporation is likely to placate that much deeper hostility. This, of course, is hardly a challenge that can be taken up by the multinationals themselves, which would involve operating well outside their boundary conditions!

It is only governments that can reframe those boundary conditions, and governments are currently unlikely to commit to anything other than piecemeal, incremental reform, nudging the pendulum of capitalism away from an almost exclusive shareholder focus back towards the interests of society and a wider group of stakeholders. The pace and depth of that reform depends, in turn, upon just how much pressure governments come under from their electorates – and from consumers – to demand more of their wealth creators in terms of higher standards and more sustainable business practices. Here, too, we will find a somewhat ambivalent picture.

REFERENCES

ACCA (Association of Chartered Certified Accountants) (2001) *Full Cost Accounting: An Agenda for Action*, ACCA, London. Available at www.accaglobal.com/research/summaries/196138

CFS (Co-operative Financial Services) (2005) *2005 Partnership Report*, CFS, Manchester

Chemistry Leadership Council (2005) *The Sustainable Production and Use of Chemicals*, Forum for the Future, London

CIMA (Chartered Institute of Management Accountants) (2002) *Environmental Accounting: An Introduction and Practical Guide*, CIMA, London

Daly, H. and Cobb, J. (1989) *For the Common Good*, Beacon Press, Boston, MA

Danon, P. (2001) *Enlightened Values: Is Shareholder or Stakeholder Value the Better Path?*, British Telecom, London

Envirowise (2004) *Using Environmental Management Accounting to Increase Profits*, Envirowise (a Government programme managed by Momenta), Didcot, UK. Website at www.envirowise.gov.uk

Hart, S. (2005) *Capitalism at the Crossroads*, Wharton School Publishing, University of Pennsylvania, Philadelphia, PA

Hawken, P. (1993) *The Ecology of Commerce*, Weidenfield and Nicholson, London

ICAEW (Institute of Chartered Accountants of England and Wales) (2004) *Sustainability: The Role of Accountants*, ICAEW, London

Prahalad, C. K. and Hammond, A. (2002) 'Serving the world's poor, profitably', *Harvard Business Review*, September

Prahalad, C. K. and Hart, S. (2002) 'The fortune at the bottom of the pyramid', *Strategy and Business*, no 26

Prince of Wales's Business and the Environment Programme (2005), *Corporate Leaders' Group on Climate Change*, University of Cambridge Programme for Industry, Cambridge, UK

WBCSD (World Business Council for Sustainable Development) (2002) *Walking the Talk: The Business Case for Sustainable Development*, WBCSD, Geneva

WBCSD (2004) *Doing Business with the Poor: A Field Guide*, WBCSD, Geneva

WDM (World Development Movement) (2005) *Dirty Aid, Dirty Water*, WDM, London

15

Civil Society

INTRODUCTION

Free market zealots (who object to *any* increase in the powers of the state) would have us believe that the only way to secure a genuinely sustainable economy is for enough consumers to be using their purchasing power (or withholding it by saving rather than consuming) in order to ensure that markets deliver sustainable development as a by-product of consumer sovereignty. It's a wonderful notion *if* one believes that we live in a world of perfect information. But given how disempowered, manipulated and deceived (not least by prices that don't reflect true costs) today's consumers really are, the concept of 'consumer sovereignty' needs to be exposed to rather more stringent analysis. This uncertainty often leaves governments uncertain of their own role – not just in terms of regulation and other direct interventions in markets, but through sustainable procurement in the public sector and other ways of 'walking the sustainable talk' rather more proactively. It doesn't help that governments (with the active connivance of today's progressive left) now choose to define all citizens as consumers – of the party brand, of policy packages, of political choices. This 'consumerization' of politics has widened the governance gaps that are already causing such concern in terms of voter disengagement and disaffection.

CONSUMERS AND CITIZENS

So here's the crunch question: even if enlightened companies were not just filling the space available to them for more sustainable behaviour, but keen for government to expand that space so that they could go even further, as in the example of the Corporate Leaders Group of the Prince of Wales's Business and the Environment Programme (see Chapter 14), and even if governments were responding to the various macro-trends laid out in Chapter 11 with real purpose and consistent leadership, would consumers and voters be going along with it? Would they be rewarding those companies through the preferential use of their purchasing power, and rewarding those politicians through the use of their votes?

Having acknowledged right up front that any reform agenda for contemporary capitalism has to be mediated through fair and efficient markets *and* through healthy, functioning democracies, there's no avoiding that question. And the harsh, unpalatable truth *as of now* is not particularly supportive of a reform agenda of this kind. Survey after survey tells us that the majority of people are broadly content with our greed-driven consumer society (even if it doesn't make them any happier), and election after election tells us that only a minority of people are prepared to vote for the only political party (the Greens) that has, as yet, honestly confronted those macro-trends.

But is this so surprising? If the vast majority of people continue to live lives that depend upon systematic denial, and if all our political leaders (and the media that feed off them and on them) are strenuously promoting such denial, it seems to me to be something of a miracle that such large minorities have so steadfastly resisted co-option until now. Whether we are talking votes or profits, a healthy interest in the 'what's in it for me/my party/my company?' is hardly surprising, and for the vast majority of politicians and business leaders, it appears that there is just not enough in it for them. The risks are too high, the potential benefits too speculative. Denial is an infinitely easier choice than commercial or political damnation.

This makes consumer behaviour the most problematic of all today's potential drivers for change. It is true, of course, that there are many inspiring examples of consumer power mobilizing in defence of both the environment and oppressed people, going right back to hugely successful campaigns in the 1980s focusing on the elimination of chlorofluorocarbons (CFCs) from aerosols, all the way through to current campaigns to promote fair trade or resist the introduction of genetically modified (GM) crops. Historically, such successes work best when it's a question of *stopping* bad things from happening rather than making good things happen. Far larger numbers of consumers can be mobilized for the former than for the latter.

Beyond that minority of concerned consumers (to which I will return in a moment), many environmentally destructive activities and products seem to remain deeply attractive to the majority of consumers. At the glamorous end of 'conspicuous consumption', which does so much to fuel mass consumer aspirations, environmentally friendly technologies are not going to find it easy to deliver the ever-expanding choice set involving speed, fashion, change, variety and luxury which the globalized affluent middle classes increasingly expect. At the more mundane level of mass consumption, there is, as yet, minimal consumer willingness to trade off the conventional consumer values of comfort, convenience and low prices against enhanced environmental or social performance. Even if it is technically possible to combine environmental sustainability and economic growth, it is by no means apparent that consumers are yet prepared to choose the kind of economic growth that this implies.

It seems likely that an environmentally sustainable form of capitalism will need to have both very large numbers of consumers who want green products enough for them to rate their sustainability value as highly as other non-price considerations, and a significant minority of consumers who are willing and able to pay more for green products on a regular basis. It will also need to have found ways of reliably informing consumers about 'sustainability best buys' and of overcoming market failures where these exist. Achieving these conditions is likely to be among the most challenging tasks involved in moving a capitalist, market-driven economy towards biophysical sustainability and simultaneously ensuring that future economic activity remains compatible with it – especially if it means that people can't have their £15 flights to Malaga, 'trophy kitchens', patio heaters or garden hot tubs.

Even more challengingly, we have to be much more realistic about the so-called 'rebound effect'. As we have seen, more efficient resource use usually reduces costs in a way that makes it naturally attractive to companies. But the responses of consumers may be rather different in that any personal efficiency savings they make may even stimulate *increased* consumption. The 'rebound effect', as this latter phenomenon is sometimes called, is well established in the field of domestic energy efficiency improvements, in which the beneficiaries regularly choose greater comfort (higher room temperature) in preference to reduced fuel use. Where the beneficiaries are less well-off, and room temperatures are excessively low, no one would grudge this extra comfort. Indeed, the efficiency gain may be justified in these social and quality of life terms alone. But rebound effects apply in other contexts, as well, and can sometimes ensure that efficiency improvements of themselves actually do little to improve the environment.

Public value and choice

One begins to wonder, in such circumstances, whether consumer-driven materialism is a beast that can ever be tamed. Might it not be more sensible for politicians explicitly to espouse a wholly different approach, based explicitly on low consumption, sufficiency, simplicity and *real* quality of life? Paul Ekins has written at length about the benefits of sufficiency as a key policy driver of this kind:

> In a society devoted to ever-greater consumption, it is hard not to identify
> sufficiency with notions of sacrifice, of 'doing without' or 'giving things
> up'. Such identifications are, however, misplaced. Certainly, sufficiency
> implies relatively modest consumption and simplicity in personal life-
> style. But these are not motivated by abstract aestheticism or self-denial,
> but arise from a perception that sufficiency in consumption permits a
> greater emphasis to be placed on other aspects of human experience,
> which are actually more personally rewarding and fulfilling than consump-
> tion. Far from entailing self-denial, sufficiency in this reading is a means
> of liberation. An all-absorbing concern with consumption is replaced by
> the pursuit of other values that yield more happiness. (Ekins, 1998)

This overall orientation has led many environmentalists to argue that the only route to sustainability is for people not just to consume more responsibly, but to consume *less*. To bring that about, the hypothesis is advanced that people who have reached a certain level of material comfort and security can (and should) be persuaded that their future quality of life resides in freeing themselves of the trappings of consumerism and in opting, instead, for low-maintenance, low-throughput, low-stress patterns of work, recreation and home life.

The clearest manifestation of this has been described as 'down-shifting', evidenced by a growing number of people quietly reconfiguring their work to spend more time at home, with their children, doing other things entailing a lower income but a higher quality of life. The fact that this is a predominantly middle-class phenomenon does not invalidate its significance; but it inevitably raises questions about its usefulness in policy-making terms. With levels of poverty as high as they still are in many developed nations, let alone in the developing world, alternatives to economic growth are non-starters unless underpinned by an equally strong commitment to eliminate poverty (particularly among the young and the old) as espoused by more conventional political paradigms.

It also has to be acknowledged that there are significant macro-economic implications in any low-consumption economic model. Lower levels of economic growth (the inevitable consequence of large numbers of people opting for lower levels of economic activity) would mean lower tax revenues, which, in turn, would necessitate lower levels of public expenditure on key public services such as health and education, as well as lower levels of capital expenditure on things such as transport. The negative impact of this upon society and people's individual quality of life is as much of concern to advocates of genuine sustainable development as the negative impacts upon the environment of current levels of economic growth.

While it's fair to say, therefore, that the concept of 'voluntary simplicity' may well have considerable resonance with a relatively small number of people in rich Northern countries, it is less likely to have much purchase either with Organisation for Economic Co-operation and Development (OECD) governments intent on addressing residual poverty within their own borders or, in global terms, where the principal challenge resides in the fate of the world's poorest 2 billion people who live on less than $2 a day. Such a crude generalization cannot, however, do justice to the rich debate about the meaning of poverty. Average income is widely and conveniently used as a proxy for human wellbeing or happiness, notwithstanding the evidence that many people in developing countries who are leading secure and dignified lives in rural areas, but on very low incomes, are often a great deal 'happier' than those on higher incomes in hellish urban slums.

From a demand-side perspective, there would appear to be very little public support for 'consume less' political alternatives. Green parties the world over have succeeded in attracting significant minorities of voters, but have rarely seen that percentage move above 10 per cent even in the world's richest countries, which one might reasonably assume to be more open to the concept of reaching some kind of 'affluence threshold' beyond which further increases in consumption or material standard of living are perceived to bring diminishing utility. With regard to the developing world, there is very little, if any, evidence that those countries are prepared in any way to forego the notional delights of Western consumerism which they see paraded in front of them through a constant battery of mass media programming and advertising that reaches into the poorest corners of the poorest countries.

Such concerns provide a formidable set of impediments to engaging in the 'consume less' debate. The concept of deferred gratification seems unlikely to make any kind of comeback in the foreseeable future. After 50 years of aspirational, growth-at-all-costs, no-holds-barred individualism, the harsh reality is that the available psychological terrain for politicians currently to operate within in pursuit of sustainable development is severely constrained. Rather than 'consume less', the thrust of any new debate here is likely to be 'consume wisely' for the foreseeable future. That may not be sufficient, but it's all that would appear to be manageable right now in terms of mainstream political responses in capitalist economies.

Every year, the Co-operative Bank, the new economics foundation and the Future Foundation combine forces to produce the Ethical Consumerism Report – a snapshot of the extent and spread of ethical purchasing power in the UK. The total value of ethical consumption in 2004 was just under £25 billion (see Table 15.1). This reveals that an extra £1 billion was spent on ethical products and services in 2003 (most significantly, sales of forest stewardship timber increased by £225 million to £869 million, and sales of energy-efficient household appliances increased by £273 million to £1.1 billion; sales of fair trade goods, such as tea, coffee and bananas, increased by £29 million to £92 million – growth of 46 per cent. A further £1.4 billion was placed in ethical investments and deposited with ethical banks and credit unions in 2003 – a rise of 18 per cent to £9 billion. This all confirms a clear trend: the overall market share of ethical consumerism in the UK has increased by almost 40 per cent in five years. The EPI now stands at 139 from a base of 100 when the index began in 1999.

The Ethical Consumer Monitor, covering the so-called 'ethical invisibles', is particularly interesting. It includes people shopping locally as part and parcel of their commitment to supporting their local communities; people explicitly opting to use public transport rather than their car to reduce their own ecological 'footprint'; people opting specifically for products that can be reused; and people avoiding or boycotting big brands because they are perceived to be unethical in one way or another – worth a substantial £3 billion to those reputation-driven brands!

This is clearly 'not insignificant', and similar results have emerged in almost all Northern European countries. Nobody should get overexcited about this – we are still talking about relatively low percentages of total market share. But as Simon Williams, director of corporate affairs at the Co-operative Bank puts it:

Table 15.1 *Ethical consumerism in the UK*

Ethical Purchasing Index (EPI)	Spend (2002) (£ million)	Spend (2003) (£ million)	Percentage growth (2002–2003)
Ethical products and services			
Food (including fair trade and organics)	1772	1946	9.8
Green household goods	1481	1989	34.3
Personal items (including cosmetics not tested on animals)	187	186	(0.5)
Responsible tourism	127	105	(17.3)
Green housing spend (including green mortgage repayments)	32	65	103.1
Green transport spend (including grants for purchase of clean fuel vehicles)	21	22	4.8
Charitable spend	4337	4662	7.5
Sub-total	**7957**	**8975**	**12.8**
Ethical finance			
Ethical banking	3886	4461	14.8
Ethical investment	3510	4214	20.1
Credit unions	283	366	29.3
Sub-total	**7679**	**9041**	**17.7**
Ethical consumer monitor			
Ethical boycotts:			
Clothing and footwear	232	273	17.7
Grocery	787	914	16.1
Food outlets	942	943	0.1
Petrol retailers	454	1040	129.1
Genetically modified (GM) food	167	–	–
Sub-total	**2582**	**3170**	**22.8**
Buying for reuse	1255	1443	15
Local shopping	1568	1724	9.9
Public transport	162	309	90.7
Sub-total	**2985**	**3476**	**16.4**
Grand total	**21,203**	**24,662**	**16.3**

Source: Ethical Purchasing Index

It's clear that UK consumers are increasingly willing to take action through their wallets to support business that they consider to be ethical and to avoid companies whom they consider to be unethical. Now may be the time for the government to recognize their wider value to the UK economy and intervene further to ensure their growth is continued. For example, the proportion of households using green electricity remains rooted at less than 1 per cent. In general, consumers must have confidence that any 'ethical' claims that a brand may make conform to certain standards which are independently accredited. (Simon Williams, cited in Ethical Consumer Monitor, 2005)

SUSTAINABLE CONSUMPTION

And that, of course, is the nub of it. The market can, indeed, be a powerful driver of more responsible behaviour, but only if market conditions are favourable. As Marcel Wissenburg concluded in his analysis of the compatibility between sustainability and market-based economic liberalism: 'Economic liberalism contains many elements that impede sustainability, but none of these threats seems invincible – assuming the right kind of preferences' (Wissenburg, 1998). The 'right kind of preferences' in this context are those that help move us faster and further down the road towards a sustainable world. And those preferences simply aren't emerging fast enough.

Ultimately, that is the stark reality that has doomed most attempts to confront sustainable consumption to predictable banality. Even the Oxford Commission on Sustainable Consumption, which convened a group of eminent international experts for two years to try and get to grips with these problems, found itself forced back into head-scratching bafflement – although it did, at least, have a crack at stiffening the resolve of governments in terms of purposeful interventions:

> *The Commission underlined the role of governments, both national and local, in making consumption more sustainable. It believes that they should not feel themselves relegated to some minor position, but should be encouraged to recover their confidence to do what is their proper work. They must set the national and international framework, and make it easier to consume sustainably than not. They have an important role as educator and enabler in setting standards and targets, and in supporting initiatives and innovations.* (Oxford Commission on Sustainable Consumption, 2004)

Fair enough; but one of the major problems about sustainable consumption is that mainstream business people and politicians are extremely reluctant to confront one of the most pernicious of all myths in this particular area: that in markets geared towards meeting consumer needs and aspirations, the consumer is assumed to be 'sovereign'. The assumption is that all the consumer needs to do is to find the most cost-effective and appropriate way of meeting their predetermined needs – a view strongly reinforced by conventional neo-liberal economics in which goods and services are simply 'the bearers of utility'. As Clive Hamilton points out, this can be disturbingly disingenuous:

> *It is perverse to characterize the market as a want-satisfying mechanism when we are exposed every day to attempts by the market to influence what we want. Consumers' preferences do not develop 'outside the system'; they are created and reinforced by the system so that consumer sovereignty is a myth. The question is not one of personal consumer choice versus elitist social engineering; it is one of corporate manipulation of consumer behaviour versus individuals in a society understanding what is in their real interests. Instead of society being populated by free agents rationally maximizing their welfare through their consumption choices, it is people as complex beings whose taste, priorities and value systems are, to a large degree, manipulated by the very 'markets' that are supposed to serve them.*
> (Hamilton, 2003)

Such a view is fiercely denied by most leading companies and retailers who hate to be portrayed as anything other than needs-meeting enterprises, and certainly not as needs-creating enterprises. Either way, consumption must be seen as a much more complex phenomenon than the conventional model would still have us believe. As many commentators have pointed out, there has been a slow but steady shift over the last few decades away from the phenomenon of people identifying themselves by reference to what they *do* in life, to people identifying themselves by reference to what they *consume*. This has hugely expanded the opportunities for marketeers to pitch their wares to consumers in terms of the identity they would like to project, rather than the needs they would like to have met for a better life. Even a humble tub of margarine can be flogged to consumers hungry not for the product itself but for the symbolic meanings associated with the product:

> *In the marketing of margarine, the product's contribution to the wellbeing of the consumer is wholly divorced from any of its physical properties. The actual usefulness of the product has become irrelevant so that the consumer does not buy something to spread on bread, but a concatenation of feelings associated with idealized family relationships. The complex, clever symbolism of the advertisement is designed to convince the viewer that a tub of vegetable fat that is identical to half a dozen other brands of other vegetable fat can give us something very special, something we really need. In a world of social disintegration, modern consumers have a powerful need for family warmth, and humans, just like Pavlov's dogs, make unconscious associations. Unmet emotional needs and unconscious association are the twin psychological pillars of the marketing society.* (Hamilton, 2003)

One can conclude from all this that working the 'sustainable consumption' end of policy-making is never going to be easy. But policy-makers in most OECD countries seem to have lapsed into a pudding-like state of inertia in which sustainable consumption is deemed to be relevant to only a tiny minority of citizens (the socially responsible niche), and where doing anything about it implies 'bucking the market' or, worse yet, limiting the range of choices available to the consumers – 'increased choice' being as sacrosanct a *desideratum* in the canon of contemporary capitalism as increased growth. Although there is much discussion in these countries on how best to decouple higher levels of economic activity from any environmental externalities, little effort is made to explore an equally important 'decoupling' issue: how to decouple unsustainable levels of consumption from real improvements in people's quality of life. As we have already seen, contemporary research clearly demonstrates that increased personal consumption does not necessarily improve people's sense of wellbeing, and may often cause severe domestic problems by accelerating unsustainable levels of debt.

One obvious way out of this dilemma is for governments to lead by example in those areas over which they do have complete control – particularly with public expenditure. If governments deployed their tax revenues in such a way as to promote sustainable consumption across the whole economy, the knock-on impacts could be enormous. The UK Government, for instance, buys £13 billion worth of goods and services each year, and directly or indirectly controls £125 billion worth of expenditure in the public sector. Until recently, there were lots of fine words flying around about how important 'sustainable procurement' could be, but little actually happening on the ground – with the exception of a few particularly sensitive issues such as sustainable timber, where previous failures to check out the origins of imported timber products had caused considerable political embarrassment.

In its recent sustainable development strategy – *Securing the Future: Delivering UK Sustainable Development Strategy* (HM Government, 2005) – the UK Government has sought to turn these fine words into changed purchasing behaviours. It has set a goal 'to be recognized as amongst the leaders in sustainable procurement across EU member states by 2009', drilling down into a host of detailed measures to oblige public-sector procurement officers to get serious about what has clearly been seen before now as a rather exotic and marginal area of concern.

But the UK debate about sustainable consumption is further confused by the Government's fixation with increasing the amount of choice available to citizens, particularly in terms of its efforts to modernize public services such as education and health. Most opinion polls indicate quite clearly that the idea of increased consumer choice in the context of improving public services just doesn't 'do it' for most people. 'Parental choice' often means very little for parents whose notional choice of schools is strictly limited in geographical terms. What most parents want is for *every* school to be resourced in such a way as to meet most of their reasonable expectations, rather than to end up with a situation in which some schools excel and others sink without trace. Anna Coote of the UK Sustainable Development Commission has highlighted a similar problem with the UK Government's almost obsessive pursuit of increased choice in the National Health Service:

'Choice' is the 'big idea' in the Government's Public Health Strategy. This is mainly devoted not to tackling the social, economic and environmental causes of illness, but to encouraging individuals to 'choose' healthy lifestyles (covering smoking, diet, exercise, alcohol and sex). Yet, health policies that focus on choice – whether it's choosing health services or healthy living – usually favour the better off. They don't have the same effect on people who are poor, disadvantaged, socially excluded – the very people whose health is most at risk. Choice may be highly desirable in theory; but individual choice as a policy driver, unless firmly rooted in policies to promote shared responsibility and equal capacity to choose, is likely to widen health inequalities and so undermine the purpose of sustainable development. (Coote, 2005)

By contrast, the work of Mark Moore at the Kennedy School of Government at Harvard University – who wrote a highly influential book called *Creating Public Value* nearly 20 years ago (Moore, 1987) – is focused on stimulating a very different kind of civic leadership, with the emphasis very much on public value rather than public choice as such. In *The Adaptive State* (a collection of short essays on 'personalizing the public realm' from the UK think tank Demos), Jake Chapman (2003) proposes a new agenda for public value, indicating that public value is increased when:

- *the level of service provision is improved;*
- *the quality of service is increased, particularly in treating all recipients with respect;*
- *the equity or fairness with which the service is delivered is increased;*
- *the service provision is more sustainable and takes into account the needs of future generations;*
- *the provision of the services is done in a way that is consistent with the expectations of a liberal civic society;*
- *the service provision enhances the level of trust between government and citizens.*

This is also a key theme in the Fabian Society's report *A Better Choice of Choice* (Levett et al, 2003), commissioned by the UK Sustainable Development Commission as part of its ongoing work on sustainable consumption. It, too, questions the desirability of politicians becoming fixated on the idea that since choice is good, more choice must necessarily be better. Yet the privilege of increased choice still features high in the pantheon of capitalism's many benefits: some economists look on the whole process of economic development as anything that increases people's options. To espouse political positions that appear to limit choice (as the green parties in Europe often do) is a high-risk and politically unpopular strategy. For the vast majority of people, it is certainly counter-intuitive to suggest that improvements in our quality of life might come about as a consequence of restricting rather than expanding choice.

For all that, it is clear that increasing individual choice does not automatically make us better off. There are several reasons for this. First, there is no such thing as a completely 'free' choice. Every choice we make is conditioned and constrained by the choices others have already made; this, in turn, conditions future choices. Individually rational choices to travel by car lead cumulatively to traffic-clogged, degraded inner cities, car-dependent suburbs and amenities accessible only by car – a mess nobody wanted or intended, in which nobody can access what they want reliably and easily, those without cars are further disadvantaged, and the unnecessary use of fossil fuel waste is structured into our lifestyles.

Choices come in 'package deals'. Claiming that a policy or decision 'increases choice' should be the beginning not the end of debate. Are the kinds of choice being increased the ones that really matter? What other choices do they curtail or foreclose? Can we be certain the gains are worth the losses? To express this, the authors of *A Better Choice of Choice* (Levett et al, 2003) have developed the idea of *the choice set* – a set of interconnected acts of consumption and other behaviours that come with them. Each choice set (the choices that are available) comes with a constraint set (the choices and options which it excludes). Box 15.1 explains what this means in terms of current transport choices.

As the authors acknowledge, there is an important connection between the idea of 'choice sets' and some of Amartya Sen's (1999) thoughts about capabilities and entitlements referred to in Chapter 2:

> *Sen notes that the access people have to goods and services depends on the 'entitlements' they enjoy – the effective economic resources over which people have control and ownership. But he also shows that the use that people can make of the benefits and services provided by commodities depends not only on their ability to buy them, but also on the 'capabilities' people have. An individual's capabilities relate to his or her psychological, physical and social characteristics and potential. The greater our set of capabilities, the more freedom we have to derive benefits and services from goods. Both entitlements and capabilities are unevenly distributed in quality and quantity, which places a further major constraint on the consumer's act of choice.* (Levett et al, 2003)

Encouragingly, *A Better Choice of Choice* received substantial media coverage when it was published in 2003, with a number of political commentators clearly delighting in the opportunity to approach some of today's same old problems from a refreshingly different perspective. It made me wonder what would happen if the media really began to open themselves up to some of these questions, or if the government really began to think seriously about working these issues into their engagement strategies with voters.

Box 15.1 Transport choice in the UK

The current transport 'choice set' maximizes:

- The freedom to drive a car wherever and whenever you want. Almost all public roads are open to car traffic. Restrictions, conditions and charges are rare exceptions requiring special justification.
- Low-cost personal mobility. Once you own a car, you can go a long way in it per pound of expenditure. People with use of a car enjoy extraordinary – historically unprecedented – freedom of mobility.
- The ability to get anywhere with a road.
- The ability (for those with cars) to choose between competing providers of many services.
- The attempt to reduce congestion (where possible). This is now an increasingly serious constraint as far as UK business is concerned.

But these choices preclude others. Very few people can now choose to:

- Live free from traffic noise and pollution, with children able to play safely in front of their homes.
- Get access to a satisfactory range of daily amenities on foot without resort to any motorized vehicle.
- Walk or cycle with much safety or pleasure.
- Make most journeys reliably, without having to make allowance for unpredictable and unavoidable problems and hold-ups.

Most households no longer have the option to live a normal full life without owning at least one car. Those who cannot afford a car, or cannot drive because of disability or age, are excluded from areas of normal life without any choice in the matter. Moreover, the patterns of behaviour that result from high car ownership deprive us of other social choices:

- Traffic is the biggest environmental problem in many town centres and unrestricted car-based mobility the biggest threat to the traditional multifunctional town or city centre. Car use is thus a 'double whammy' against urban vitality.
- Hyper-mobility undermines community vitality.
- Personal transport accounts for over one quarter of greenhouse emissions and is still rising. The freedom to drive is one of the main threats to future climate security.

Apparently innocuous and perfectly rational choices by individuals – to buy and drive cars more since other transport options appear less able to provide access to amenities wanted – have led cumulatively to disbenefits which nobody consciously sought. At no stage was an explicit decision taken that the benefits justified the disbenefits. In consciously exercising our individual, incremental choices, we have sleepwalked into some larger choices and foreclosed others without even realizing it. In this respect, the market can be an 'invisible elbow', shoving us into an unwanted corner, as well as Adam Smith's 'invisible hand'.

Individual rational choices do not necessarily add up to the best overall outcome because of the way in which each choice alters the choices available to others. For example, each perfectly sensible choice to make a journey by car instead of bus will slightly:

- Reduce the fare income to the buses while increasing the congestion they face, thus making the service a bit less effective.
- Reduce the safety and attractiveness of cycling.
- Encourage shops and other amenities to move to car-accessible rather than bus-accessible locations.
- Encourage better-off people to move out of more heavily trafficked central areas to suburbs with better car access to the new amenities.

Source: Levett (2003)

ADDRESSING THE GOVERNANCE GAP

As we have seen, one of the most profound consequences of our 25-year love affair with economic neo-liberalism is that more and more of the management of people's lives in most OECD countries has been consigned to the marketplace, with politicians across the entire political spectrum increasingly disinclined to intervene through discredited 'command and control' measures. Governance as such would appear to have become more about individual consumer choice than about decisions taken through the ballot box. This worldview has, of course, always been popular with the right, but is now promoted with equal vigour by today's progressive 'centre-left' think tanks, such as Demos in the UK:

> Command and control is a framework unsuited to the complex, unpredictable demands of contemporary organizational life. Command and control systems tend to treat people in instrumental ways, a feature they share with unrestrained market liberalism. They assume a directive model of institutional authority in which the priorities, values and knowledge held at the centre of an institution or community will shape and control the behaviour of those who make up the wider system.
>
> Clinging to command and control as a method of social intervention and a defence of the legitimacy of collective action in such an environment is a self-defeating strategy. The challenge is to recreate public institutions and governance regimes as open, porous and decentred systems which can thrive on diversity, adapt to radical innovation and still maintain coherent purpose and progress . . . in seeking to stimulate and influence such change, the underlying goal of political intervention should be seen as developing or supporting systems of self-governance in a complex and fluid environment, rather than simply establishing institutional control or imposing a simplified set of priorities on existing systems. (Bentley, 2002)

But what the devil does that mean in practice? From a sustainability perspective, how does 'self-governance' play out in a world where (as we have seen) short-term personal gratification and corporate profit maximization remain utterly dominant? Where many people's favourite 'coping strategy' is simply to deny the reality of what is happening around them and cheer themselves up by doing some serious shopping? Where the global media are managing and manipulating coverage of the 'state of the world' explicitly to protect the interests of a tiny elite of the unelected super-rich – described by some as a 'corporatocracy' or 'global monetocracy'? Where politicians themselves seem disinclined even to participate in a more intelligent discourse about the viability of today's model of progress? In such a world, talk of authentic self-governance, let alone 'open, porous and decentred systems', is clearly vulnerable to a charge of extreme naivety.

This may explain why the different approaches to governance adopted by many of the international NGOs at the heart of these issues remain rather more *dirigiste* and open to the possibility of 'command and control' still having an important role to play. This balance is pragmatically captured in the Real World Coalition's *From Here to Sustainability* (Christie and Warburton, 2001), which identifies the four critical linkages between sustainable development and better governance:

1   *Movement away from unsustainable 'business as usual' can only be based on consent, democratically given. We need a system that promotes rich debate about the state we're in. This means a thorough renewal of the institutions that have seen public trust and enthusiasm leak away over the years in order to re-engage citizens with politics. It also means devising better systems for civic and moral education so that everyone is equipped with the 'moral fluency' to participate in debate and make informed choices.*

2   *We need a renewal of trust between citizens and government simply because sustainable development cannot be delivered solely through individual choices, business innovation and voluntary action. It requires a huge and complex long-term negotiation of change; trade-offs between private choices and public goods; changes to market frameworks; and strategic investment in public services and new technologies. All this requires an effective, legitimate and trusted state.*

3   *Sustainable development demands a renewal of local democracy. We know that national and global frameworks can only sketch the direction and principles for action. As the Agenda 21 statement from the 1992 Earth Summit underlined, effective measures for sustainable development must, to a large extent, be devised and implemented through democratic local government and partnerships at the local level between communities, public agencies and business.*

4   *The nature of the present phase of globalization emphasizes the need for democratic accountability and deliberation to be extended to the international level, and for global institutions and corporations to be more open, democratic and accountable. The greatest challenge for democratic governments is to find ways to foster a global democratic culture and process so that international agencies that shape strategies on development work better, more accountably, and in the interests of environmental sustainability and wellbeing for all.*
    (Christie and Warburton, 2001)

This book cannot examine in detail the kind of reform processes which might be necessary to restore confidence in systems of governance; but there is now an extraordinary array of innovative and challenging work doing precisely that, all the way through from mainstream texts such as David Held's *Democracy and the Global Order* (1995) and *Future Positive* by Michael Edwards (1999), to more radical offerings from Jeff Gates (1998, 2000), George Monbiot (2004) and Colin Hines (2000) referred to elsewhere in this work. It has to be said, however, that many of these works still don't reflect the preconditional importance of aligning *our* systems of governance with the way in which *nature's* systems work.

Beyond that, there are two further layers of complexity in advocating any wholesale reform of existing governance systems. The first is the astonishing collapse in levels of trust between the governed and their governments. In 2002, the World Economic Forum asked 36,000 people to rate their 'level of trust' for 17 different institutions involved in protecting the interests of society. Two-thirds of them did not believe that their country was 'governed by the will of the people'. Across the world, the principal democratic institution in each country (for example, parliament or congress) is the least trusted of the 17 institutions tested. Global companies and large domestic companies are equally distrusted, ranking next to national legislative bodies at the bottom of the trust ratings.

Second, there remains a serious tension for anyone involved in promoting an accelerated move to a more sustainable world: how is this to be done in ways that strengthen rather than erode democracy? Simon Dresner painfully exposes this dilemma:

> *The paradox is that sustainability is a philosophy firmly based on the notion that attempts to transform Nature are likely to be self-defeating, but is itself committed to attempting to transform society and control its future direction. The Green movement attempts to get round this problem by advocating radical decentralization of decision-making so that sustainability can be implemented from the grassroots upwards. One difficulty with that answer is that sustainability is a global problem requiring global coordination of action. Leaving all decisions to local communities is not very different from the neo-liberal solution of leaving everything to the market to decide; there is every possibility for free-riding and the tragedy of the commons.* (Dresner, 2002)

I know of no easy way of resolving that paradox. But I do know that the best starting point is for people to make a rather better job of articulating what a sustainable society would actually look like, both in aspirational and in operational terms.

REFERENCES

Bentley, T. (2002) 'Letting go: Complexity, individualism and the left', *Renewal*, vol 10
Chapman, J. (2003) *The Adaptive State*, Demos, London
Christie, I. and Warburton, D. (2001) *From Here to Sustainability*, Real World Coalition/Earthscan, London

Coote, A. (2005) *Sustainable Development and Public Health*, UK Sustainable Development Commission, London

Dresner, S. (2002) *The Principles of Sustainability*, Earthscan, London

Edwards, M. (1999) *Future Positive: International Co-operation in the 21st Century*, Earthscan, London

Ekins, P. (1998) 'Can humanity go beyond consumerism?', in *1998 Development Report*, Society for International Development, Rome

Ethical Consumer Monitor (2005) *Ethical Consumerism in the UK*, The Co-operative Bank, Manchester

Gates, J. (1998) *The Ownership Solution*, Penguin, London

Gates, J. (2000) *Democracy at Risk*, Perseus Publishing, Cambridge, MA

Hamilton, C. (2003) *Growth Fetish*, Allen and Unwin, Sydney

Held, D. (1995) *Democracy and the Global Order*, Polity Press, Cambridge, UK

Hines, C. (2000) *Localization: A Global Manifesto*, Earthscan, London

HM Government (2005) *Securing the Future: Delivering UK Sustainable Development Strategy*, TSO, London

Levett, R., with Christie, I., Jacobs, M. and Therivel, R. (2003) *A Better Choice of Choice*, Fabian Society, London

Monbiot, G. (2004) *Age of Consent: A Manifesto for a New World Order*, HarperCollins, London

Moore, M. (1987) *Creating Public Value*, Harvard University Press, Cambridge, MA

Oxford Commission on Sustainable Consumption (2004) 'Official report', Mansfield College, Oxford

Sen, A. (1999) *Development as Freedom*, Oxford University Press, Oxford

Wissenburg, M. (1998) *Green Liberalism*, UCL Press, London

16

Visions and Values

INTRODUCTION

Utopias have been out of fashion for a long time now, and the nearest thing to a sustainability Utopia (Ernest Callenbach's 'Ecotopia') is now 30 years' old. That leaves sustainable development advocates struggling to explain what life would really be like if we did, indeed, get on top of today's sustainability challenges. Is it really possible to retain the best of the dynamism and efficiency of capitalism while simultaneously learning to abide by the laws of nature? This chapter seeks to address that conundrum by looking at the kind of values upon which the attaining of a sustainable society depends (interdependence, empathy, equity, personal responsibility and intergenerational justice), and explores the degree to which it is possible to be optimistic about such values 'winning out' in a world such as ours. It also examines how it is that the religious right in the US has been able to 'see off' environmentalism and every other progressive cause by making such strong play on the American dream and core American values.

DEFINING THE UNIVERSAL DREAM

There was a time in the affairs of humankind when the only vision on offer was a vision of life after death – for the virtuous, of an eternity in the company of angels somewhere in the celestial beyond; for the wicked, of an eternity in hell. Through-out most of human history, notwithstanding literary gems such as Thomas More's *Utopia*, published in 1518, there wasn't much point in offering people any vision of a better life on Earth. For the vast majority of people, such a vision would have been neither conceivable nor deliverable. In modern times, from the 18th century onwards, Earth-bound visions of a better world have taken on an increasingly important role as part and parcel of various secular models of progress. The sheer dynamism of the capitalist economy, as it gradually extended its reach to embrace most of the world, has ensured that those secular visions of a better world have become all but synonymous with personal visions of being better off (for oneself or for one's children) or more secure in material terms.

The American dream is well on the way to becoming today's universal dream, even if the ways in which different nations pursue it remain sharply differentiated, as explored in the context of the debate about globalization in Chapter 5. A powerful combination of economic and psychological drivers keeps that dream alive and well. Some of those drivers are largely, if not wholly, altruistic, inspired by a commitment to social justice, and to the elimination of poverty in the rich world and of the increasingly grotesque disparities in wealth between the rich and the poor world – the solutions to which are understandably assumed to depend upon the generation of yet more wealth rather than the more effective distribution of the wealth that has already been amassed. Other drivers are largely, if not entirely, venal and self-interested, underpinned by some sense of 'rightful entitlement', however spurious, or by insecurity, greed or envy. But for most, those who are neither ultra-rich nor desperately poor, the principal driver is material independence, to secure one's old age, to look after one's children, and to have something set aside against disaster or tragedy. One way or another, personal visions of a better world usually entail some constant improvement in one's own financial situation.

This poses a rarely acknowledged dilemma for advocates of sustainable capitalism: is it possible to offer people a vision of a better world in which each and every individual in that world will not necessarily be seeing their material standard of living improving year on year, and in which the imperative of 9 billion people learning to live sustainably within the Earth's biophysical limits will demand that missing ingredient so dangerously absent from today's universal dream – namely, the *truth*? For the truth of it is that if 9 billion people want to live like the richest 1 billion live right now (and we don't seem to be particularly satisfied with what we've already got anyway), we will need the resources and natural services of at least three – and probably five – more planet Earth look-alikes. At the risk of over-egging the message, just the one planet Earth is all we've got.

And that's the dilemma. Is this fragile, seemingly preposterous, notion of sustainable capitalism all but dead in the water not just (as many orthodox economists would have us believe) because it can't be made to work anyway, but because the vision of what such an economy might mean for people and their communities is inherently 'unsellable', being constantly overwhelmed by the universal dream and its promise of ever greater wealth forever for everyone – however dishonest and truly preposterous such a promise might really be? And if it's *not* possible, in today's mature, well-educated and largely well-fed democracies, to win serious support for a vision of a better world secured by virtue of the global economy evolving its way towards something resembling sustainable capitalism, then we are inevitably stuck with business as usual – that is to say, utterly unsustainable capitalism, all but guaranteeing the acceleration of every one of the destructive trends identified in Chapters 1 and 12.

GETTING VISIONARY

It might help to be a little bit more explicit about what exactly this 'vision of a better world' might look like. In 1975, Ernest Callenbach published his hugely stimulating novel *Ecotopia*, set in California in 1999 – that is to say, looking forward over a quarter of a century. *Ecotopia* is made up of California, Oregon and Washington State, which seceded from the US in 1980 after threatening to detonate nuclear mines in New York and Washington, DC, unless they were allowed to go their independent way! Twenty years on, after total isolation, a leading US journalist is allowed to visit to see the ways in which Ecotopia has evolved in the meantime. Many of the developments are not that surprising now: organic food; balanced diets; everyone involved in food production in one way or another; hyper-efficient public transport, walking and cycling, and very few cars; 100 per cent recycling and incredibly strict pollution controls; small-scale, close-knit communities with access to work shared much more equitably – with a return to the Protestant work ethic; a free and easy approach to sexuality – it is California, after all; a dynamic population reduction programme; all buildings made of renewable and biodegradable materials, and 100 per cent renewable energy.

Nothing too outrageous – but this just shows the degree to which a huge number of green ideas that were considered to be totally outlandish back in the mid 1970s have now entered the political mainstream. Nevertheless, *Ecotopia* still has the potential to surprise with some of its more radical ideas: no advertising whatsoever and a hugely reduced use of the TV; ritual war games to 'manage' inherent violent tendencies, predominantly in men; political parties dominated almost entirely by women (who make up a substantial majority of the population of Ecotopia); no income tax, sales tax or property tax – with all tax revenues based upon a turnover tax on productive enterprise; schools that are more like farms or outward-bound centres; and so on.

Ever since then, green theorists and activists have spent countless person years drafting and redrafting an almost limitless multiplicity of visions. Off-the-shelf hand-me-downs just don't cut it; every organization and every newcomer to the embrace of sustainable development seem to be seized with the need to work out for themselves what a sustainable future might actually look like – even though there has always been an intense, ongoing debate about whether the very process of 'visioning a sustainable society' has any real legitimacy or usefulness. Some 'vision critics' believe all such ecotopias to be either childish or, much more seriously, an opening of the door to lurking totalitarian tendencies in the green movement: 'we know what's good for you, and this really will make you a lot happier'.

Others find such visions predictable, formulaic or stultifyingly monolithic, a real turn-off for today's pragmatic politicians, unappealingly presenting the sustainable development project as a take-it-or-leave-it blockbuster in which organics, fair trade, beards, human rights, photovoltaics, bicycles, animal welfare and an end to global poverty are all inextricably woven together. Michael Jacobs, the former director general of the Fabian Society and now a political adviser to UK

Chancellor of the Exchequer Gordon Brown, captured this sentiment perfectly in his 1999 pamphlet on *Environmental Modernization* (Jacobs, 1999), in which he advocated a series of ideology-free, vision-lite and resolutely pragmatic campaigns to overcome the deep instinctive antipathy of most Labour politicians (new or old) to the environment movement, let alone to the sustainable development cause. He highlighted five key aspects that would make an environmental modernization agenda 'acceptable' to mainstream Labour politicians:

> *First, it is intended to 'go with the grain' of globalization. Second, it acknowledges the trend towards individualization and understands the role of consumption in modern life, but seeks to encourage consumption towards environmentally benign forms. Third, environmental modernization gives a central place to the perception of risk and scientific uncertainty, and makes risk management a key policy field. Fourth, it seeks to counter the trend towards greater environmental inequality or exclusion. Fifth, it is firmly a modernist project, accepting the central role of science and technology in tackling as well as contributing to environmental problems. It sees the future as essentially optimistic and environmental problems as soluble.* (Jacobs, 1999)

By implication, therefore, there are no 'limits to growth' ideas, no suggestions of any *structural* problems within the conventional model of progress, and nothing that might scare the horses about consuming less, demand management through radical tax reform and so on. Everything is 100 per cent compatible with mainstream ideas about globalization, free markets, constant economic growth and technocratic progress.

I for one find it hard to accept that this is likely to be the best way of getting real traction for the uncompromisingly radical ideas that lie behind sustainable development – a theme to which I will return in Chapter 17. But it has to be acknowledged that there *is* a genuine problem in contemplating a vision of a sustainable society. If sustainability is, indeed, the 'end goal' – the 'stable state' which we need to arrive at to ensure compatibility with the life-support systems upon which we depend – how do we then avoid stagnation? More specifically, in the context of trying to define what sustainable capitalism might look like, how do we retain capitalism's dynamism, creativity, innovation and hunger for change and 'progress' that has made it one of the most powerful forces in the history of humankind, and yet still stay within those biophysical limits? Apart from resorting to slightly pretentious analogies – 'Think of Shakespeare's sonnets: do you suppose for a moment that his creativity was stifled by the fact that he had to stick to a given number of lines, each containing a given number of syllables?' – this tension between the imperative of a biophysical 'steady state' (albeit with some room for manoeuvre around what science determines as the limits) and the life blood of capitalism at its best remains hugely problematic.

It's a dilemma that goes back to J. S. Mill's exploration during the 1860s of the notion of the 'stationary state'. Unlike most of his contemporaries, he felt that it was critical to keep interrogating the fundamental *objectives* of industrialism at that time – where was it all headed and what would happen when society actually got there? Would people be better or worse off? Although his articulation of this sometimes makes him sound like an old fogey ('I confess I'm not charmed with the ideal of life held out by those who think that the normal state of human beings is that of struggling to get on; that the trampling, crushing, elbowing and treading on each other's heels, which forms the existing type of social life, are the most desirable lot of humankind'), his understanding of the trade-offs involved in the pursuit of constant expansion and growth ring as true today as they did then:

> *If the Earth must lose that great portion of its pleasantness which it owes to things that the unlimited increase of wealth and population would extirpate from it, for the mere purpose of enabling it to support a larger but not a better or happier population, I sincerely hope, for the sake of posterity, that they will be content to be stationary long before necessity compels them to it.* (Mill, 1861)

Orthodox economists have never been happy with the notion of the stationary state, and there is, indeed, something both absurd and deeply unappealing about the idea of aiming at a future state of equilibrium which from that point on would remain constant – especially in an age where the only thing that seems to be constant is change itself. But it would be wrong to dismiss J. S. Mill's anxieties too quickly. What do we really gain if, in the process of gaining it, we lose both 'the art of living' and that indispensable harmony between ourselves and the natural world? Jay Griffiths, the author of *Pip Pip: A Sideways Look at Time* (1999), offers her own lyrical riposte to the idea that sustainability is incompatible with any true sense of progress:

> *'Sustainability' seems to weigh in with the burden of a heavy stasis. A life half-lived and a death half-died, all the dirgey effort of a worthy cause and none of the dynamite of 'progress'. But the opposite is true. Progress, along the trajectory Euro-American culture is now on, is a one-word lie; it is neither the travel nor the arrival, but the ultimate ending; not the flame of thought, but a bonfire of humanity: the vaunted 'progress' of cars and unlimited plane travel leading to global warming and millions of environmental refugees – this so-called progress is a politics which tends towards death. Sustainability, on the other hand, is where the life lies, where time touches eternity, the time of the natural world, of ice and melt, of the seas' times and tides. Both sustainability and progress need to be redefined and reclaimed. In order to do this, Western culture needs to listen to indigenous peoples because in their ideas of cyclical time, time is constantly restored, nature sustained and*

sustaining. These are the very ideas the world needs most. (Griffiths, 2005)

Finding an elegant way out of this impasse (how to be visionary about a sustainable future without coming up with completely unworldly or static visions) is not easy. Some resort to finely honed *principles* intended to speak to such a vision, but framed as contemporaneously as possible (see Box 16.1). Others prefer to rely upon defining the kind of *values* that will inform a sustainable society without necessarily going to the extent of defining what that society would look like. There is, after all, a very powerful *moral* case for sustainable development – notwithstanding the fact that these days we tend to hear far more about the *business* case for sustainable development rather than we do about the moral case. As we saw in Part I, that moral case rests on a fundamental commitment both to greater equity and social justice (within and between different generations, and within and between different countries), and on the recognition that we have a moral obligation to secure the wellbeing of other creatures regardless of whether or not they bring any benefit to humankind. The concept of 'stewardship', of taking responsibility in so far as we can for the whole of life on Earth, is a powerful source of moral inspiration for hundreds of millions of people and an important element in all the world's major religions and faith systems.

SUSTAINABILITY VALUES

Within that kind of moral framework, is it possible to advocate a set of generic values (regardless of cultural diversity, different norms and lifestyles) that would be conducive to establishing a genuinely sustainable way of life? Promoting equity and social justice requires awareness of the difficulties of others and compassion for the disadvantaged; recognition of the value of difference, tolerance and freedom is critical; living within environmental limits calls for a much deeper understanding of nature; intergenerational equity rests on the simple notion that no one generation should promote its own material interests at the expense of succeeding generations. Putting these together, we come up with a list of values that might look something like this:

- recognition of interdependence;
- self-determination;
- diversity and tolerance;
- compassion for others;
- upholding the principle of equity;
- recognition of the rights and interests of non-humans;
- respect for the integrity of natural systems; and
- respect for the interests of future generations.

BOX 16.1 THE UK SUSTAINABLE DEVELOPMENT COMMISSION'S PRINCIPLES FOR SUSTAINABLE DEVELOPMENT

Sustainable development provides a framework for redefining progress and redirecting our economies to enable all people to meet their basic needs and improve their quality of life, while ensuring that the natural systems, resources and biological diversity upon which they depend are maintained and enhanced both for their benefit and for that of future generations. This is inevitably a contested idea, dependent upon finding the right balance between different and often conflicting objectives though much more integrated policy-making and planning processes. Putting its principles into practices demands debate, experimentation and continuous learning, and therefore requires a thriving democracy to allow it to evolve and flourish.

PUTTING SUSTAINABLE DEVELOPMENT AT THE CENTRE

Sustainable development should be the organizing principle of all democratic societies, underpinning all other goals, policies and processes. It provides a framework for integrating economic, social and environmental concern over time, not through crude trade-offs, but through the pursuit of mutually reinforcing benefits. It promotes good governance, healthy living, innovation, life-long learning and all forms of economic growth which secure the natural capital upon which we depend. It reinforces social harmony and seeks to secure each individual's prospects of leading a fulfilling life.

VALUING NATURE

We are and always will be part of nature, embedded in the natural world, and totally dependent for our own economic and social wellbeing upon the resources and systems that sustain life on Earth. These systems have limits, which we breach at our peril. All economic activity must be constrained within those limits. We have an inescapable moral responsibility to pass on to future generations a healthy and diverse environment, and critical natural capital unimpaired by economic development. Even as we learn to manage our use of the natural world more efficiently, so we must affirm those individual beliefs and belief systems which revere nature for its intrinsic value, regardless of its economic and aesthetic value to humankind.

FAIR SHARES

Sustainable economic development means 'fair shares for all', ensuring that people's basic needs are properly met across the world, while securing constant improvements in the quality of people's lives through efficient, inclusive economies. 'Efficient' simply means generating as much economic value as possible from the lowest possible throughput of raw materials and energy. 'Inclusive' means securing high levels of paid, high-quality employment, with internationally recognized labour rights and fair trade principles vigorously defended, while properly acknowledging the value to our wellbeing of unpaid family work, caring, parenting, volunteering and other informal livelihoods. Once basic needs are met, the goal is to achieve the highest quality of life for individuals and communities, within the Earth's carrying capacity, through transparent, properly regulated markets which promote both social equity and personal prosperity.

POLLUTER PAYS

Sustainable development requires that we make explicit the costs of pollution and inefficient resource use, and reflect those in the prices we pay for all products and services, recycling the revenues from higher prices to drive the sustainability revolution that is now so urgently needed and compensating those whose environments have been damaged. In pursuit of environmental justice, no part of society should be disproportionately affected by environmental pollution or blight, and all people should have the same right to pure water, clean air, nutritious food and other key attributes of a healthy, life-sustaining environment.

GOOD GOVERNANCE

There is no one blueprint for delivering sustainable development. It requires different strategies in different societies. But *all* strategies will depend upon effective, participative systems of governance and institutions, engaging the interest, creativity and energy of all citizens. We must, therefore, celebrate diversity, and practise tolerance and respect. However, good governance is a two-way process. We should all take responsibility for promoting sustainability in our own lives and for engaging with others to secure more sustainable outcomes in society.

ADOPTING A PRECAUTIONARY APPROACH

Scientists, innovators and wealth creators have a crucial part to play in creating genuinely sustainable economic progress. But human ingenuity and technological power is now so great that we are capable of causing serious damage to the environment or to people's health through unsustainable development that pays insufficient regard to wider impacts. Society needs to ensure that there is full evaluation of potentially damaging activities so as to avoid or minimize risks. Where there are threats of serious or irreversible damage to the environment or human health, the lack of full scientific certainty should not be used as a reason to delay taking cost-effective action to prevent or minimize such damage.

Source: Sustainable Development Commission (2001)

Some of those values overlap substantively with the core values of most progressive organizations and individuals broadly seeking to make the world a better place. But some are very different – intergenerational justice (justice between different generations), concern for the non-human world of natural systems, and a desire to see the rights of the individual to determine as much as possible of his or her own life properly balanced with the recognition of our dependence upon everyone else and everything else. The *Declaration of Interdependence* developed by the Canadian environmental activist David Suzuki takes us one stage further in terms of unpacking that notion of interdependence, widening the circle of relationships not just to embrace all human beings within the meaning of 'one world' but all living creatures (see Box 16.2).

BOX 16.2 DECLARATION OF INTERDEPENDENCE

THIS WE KNOW

We are the Earth, through the plants and animals that nourish us. We are the rains and the oceans that flow through our veins. We are the breath of the forests of the land, and the plants of the sea. We are human animals, related to all other life as descendants of the firstborn cell.

We share with these kin a common history, written in our genes. We share a common present, filled with uncertainty. And we share a common future, as yet untold.

We humans are but one of 30 million species weaving the thin layer of life enveloping the world. The stability of communities of living things depends upon this diversity. Linked in that web, we are interconnected – using, cleansing, sharing and replenishing the fundamental elements of life. Our home, planet Earth, is finite; all life shares its resources and the energy from the sun and therefore has limits to growth. For the first time, we have touched those limits.

When we compromise the air, the water, the soil and the variety of life, we steal from the endless future to serve the fleeting present.

THIS WE BELIEVE

Humans have become so numerous and our tools so powerful that we have driven fellow creatures to extinction, dammed the great rivers, torn down ancient forests, poisoned the Earth, rain and wind, and ripped holes in the sky. Our science has brought pain as well as joy; our comfort is paid for by the suffering of millions. We are learning from our mistakes, we are mourning our vanished kin and we now build a new politics of hope. We respect and uphold the absolute need for clean air, water and soil. We see that economic activities that benefit the few while shrinking the inheritance of many are wrong. And since environmental degradation erodes biological capital forever, full ecological and social cost must enter all equations of development. We are one brief generation in the long march of time; the future is not ours to erase. So where knowledge is limited, we will remember all those who will walk after us and err on the side of caution.

THIS WE RESOLVE

All this that we know and believe must now become the foundation of the way we live. At this turning point in our relationship with Earth, we work for an evolution: from dominance to partnership; from fragmentation to connection; from insecurity to interdependence.

Source: Suzuki (1997)

Box 16.3 The Five Capitals Framework and key features of a sustainable society

Natural capital

1   In their extraction and use, substances taken from the Earth do not exceed the environment's capacity to disperse, absorb, recycle or otherwise neutralize their harmful effects (to humans and/or the environment).

2   In their manufacture and use, artificial substances do not exceed the environment's capacity to disperse, absorb, recycle or otherwise neutralize their harmful effects (to humans and/or the environment).

3   The capacity of the environment to provide ecological system integrity, biological diversity and productivity is protected or enhanced.

Human capital

4   At all ages, individuals enjoy a high standard of health.

5   Individuals are adept at relationships and social participation, and throughout life set and achieve high personal standards of their development and learning.

6   There is access to varied and satisfying opportunities for work, personal creativity and recreation.

Social capital

7   There are trusted and accessible systems of governance and justice.

8   Communities and society at large share key positive values and a sense of purpose.

9   The structures and institutions of society promote stewardship of natural resources and development of people.

10   Homes, communities and society at large provide safe, supportive living and working environments.

Manufactured capital

11   All infrastructure, technologies and processes make minimum use of natural resources and maximum use of human innovation and skills.

Financial capital

12   Financial capital accurately represents the value of natural, human, social and manufactured capital.

Source: Forum for the Future

Values can be thought of as a system of implicitly agreed norms that enable the smooth running of society; they are not agreed by committee or imposed upon societies from above. They emerge from the collective behaviour of individuals and respond to the needs of society as a whole. For this system to function, a feedback mechanism needs to be in place; people need to be able to see the effects of their actions on others. In a small community, this is a straightforward process. But sustainable development is a global problem and the effects of our actions are often indirect, taking place thousands of miles away. For values to develop that are aligned to sustainable development, adequate feedback mechanisms are required – mechanisms that nurture empathy, and that allow us to witness global problems and connect them to their cause.

There are many who believe that the Indian Ocean tsunami in December 2004 marked a decisive turning point in the way in which people in the rich world were able to empathize with the millions of people in the poor world affected by this terrible natural disaster. Many commentators drew an analogy between the impetus given to the 'war on terror' by the attack on the Twin Towers in New York on 11 September 2001 and the impetus given to the 'war on poverty' from the Indian Ocean tsunami. For the first time, the rhetorical notion of 'one world' could be seen to have some direct, tangible manifestation, a beating heart in the theoretical concept of global solidarity.

As the first few months of the Making Poverty History campaign in 2005 demonstrated, converting even the deepest up-welling of 'empathy in adversity' into focused political action to address the root causes of chronic poverty in the world today has been an enormous challenge. That should not detract from the possibility of there having been a profound and lasting shift in people's values as a direct consequence of the tsunami; it is invariably the case that a shift in values has to precede a shift in behaviour, and the time lag between the two can often be protracted.

However, today's champions of sustainable development clearly need something more substantive than a high-level set of values or beliefs that might be conducive to ushering in a more sustainable global order. We need to be able to delineate some of the key features that would characterize a genuinely sustainable society, and in Forum for the Future's case, that means correlating those features with the Five Capitals Framework outlined in Part II (see Box 16.3).

More recently, Forum for the Future has started to get its own 'vision itch', partly because so many of our partners (in all different sectors) tend to end up asking us what this elusive 'sustainable society' would actually look like, and partly because of what we are – an organization made up of 70 people single-mindedly intent on helping others to deliver solutions to today's environmental, social and economic problems. Here is the latest version – as of 2005 – offered very much as 'work in progress':

In a sustainable society, everyone's human rights and basic needs are met. Everyone has access to good food, water, shelter and sustainable sources of energy at reasonable cost. People's health is protected by creating safe, clean and pleasant environments, as well as health services that prioritize the prevention of illness while providing proper care for the sick. People live without fear of personal violence from crime or persecution on account of their personal beliefs, race, gender or sexuality.

The economic system serves people and the environment. It is market based to ensure innovation and efficiency, but rigorously regulated to secure social and environmental benefits as well as economic benefits. Where practical, local needs are met locally. The ambition of politicians and community leaders is to ensure the highest possible quality of life within the operating limits of the natural world. Everyone has access to the skills, knowledge and information needed to enable them to play a full part in society, and everyone has the opportunity to undertake satisfying work in a diverse economy. The value of unpaid work is recognized, while payments for work are fair and fairly distributed.

Society is founded on democracy, tolerance and diversity. All sections of the community are empowered to participate in decision-making. Opportunities for culture, leisure and recreation are readily available to all, and places, spaces and objects combine meaning and beauty with utility. Settlements are 'human' in scale and form. Ethnic and cultural diversity and local distinctiveness are valued and protected.

The Earth is nurtured as a single community, bound together with interdependent relationships. Our life-support systems are afforded the highest political priority. Resources are used ultra-efficiently, waste is minimized by closing cycles, and pollution is limited to levels which natural systems can cope with without damage. The diversity of nature is valued and protected, regardless of its usefulness to humankind. (Forum for the Future, 2005)

For those who want them, there are many visions of a sustainable society to inform and inspire. And there are literally dozens of books mapping out in varying degrees of detail how a sustainable economy might work; how sustainable lifestyles would transform current living patterns; and how radical policy change in different areas would rise to the challenge of providing health services, education, transportation, planning, food, leisure and so on – all on a genuinely sustainable basis. Although many in the green movement perceive themselves to have been in the political wilderness over the last 30 years, a huge amount of creative and intellectually rigorous endeavour has been invested in preparing the policy seedbeds for a more sustainable future.

It is important not to pass too quickly over the role that a compelling vision can play in transforming people's views and even their voting habits. Adam Werbach's speech *Is Environmentalism Dead?* (2004) homes in on the way in which the neo-conservatives in the US gradually built a vision that played so effectively to core American values that it eventually won out over every progressive cause it came up against, including environmentalism. Throughout the 1970s and 1980s, the US environment movement stuck to its narrow, regulatory guns ('polluter pays',

'command-and-control regulation', detailed inventories of toxic substances, etc.),
much of it working against the kind of 'frontier values' and aspirational culture of
the typical American. Meanwhile, the conservative right went broad rather than
narrow, appealing directly to those aspirational values (based on individual liberty,
limited government, free enterprise and the right to own and use property),
persuading Americans that a free market was pretty much ordained by God and
that it was both 'un-American' and morally wrong to regulate the hell out of God-
fearing Americans intent on building responsible businesses here on Earth.

That kind of alignment with core American values eventually enabled the neo-
conservatives to take control of all three branches of the federal government – and
the state governorships and the school boards, as we will see in Chapter 17. Soon
the US Supreme Court will follow. From these commanding heights the neo-
conservatives have set about systematically dismantling all of the key institutions –
the taxation system, the United Nations, federal research budgets, the public
schools, core environmental legislation – upon which any resolution to today's
interlocking sustainability crises depends.

In asserting that environmentalism is dead in no small part because it could
never match the right wing's power to narrate a compelling vision of America's
future, Werbach's (2004) real challenge to a substantially weakened environment
movement in the US is to step outside the confines of the standard environmental
discourse that it has relied upon for 40 years in order 'to articulate a more expansive,
more inclusive and more compelling vision for the future'.

This is controversial stuff and is fiercely resisted by many mainstream American
environmentalists who point to the fact that, paradoxically, both membership and
income has been on the rise in the US over the last four or five years, not least
because of the role that President Bush and his Administration play as 'recruiting
sergeants'. And such a transformation would exact a heavy price: it would mean all
the big environmental organizations downplaying their environmental or conservation labels and identifying themselves more as 'American progressives'. This is not
too hard, perhaps, for the likes of the Sierra Club or Greenpeace, but is a bit of a
stretch for Conservation International (CI) or even the World Wide Fund for
Nature (WWF). Nonetheless, Werbach believes this is the price that has to be paid
for having wasted so many years addressing 'the environment' as a compendium
of scientific and technical issues, rather than the territory upon which to engage
with American citizens about core values and aspirations. Whether the same
strictures can be levelled against UK environmentalists is a controversy to which I
will return in the final chapter.

CONFRONTING THE SCEPTICS

For some, however, this is all just so much moonshine – as are all the transitional
strategies for government, business and civil society sketched out in Part III.

However much sense they might make, however desirable and even preferable they might be, there is one overwhelmingly powerful reason why they are seen to be doomed to failure: human nature.

There are a very large number of people whose view of human nature is so gloomy that no amount of well-meaning endeavour to reform or even transform contemporary capitalism warrants any credibility whatsoever. According to this worldview, we've got the economic system that we've got (triumphalist, all pervading, hugely resilient and creative, on the one hand, hugely destructive and inequitable, on the other) because it's the one that most powerfully reflects our *true* human nature: greedy, aggressive, self-interested, short-termist, irresponsible and cruel. It is the job of politicians and social institutions to 'manage' those characteristics and to mitigate their most destructive impacts; but that's the way we are because evolution made us that way and those characteristics are unalterably encoded in our genes. So, set aside unworldly dreams of some kind of sustainable capitalism and let rip the red-in-tooth-and-claw version that we've ended up with today until its destructive force is spent and something else (about which there is little point speculating) arises from its ashes.

We have all met those who subscribe to such a worldview. A steely, contemptuous look comes into their eye in the presence even of tentative optimism. Look around you, it says. Check out your *own* analysis of the state of the world and its people. What further proof could you possibly require to demonstrate that the 'perfectibility of the human spirit' is and always will be an utterly forlorn notion?

There are many personal attributes that one needs to be a sustainable development activist or a campaigner for human rights, the environment and social justice – but perhaps the most important of all is a lack of fatalism about human nature! One has to have faith in humankind's capacity for good ultimately winning out over humankind's capacity for evil – both at a societal and an individual level. It doesn't matter how marginal that faith may be, how attenuated it may have become in the face of 'man's inhumanity to man' (let alone to the rest of life on Earth), or how hard one has to work to keep it alive: one has to be able to take on those steely-eyed fatalists lest one's vision of a better world gets smothered under their cynical negativity.

Realistically, it is only in the last 30 years or so (if you go back to the first United Nations Conference on the Environment and Human Development in Stockholm in 1972) that we have woken up to today's sustainability crisis. There were a few voices in the wilderness before then, but no concerted movement for change. In the intervening 30 years, a huge amount of scientific data has been generated, providing us with an extraordinary wealth of knowledge and practical know-how about learning to live more sustainably on planet Earth. The fact that we don't yet take advantage of that science (the gap between what we know about the state of the Earth and what we are doing about it remains as large as ever) is massively regrettable; but this vast store of intellectual capital is not going to disappear just because we don't value it properly today. Indeed, it is growing all the time.

And that, in turn, drives a powerful process of technological innovation. Notwithstanding the worst prognostications of Sir Martin Rees (2003) and Bill Joy (2000) (see Chapter 12), only the most churlish of fatalists would deny the potential for benign change through the next generation of sustainable technologies. The fact that it is possible, for instance, even now, to map out a 30-year transition from a world powered predominantly by fossil fuels to one powered predominantly by renewable energy is extraordinary. There are, of course, huge structural and institutional hurdles to be overcome (not least the fact that the current power brokers in the world of renewables are the self-same multinational companies whose short-term commercial fortunes depend utterly upon maximizing the value of their hydrocarbon assets); but the renewables revolution is at last under way.

For others, the source of their optimism is much more cultural than technological. It often rests upon the hypothesis that underneath all the hurly-burly of crass consumerism there is, in all OECD countries, a nation of caring 'inner-directeds' struggling to get out. During the 1950s, the sociologist David Riesman divided consumers into three categories: sustenance driven – insecure and driven primarily by where the next meal would come from; outer-directeds – in control of their insecurity, but busy consuming as conspicuously as possible; and inner-directeds. This category has been defined as follows:

> . . . people whose prime motivation is no longer conspicuous consumption or keeping up with their neighbours, but autonomy, self-expression, health and independence. These are people who are suspicious of mass production, who want things customized or tailor made, who may or may not be excited by information technology and computers, but who are definitely part of the world of self-actualization and may be self-employed. (Boyle, 2004)

By some calculations, up to 50 per cent of people in a country such as the UK can now be categorized as *potentially* inner-directed. The same kind of analysis in the US shows something like 25 per cent of people who can be classified as 'cultural creatives', to use Paul Ray's terminology, interested in health and spirituality, and searching for integrity and quality in everything they buy.

The key to all this is the notion of *authenticity*. David Boyle's book *Authenticity: Brands, Fakes, Spin and the Lust for Real Life* (2004) provides a wonderfully stimulating review of all the different ways in which the quest for the authentic is influencing more and more aspects of our lives – in terms of food, culture, relationships, politics, consumerism and technology. He sums up the debate as follows:

> In the blue corner, we have the moderns and post-moderns, thrilled by technological advance and extrapolating it as the key driver of humanity's future. Human intelligence is just a complex manipulation of information, and genetic code just a version of digital code. They can't pin down any

fundamental difference between real and virtual, between authentic and fake. And, thus, authenticity for them is an almost meaningless term – certainly a relative term (as in 'is this authentic artificial intelligence?').

For the spirituals and creatives in the red corner, the next stage of human evolution isn't primarily technological – it's rather to do with the human mind and its limitless potential. Suspicious of the calamities that technology seems constantly on the verge of visiting on the planet, they are nostalgic for the mythical time when people interacted successfully in communities and with the environment – believing that the natural world holds within it its own kind of wisdom.

This is the great divide that will shape the next century between those who want to entrust humanity to technology alone and those who want to embrace something inside people and planet that takes us beyond ourselves. This is an old struggle – between classical and romantic, between Aristotle and Plato – but it is bursting out again in a new definition of authenticity, and between two different interpretations of human potential. (Boyle, 2004)

In seeking to delineate the edges of that confrontation he devotes considerable attention in his book to an enquiry into the notion of authenticity within the business community. To what extent can one really claim that significant elements in the modern business world are now part of the solution rather than still being part of the problem? If our knowledge base has been growing for the last 30 years, it is only during the last ten or so that some of the world's most powerful multinationals have begun to internalize that knowledge about the state of the world and to change their ways. The scale and potential significance of these changes has been covered in earlier chapters of this book, and is now the source of a huge numbers of books, journals and newsletters trying to track and promote ever deeper engagement on the part of multinational companies today.

It's unwise to get all this out of proportion. The changes to date are modest, slow, inadequate and inconsistent. There are still *very* few companies that have really got to grips with sustainable development; for most, the business model remains largely unchanged. But it *is* happening, and it's not all for show and public relations glory, as so many campaigners would still have you believe. For whatever reason, this is an upward curve moving in the right direction – and, even more astonishingly, doing so at a time when the utterly aberrant pressures of short-term profit maximization to boost shareholder value have been at their most intense and most destructive.

RAISING OUR SPIRITS

By contrast, David Boyle devotes surprisingly little attention to the areas of religion and spirituality, seen by other commentators as absolutely central to the pursuit of a more authentic and more sustainable way of life. Fritjof Capra, for instance, has written:

> *Ultimately, deep ecological awareness is spiritual or religious awareness. When the concept of the human spirit is understood as the mode of consciousness in which the individual feels a sense of belonging, of connectedness, to the cosmos as a whole, it becomes clear that ecological awareness is spiritual in its deepest essence.* (Capra, 2000)

Interestingly, such views command much less support than might be supposed in the wider green movement. As covered in Chapter 3, there is often hostility to those who promote a spiritually inspired perspective on today's sustainable development challenges, the roots of which tell us a lot about some of the barriers that will need to be overcome if we are to fashion a genuinely sustainable future for the whole of humankind. For some, that hostility is simply part and parcel of a completely consistent antagonism to anything non-rational or 'unscientific', as they would see it. For others, it goes deeper than that. They are hugely suspicious of anything with a whiff of 'New Age' mysticism about it, seeing such perspectives as both intellectually defective and prejudicial to their constant, ongoing efforts to mainstream environmental and social justice issues on the basis of scientific credibility.

One might be amused by this defensive secularism were it not such an impediment to accelerating the uptake of more sustainable behaviours and mindsets. As I have pointed out before, we are unlikely to counter the all-but-universal seduction of consumerism or to meet the need for people to go beyond 'detached respect' for the natural systems upon which we depend by developing a much more humble, reverential ethos without some kind of spiritual support. There are few voices of authority (let alone wisdom) in addressing these two challenges that are not derived from religious or spiritual sources. Commenting upon the life of St Francis of Assisi, Richard Chartres (the Bishop of London) concluded quite simply that 'we move towards God by subtraction rather than accumulation'. Yet, that critical inheritance is deemed irrelevant by those who continue, often rather forlornly, to exhort people to 'respect nature' and 'consume responsibly' from a purely secular perspective. In his 'Reflection on the Reith Lectures' in 2000, HRH The Prince of Wales staked out the ground for a more spiritual perspective:

> *The idea that there is a sacred trust between mankind and our Creator, under which we accept a duty of stewardship for the Earth, has been an important feature of most religious and spiritual thought throughout the ages. Even those whose beliefs have not included the existence of a Creator have, nevertheless, adopted a similar position on moral and ethical grounds. I believe that if we are to achieve genuinely sustainable development we will first have to rediscover, or re-acknowledge, a sense of the sacred in our dealings with the natural world and with each other.*

> *If literally nothing is held sacred any more – because it is considered to
> be synonymous with superstition or in some other way 'irrational' – what
> is there to prevent us treating our entire world as some 'great laboratory
> of life', with potentially disastrous long-term consequences?* (HRH
> Prince of Wales, 2000, cited in Lorimer, 2003)

My own feeling is that we constantly underestimate this hunger for transcendence,
just as we underestimate our extraordinary capacity for the deepest feelings of
empathy and compassion for other people and for the living world. Too much is
made of the highly visible manifestations of self-interest and apparent indifference;
the less visible (and often completely invisible) outpouring of acts of altruism and
selflessness are rarely factored into the rather crude generalizations that those steely-
eyed fatalists tend to make about human nature. One has only to take account of
the countless millions of people in most developed countries involved in volunteering or charity work of one kind or another to realize how misleading this can be.

This, of course, is standard fare for humanitarian idealists of every description,
whatever the cause of their optimism. It has taken on an added dimension in the
green movement where the natural world itself is still held to have some influence
over the behaviour and, indeed, the aspirations of humankind. That sense of
interdependence referred to above (regardless of whether it is intuited in a secular
or spiritual way) connects many environmentalists into a richer perception of their
evolutionary origins. For many years, a number of so-called 'eco-psychologists' have
argued that one of the principal reasons why so many people in the developed world
are unhappy, unfulfilled and generally out of sorts is that they are 'alienated from
the rest of life on Earth'. Theodore Roszak articulates this most powerfully in his
book *The Voice of the Earth*:

> *A culture that can do so much to damage the planetary fabric that
> sustains it, and yet continues along its course unimpeded, is mad with
> the madness of a deadly compulsion that reaches beyond our own kind
> to all the brute innocence about us. We are pressing forward to create a
> monocultural world society in which whatever survives must do so as the
> adjunct of urban-industrial civilization. And the loss that comes of that
> crime falls upon us as much as on any species of plant or animal we
> annihilate; for the planet will, of course, endure, perhaps to generate new
> adventures in life in the aeons to come. But we are being diminished by
> our destructive insensitivity in ways that cripple our ability to enjoy,
> grow, create. By becoming so aggressively and masterfully 'human', we
> lose our essential humanity.* (Roszak, 1993)

Our 'essential humanity' is necessarily Earth-bound, contextualized both physically
and cosmologically by the evolution of life on Earth and our part in it. Despite
our every effort, we cannot disconnect from that context. The great biologist

E. O. Wilson suggests in *Biophilia* (1984) that 'the urge to affiliate with other forms of life is to some degree innate', and ascribes all sorts of basic behaviours (gardening, keeping pets, rambling, watching natural history programmes on television and even golf!) to a genetic, Earth-loving inheritance that we can temporarily ignore but never entirely suppress.

For many, however, all of these upbeat 'reasons to be cheerful' look very frail indeed when set against the massively powerful onward momentum of the particular model of capitalism that has dominated the world for at least the last 30 years. For them, uncompromising resistance and opposition is the only course of action which provides any cause for optimism. I will return to that theme in Chapter 17, as it goes right to the heart of whether or not some kind of accommodation with this particular model of capitalism is feasible. But one thing is for sure: those forces of opposition and resistance are still growing, all around the world, in all sorts of different ways. Nowhere has this been made more compelling (and more personal, in terms of the individual stories that it tells) than in Paul Kingsnorth's powerful book *One No, Many Yeses:*

> *I can't help being optimistic, and my optimism comes from the answers I find to a few simple questions. Has a movement this big ever existed before? Has such a diversity of forces, uncontrolled, decentralized, egalitarian, ever existed on a global scale? Has a movement led by the poor, the disenfranchised, the South, ever existed at all, without being hijacked by intellectual demagogues or party politicians in a way that this movement looks unlikely, because of both its principles and its organizing methods, ever to do? How have we achieved so much in such a short time? Do the world's people want to listen? Are we going in the right direction? Are we gaining in momentum? I get the right answer to every one of those questions, and every one of those answers helps to answer another: can the world afford to ignore this any more?* (Kingsnorth, 2003)

There are, of course, lots of mainstream commentators who would have us all believe that this is a movement that's actually going nowhere – that it's too negative, too marginal, too disunited, too incoherent. That kind of dismissive editorializing became particularly strident after the events of 11 September 2001 in the apparent belief that 'all anti-globalization campaigners in the West' would just melt away as the rest of the world dedicated itself to the war against terror. I return to the figures provided by the *New Internationalist* (2001) and cited in Box 12.2 ('The war against terror in context') in order to demonstrate why such beliefs are so ill-founded and, indeed, so arrogant:

- the number of people who died in the 11 September 2001 attack on the New York Twin Towers: 3000;
- the number of people who died of hunger on 11 September 2001: 24,000;

- the number of children who died of diarrhoea on 11 September 2001: 6020;
- the number of children who died of measles on 11 September 2001: 2700.

It isn't just the anger and passion at such enduring global injustice that keeps campaigners going. They know from their own experiences, at the local and community level, that the vast majority of people are far more hungry for change than you would ever guess if you are stuck with our lamentably biased mainstream media for insights into the world around you. For instance, when Local Agenda 21 was at its most influential in the UK, during 1999 and 2000, literally thousands of 'visioning exercises' across the country asked people what they hoped the future would look like. They may not have been familiar with the concept of sustainable development and all the jargon that goes with it; but time after time they identified the key social, environmental and economic foundations of sustainable development as central to their own personal visions. Many had come to those conclusions not just because of anxieties about the present, but because they were already seeing the future through the eyes of their children and grandchildren. And that's when sustainable development really begins to bite.

REFERENCES

Boyle, D. (2004) *Authenticity: Brands, Fakes, Spin and the Lust for Real Life*, Harper Perennial, London

Callenbach, E. (1975) *Ecotopia*, Banyan Tree Books, Berkeley, CA

Capra, F. (2002) *The Hidden Connections*, HarperCollins, London

Forum for the Future (2005) 'A vision of a sustainable future', internal paper

Griffiths, J. (1999) *Pip Pip: A Sideways Look at Time*, Flamingo, London

Griffiths, J. (2005) 'Living time', *Green Futures*, no 51

Jacobs, M. (1999) *Environmental Modernisation: The New Labour Agenda*, Fabian Society, London

Joy, B. (2000) 'Why the future doesn't need us', *Wired*, April

Kingsnorth, P. (2003) *One No, Many Yeses*, Free Press, London

Lorimer, D. (2003) *Radical Prince*, Floris Books, Edinburgh

Mill, J. S. (1861) *Utilitarianism*, first published in three issues of *Fraser's Magazine*, first book publication by Parker, Son and Bourn, London (1863)

New Internationalist (2001) 'Enduring terrors', *New Internationalist*, November

Rees, M (2003) *Our Final Century*, William Heinemann, London

Roszak, T. (1993) *The Voice of the Earth*, Bantam Press, London

Sustainable Development Commission (2001) *Principles for a Sustainable World*, Sustainable Development Commission, London

Suzuki, D. (1997) *Declaration of Interdependence*, David Suzuki Foundation, Vancouver, Canada

Werbach, A. (2004) *Is Environmentalism Dead?*, speech at The Commonwealth Club, San Francisco, 8 December. Text available at www.grist.org/news/maindish/2005/01/13/werbach-reprint/

Wilson, E. O. (1984) *Biophilia*, Harvard University Press, Cambridge, MA

17

Converging Imperatives

INTRODUCTION

So, does it all come down to how we interpret human nature? Are we genetically predisposed, as Richard Dawkins (2002) argues, to raise up the short term and the selfish over the long term and the altruistic? Sustainable development activists have to resist such genetic determinism, not least in terms of the influence they can bring to bear on both formal and informal educational systems. But a lot more needs to be done to persuade people that a more sustainable system of wealth creation would not only enhance security in such a troubled world, but would enable them to enjoy a higher quality of life, and to be *happier* in themselves, in their work and their communities. Unfortunately, sustainable development activists are unlikely to get much support in this either from the progressive left (which has been largely co-opted by the myth of permanent economic growth as the answer to everything), or from mainstream environmentalists who are now so depoliticized as to be unable to confront today's ideological reality. Until sustainable development is embraced as the genuinely 'big idea' that it really is, then things are likely to get a very great deal worse before they start to get any better. And it is only a transformation towards a very different kind of capitalism – as if the world really matters – that offers any kind of prospect of a sustainable future.

PROGRAMMED FOR SUSTAINABILITY?

As will by now be abundantly clear, sustainability and capitalism do not automatic-ally make natural bedfellows. Sustainability is all about the long term, about working within limits, about making more from less, about accommodation with others to secure equilibrium – and it demands a deep and often disconcerting re-engagement with the natural world. Contemporary capitalism responds to the shortest of short terms, abominates the very notion of limits, celebrates excess, accepts that its 'invisible hand' will fashion as many losers as winners – and has no connectedness with the natural world other than as a dumping ground and a store of raw materials.

In this regard, regrettably, defenders of contemporary capitalism can justifiably claim that it would appear to be aligned a great deal more closely with human nature (as we understand human nature today) than the precepts of sustainability. And that's a tough call for the emerging sustainable development movement. In a fascinating lecture given at the Royal Institution in London in 2002, Richard Dawkins rubbed our sensitive little noses in this particular aspect of Darwinian *realpolitik*:

> *There is something profoundly anti-Darwinian about the very idea of sustainability. Sustainability is all about long-term benefits of the world at the expense of short-term benefits. But short-term genetic benefit is all that matters in a Darwinian world. Superficially, the values that will have been built into us will have been short-term values, not long-term ones. If it were left to Darwinism alone, there would be no hope. Short-term greed is bound to win.* (Dawkins, 2002)

And frankly, it's hard to come to any other conclusion at the moment. In all sorts of ways, consumerism has more or less established itself as the new religion in the rich world. In rallying US citizens after the 11 September 2001 terrorist attacks, President Bush was quick to exhort them to get out there and go shopping, as proof positive that the American way of life was untouched by such a trauma. Every year, the story of Christmas is the story of just how much consumption people can pack in to the festive season, with what impact on the national economy. And year on year, a few more tens of millions of people are conscripted into a global 'consumertariat' – the sole task of which is to keep on shopping, and throwing away, and shopping some more.

Yet Richard Dawkins went on to suggest that we should not despair:

> *If any species in the history of life has the possibility of breaking away from short-term Darwinian selfishness, and of planning for the distant future, it is our species. Although we are products of Darwinism, we are not slaves to it. Using the large brains that Darwinian natural selection has given us, it is possible to fashion new values that contradict Darwinian values. What it does mean is that we must work all the harder for the long-term future, in spite of getting no help from nature, precisely because nature is not on our side.* (Dawkins, 2002)

MAKING SENSE OF EVOLUTION

That's an intriguing way of articulating the sustainability challenge for humankind: to overcome our natural tendencies, encoded ineluctably in our selfish genes, to enable us to put long-term species survival and the prospect of a better life ahead of instantaneous, selfish gratification. A tough call! But even this may represent a rather grimmer understanding of our evolutionary destiny than may be warranted. It all depends upon how one reads the relative importance of 'competition versus collaboration' in our evolutionary history – and in this regard the work of Herbert Spencer may have had a more influential role even than that of Charles Darwin himself.

It was Spencer who seized hold of Darwin's ideas about natural selection and sought to apply them in every particular to the human species. If competition and 'survival of the fittest' were the laws that drove natural selection for all other organisms, then these had to be the laws for human beings since we were no more than very smart animals in evolutionary terms. So, shed no tears for those who fall by the wayside. Social Darwinism was born, in its crudest, cruellest form, allowing no room for any other human instinct or impulse other than all-out self-interest and power-hungry aggression.

As already explored in Chapter 4, we now know that this kind of 'red in tooth and claw' interpretation of evolution is a grotesque distortion of a much more subtle balance of competitive and collaborative behaviours among organisms sharing the same ecosystem. And these rival interpretations of evolution have had a big impact upon different variations of capitalism. In *Moral Capitalism*, Stephen Young holds up Enron as an archetypal manifestation of 'brute capitalism', descended (via various pathways) from the social Darwinism of Herbert Spencer – and he reminds us in no uncertain terms of just how dangerous it is to raise up Herbert Spencer over Adam Smith:

> *Spencer did not see any value in symbiosis. To analogize people to animals in every important sense, as Spencer did, is a mistake. Perhaps in the excitement of his conceptual breakthrough, Spencer overlooked just how inconsistent his theory was with the insights of Adam Smith. Where Smith had seen specialization and accelerating divisions of labour producing more and more cross-dependencies and interdependencies as capitalist economic growth expanded, Spencer only saw more and more autonomy, independence and conflict to get one's way in the world.*
> (Young, 2003)

So perhaps Adam Smith was just the first of many individuals intent on using 'the large brains that Darwinian natural selection has given us' to fashion the kind of values that will dig us out of our Darwinian heritage! Darwin himself would have acknowledged the feasibility of such a shift, with his pertinent reminder that 'it is not the strongest or most intelligent that survive, but the ones that are most responsive to change' (Darwin, 1859).

Given the dominant role of the US in the world today, it seems improbable that there's going to be much of a global shift without a shift in the US. The impact of Hurricane Katrina on the political scene is therefore being analysed with particular attention. What was initially described as 'the worst natural disaster in the history of the US' is already being reinterpreted (as with the Indian Ocean tsunami) as a disaster that was as much man-made as natural. For decades, US business interests (particularly the oil sector) have been eroding the natural defences of the Louisiana and Mississippi coastline, destroying mangrove swamps, driving through canals, reclaiming land for industrial development and so on. For years, critics had been warning that this had reached such a point that the impact of *any* major wind storm, let alone a hurricane of the strength of Katrina, would inevitably be greatly exacerbated. Add to that the decision by the Bush Administration to cut by nearly 50 per cent budgets appropriated for maintaining flood defences around New Orleans, and the man-made elements in this disaster become all the clearer.

The ensuing chaos and horror that engulfed so many of the poorer, black citizens of New Orleans has burned itself into the collective US psyche, leaving Americans deeply uneasy about the picture of the divided, cruel and uncaring America that opened up in front of them. Shame, anger and astonishment are all part of the complex emotional response that has led commentators such as Simon Schama to anticipate a profound turning away from the neo-conservative free market model that underpins today's US politics and values.

> *Historians ought not to be in the prophecy business, but I'll venture this one: Katrina will be seen as a watershed in the public and political life of the US, because it has put back into play the profound question of American government. Ever since Ronald Reagan proclaimed that government was not the answer but the problem, conservatism has stigmatized public service as parasitically unpatriotic, an anomaly in the robust self-sufficiency of American life. For the most part, Democrats have been too supine, too embarrassed and too inarticulate to fight back with a coherent defence of the legitimacy of democratic government. Now, if ever, is their moment.* (Schama, 2005)

One of the principal implications of this is that our political and business leaders have got to explicitly align themselves with those long-term values of interdependence, solidarity and empathy. And one can take little succour when one looks out at a world seemingly bereft of any serious sustainability leadership in this respect or, indeed, of any serious readiness to respond to the scientific knowledge which is now available to our decision-makers. The idea that we now live in an age of evidence-based policy-making is preposterous. Although it's true that the unfolding empirical reality of a changing climate is forcing politicians to accept that it is their responsibility in their own term of office to do something about it, this for the most part is the only bit of the evidence base they seem prepared to address. Talk of the cumulative and seemingly inexorable build-up of toxic chemicals in the environment, and that's a different story. Talk of the incremental but seemingly inexorable loss of land to new development, and that's a different story again. Talk of a whole host of natural limits to economic growth as presented in the Millennium Eco-system Assessment report (MA, 2005), and that's a *completely* different story. You're suddenly a radical subversive beyond the pale of intelligent discourse.

Looking back on 20 years as an 'economic hit man' serving the interests of today's American imperium, John Perkins expresses his anger at the continuing act of collective denial on the part of so many people in that political and business elite:

> *We prefer to believe the myth that thousands of years of human social evolution has finally perfected the ideal economic system, rather than to face the fact that we have merely bought into a false concept and accepted it as gospel. We have convinced ourselves that all economic growth benefits humankind, and that the greater the growth, the more wide-spread the benefits. Finally, we have persuaded one another that the corollary to this concept is valid and morally just: that people who excel at stoking the fires of economic growth should be exalted, and rewarded, while those born at the fringes are available for exploitation. The real story is that we are living a lie.* (Perkins, 2004)

To observe how the so-called 'progressive left' here in the UK, or the recovering Democrats in the US, find it so easy to go on living that lie, continuing to shy away from the incontrovertible physical reality of the continuing damage we are doing both to the Earth and to a very large number of its people on the grounds that sustainability is an 'unsellable concept', demonstrates a degree of co-option that is sometimes hard to believe. Deep down, they know that to embrace sustainable development as the 'big idea' that it indisputably is would call into question the deeply compromised accommodation they have come to with today's neo-conservative, globalized 'growthism'. It's just that they are a great deal less open about their fear of sustainable development (at this more ideological level) than the American Policy Center, which was quoted earlier on describing sustainable development as 'the enemy' of all self-respecting Americans fighting to keep their guns, property, children and God!

But as Perkins says, it's all too easy to blame such a regrettable state of affairs on anybody but ourselves: on the 'corporatocracy' that has taken so much power and such undeserved wealth unto itself; on our largely corrupted media that live so clearly (and, these days, unapologetically) in the pockets of the corporatocracy without whose advertising revenue they could no longer survive; on some surreal conspiracy of fundamentalist Christians and neo-conservative imperialists who would appear to have taken over the White House; or on a generation of economists who have perpetuated the impossibilism of exponential economic growth, forever, on a finite planet.

This is one of the reasons why I feel increasingly disinclined to give an inch to those who complain about the inadequacy of sustainable development as a mobilizing concept in such a troubled world. Behind all their slick protestations about its un-sellability, its inaccessibility, its indeterminacy or its openness to linguistic abuse, there lurks an extraordinarily persistent reluctance to confront the limits to growth head on, to explore what today's chronic lack of biophysical headroom means in practice, right now, for a Spencerian model of brute capitalism that could never in a million years accommodate itself to anything as irrelevant to it as the laws of nature. As Richard Reeves puts it:

> But the penny hasn't dropped yet. Our cultures, political systems, yardsticks of success have utterly failed to adapt to the new world – one in which economics does not equal or even equate to progress. Governments remain as obsessed as ever with economic productivity and growth. No serious challenge has yet been mounted to the Enlightenment model of rationalist economic growth – a model that served us so well for so long, but is now past its sell-by date. (Reeves, 2002)

From that perspective, the tactics of environmental and development non-governmental organizations (NGOs) around the world must be called into question. The argument developed in this book – that sustainable development provides the only intellectually coherent basis upon which to transform contemporary capitalism – is not one that commands a huge groundswell of support among the NGO community at large. Indeed, the acute reluctance on the part of tens of millions of activists around the world who are happy to be described as 'environmentalists' even to acknowledge the ideological heartland of what they call 'environmentalism' has become a major problem. If the future of humankind depends upon transforming this particular model of capitalism into one that has a rather better chance of embracing both equity and sustainability (as sketched out in Part II of this book), then it is a massive problem if the vast majority of environmentalists choose to remain semi-detached and so depoliticized that any mention of the bigger picture (namely, a root-and-branch transformation of today's capitalism) sends them running off back to their bird-boxes and gently simmering organic lentils.

I hope it is clear that I am *not* talking about some revolutionary taking to the barricades. The notion of 'capitalism as if the world matters' demands a *reform* agenda, however radical it may appear to some, not a *revolutionary* agenda. But it does require a different level of engagement, both as citizens and as consumers, and a much greater readiness to confront denial at every point, to challenge the slow, soul-destroying descent into displacement consumerism, and to take on today's all too dominant 'I consume therefore I am' mindsets and lifestyles.

EDUCATION FOR SUSTAINABLE DEVELOPMENT

Whichever way one looks at this, education is absolutely at the heart of the transformation process – starting in our own homes, workplaces, leisure centres, professional bodies or institutions, clubs, trade unions and so on. And it's as much a re-education of the heart that we are talking about here as the continuing education of the mind. Janine Benyus is lucky enough to live in one of the most beautiful valleys of one of the most beautiful states of the US (Montana), but her guidance here should have some resonance with all of us, however gritty our suburban or urban confines may be:

> *We need to put down our books about nature and actually get into a rain storm, be startled by the deer we startle, climb a tree like a chameleon. It's good for the soul to go where humans do not have a great say about what happens. Between these trips to 'the big outside', we need only open our hearts to the smaller encounters: the smell of old sunlight in a leaf pile, the chrysalis of a butterfly inside our mailbox, the glimpse of that earthworm that helps us grow tomatoes. This literal immersion in nature prepares us for the figurative immersion. This is where we take our reasoned minds and stuff them back into our bodies, realizing that there is no membrane separating us from the natural world.* (Benyus, 1997)

By emphasizing this more informal education, I am in no way downgrading the importance of more formal educational systems in our schools, colleges and universities. The battle here is well and truly joined in most OECD countries, both in terms of claims now made by 'education for sustainable development' (ESD) on the formal curriculum, competing for space and funds to find creative and intelligent ways of enabling young people to learn and experience what it means, in practice, to be a citizen of our living Earth, and in terms of making sure that *all* places of learning embody that heightened awareness about responsibility to the world and its people in their design, construction, management and engagement with their surrounding communities. If one subscribes to the inspirational rallying cry of the annual World Social Forum in Porto Alegre that 'another world *is* possible', then we have to start to make it possible first and foremost for young people. From the relatively privileged position of the UK, the signs here are hopeful, with a lot of smart NGOs working away at both the curriculum end of things (with a fantastic array of ESD materials now available to schools and colleges) and the practical end of things around the broad concepts of eco-schools, playground regeneration and so on. A lot of schools, colleges and individual teachers are intent on finding the time and resources to make these things happen, and are now doing so within a political system that has finally woken up to the urgency of getting our own educational house in order.

It's hard not to compare that reasonably encouraging outlook with that which confronts ESD activists in the US. Tim Kasser reminds us of the way in which American educational systems have been comprehensively co-opted into promoting crude consumerist values:

Society works through various means to indoctrinate children, including the school system, behaviour of parents, mass media and the internet. As the world has become increasingly materialistic, so have our children. Since the mid 1960s, Alexander Astin and his colleagues have been asking over 200,000 first-year college students in the United States what is important to them in life. The percentage of students who believe that it is very important or essential to 'develop a meaningful philosophy of life' decreased from over 80 per cent in the late 1960s to around 40 per cent in the late 1990s. At the same time, the percentage who believe that it is very important or essential to be 'very well off financially' has risen from just over 40 per cent to over 70 per cent. Society's value-making machine is an effective one. (Kasser, 2002)

Right now, however, the principal battle in the US is to hold the line on teaching some of the scientific building blocks that underpin any real understanding of sustainability. According to the National Center for Science Education, 17 states are now embroiled in legal and political battles over the way in which evolution is taught in schools and colleges. For the last 20 years or more, Christian fundamentalists have been seeking to have evolution described as 'a theory' so that their version of creationism (the belief that God created the Earth and all its species – and, indeed, all its fossils! – in just six days around 6000 years ago) can be taught as a rival theory alongside evolution.

The teaching of creationism in American schools was explicitly outlawed in 1987 when the US Supreme Court confirmed that it was unconstitutional to bring any such religious perspectives to bear on the school curriculum. Since then, however, the religious right has regrouped and, under the new banner of Intelligent Design, is now intent on challenging what it sees as the atheistic domination of science in American education. Intelligent Design maintains that there is no definitive proof for the theory of evolution, and that the complexity and diversity of life on Earth can only be explained in terms of some purposeful act of creation by 'an intelligent designer'.

Again, it's easy for Europeans to snicker away about these outlandish intellectual eccentricities, and to justifiably point out that the majority of Christians in the US still see no profound clash between religion and science – and with the theory of evolution in particular. Suzanne Goldenberg offers a corrective to that kind of complacency:

For the conservative forces engaged in the struggle for America's soul, the true battleground is public education, the laboratory of the next generation and an opportunity for the religious Right to effect lasting change on popular culture. Science teachers believe that the genteel questioning of the Intelligent Design movement masks a larger project to discredit an entire body of rational thought. (Goldenberg, 2005)

Some may feel that I am setting too much store on what is happening in the US in terms of the gradual annexation of the 'commanding heights' of that country (Capitol Hill, government agencies, the educational system and so on) by the religious right. If I am, it is only to challenge the often unspoken assumption on the part of most reasonable, decent people that we don't really have to stir ourselves too much here, and that we are slowly getting these big picture environmental and social justice challenges under control. So just keep pushing things along in the same old dogged, incrementalist way that we all feel so comfortable with.

But who knows what kind of backlash we might witness in our own more reasonable European backyards when some of the worst effects of extreme weather events and climate change converge with the already severe impacts of chronic poverty in Africa and elsewhere? In most European countries, there is already a powerful political backlash against the European Union's (EU's) 'open borders' philosophy, with a growing number of political parties (and not just on the extreme or centre right) calling for much stricter controls on immigration and on the movement of people between countries. Facing up to this threat to political stability in advance, rather than waiting for it to catch us 'unawares', would seem to make a lot of sense.

What is currently happening in The Netherlands may turn out to be the most interesting of these European test cases. The resurgence of a much less tolerant anti-immigration political creed, under the leadership of Pim Fortuyn's party (*Lijst Pim Fortuyn*) until his murder in May 2002, has shocked many people both within and outside this traditionally welcoming and consensus-seeking country. Interestingly, there is a widely accepted school of thought among Dutch people that this historical readiness to play down conflicting social and political interests has much to do with the country's uniquely vulnerable geography. One fifth of the total land mass of The Netherlands is below sea level, some of it by as much as 6 metres, reclaimed from the sea over the centuries. These reclaimed lands are called 'polders' and are protected from the sea by an extraordinarily complex system of dykes, ditches and pumping operations. One of their favourite catchphrases is 'God created the Earth, but we Dutch created The Netherlands' – though they would be unwise to give voice to such a blasphemy in the US!

In *Collapse*, Jared Diamond (2005) was so taken with the effect of this engineering triumph on the populace ('We feel that we're all down in the polders together – it's not the case that rich people live safely up on the tops of the dykes while poor people live down in the polder bottoms below sea level: if the dykes and pumps fail, we'll all drown together, so we've learned through our history that we're all living in the same polder, and that our survival depends on each other's survival') that he used it for the title of his book's final chapter – 'The world as a polder' (Diamond, 2005). In a wonderful expression of 'against the odds' optimism, many people subscribe to that kind of 'polder mindset'. As the threat of ecological meltdown seems to become greater by year, so, too, does our awareness of our interdependence and the need for unprecedented solidarity if we are to secure any kind of sustainable future. There is no other planet to which we can turn for help or to which we can export our problems. Indeed, earlier in the year, many saw in the generous response of the rich world to those countries shattered by the Indian Ocean tsunami precisely the kind of empathy and engagement upon which our ability to avoid ecological collapse will surely depend.

Or will it go the other way? If the Greenland ice sheet starts to melt at an accelerated rate (as many scientists believe is all but inevitable) and sea level rises of one metre or more become a reality within the next 20 years, the consequences will be more severe for The Netherlands than for any other country in the northern hemisphere. Will that threat inspire a recasting of their traditional solidarity and interdependence, maintaining that special Dutch balance of mutuality and individualism, or usher in a new dark age of intolerance, xenophobia and isolationism?

This goes to the heart of just how resilient our societies are likely to be in the event not just of the occasional discontinuity but of cataclysmic shocks. Very sensibly, there is now growing interest in planning for and funding a wide range of what are called 'adaptation strategies' regarding some of the likely impacts of climate change. But the adaptations pursued are almost invariably *physical*: higher flood defences or levees, 'climate-proofed' buildings, transport infrastructure built to higher engineering specifications, and so on. There would appear to be little interest in what might be described as 'psychological adaptation' either at the level of the individual or of whole communities.

Yet Hurricane Katrina offered a deeply disturbing insight into how people might behave in the event of similar disasters. The outbreak of widespread looting, violence and something resembling general anarchy can, on the one hand, be interpreted as a phenomenon specific to New Orleans, a city fractured for many years by some of the highest levels of murder, gun crime and drug abuse anywhere in the US. On the other hand, it can be seen as a more chilling reflection of how the majority of people are likely to behave in circumstances where law and order have so clearly broken down. Raising the nightmarish prospect of 'decivilization', Timothy Garton Ash (2005) draws precisely that conclusion:

> *Katrina's big lesson is that the crust of civilisation on which we tread is always wafer thin. One tremor, and you've fallen through, scratching and gouging for your life like a wild dog. Remove the elementary staples of organized, civilized life – food, shelter, drinkable water, minimal security – and we go back within hours to a Hobbesian state of nature, a war of all against all. Some people, for a time, behave with heroic solidarity; most people, most of the time, engage in a ruthless fight for individual and genetic survival. A few become temporary angels, most revert to being apes.* (Ash, 2005)

As referenced in Chapter 12, there are many potential shocks to our all too vulnerable systems that might trigger such reaction – not just climate change (though the increasing likelihood of some kind of 'runaway' effect may in retrospect make Hurricane Katrina look like a rather gentle wake-up call), but terrorism, resource wars, mass migration, or any combination of the same. Timothy Garton Ash's crystal ball may reveal a rather gloomier outlook than most of us have as yet entertained ('I see the advancing shadow of a new European barbarism'), but the signs are there – in Bosnia as much as in Rwanda, in Abu-Ghraib as much as in Chechnya.

Grimly sobering though it may be, I believe this kind of analysis has a direct bearing on our responsibility as citizens to redouble our collective and individual efforts in transforming today's particular manifestation of capitalism. There are of course those who believe that *any* transformation agenda is misguided, and even self-indulgent; for them, there can be no accommodation with a system that is clearly exacerbating so many of today's symptoms of stress and potential collapse. But the idea that we might transition calmly and peacefully from where we are now to some non-capitalist system in the near future (it has to be soon, after all, or not at all) seems fantastical. Far more probable is a grim descent into the kind of Hobbesian nightmare that dominated the global coverage of Hurricane Katrina.

For all that it's a compromise, radical and urgent transformation of the worst dysfunctionalities of contemporary capitalism, based on the kind of principles and practice of sustainable capitalism outlined in Parts II and III of this book, must therefore constitute a more realistic strategy than urging people to take to some anti-capitalist barricade. This side of a precipitate descent into a new 'barbarism' (a real possibility, even in Europe, according to Timothy Garton Ash, let alone in much more troubled parts of the world), we still have a time-limited opportunity to make the necessary changes democratically and through effective international consensus.

It's not as if we don't know that these dilemmas will be upon us in the not so distant future. Much of this book has emphasized the *inevitability* of change, and the *necessity* of adapting our political and economic systems to cope with that change. Even if politicians have not yet internalized the degree to which things must change on account of this broader limits-to-growth analysis (looking at the relationship between humankind and the natural world from a systems perspective), most have now started to internalize the implications of having to cope with climate change – treated in this case as a symptom of the inherent unsustainability of the broader system. But the degree of internalization remains remarkably shallow.

MAKING SUSTAINABLE DEVELOPMENT DESIRABLE

My explanation for this (sketched out in earlier chapters) is that proof of the necessity of change, however incontrovertible it may be, is a necessary but not sufficient condition for change actually to happen. It is not sufficient because at the moment it doesn't come with any compelling explanation of how to make that necessary change desirable to the people who are going to have to change! In this respect, our contemporary model of consumer capitalism sets a very stiff challenge indeed. Ideas have to be *sold*; our citizenry (or 'consumertariat', as I think more accurately defines the body politic today) has to be *seduced* into seeing the world in a different way; and increased choice, increased private benefits, and increased material wellbeing would all appear to have to be part of that kind of offer. Is it any wonder that politicians are struggling to find either the language or the incentives to start bringing people into a shared sense of the need for radical change?

It's not that people haven't tried to come up with one or two bridging devices to achieve this 'desirability element'. From time to time, for instance, there are great flurries of excitement about the potential for 'green consumerism' to become a sufficiently significant force to bring about substantial market shifts. And as we saw in Chapter 15, this remains an important element in the mix and continues to grow from year to year. But as a genuinely transformative influence, this kind of approach has always been constrained by the rather dowdy niche psychology that seems to go with it. Efforts to convert that niche into a dynamic, mainstream consumer movement have had very limited success.

Others are out there cranking away at a much more technocratic approach to demonstrating desirability, emphasizing the potential for a 'green industrial revolution' in terms of massive efficiency gains, reduced material throughput, strict carbon neutrality, industrial symbiosis and so on. This is very much part of the 'opportunity agenda' that I've emphasized time after time throughout this book. It's what gets many individual business leaders really fired up, positioning sustainable development in the zone of innovation, creativity and making money rather than as a constraint or regulated burden. But this, too, has proved to have a limited appeal so far; beyond the geeks and the techies, most people are not interested in the technologies per se, but primarily in the value, service or functionality that any particular technology may give them.

That may have something to do with the way in which we articulate that particular technocratic vision. In the US, the campaign behind the New Apollo Project for Energy Independence and Good Jobs (which was set up in 2003) succeeded in getting out of the technocratic, environmental box by appealing directly to US workers whose principal concern is the loss of jobs in manufacturing, particularly to new economies such as India and China. The campaign wasn't billed as an 'environmental' or 'green' project, and tried hard not to present climate change as a problem of pollution to be sorted out by getting after the polluters or making everybody pay more for their oil and gas. The purpose was to stop trying to shock people with horrific scenarios about climate change (the only consequence of which, in the US, is to persuade people to go out and buy an even bigger SUV so that they're properly prepared for the coming meltdown!) and to inspire them, instead, with a vision of economic opportunity, new jobs and energy security. The New Apollo Project would have been paid for by a new $30 billion investment fund, and 'sold' to US voters on the basis that this represented much better value for money than trying to secure energy independence by annexing Iraq and any other oil-rich country. Unfortunately, John Kerry's advisers baulked at the price, and the New Apollo Project remains little more than an ambitious dream.

A third group of seekers after the missing aspect of desirability (apart from the 'green consumers' and the 'eco-technocrats') have been the 'down-shifters' and the advocates of 'voluntary simplicity'. Again, as we saw in Chapter 15, although a surprisingly large number of people sympathize with the ideals and some of the practicalities of leading a simpler, less materialistic lifestyle, there is still too much of the 'giving up' about it, and too much about sacrifice and self-denial – however unfair a representation of the art of living a simpler life that may really be.

For me, all three of those directional trends have enormous importance; they clearly constitute a very significant part of what might be described as 'our sustainable world in waiting'. Many of the details of the new thinking will come through one of these three strands, though *not* in isolation from each other. But over the years, it's been sobering to see how disparaging and dismissive mainstream politicians, commentators and business people can be about these trends, seeing them as utterly marginal to the core tasks of meeting mass consumer demand, or making markets deliver more efficiently, or providing an ever higher material standard of living. That is what keeps shareholders content and gets politicians elected – even if it doesn't seem to be making people any happier.

This brings me back to Figures 3.2 and 3.3 in Chapter 3, comparing constantly rising economic growth with levels of perceived happiness or contentment. If anything is ever going to make sustainable development genuinely desirable to very large numbers of people in such a compelling way that they come to embrace the necessity of change, it must surely be the possibility that sustainable development could change their lives by putting personal wellbeing and happiness at the very heart of its 'offer' to citizens. For all sorts of reasons, that is *not* the principal objective of today's economies. Macro-economic goals might include financial stability, fair taxation, low inflation, high levels of employment, a reliable and cost-effective welfare system and, of course, year-on-year increases in exponential economic growth – but absolutely *not* making more people feel happier about themselves and their lives. If that has any political salience at all, it is as the assumed by-product of achieving all those other 'grown-up goals'.

The validity of that assumption is rarely questioned. When the UK Sustainable Development Commission petitioned the UK Treasury on a number of occasions to begin investigating this assumption as an important macro-economic issue, it was brushed off with the kind of *de-haut-en-bas* 'politeness' that only the Treasury can manage. And none of the political parties has shown the remotest interest in pursuing the implications for policy-making of this major disconnection at the heart of the UK's long-term economic strategy.

THE HIGH PRICE OF MATERIALISM

Yet the conclusions from more than 20 years of psychological and social research are crystal clear. Those people who are driven predominantly by *extrinsic goals* (money, relative status, exhibitionistic affluence and so on) are far more likely to experience a lower quality of life than those driven by *intrinsic goals* (such as good relationships, personal growth, a meaningful job, and being 'at home' in the community and useful to others). By far the most elegant exposition of this research (and its implications) can be found in a helpfully slim book *The High Price of Materialism*, by Tim Kasser (2002). For me, it turned out to be one of those books that transformed an intuitive gut feeling (in this instance, astonishment that such an important reflection on the relative success or failure of contemporary capitalism was being so comprehensively ignored) into a much better-informed realization that this issue lies as much at the heart of sustainable development as the limits-to-growth thesis.

What makes the book so special is that it is very dry, very understated and very cautious in the inferences that the author draws from an extraordinary wealth of empirical and perceptual data – largely drawn from studies in the US. In elaborating upon the familiar but still controversial view that all people have psychological needs just as they have physical needs, Kasser advances the hypothesis that at least four sets of needs are basic to the motivation, functioning and wellbeing of all humans. These are the needs for safety, security and sustenance; for basic competency and self-esteem; for connectedness; and for autonomy and authenticity. Substantial research suggests that people are highly motivated to feel safe and secure, competent, connected to others, and autonomous and authentically engaged in the way that they lead their lives. 'This literature proposes that wellbeing and quality of life increases when these four sets of needs are satisfied, and decreases when they are not', is Tim Kasser's (2002) overall conclusion. Yet, it seems to me that the sum of the book's modestly stated conclusions is the equivalent of political dynamite:

- *People who are highly focused on materialistic values have lower personal wellbeing and psychological health than those who believe that materialistic pursuits are relatively unimportant.*
- *When needs for security, safety and sustenance are not fully satisfied, people place a strong focus on materialistic values and desires. Insecurity also makes it likely that people will pursue materialistic aims, as both inner predispositions and external consumer culture suggest that resources can purchase security.*
- *Children who feel insecure about themselves may be likely to look for approval from other people in order to feel better about themselves. Because they are exposed to frequent messages in society glorifying image, fame and wealth, they may strongly pursue materialistic aspirations as a way to obtain that approval.*

- *When women have less opportunity to become educated or to control their reproduction, they are likely to feel less secure about their abilities to fend for themselves and, thus, are more materialistic in the desires they have for mates.*
- *Beyond the point of providing for food, shelter and safety, increases in wealth do little to improve people's wellbeing and happiness.*
- *People with a strong materialistic orientation are likely to watch a lot of television, compare themselves unfavourably with people whom they see on television, be dissatisfied with their standard of living, and have low life satisfaction.*
- *When people and nations make progress in their materialistic ambitions, they may experience some temporary improvement of mood, but it is likely to be short lived and superficial. Furthermore, some of the psychological dynamics related to the strong pursuit of materialistic goals keep individuals' wellbeing from improving as their wealth and status increase.*
- *People who hold materialistic aims as central to their values have shorter, more conflicting relationships with friends and lovers, feel alienated and disconnected from others in society, and have dreams in which they move away from intimate connections with others.*
- *When people highly value wealth, possessions, status and image, the emphasis they place upon interpersonal relationships and contributions to their community declines.*
- *Materialistic values of wealth, status and image work against close interpersonal relationships and connection to others – thus, materialistic values lead people to 'invest' less in their relationships and in their communities.*
- *People with a strong orientation to materialism tend to place less value on freedom and self-expression.*
- *Materialistic values are associated with making more anti-social and self-centred decisions involving getting ahead rather than cooperating.*
- *Materialistic values are associated with low interest in environmental and ecological issues.*
- *Materialistic values not only undermine the wellbeing of those who strongly hold them, but also negatively affect the health and happiness of many others. When interactions with people are based upon such values, less empathy and intimacy are present in relationships, and materialistic values are more likely to be transmitted to the next generation.*
- *People believe in materialism because society is so materialistic, and society is so materialistic because many people believe that materialistic pursuits are a path to happiness.* (Kasser, 2002)

How else can we interpret findings of this kind (which are backed by literally dozens of studies in many different countries going back over many years) than to conclude quite simply that the kind of materialism driven on by our contemporary consumer capitalism is leaving people unfulfilled and is killing the human spirit even as it degrades and despoils the natural world. This is, indeed, the dark side of the American dream, as the richest nation on Earth is traumatized by an epidemic of psychological disorders and dysfunctionalities. And there is little reason to suppose that European countries will be far behind.

It must, in part, have been this realization that persuaded Richard Layard to leave behind the safe but often irrelevant confines of conventional economics, and recommend a wholesale transformation in the way in which economists set about their trade. In *Happiness* (Layard, 2005), he exhorts his professional colleagues to reconnect with the real world by looking at how and why people really behave the way they do, and to be far more open to the insights of psychology, neuroscience, sociology and philosophy – 'to learn the lessons of a new science'. In that regard, he still believes that Jeremy Bentham has more to teach us about a new definition of progress for the 21st century than any other contemporary thinker:

> *Create all the happiness you are able to create: remove all the misery you are able to remove. Every day will allow you to add something to the pleasure of others or to diminish something of their pains. And for every grain of enjoyment you sow in the bosom of another, you shall find a harvest in your own bosom; while every sorrow which you pluck out from the thoughts and feelings of a fellow creature shall be replaced by beautiful peace and joy in the sanctuary of your soul.* (Bentham, *An Introduction to the Principles of Morals and Legislation*, 1789, cited in Layard, 2005)

In policy terms, that throws up some interesting challenges for our politicians. If we are to 'rededicate our society to the pursuit of happiness' rather than the goals of growth, efficiency and competitiveness, then we will need to be monitoring people's wellbeing and happiness just as closely as we measure income and gross domestic product (GDP). We should be focusing far more on the problems of mental health; we should be actively investing in activities that promote community life and build social capital; we should eliminate high unemployment altogether; we should rethink our education system – 'we should teach the systematic practice of empathy and the desire to serve others' – and be less coy about the importance of moral education; we should get real about family-friendly practices at work; and we should ban all advertising to children!

As I made clear in Chapter 2, one of the principal differences between sustainable development and conventional environmentalism is that sustainable development is as much about the wellbeing of the human species as about the wellbeing of the natural world. The idea of an environmental organization devoting as much time and effort to the erosion of the human spirit as it does to the erosion of our physical life-support systems is all but unthinkable. For sustainable development activists, on the other hand, not to be as concerned about the impacts of unsustainable capitalism upon the individual, the community and society at large as upon the natural world would represent a betrayal of what sustainable development really stands for.

THE POLITICS OF INTERDEPENDENCE

So, is that where the progressive politics of the 21st century will begin to redefine itself: at the interface between the non-negotiable *necessity* of profound and radical change in the face of climate change and environmental collapse, and the *desirability* of putting the physical, psychological and spiritual wellbeing of people absolutely at the heart of our political and economic systems? And will the gradual realization of total interdependence (upon each other and upon the Earth's life-support systems) lead to a reconfiguring of the progressive forces in society to reshape that political landscape? Will it transform the way in which we use capitalism to help meet our real needs for security, happiness, self-esteem and connectedness, rather than remain enslaved to today's abhorrent, neo-conservative travesty of capitalism that brings misery for the majority of humankind and mayhem for the planet?

This awareness of *interdependence* (between ourselves and the natural world) is undoubtedly the most powerful driver of psychological change available to us today – the necessary stimulus to engage those big brains of ours (to return to the challenge of Richard Dawkins) to overcome our selfish genes. It remains the deepest disappointment of my life as a political activist to see how alien an insight this still is to those on the progressive or centre left in the UK or in the Democratic party in the US. How is it that they have become so alienated from the natural world that there is just no deeper connection within them at all? For many, embarrassment is the principal reaction to the lyricism of seers and philosophers such as Thomas Berry:

> We cannot have well humans on a sick planet. We cannot have a viable human economy by devastating the Earth's economy. We cannot survive if the conditions of life itself are not protected. Not only our physical being, but our souls, our minds, imagination and emotions depend on our immediate experience of the natural world. There is in the industrial process no poetry, no elevation or fulfilment of mind or emotions comparable to that experienced in the magnificence of the sea, the mountains, the sky, the stars at night, the flowers blooming in the meadows, the flights and song of the birds. As the natural world diminishes in its splendour, so human life diminishes in its fulfilment

of both the physical and the spiritual aspects of our being. Not only is it the case with humans, but with every mode of being. The wellbeing of each member of the Earth community is dependent on the wellbeing of the Earth itself. (Berry, 2003)

Reluctantly, I've come to the conclusion that the progressive left – as it chooses to define itself today – has simply run out of relevance on two counts. So preoccupied has it been with the challenges of material poverty and inequity that it simply hasn't noticed the simultaneous impoverishment of the human spirit. Its sole prescription for any social ill is to press down ever harder on the pedal of economic growth to generate enough tax revenues to chuck yet more money at the problems caused by the economic model itself. You have only to look at the inherent irrationality (let alone unsustainability) of most healthcare systems in the developed world, with demand for illness services of every conceivable kind increasing every year, even as the macro-economic policies that provide the cash to pay for those services contribute *directly* and massively to worsening patterns of physical and mental ill health. And what does the progressive left offer here in the UK in response to that structural absurdity: increased consumer choice in the range of illness services available to us!

Second, the progressive left has largely failed to understand the environmental agenda, and continues to see it as a second-order priority of little direct interest to them or the people whom they claim to represent. This is a more complicated charge, as I suspect that the responsibility for this lies as much with today's environmental movements as with the progressive left. By sticking to their single issues, their narrow protectionist agenda, their nay-saying tactics, and their (explicit or implicit) prioritizing of the interests of the natural world over those of the disenfranchised and disadvantaged, many environmentalists have hardly endeared themselves to those whose principal concerns are social justice and increased equity.

One area where environmentalists and the progressive left are 'as one' is in their out-and-out refusal even to discuss the importance of population. While recognizing the political and religious sensitivities associated with population issues, it's hard to explain this continuing conspiracy of silence. Whichever way you look at it, managing climate change, declining resources and collapsing ecosystem services is going to be a great deal harder for 9 billion people than it would be for 8 billion, 7 billion or even 6 billion. While many environmentalists wax eloquent about the impending horrors of global oil production peaking within the next decade, or about runaway climate change, the next logical step (in terms of thinking through the demographic implications) is constantly shied away from. But just try answering this one question: how are we going to feed 9 billion people, in the middle of this century, when the agricultural systems on which most nations depend are no longer underpinned by cheap and easily available fossil fuels?

This silence is all the more strange given that the evidence demonstrates incontrovertibly that investment in enlightened family planning (with the focus on education and better healthcare for girls and women, combined with easy access to safe and reliable contraception) is not just *the* most effective way of reducing average fertility, but supportive of every other economic and social aspiration that developing countries may have. Bizarrely, by turning their back on this available synergy, environmentalists and the progressive left have chosen to align themselves in practice with the Bush Administration that has so disastrously cut back on funding for family planning – even in those countries that are crying out for financial support.

Nor should this focus on population be restricted to the developing world. It's important that OECD countries should be seeking actively to manage down their own population, as has already been happening in several European countries. But not in the UK. Figures from the Office of National Statistics earlier this year show that there are now more than 60 million people in the UK, with forecasts showing continuing growth for several decades to come. And there is still significant growth, year on year, in the population of the US, though this critical issue is nowhere to be seen on the mainstream environmental agenda in the US today.

In Adam Werbach's speech *Is Environmentalism Dead?* (2004), he calls for a total overhaul of traditional environmentalism in the US, a stepping away from the single-issue 'problem categories' that have characterized environmental campaigning in the US for more than 30 years – as embodied, for example, in the Clean Air Act and the Endangered Species Act. He exhorts US environmentalists to throw in their lot with a broader coalition of progressive causes, all of which have been as comprehensively routed by the religious right and the neo-conservatives as environmentalism has been. 'I'm done calling myself an environmentalist', he declares:

> *For 30 years, American liberals have defined themselves according to a set of problem-categories that divide us, whether they be racial, gender, economic or environmental. We have spent far less time defining ourselves according to the values that unite us, such as shared prosperity, progress, interdependence, fairness, ecological restoration and equality. We can no longer afford the laundry list of 'isms' to define and divide our world and ourselves.* (Werbach, 2004)

Werbach also wants environmentalists to stop playing around with the illusion of being 'above party politics'. He argues that there's an extremely clear choice between being a progressive or a conservative. If people are conservatives, however much they might love nature, then they have no part to play in this new movement. And that leads him on to his recommendations for the Democratic party: 'The Republican party – as an institution – has declared war on us. The Democratic party claims to be our ally, yet fails us. It's time for us to drop our veil of bipartisanship and fight to fix the deeply broken Democratic party' (Werbach, 2004).

From this side of the Atlantic, it's interesting that Werbach's stirring polemic makes not one single mention of either sustainable development or capitalism itself – in its current or any other manifestation. Sustainable development just doesn't do it for most people in the US, and it plays little part in the current debate about reconfiguring progressive politics. Nonetheless, the 'coalition of progressive causes' that Werbach talks about (unavoidably triggering a nostalgic resonance with Jesse Jackson's erstwhile 'Rainbow Coalition') would bring together a combination of environmental, fair trade, development, social justice and human rights organizations that looks pretty much like sustainable development to me – indeed, pretty close to the Real World Coalition here in the UK.

The lack of any reference to capitalism is also not that surprising. US politics does not yet allow for much subtlety about different expressions of capitalism; if you criticize capitalism, you're a communist. It's pretty much as simple as that. The idea of some 'root-and-branch transformation of contemporary capitalism' would mean instant and total oblivion.

This is not the case in Europe, where there is already a lively debate about the most appropriate way of harnessing the dynamism of capitalist systems to help secure central social and economic objectives – and substantial disagreement among EU members, old and new. However, it is a debate that most environmentalists have been slow to engage in substantively for fear of undermining their credibility as technical and policy experts, as well as their lobbying access to the EU Commission and the EU Parliament. There are, indeed, significant risks entailed in taking on such politicized tasks, and given that European environmentalists do not currently see themselves in quite such an endangered status as US environmentalists would appear to do, I suspect there will be little appetite for setting out to 'fix something' that isn't actually perceived to be broken.

Yet you have to wonder about this. Those who are pushing the EU's Lisbon agenda on competitiveness and liberalization are not that different from the less rabid wing of the neo-conservatives in the US. European environmentalists might have been more successful than their US counterparts in holding their ground on core environmental regulations and standards; but this demands a growing investment in defensive campaigning and lobbying to prevent the constant erosion that threatens. Public support is both shallow and fickle. In real terms, it can hardly be claimed that environmentalists are having much success in addressing new environmental challenges – on aviation or other transport issues, for instance, or the build-up of toxics in the environment. The measures taken, to date, to address climate change are almost universally acknowledged to be hopelessly inadequate.

So, while we bang on about the burning *necessity* of urgent and comprehensive change, electorates remain unmoved by this rhetoric and apprehensive about the implications of any such change for their own quality of life. Although they know our current system of capitalism is seriously flawed, there is little recognition that it is completely unsustainable. There's little deep awareness of what interdependence really means – even down in the Dutch polders. John Muir's observation that 'when we try to pick out anything by itself, we find it hitched to everything else in the universe' means little if anything in today's culture of instant gratification and atomized self-indulgence. Meanwhile, as catalogued at length in this final chapter, few people in the rich world seem to be getting any happier – and neither the environmental movement nor the progressive left have anything much to say about that extraordinary state of affairs. The new European Constitution fails to find any form of words that reflects either real awareness of the biophysical limits to future growth, or any equivalent to those stirring words in the US Declaration of Independence: 'We hold these truths to be self-evident, that all men are created equal, that they are endowed by their Creator with certain unalienable Rights, that among these are Life, Liberty and the pursuit of Happiness.'

I have set out to demonstrate in this book that the bipolar challenges of, on the one hand, the biophysical limits to growth and, on the other, of the terrible damage being done to the human spirit through the pursuit of unbridled material-ism, will compel a profound transformation of contemporary capitalism – and sooner rather than later if we want to avoid dramatic social and economic disrup-tion. Hence this book has advocated the idea of capitalism as if the world matters: an evolved, intelligent and elegant form of capitalism that puts the Earth at its very centre (as our one and only world) and ensures that all people are its beneficiaries in recognition of our unavoidable interdependence.

And I have argued, perhaps more controversially, that it is only sustainable development that can provide both the intellectual foundations and the operational pragmatism upon which to base such a transformation. This is why sustainable development remains for me the only seriously 'big idea' that can bear the weight of that challenge, and why the core values that underpin sustainable development – interdependence, empathy, equity, personal responsibility and intergenerational justice – are the only foundation upon which any viable vision of a better world can possibly be constructed.

REFERENCES

Ash, T. G. (2005) 'It always lies below', *Guardian*, 8 September

Benyus, J. (1997) *Biomimicry: Innovation Inspired by Nature*, Quill, William Morrow, New York

Berry, T. (2003) 'The legal foundation for Earth survival', unpublished paper for Gaia Foundation, London

Darwin, C. (1859) *On the Origin of Species by Means of Natural Selection, or the Preservation of Favoured Races in the Struggle for Life*, John Murray, London

Dawkins, R. (2002) 'Our big brains can overcome our selfish genes', *Independent*, 2 September 2002

Diamond, J. (2005) *Collapse: How Societies Choose to Fail or Succeed*, Allen Lane, London

Goldenberg, S. (2005) 'Religious right fights science for the heart of America', *Guardian*, 7 February

Kasser, T. (2002) *The High Price of Materialism*, MIT Press, Cambridge, MA

Layard, R. (2005) *Happiness*, Allen Lane, London

MA (2005) *Ecosystems and Human Well-being: Opportunities and Challenges for Business and Industry*, the fourth Millennium Ecosystem Assessment report, available at www.millenniumassessment.org

Perkins, J. (2004) *Confessions of an Economic Hit Man*, Berrett-Koehler, San Francisco, CA

Reeves, R. (2002) 'The sun sets on the enlightenment', *RSA Journal*, December

Schama, S. (2005) 'Sorry Mr President, Katrina is not 9/11', *Guardian*, 12 September

Werbach, A. (2004) *Is Environmentalism Dead?*, speech at The Commonwealth Club, San Francisco, 8 December. Text available at www.grist.org/news/maindish/2005/01/13/werbach-reprint/

Young, S. (2003) *Moral Capitalism: Reconciling Private Interest with the Public Good*, Berrett-Koehler, San Francisco, CA

Index

Page numbers in *italic* refer to Figures, Tables and Boxes